Take A Break In Ireland

Pat Preston, widely acknowledged as the 'Ireland expert', has thirty-five years of experience of writing about Ireland. She has written nine previous books on travel in Ireland, and contributed to nineteen others from all the major guidebook publishers, as well as writing for numerous magazines and major US and Canadian newspapers. She is also the author of more than a dozen travel guidebooks on US destinations. In 1997, she and her husband John Preston were the first ever recipients of the Travel Writer of the Year award from the state of Delaware. Pat and John live in Red Hook, NY, but travel to Ireland frequently accompanying group tours.

Take a Break
IN IRELAND

Pat Preston

With photographs by Pat Preston

THE O'BRIEN PRESS
DUBLIN

First published 2004 by The O'Brien Press Ltd,
20 Victoria Road, Dublin 6, Ireland.
Tel: +353 1 4923333; Fax: +353 1 4922777
E-mail: books@obrien.ie
Website: www.obrien.ie

ISBN: 0-86278-839-0

British Library Cataloguing-in-Publication Data
A catalogue record for this title is available from the British Library

1 2 3 4 5 6 7 8 9 10
04 05 06 07

Layout, editing, typesetting and design: The O'Brien Press Ltd.
Printing: Nørhaven Paperback A/S

Contents

Introduction

Taking a break in Ireland – whether for a day, weekend, week or longer – is a smart choice. Whether you reside in Ireland and want a change of scenery, or come from afar and yearn to see the forty shades of green, the Emerald Isle is a refreshing destination. Play a few rounds of golf, hike in the hills, sail along the coast, swim with a dolphin, fish in the rivers, go racing, join in a festival, indulge in gourmet food or just settle into a pub and chat with the locals. Ireland brings out the best in all of us.

As an island just over 483 kilometres (300 miles) long and 274 km (170 miles) wide, Ireland is a small and compact destination. No part of Ireland is more than 113 km (70 miles) from the sea, and no city is more than 80–160 km (50–100 miles) from a neighbouring city.

It is possible to drive cross-country between east and west in a few hours, or to travel from the southern edge of the country to the northern rim in a day. But why rush? The optimum distance to travel in a day is about 200–240 km (125–150 miles) and less than 160 km (100 miles) a day is best, especially in scenic areas.

Because distances are relatively short, the ideal way to enjoy Ireland is to base yourself in one area for two or three days and take day tours in various directions, and then move on to a new destination for a few more days. Why pack and unpack and change hotels every day? There is so much to see and to do, and all within close range of the major cities.

This book describes 38 of the most enjoyable destinations, giving a step-by-step itinerary, whether it is a walking tour or a driving route. It's a simple and enriching way to go around on your own, taking in all the major sites, yet allowing plenty of time for options and digressions. Whether you take a break for one or two days or for longer, this book gives you all the ingredients to put together a fun trip.

So, start to plan your travels now. You will soon discover that Ireland holds many unique experiences, and a few surprises, too.

CLIMATE AND WEATHER

Weather is a constant topic of conversation in Ireland because it is so changeable – and unpredictable! As an island warmed by the Gulf Stream and surrounded by the sea, Ireland has a temperate (but erratic) climate all year – it has been described aptly as 'the land of perpetual spring' and can experience 'four seasons in one day'.

Temperatures generally average:
Summer 15°C/60°F to 20°C/70°F
Spring/Autumn 10°C/50F° to 15°C/60°F
Winter 5°C/40°F to 8°C/46°F

It is never very cold or too hot – so don't expect to acquire a suntan. Showers are ever-present but snow and ice are rare. The grass is as green in January as in June, flowers begin to bloom in February, and palm trees flourish all year.

Warmer temperatures and longer hours of daylight prevail from May through September, but fewer crowds and lower prices are the benefits of visiting in the October–April period.

TRIP TIMING

When to go? Any month of the year is a good time to take a break in Ireland. Summer remains the most popular time, with long hours of daylight and attractions in full swing, but spring and autumn are also very enticing, with festivals and fewer crowds. The winter, especially November–February, brings the lowest airfares and all-inclusive package deals at prices that can seem cheaper than staying at home!

Weekends are less crowded at city hotels (because business traffic is light), so many hotels offer weekend breaks at alluring rates. Likewise, midweek can be slow at resorts and rural areas, so three- and four-night breaks are offered by country hotels.

Some lodging places offer special deals such as 'short breaks', 'getaway packages', and 'stay three nights, get the fourth night free' deals. Watch the Irish newspapers and hotel internet websites to catch the best offers. Be prepared to travel at short notice to get a good deal.

TOURING V. CHILLING OUT

What to do? See the sights, savour the spa, or steal away to an off-the-beaten-path place? The best answer is to plan for a combination of all of these – stay a few nights at one destination and allow time to tour and time for relaxing. In each chapter, I have outlined a walking or driving tour, and also described several 'digressions', designed to help you experience alternative plans – from island-hopping and river cruising to visiting medieval towns and Gaeltacht areas, or tracing historic footsteps.

SPECIAL INTEREST ACTIVITIES

From angling to archaeology, horse riding to hiking, golf to gardens, painting to pottery classes, Ireland presents a wealth of sport and leisure activities to enjoy on a short or long break. In each chapter is listed the addresses and phone numbers of local tourist information offices. Contact these offices to get the latest information on indoor and outdoor activities. Also use Internet websites to gather information on your favourite sport or special interest.

BRINGING ALONG THE CHILDREN

Ireland has long been known as the 'land of youth', and for good reason. This small island has many activities and attractions that fascinate kids. In the chapters of this book, dozens of family-friendly attractions are included as part of the driving or walking tours and as digressions – from theme parks and castles to steam railways, horse-drawn jaunting cars, boat rides and aquariums. In addition, all over Ireland there are 'open farms' that invite children of all ages to sample agrarian life and see farm animals up-close.

SOURCES OF INFORMATION

Within the Republic of Ireland, the office that prepares and dispenses tourist information is called Fáilte Ireland (formerly Bord Fáilte), a name that literally means 'Welcome (to) Ireland'. The Northern Ireland Tourist Board does the same for the six counties of Northern Ireland. Outside Ireland, a separate organisation, known as Tourism Ireland, is responsible for marketing the entire island of Ireland worldwide. Fáilte Ireland and the Northern Ireland Tourist Board maintain more than 100 tourist information offices in cities, towns and resorts of the 32 counties. Each tourist office is usually identified with a sign showing a large 'i' (for information).

Most tourist information offices are open year-round but some are seasonal. Details of tourist offices, where applicable, are given in the various chapters of this book. In addition to providing information, tourist offices also make reservations for accommodation in their particular area and throughout the rest of the country.

Using the internet, you can also log on to the following websites: www.ireland.travel.ie, www.tourismireland.com or www.discovernorthernireland.com.

Please also visit my website – www.IrelandExpert.com – for the latest travel planning tips and my original photographs of Ireland. A special feature of the site is the 'Ask Pat Q&A'. Post your question and I'll provide a personalised online answer within 24 hours. The IrelandExpert website is designed to supplement and enhance this book by providing a continuous online update for readers.

We hope you enjoy this book and find it to be a helpful companion in your travels. Your comments and suggestions (and trip reports) are always welcomed. Please direct all to:

Pat Preston, Author, *Take a Break in Ireland*, c/o The O'Brien Press, 20 Victoria Road, Dublin 6, Ireland, or via email to TheIrelandExpert@aol.com.

Happy travels!

Pat Preston

2. Planning Strategies

The mission of this guide is simple – to impart the best advice and up-to-date information for taking a break in Ireland. And a 'break' can take many shapes and sizes, from a quick two-day getaway to a full-blown two-week grand tour.

Whether you go to cities or to the countryside, stay put or drive about, the information on these pages is designed to give you optimum enjoyment in your travels.

There are two ways to make the most of this book:

1.SHORT BREAKS – If you are heading to one town, city or region (for example, a weekend in Dingle or Derry, or a mid-week break in the west or southeast), use this book one chapter at a time, or group together two or more itineraries that are geographically close. You can rely on this book over and over as you plan short breaks for every season – and every reason.

2.COMPLETE ITINERARIES – If you are taking a longer multi-destination trip (covering two, three or four regions of Ireland), use this book in a 'modular' style – linking together a series of chapters to build a one- or two-week itinerary. This one trip can easily be the

trip of a lifetime! Flexibility is the forte of this guide – so you can build a travel plan to suit your own tastes and timing. Before you delve into our trip suggestions and ideas, here are a few 'basics' about travelling in Ireland.

DRIVING IN IRELAND

Meandering along the open roads is one of the best ways to enjoy Ireland. Get out into the countryside and meet the people. In some rural parts of the country, the only 'traffic' you'll meet is of the four-legged variety – sheep or cows crossing the road.

Distances and speed limits are posted in miles and kilometres. Speed limits, currently shown in miles per hour (mph), are gradually being converted to kilometres per hour (kph) – 30mph (48kph) in cities and towns, 60mph (96kph) on the open road, and 70mph (112kph) on divided highways and motorways. (1 mile = 1.6km; 1km = 0.6 miles).

Seat belts are required for the driver and all passengers. Pedestrians have right of way, especially at marked crossings. Ireland has strict rules against mixing driving with alcohol; do not drink and drive. Ireland also has strict enforcement of speed limits.

SIGHTSEEING ATTRACTIONS AND ACTIVITIES

In the course of outlining the suggested itineraries in this book, we make specific recommendations for attractions, historic sites and castles to visit, and other things to do. Since opening times and admission rates change from year to year and sometimes with the seasons, we have not listed any specific prices or hours, but we do state what days of the week a place is open. Unless otherwise indicated, attractions are open all year including Easter and other bank-holiday weekends, but are closed for a few days at Christmas/New Year and on Good Friday.

If there is an admission charge, we use the following code (€ as the symbol for the euro in the Republic of Ireland, and £ as a symbol for pound sterling in Northern Ireland):

REPUBLIC OF IRELAND	NORTHERN IRELAND
€ – under €6 per person	£ – under £5 per person
€€ – €6 to €12 per person	££ – £5 to £10 per person
€€€ – over €12 per person	£££ – over £10 per person

Admission for children is generally about half of adult admission, and seniors usually get a discount of ten percent or more.

MONEY-SAVING IDEAS

Although Ireland is not a travel bargain, here are some good ways to trim costs:

MEALS: Ask at any tourist office for a copy of the *Value Menu Restaurant Guide*. This free pocket-sized guide provides details on more than 200 restaurants in three price categories – €10, €20 and €30 (per person meal prices for a minimum of two courses including service charge). This guide also lists the times and days when these special-value meals are available. In addition, if you are willing to dine early (seatings usually before 6.30pm or 7pm), some restaurants offer reduced-price 'early bird' dinner menus, providing savings of twenty to thirty percent off usual dinner menus. In the larger cities, early-dining choices are usually known as 'pre-theatre' menus.

ATTRACTIONS: Invest in a discount card or publication that provides reduced admission charges at sightseeing attractions. The three main choices are:

Heritage Card – this credit-card-sized pass is valid for reduced admissions at over sixty-five heritage sites. Valid for one year from date of purchase, it's available at individual heritage sites in Ireland or in advance by contacting the Heritage Service, 6 Upper Ely Place, Dublin 2 (tel. 01 647 2461, or CALLSAVE 1850 600 601 within Ireland only; or www.heritageireland.ie).

Ireland at a Glimpse – provides two-for-one admission coupons at over 100 attractions. It's sold at most bookshops and tourist offices throughout Ireland and Northern Ireland; also from the publisher:

Peter Little Publications, Ards Business Centre Ltd, Jubilee Road, Newtownards, Co. Down BT23 4YH (tel. 028 9182 3331 or www.take-a-glimpse.com).

Inside Ireland – a quarterly newsletter and information service that includes money-saving travel tips and centrefold discount coupons for accommodation, restaurants and activities. To subscribe, contact: Brenda Weir, Editor, *Inside Ireland*, PO Box 1886, Dublin 16 (tel. 01 493 1906 or www.insideireland.com).

SHOPPING: Almost all souvenirs and gifts purchased in Ireland are subject to VAT (Value Added Tax) at point of sale. This tax is built into the ticket price. Non-EU residents can get a refund of the tax paid (on all goods taken out of Ireland) by requesting a VAT refund form and submitting it on departure from Shannon or Dublin. Refunds are given in cash or processed to a credit card. More information is available from tourist offices or Global Refund, www.globalrefund.ie.

WHAT ARE 'PAT'S PICKS'?

Quite simply, these are some of my favourite restaurants, pubs and digressions, over and above the itineraries. For every chapter, I list a few of my 'picks' in each category. These recommendations are based on my own experience over the years and are not meant to be comprehensive – just a few ideas to start off your travels in each new area.

RESTAURANTS: More than 230 restaurants and cafés are described in this book. As you explore Ireland, you'll be on the lookout for good places to stop for snacks or lunch during the day, and good restaurants for evening meals. Prices will vary according to what you eat or drink but menus are normally posted outside in a window or beside the entrance. For a directory, contact: Restaurants Association of Ireland, 11 Bridge Court, City Gate, St Augustine Street, Dublin 8 (tel. 01 677 9901). The Adlib eatery website features Irish restaurants by category online at www.adlib.ie.

PUBS: In the chapters that follow, we provide short descriptions for over 180 pubs in towns and cities, and scattered throughout the countryside. As the social hubs of Ireland, pubs are an integral part of any short or long break. Stop in for a drink, a cup of coffee or tea or 'pub grub'. We also include some pubs known for music sessions at night (sessions normally start after 9 or 9.30pm). Helpful pub websites include Irish Pub Guides, www.IrishPubGuides.com, and Irish Music Bars, www.IrishMusicBars.com.

DIGRESSIONS: In all of our chapters, we add a few lines about nearby places of interest, special scenic drives, car ferries, or local tours via boat, train, or other conveyance such as horse-drawn traps or carriages. Such digressions can add zest to your trip and are well worth taking a slight detour to sample. We have more than 125 digressions on these pages for you to consider.

A FINAL WORD OF ADVICE

Be selective in your travels. It isn't necessary to see or do everything at any given destination. Choose what appeals to you. Some buildings can be enjoyed from the outside; you don't have to trudge through every corridor. Conversely, if one attraction really wins your fancy, you can devote a half-day or more to it. Your breaks (whether short or long) should be fun, not a stamina test. If time starts to run out, just amble into the nearest café or pub, sit down, and savour the moment. That's what 'taking a break in Ireland' is all about …

Dublin and
the East Coast

3. Dublin – Ireland's Capital

Over the years, a walk around Dublin's Fair City has always come highly recommended. The Vikings braved fierce seas in long wooden ships to reach Dublin's shores and settle in. The Normans came as conquerors but made themselves at home, sauntering along the cobbled streets. The English invaded and stayed 800 years. Molly Malone made a career out of walking the streets with her wheelbarrow. James Joyce chronicled almost every nook and cranny of the city. The list goes on, right up until today as Dublin continues to delight residents and visitors alike. It's no secret that this is one of the top cities of Europe for short breaks, whether at weekends or midweek.

And why wouldn't it be? Bordered by the Irish Sea and sheltered on three sides by mountains, Dublin is one of Europe's most picturesque capitals. It is bisected from west to east by the River Liffey, which has no fewer than fifteen bridges spanning its wide embrace.

Rich in history and steeped in progress, Dublin's streetscapes are a harmonious blend of narrow laneways and wide avenues, medieval castles and multi-storey shopping centres, eighteenth-century Georgian landmarks and glassy contemporary skyscrapers, horse-drawn carriages and double-decker buses, dozens of chic pavement cafés and over 1,000 friendly pubs.

Stroll the streets of Dublin and experience more than 1,000 years of history, interspersed with an exciting mix of new hotels, multicultural restaurants, theatres, galleries, transport systems, world-class shops, pedestrianised streets and squares, and indeed whole new residential areas like Smithfield, Customs House Quay and Temple Bar. If you haven't been to Dublin in a few years, you'll hardly recognise it. And if you have never been here before, you have a real treat ahead. Get out your best walking shoes and enjoy – three different Dublin walking tours are outlined on the following pages.

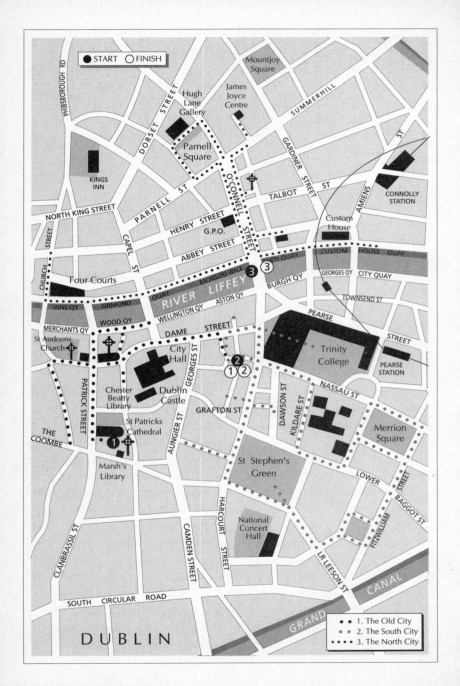

● START ○ FINISH

Mountjoy Square

PHIBSBOROUGH RD

DORSET STREET

Hugh Lane Gallery

James Joyce Centre

SUMMERHILL

Parnell Square

KINGS INN

PARNELL ST

O'CONNELL STREET

GARDINER STREET

ST

CONNOLLY STATION

TALBOT

AMIENS ST

NORTH KING STREET

HENRY STREET

G.P.O.

Custom House

CAPEL ST

ABBEY STREET

STREET

CUSTOM HOUSE QUAY

CHURCH

STREET

Four Courts

BACHELORS WALK

QUAY

RIVER LIFFEY

GREEN QUAY

BURGH QY

GEORGES QY

CITY QUAY

3

3

INNS QY

ORMOND

WOOD QY

WELLINGTON QY

ASTON QY

TOWNSEND ST

MERCHANTS QY

St Audoens Church

DAME

STREET

PEARSE

STREET

City Hall

GEORGES ST

Trinity College

PEARSE STATION

PATRICK STREET

Chester Beatty Library

Dublin Castle

2
1 2

NASSAU ST

GRAFTON ST

DAWSON ST

KILDARE ST

St Patricks Cathedral

AUNGIER ST

Merrion Square

THE COOMBE

1

Marsh's Library

St Stephen's Green

LOWER

STREET

BAGGOT ST

CLANBRASSIL ST

CAMDEN STREET

HARCOURT STREET

National Concert Hall

FITZWILLIAM

LR LEESON ST

GRAND

CANAL

SOUTH   CIRCULAR   ROAD

DUBLIN

●━● 1. The Old City
● ● 2. The South City
●●●● 3. The North City

16 TAKE A BREAK IN IRELAND

FAST FACTS

Travel Information Offices

DUBLIN TOURISM CENTRE, Suffolk Street, Dublin 2 (tel. 605 7725), with other branches at the following locations: Arrivals Hall, Dublin Airport; 14 Upper O'Connell Street, Dublin 1; Dún Laoghaire Ferry Terminal, Dún Laoghaire Harbour, Co. Dublin; Baggot Street Bridge, Dublin 2; and the Square Town Centre, Tallaght, Dublin 24. Open all year.

TRAVEL INFORMATION ONLINE: www.visitdublin.com

TELEPHONE AREA CODE: The telephone area code for all numbers in Dublin is 01.

MAJOR EVENTS

ST PATRICK'S FESTIVAL – Although St Patrick's Day is a national holiday, no city or town celebrates it in such a big way as Dublin, with a week-long schedule of events. The programme includes a huge parade, plus street theatre, fireworks, treasure hunt, *céilithe* and more. Information: St Patrick's Festival Office, tel. 676 3205 or www.stpatricksday.ie. (Mid-March)

DUBLIN HORSE SHOW – This is the principal sporting and social event on the Irish calendar, attracting visitors from all parts of the world. More than 2,000 horses also travel to Dublin for showjumping and dressage competitions. Highlights of the week include a fashionable 'ladies day', formal balls and trophy presentations. Information: Royal Dublin Society, Ballsbridge, tel. 668 0866 or www.rds.ie. (Early August)

DUBLIN THEATRE FESTIVAL – As Europe's oldest specialist theatre festival, this two-week event offers the best of world theatre, as well as new productions from all the major Irish companies, including the Abbey and the Gate. Information: Dublin Theatre Festival, tel. 677 8439 or www.dublintheatrefestival.com. (End of September into early October)

DUBLIN CITY MARATHON – Competitors from all over the world gather to run through the Georgian streets and suburbs of Dublin's fair city. Information: Dublin City Marathon, tel. 626 3757 or www.dublincitymarathon.ie. (Last Monday of October)

DUBLIN CITY WALKING TOUR – THE OLD CITY

Duration: 2–5 hours plus stops

Where and when did Dublin begin? This tour traces the path of Dublin's earliest recorded history, a walking route to places of early Christian, Viking, Norman and medieval heritage. Although evidence of human life in Ireland can be traced back at least 10,000 years, published accounts of

Dublin go back only to 130–180AD, when the geographer Ptolemy pinpointed it on the map as a place of note, labelling it *Eblana*. Like most great European cities, Dublin sprang up beside a body of water, the **River Liffey**. The settlement began as a ford at the junction of two important trading routes – the Liffey and its tributary, the Poddle. It became known as *Baile Átha Cliath*, a name that means 'town of the hurdle ford'. Eventually, it was referred to as *Dubhlinn,* an Irish or Gaelic word meaning 'black pool'. From those days, all that remains visible today is the River Liffey.

In the fifth century Dublin became a focal point when St Patrick visited and converted the inhabitants to Christianity. Start your tour at **St Patrick's Cathedral**, Patrick's Close (tel. 475 4817). This is Dublin's oldest Christian site, built on land that was known as Cross Poddle, because the River Poddle flowed beside it. It was here, on the grounds now known as St Patrick's Park, that Patrick baptised converts at a small spring. Just inside the entrance gate of the park, a small stone marks the site of the spring, known today as St Patrick's Well. A church of some sort and size has stood on this site since Patrick's time, but it was not elevated to the status of cathedral until 1213. Today, St Patrick's is the longest church in Ireland, with a 91.5-metre (300-foot) interior, and walls covered with memorials of the past. The massive west tower, dating from 1370, houses the largest ringing peal bells in Ireland. Although the cathedral has had many deans, by far the most celebrated was Jonathan Swift, author of *Gulliver's Travels*, who presided here from 1713 to 1744. Swift is buried here, as is his beloved 'Stella' (Esther Johnson). His pulpit and chair and other belongings are on display in the north transept. Open daily. Admission: €

The focus of the city shifted to the banks of the River Liffey in the ninth century when the Vikings sailed into Dublin Bay. The Norse built a seafort beside the River Liffey in 841 and the Danes took possession of the town twelve years later. These Viking raiders called the settlement *Dyflin,* to suit their language.

Follow Patrick Street northward, the pathway of the original River Poddle, to **Christ Church Cathedral**, Christ Church Place (tel. 677 8099), Dublin's other great cathedral and the centrepiece of the city's Viking heritage. Officially named the Cathedral of the Holy Trinity, it was built as a wooden church in cruciform style in 1038 for Sitric Silkenbeard, the Norse king of Dublin, and has been enlarged and rebuilt over the years. Highlights include magnificent stonework and graceful pointed arches, with delicately chiselled supporting columns; the tomb of Strongbow, the Norman earl of Pembroke; and a crypt considered Dublin's oldest surviving building, which includes the official Stocks of the Liberty of Christchurch, made in 1670, where criminals were fastened for public ridicule. Today, the Cathedral is the mother church for the Diocese of Dublin and Glendalough of the Church of Ireland (Anglican/Episcopal). Open daily. Admission: €

From Christ Church, walk down **Winetavern Street**, which, as its name suggests, was originally a medieval drinking centre. Once lined with taverns and alehouses, it was the hub of trades related to drinking, such as cask-making. In a different vein, Pickett's Tower, a square stone building, once stood at the bottom of the street. A publishing house, it produced the first book printed in Ireland in 1551 – an edition of *The Book of Common Prayer*. Beside the Liffey is **Wood Quay**. Although today you will see a modern office complex, the home of the Dublin Corporation Civic Offices, this was the site of the original Viking city of Dublin. During recent excavations, before the offices were built, archaeological digs revealed the layout, houses, walls and quays of Dublin as they existed in the ninth to eleventh centuries.

From Wood Quay, walk east along the River Liffey. On the right is **Fishamble Street**, a narrow passage that was once a Viking fish market. In subsequent years it was a fashionable street and home to a music hall that opened in 1741. Although the music hall is long gone, a plaque on a remaining building indicates that the first performance of Handel's *Messiah* was given here on 13 April 1742.

Continue east to Essex Quay. The building on the right is the former Franciscan church of Saints Michael and John, built in 1815. Prior to that, it was one of Dublin's most notable playhouses, the Smock Alley Theatre (1661–1790).

After this short diversion, return to Christchurch Place (via Fishamble Street) and continue walking west to **High Street**, one of Dublin's principal streets in the Middle Ages. On the right-hand side are the two churches named St Audoen, in honour of St Ouen of Rouen, patron saint of the Normans who came to conquer the Irish after the Vikings. The first church, with a dark stone exterior and Corinthian portico, is relatively modern, dating back to the nineteenth century. The second, smaller, church is the original **St Audoen's Church** (tel. 677 0088), built by the Normans *c*.1190 and said to be the only surviving medieval parish church in Dublin. The churchyard has been turned into a park to showcase the old city walls, dating back to 1214. A set of steps leads down to **St Audoen's Arch**, the only gateway of the old city that is still standing. The gate and surrounding walls were restored in the 1880s. Although the church is partly in ruins, significant sections have survived, including the west doorway, which dates from 1190, and the nave from the thirteenth century. In addition, the seventeenth-century bell tower houses three bells that were cast in 1423, making them the oldest in Ireland. The grounds also include an early Christian gravestone, dating to the eighth century. Open daily, June–September. Admission: €

The avenue in front of St Audoen's is known as **The Cornmarket** because in the thirteenth century it was an important trade and street-market site. Nothing remains of the original cornmarket except the name.

For a slight detour, turn right from the Cornmarket and follow **Bridge Street** down towards the Liffey. On the left-hand side, you will come to **The Brazen Head** (see Pubs below), dating back to 1198 and reputed to be the city's oldest pub. Step inside and explore the various rooms filled with Dublin city memorabilia.

Return to the Cornmarket and then cross over to **Francis Street**, known as Dublin's 'antiques row' because of its abundance of fine antique shops. A notable building, about mid-way along the street, is the church of **St Nicholas in Myra**, a handsome neoclassical structure of fairly recent vintage, dating back to the 1830s.

From Francis Street, return to the Cornmarket and make a right onto **High Street**. Take the cut-off to the right for **Back Lane**, a narrow thoroughfare dating from 1610 and once the location of a Jesuit university and chapel. Back Lane is today the address of **Tailors'**

Hall, *c.*1418 and 1706, Dublin's last-surviving guildhall, set up in the Middle Ages to represent the interests of craftsmen and traders. Built for the guild of tailors, it was also used by other guilds – hosiers, tanners, saddlers and barber-surgeons. Since 1983, it has been the headquarters of An Taisce (the National Trust for Ireland), and is not open to the public for tours.

Return to High Street, and at the corner of High and Winetavern Streets, you will see a picturesque bridge linking Christchurch Cathedral with its Synod Hall. In recent years, the hall has been converted into a heritage attraction known as **Dublinia**, St Michael's Hill, Christ Church Place (tel. 679 4611). Dublinia depicts Dublin as a medieval city – from the coming of the Anglo-Normans in 1170 to the Reformation and the closure of the monasteries in the 1530s. A tour starts with a scale model of the old city and an illuminated Medieval Maze, complete with visual effects, background sounds and aromas. The next segment depicts everyday life in medieval Dublin, with a diorama, as well as a prototype of a thirteenth-century quay along the banks of the Liffey. You can roam among craftsmen and guildsmen at work, learn what they were paid, visit a typical merchant's house of the fifteenth century, and enter a medieval parish church. The final segment takes you into the Great Hall for a 360-degree wraparound portrait of medieval Dublin via a twelve-minute cyclorama-style audiovisual. Afterwards, you can also climb the seventeenth-century St Michael's Tower, for a panoramic view of modern Dublin. Allow one to two hours to complete a visit. Open daily. Admission: €€

From Christchurch Place, continue one block east to Castle Street and **St Werburgh's Church** (tel. 478 3710), a seventeenth- to eighteenth-century structure of Anglo-Norman origin on the site of an earlier Viking foundation. Open by appointment or at services each Sunday at 10.30. Admission: free

St Werburgh's was once the parish church of **Dublin Castle**, Castle Street, off Dame Street (tel. 677 7129). Built between 1208 and 1220, Dublin Castle is the historic centre of Dublin. It sits on ground that was part of an original ninth-century Viking fortress and moat, and it is believed that a defensive rath or earthwork stood here before that. Representing some of the oldest surviving architecture in the city, this building was the focal point of British power in Ireland for seven centuries until it was taken over by the Irish in 1922. It is now owned by the Irish state. The circular keep known as the Record Tower, built in 1204, and the Bermingham Tower which was added in the fourteenth century, are the only remaining features of the original castle. The most important section is the State Apartments, once the residence of English viceroys and now the setting for government ceremonial functions, such as the inauguration of Ireland's presidents, state receptions and meetings of heads of state of the European Union. The castle complex also includes the Chapel Royal, built between 1807 and 1814; an undercroft showcasing recent archaeological excavations; and the Treasury, built in 1712–1715 and believed to be the oldest surviving purpose-built office building in Ireland. Open daily. Admission: €

The eighteenth-century Clock Tower building on the Dublin Castle grounds is home to one of Ireland's most significant art attractions – **The Chester Beatty Library** (tel. 407 0750), a world-famous collection of Early Christian writings, Islamic and East Asian manuscripts, paintings, prints and printed books. The works were assembled by a single collector, Sir Alfred Chester Beatty, who bequeathed his treasures to the Irish people on his death in 1968. Outstanding exhibits in these galleries range from great illuminated copies of the Qur'an dating from the ninth to the nineteenth century AD; and ancient papyri, including the famous Egyptian love poems of $c.1100$BC; to some of the earliest Gospels and other New Testament texts, dating to $c.200$AD. Works of art include some of the finest Chinese jade books in the world, exquisite calligraphy and miniature paintings. The Clock Tower building sits next to the castle's walled gardens, which offer a refreshing respite in the centre of the city. Open daily except Mondays in October–April. Admission: free

To the east of Dublin Castle, as Dame Street meets Parliament Street, is **City Hall** (tel. 672 2204), recently restored at a cost of €5 million. Designed in 1769 by Thomas Cooley, and built in 1769–79, it was originally the city's Royal Exchange where Dublin merchants came to trade stocks and shares. It was taken over by Dublin Corporation in 1851 and renamed Dublin City Hall. A fine example of neoclassical architecture, the building pre-dates the Four Courts and the Custom House. In addition to cleaning the Portland stone exterior, the restoration has brought the interior back to its original design – a massive domed rotunda with marble columns and flooring, huge windows and doors, elaborate plasterwork on the ceiling beams, a pair of cantilevered stone staircases, frescoes depicting Dublin history, statues of Daniel O'Connell and other prominent Dubliners, and a distinctive circular mosaic of the Dublin coat-of-arms (granted to the city in 1607).

Meander down the stairs (or use the new lift) to explore the vaulted basement that has been transformed into a museum focusing on 'The Story of the Capital'. It offers displays of Dublin treasures such as the Great Sword given by Henry VI, moulds for the thirteenth-century city seal, early charters and manuscripts and other civic regalia, as well as timelines, audiovisuals and a café. Open daily except Sunday mornings. Admission: €

From City Hall, continue eastward along Dame Street until you reach Trinity Street; turn right and at the corner of Trinity and Andrew Streets is the former **St Andrews's Church** – a Gothic-style building dating back to 1866 and reputed to have Viking and medieval roots – recently given new life as the **Dublin Tourism Centre**. It's no wonder that the city's main visitor centre/tourist information office is housed in such a historic site – just read on to learn what was once across the street.

Continuing past the tourism centre to Suffolk Street, cross over to **Church Lane**. Use your imagination to picture what stood here 1,000 years ago – *Thingmote*, a 12-metre (40-foot) high earth mound built by the Vikings as the location of their parliaments and assemblies. A temporary palace was built on the site in 1172 for meetings between the Norman King Henry II and Irish chieftains. In medieval times, it served as a place for public entertainment and executions until it was levelled in 1681. Excavations along Suffolk Street have unearthed weapons from the Norse period, which are now in the National Museum. End your tour here or by returning to the tourist office, an excellent source for books and brochures about Dublin's early years.

DUBLIN CITY WALKING TOUR – THE SOUTH SIDE

Half-day or full-day, depending on stops

In recent years, the heart of Dublin has shifted from O'Connell Street, on the north side of the River Liffey, to Grafton Street on the south side of the river. The focal point is the sector stretching just south of O'Connell Bridge, from Trinity College to St Stephen's Green, with Grafton Street as the connection. A busy shopping thoroughfare, Grafton Street is a buzz of activity, from buskers and sidewalk artists to a constant stream of shoppers and browsers. Restricted to pedestrians during prime business hours, Grafton Street has experienced a ripple effect – with the attractions of that street fanning out to a ring of surrounding streets where still more shops are situated, plus a variety of museums, government buildings, cultural centres, eighteenth-century architectural landmarks and squares, restaurants and hotels. This area is 'the place' to be in Dublin, for locals and visitors alike.

Start this tour at the Dublin Tourism Centre (where the Old City tour concluded) on Suffolk Street, just off the north end of Grafton Street. Cross over to Trinity Street, a small corridor facing the front of the tourist office, leading into Dame Street. To the right is College Green and the setting of one of Dublin's prime visitor attractions – **Trinity College** (tel. 608 2320). With an impressive 90-metre (300-foot) wide Palladian façade, Trinity College stands out on the Dublin streetscape. Founded in 1592 by Queen Elizabeth I, Trinity is the oldest university in Ireland, and the sole constituent college of the University of Dublin, although most of the buildings in the current layout were erected over the period 1752–1759. Over the centuries, Trinity has turned out some very impressive alumni – from Jonathan Swift and Oscar Wilde to Nobel Prize-winner Samuel Beckett, and Bram Stoker (author of *Dracula*), as well as Ireland's first president, Douglas Hyde, and Ireland's first woman president, Mary Robinson.

On either side of the main gate are statues of two other famous graduates, the orator Edmund Burke (left, as you enter), and the playwright and poet, Oliver Goldsmith. Passing under the archway, you will enter the wide cobbled quadrangle called **Parliament Square**, commonly known as Front Square. Directly ahead is the **Campanile**, donated in 1853 by the Archbishop of Armagh, Lord Beresford. Behind the Campanile, at the far end of the square, is a row of red-brick buildings, the **Rubrics**, dating from 1700 – the oldest surviving buildings of the College. To the right is the **Examination Hall**, designed by Sir William Chambers and built between 1779 and the mid-1780s, and to the left is the **Chapel**, also designed by Chambers, added in 1798. The only chapel in Ireland that is shared by all Christian denominations, it also has a small adjacent cemetery, known as **Challoner's Corner**, reserved for burials of Provosts of the College. Beside the Chapel is the **Dining Hall**, designed in 1743 by Richard Castle.

To the right of the square is the **Old Library**, designed by Thomas Burgh and built between 1712 and 1732. The centrepiece of this building is the Colonnades Gallery on the ground floor. This exhibition space contains some of the college's greatest treasures including the world famous **Book of Kells**, a handscripted and illuminated edition of the Four Gospels, dating back to the ninth century or earlier. Each day a new page is turned for visitor viewing. Other ancient items on permanent exhibit include the Book of Armagh and the Book of Durrow, a copy of the 1916 Proclamation of the Irish Republic, and an elaborately carved harp, dating to the fifteenth/sixteenth century, and considered to be Ireland's oldest harp, made of willow with 29 strings. Open daily, year-round, except Sunday mornings during October–May. Admission: €€

After passing through the exhibition area, visitors are directed upstairs for a walk-through tour of the library's most celebrated room, the 64-metre (210-foot) long and 12-metre (40-foot) high **Long Room**. Recognised as the largest single-chamber library in Europe, the Long Room contains over 200,000 of the library's oldest books. The total Trinity library collection, spread over eight buildings, consists of more than 3 million volumes published from the sixteenth to the twentieth century – a figure that is always growing, thanks to the copyright law of 1801 specifying that a copy of every book printed in Britain or Ireland must be sent here.

Beyond the Rubrics is **New Square**, built in 1838–44, containing a printing house and a museum. A multimedia audiovisual exhibition, 'The Dublin Experience', which tells the story of Dublin from its origins to the present day, is on view from late May through early October in the Davis Theatre. Admission: €

Return to the front gate of Trinity and cross over College Green to see the **Bank of Ireland**, 2 College Green (tel. 677 6801). Built originally to house the Irish Parliament, this unique windowless structure is regarded as one of the finest specimens of Dublin's eighteenth-century architecture. Begun in 1729 from the design of Sir Edward Lovett Pearce, the surveyor-general of Ireland, the building was enhanced in 1765 by the work of James Gandon. Initially, this grand Georgian-era symbol enjoyed a short-lived glory as the seat of government, but when the Irish Parliament voted itself out of existence in 1800 (the only recorded Parliament in history to do so), power shifted back to London. It became the headquarters of the Bank of Ireland in 1801. Even though it has served as a working bank ever since, you can still tour the original House of Lords room (guided tours on Tuesdays only), with its elaborate coffered ceilings, heirloom tapestries, and a Waterford Crystal chandelier dating back to 1765. Open Monday–Friday. Admission: free

The adjacent **Bank of Ireland Arts Centre** (tel. 677 6801), in the old bank armoury, is the setting for 'A Journey through 2,000 Years of Irish History' museum. Spread over three floors, the exhibition reflects the role played by banking in the economic and social development of Ireland in the past two centuries. Open Tuesday–Friday. Admission: €

From the Bank, cross back over College Green to the front of Trinity and then take a left turn onto Nassau Street which runs along the south border of the college grounds. Continue along Nassau Street, a busy shopping strip, and then make a right on to Kildare Street. On the left-hand side is the **Heraldic Museum**, 2 Kildare Street (tel. 603 0311), the home of Ireland's chief herald and the only museum of its kind in the world that focuses exclusively on the uses of heraldry. Exhibits include shields, banners, coins, paintings, porcelain, and stamps depicting coats of arms. If you are interested in tracing your Irish family name or ancestral roots, this is the place to start. The building itself, originally used as the

Kildare Street Club for the Dublin élite, was erected in 1861 in a Venetian style. The intricate and witty carvings of animals around the window ledges have been well preserved. Open Monday–Friday, and Saturday morning. Admission: free

Next door is the **National Library of Ireland** (tel. 603 0200). Founded in 1877, this is the largest public library in the country, the repository for half a million books, prints and manuscripts. It has an unrivalled collection of maps of Ireland and an extensive accumulation of Irish newspapers, as well as first editions of many Irish authors such as Swift, Yeats, Shaw, Joyce and Goldsmith. It also has an extensive collection of ancestral information and records, to help in family searches. Open Monday–Friday, and Saturday morning. Admission: free

As you exit the National Library, turn left for the **National Museum of Archaeology and History**, Kildare Street (tel. 677 7444). Home of many great historic treasures, this museum is worth several hours of time to learn about Ireland's heritage. Opened in 1890, it displays many archaeological treasures, dating from 2000BC to the twentieth century. The collections consist of five distinct areas: 'The Treasury', a suite of rooms housing a collection of Celtic antiquities including such one-of-a-kind pieces as the Tara Brooch, Ardagh Chalice and Cross of

Cong; 'Ór – Ireland's Gold', the finest collection of prehistoric gold artefacts in Europe; 'Prehistoric Ireland', an exhibition spotlighting the everyday material culture of the time; 'Viking Ireland', focusing on Irish archaeology from 800–1200AD; and 'Medieval Ireland' (1150–1550), depicting life in Ireland in the age of cathedrals, monasteries and castles. Open Tuesday–Saturday, and Sunday afternoon. Admission: free

At the foot of Kildare Street, make a left to see the fanciful brick and white-trimmed façade of **Le Meridien Shelbourne Hotel**, 27 St Stephen's Green. One of Dublin's landmark hotels, the Shelbourne dates back to 1824 and played an important role in Irish history (the Irish constitution was signed in room 112 in 1921), and it has often been host to world leaders, literary giants, and stars of stage and screen. Just past the hotel, on Merrion Row, you'll see a set of wrought-iron gates of a small seventeenth- to eighteenth-century cemetery – the **Huguenot Graveyard**. Last used in 1901, it is usually locked.

Continue along Merrion Row and make a left at Upper Merrion Street. On the left, you will pass a series of government buildings, including the Department of the Taoiseach, followed by the entrance to the **National Museum of Natural History** (tel. 677 7444), another division of the National Museum of Ireland. This branch focuses on the zoological aspect of Ireland's history, with collections on wildlife, ranging from mammals and birds, to butterflies and insects. Open Tuesday–Saturday, and Sunday afternoon. Admission: free

Merrion Street now merges into Merrion Square West, a segment of the rectangular park known as **Merrion Square**. Laid out in 1762, it is considered to be the core of the best-preserved section of Georgian Dublin. The park contains flowers, shrubs, trees and benches, as well as the Rutland Fountain of 1791, one of the few Georgian drinking fountains left in the city.

The leafy park is bordered by four streets of impressive Georgian townhouses. It has always been a distinguished address for Dubliners, from Daniel O'Connell (number 50), William Butler Yeats (number 82) and George Russell, otherwise known as AE (number 84), to Oscar Wilde and his parents, Sir William and Lady Jane Wilde (who wrote under the pen-name, 'Speranza') (number 1). This house, **Oscar Wilde House**, 1 Merrion Square North (tel. 662 0281), is open to the public and is an excellent example of Georgian architecture, with many remarkable cornices, architraves and decorative centrepieces. The Wilde family took up residence in 1855, and Oscar lived here until 1876. An assortment of Wilde's books and memorabilia is on display. The American College of Dublin currently owns the building. Open Monday, Wednesday and Thursday morning. Admission: €

The most important building facing Merrion Square is **Leinster House**, Kildare Street and Merrion Square (tel. 678 9911). Set back from the street and surrounded by wrought-iron railings and entrance gates, this impressive building is the meeting place of Ireland's government, Dáil Éireann (the parliament of Ireland) and An Seanad (the senate). Dating back to 1745 and designed with a 42.5-metre (140-foot) façade, this building once ranked as the largest Georgian building in Dublin. With an impressive central pediment and Corinthian columns, it is said to have been the model from which James Hogan, the Irish-born architect, later designed the White House in Washington DC. It is usually open for tours when the Dáil is not in session, but phoning in advance is strongly recommended. Open Tuesday–Thursday during May–September. Admission: free

The adjacent building is the **National Gallery of Ireland**, Merrion Square West (tel. 661 5133). A cultural hub of Dublin, this expansive art museum, which welcomes over one million visitors a year, is home to an outstanding collection of European works, from Rembrandt and Caravaggio to Goya, with particular emphasis on Dutch, French, German and Italian paintings.

As might be expected, the gallery also houses an extensive collection of works by Irish artists, including a Yeats Museum, showing paintings by Jack B Yeats, one of the foremost Irish painters of the twentieth century, and his father John Butler Yeats. There is also a print room and icon collection area.

Among the gallery's staunchest supporters over the years was Dublin writer and Nobel Prize-winner George Bernard Shaw, author of *Pygmalion* (on which the musical *My Fair Lady* was based), who spent many of his early days studying informally here instead of at school. Shaw bequeathed one-third of his royalties to the gallery and hence it is often referred to as 'The My Fair Lady Gallery'. Open Monday–Saturday, and Sunday afternoon. Admission: free

Walk along Merrion Square to see the splendid array of brick-fronted Georgian houses, each with its own colourful door, or a distinctive knocker, fanlight, ornamental balcony or iron foot-scraper.

Turn right onto Merrion Square East, which then leads into Lower Fitzwilliam Street, another thoroughfare distinguished by its Georgian buildings. To see what the complete interior of a Georgian townhouse looks like, step into **Number Twenty-Nine**, 29 Lower Fitzwilliam Street (tel. 702 6165). This four-storey townhouse has been restored from the basement to the attic as a walk-through museum depicting the lifestyle of a Dublin middle-class family during the period 1790–1820 – including prototypes of a family livingroom, bedrooms, playroom, nursery and kitchen.

The displays include works of art of the time, carpets, curtains, floor coverings, decorations, paintwork, plasterwork and bell pulls. This museum is the joint effort of Ireland's National Museum and the Electricity Supply Board (ESB). Open Tuesday–Saturday, and Sunday afternoon. Admission: €

Cross from Lower Fitzwilliam to Upper Fitzwilliam Street, via Baggot Street, to see **Fitzwilliam Square**, dating back to 1820, and the last and smallest of the great Georgian squares to be developed. It is also the only city-centre park of its kind to remain private, for use of the residents of the square only. The Georgian buildings that surround this square are today primarily offices for doctors, dentists and other professionals. Walk around Fitzwilliam Square and take a left onto Pembroke Street, also lined with impressive Georgian town houses, which leads into Lower Leeson Street.

Make a right and follow this street for one block to the southeast corner of **St Stephen's Green**, a mid-city park enclosed by wrought-iron railings. Enter via the nearest gate and then take a stroll, or sit back and relax on a bench, to enjoy this magnificent 9-hectare (22-acre) patch of greenery. Usually referred to by locals simply as 'Stephen's Green' or 'The Green', this leafy oasis is the oldest of Dublin's park-like squares. Dating back to medieval times, it was first enclosed in 1670 and formally laid out as a public park in 1880. It contains flowers, trees and shrubs of all types, as well as statuary, gazebos, an ornamental lake and a scented garden for the blind, with plants identified on Braille tags. In the summer months, a Victorian bandstand is the setting for free lunchtime concerts and Shakespearean plays.

Return to the outer footpath outside the railings to continue your walking tour along the south and west sides of the Green, passing a series of interesting buildings, such as **Iveagh House**, 80 St Stephen's Green. Built for a bishop in 1736, it is currently used as the offices for Ireland's Department of Foreign Affairs, and is not open to the public.

Several doors away is **Newman House**, 85–86 St Stephen's Green (tel. 716 7422). Dating back to 1740 and the historic seat of the University of Ireland, this building is named after John Henry Newman, first rector of the university and celebrated cardinal who wrote the influential *Discourses on the Scope and Nature of University Education.* The structure is a blend of two restored town houses, distinguished for their elaborate plasterwork and interior design. A visit to Newman House includes a guided tour and exhibition on recent restoration work. Open Tuesday–Friday in June–August. Admission: €

From St Stephen's Green West, make a short detour one block west at York Street to Aungier Street, to visit

Whitefriar Street Carmelite Church, 57 Aungier Street (tel. 475 8821). One of the largest churches in the city, it was built in 1825–27 on the site of a pre-Reformation Carmelite priory (c.1539) and an earlier (thirteenth-century) Carmelite abbey. Extended over the years, it contains the fifteenth-century black oak Madonna, known as 'Our Lady of Dublin'. This church is also a popular place to visit in mid-February because the body of St Valentine is enshrined here, a gift to the people of Dublin from Pope Gregory XVI in 1836. Open daily. Admission: free

Returning to St Stephen's Green West, one of the most eye-catching buildings along this route is the **St Stephen's Green Shopping Centre** (tel. 478 0888), on the northwest corner of the Green. It is a modern multi-storey indoor shopping mall with a fanciful domed Victorian façade. At this juncture begins the southern end of Grafton Street, Dublin's fashionable shopping corridor. Stroll up Grafton Street, making a few stops en route.

At Anne Street, take a slight detour to the right for one block. Straight ahead is **St Anne's Church**, 18 Dawson Street (tel. 676 7727). It dates back to 1720, but the present structure is mainly from 1868. On the right is the **Mansion House**, the home of Dublin's Lord Mayor. Dating back to 1710, it is a study in Queen Anne-style architecture. It is not open to the public, but the fanciful exterior is well worth a look or a photograph.

Return to Grafton Street, continue northwards, and on your left is **Bewley's Café**, 78–79 Grafton Street (See Restaurants below). This three-storey landmark is the city's quintessential coffee (and tea) house. There is also a coffee museum on the second floor, and lunchtime theatre.

Leave Bewley's by the side exit (Johnson's Court) and follow the narrow laneway to **St Teresa's Church**, Clarendon Street (tel. 671 8466 or 671 8127). Dating back to 1793, this was the first post-Penal church to be legally erected in Dublin for Catholics. One of Dublin's busiest inner-city churches today, St Teresa's is known for its beautiful stained-glass windows.

While on Clarendon Street, take a few moments to enter the **Powerscourt Townhouse Centre** (tel. 679 4144), stretching a full block from Clarendon Street to South William Street. Housed in a restored 1774 townhouse, this four-storey complex consists of over 40 craft and antique shops, boutiques and art galleries.

Return to Grafton Street, in the pathway of leading department stores such as Brown Thomas and Marks & Spencer, to the north end of the street, marked by a bronze statue of **Molly Malone** with her wheelbarrow. The statue was erected in 1988 as part of Dublin's celebration of its 1,000th anniversary as a city.

Take a left onto Suffolk Street and walk one block to **St Andrew's Church**, a building dating back to 1866 and said to have Viking and medieval roots, now serving as the new **Dublin Tourism Centre**, the end of this tour.

DUBLIN CITY WALKING TOUR – THE NORTH SIDE

Duration: Half-day or full-day, depending on stops

Dublin's historic north side, after several decades of stagnation, is enjoying a renaissance – a new buzz of development, activity, and civic pride. From O'Connell Bridge to Parnell Square, things are perking up. It all started in 1988 as Dublin celebrated its 1,000th anniversary. All parts of the city vied to put on the 'best face' for the world. Many of the north side's impressive eighteenth-century buildings were restored and spruced up.

The early 1990s brought a new energiser – the International Financial Services Centre (IFSC) at Custom House Quay, attracting dozens of multinational financial and banking interests. A fine example of urban renewal, the IFSC injected new life into a once-seedy area along the river, with high-rise office buildings, river-view hotels, restaurants and shops. So, step out and enjoy the 'new face' of the north side.

Start your tour at the south end of **O'Connell Street**, Dublin's broad main ceremonial boulevard. Originally known as Drogheda Street, later Gardiner's Mall and then Sackville Street, in the mid-nineteenth century it was renamed in honour of Daniel O'Connell, the 'Liberator', champion of Catholic emancipation in Ireland, and also a former lord mayor of Dublin. The adjoining bridge over the River Liffey was also renamed in tribute to O'Connell, and the monument beside the bridge is a statue of him. O'Connell Street was the hub of patriotic activity during the Irish Rising of 1916, when the Volunteers made their headquarters there.

Walk north from the bridge along O'Connell Street on the left side, crossing over Middle Abbey Street. On the left, you will see **Eason & Son Ltd**, 40–42 Lower O'Connell Street, which has operated as a bookshop for over 100 years at this location, and is a landmark in its own right. Continue for one block to visit the **General Post Office (GPO)**, O'Connell Street (tel. 705 7000), one of Dublin's great historic icons. Built between 1814 and 1818 according to the designs of noted architect Francis Johnston, this was one of the last great public buildings of the Georgian era, but its prime claim to fame is that it was a pivotal point of the Irish struggle for freedom. The Republic of Ireland was proclaimed here in 1916 when the Irish Volunteers commandeered the GPO as their headquarters. Although the patriots put up a brave fight, the building was shelled by a British gunboat anchored in the River Liffey and completely gutted by fire.

Now fully restored, the GPO commemorates the Irish Rising in one of its front windows with a huge bronze statue of the dying *Cú Chulainn*, a legendary Irish folk hero. The building's outer façade still bears bullet holes, as well as the words of the Proclamation of the Irish Republic etched in stone. On an architectural note, the GPO is noted for its giant front Ionic portico, with six fluted columns topped by three stone figures, representing *Mercury*, *Fidelity* and *Hibernia*. It is a full-service post office, as well as a revered landmark. Open daily. Admission: free

As you exit the GPO, look upward at the centre of O'Connell Street to see the **The Spire**, a 120-metre (394-foot) needle-shaped stainless-steel monument that sits in the centre of the median dividing north and south traffic. Erected in six sections in early 2003 at a cost of €4.5 million, this spire is Dublin's (and Ireland's) tallest structure, seven times the height of the surrounding buildings and twice as high as the capital's tallest building, Liberty Hall. Although officially known as 'The Spire', many locals have dubbed it 'The Spike' and predict it will eventually be to Dublin what the Eiffel Tower is to Paris or the Empire State Building to New York.

Take the next turn left onto Henry Street, a busy pedestrianised shopping thoroughfare, with several major department stores, such as Arnott's, Debenham's and Marks & Spencer, as well as the ILAC and Jervis Street Shopping Centres. A right turn off Henry Street will thrust you into one of Dublin's noisiest and most aromatic attractions – **Moore Street**, an open-air market for fresh fish, fruit, vegetables, flowers, and more. Molly Malone would be at home here, except nowadays the street vendors usually arrive each morning with their wares loaded onto four-wheel carts or vans instead of wheelbarrows. You'll find it hard to resist the feisty salesmanship, sharp wit and rich Dublin accents.

Return to O'Connell Street, and continue northwards. Straight ahead are the **Parnell Monument** and **Parnell Square**. Dating back to 1748, this is the oldest of the city's squares after St Stephen's Green. In the mid-eighteenth century, this was one of the most fashionable places to live in Dublin, with palatial town houses occupied by more peers, bishops and members of Parliament than any other part of the city. Both the statue and the square are named after Charles Stewart Parnell, a nineteenth-century Irish leader and advocate of Irish Home Rule, who is fondly referred to as 'the uncrowned king of Ireland'. Today, Parnell Square is a mainly commercial area, with several notable landmarks.

On Parnell Square West is the **Rotunda Hospital**, the oldest maternity hospital in Ireland or Britain (built in 1751–55). Built in the Palladian style, the hospital includes a chapel decorated in Baroque style with very ornate and figurative plasterwork.

As you approach Parnell Square North, a slight cut-off to Granby Row will bring you to the **National Wax Museum**, Upper Dorset Street (tel. 872 6340). It presents an interesting collection of Irish historical and political figures, as well as world leaders and contemporary music stars, and is a great refuge on a rainy day. Open Monday–Saturday, and Sunday afternoon. Admission: €€

Return to the square and continue for half a block to **Dublin City Gallery – The Hugh Lane**, Parnell Square North (tel. 874 1903). The first-ever public gallery of modern art in Ireland, the Hugh Lane gallery opened in 1908 with over 300 works by Irish and continental artists. It was launched with the initiative and resources of art collector Sir Hugh Lane, who subsequently died in the sinking of the *Lusitania* in 1915. With the Lane collection as its core, this art gallery has continued to grow in the past century, with heavy emphasis on Impressionists including works by Monet, Degas and Renoir. The Stained Glass Room contains noteworthy works by Irish artists Harry Clarke, Evie Hone, and James Scanlon. In 1993, it moved to its present location – a building that is an attraction in itself – Charlemont House, one of Dublin's finest houses and often compared to a palace, erected between 1762 and 1765.

One of the most intriguing features of this museum is the art studio of Francis Bacon, an internationally renowned artist who was born in Dublin in 1909 and lived in London until 1925. The contents of his studio, transferred from South Kensington, London, and re-assembled here, reflect the last 30 years of the artist's life including drawings, canvasses and brushes, as well as books and photographs. The studio is accompanied by an audiovisual room, micro gallery, touch-screen terminals, and an exhibition of unfinished Bacon works. Open Tuesday–Sunday. Gallery admission is free; Bacon Studio admission: €€

The adjacent building is the **Dublin Writers' Museum**, 18 Parnell Square North (tel. 872 2077), a showcase of Dublin's (and Ireland's) great literary achievements. Housed in two restored eighteenth-century buildings, it offers literary exhibits focusing on Ireland's four Nobel Prize winners – Shaw, Yeats, Beckett, and Heaney – as well as other famous writers, from Swift and Wilde, to O'Casey, Joyce, Behan and Binchy. Exhibits focus on the history of Irish literature over the past 300 years, with displays of rare editions, manuscript notes, and assorted memorabilia. There is also a gallery of portraits and busts, library, and meeting rooms for writers of today. Open daily. Admission: €€

The distinctive spires of the **Abbey Presbyterian Church** stand out at the juncture of Parnell Square North and North Frederick Street. Although the current Gothic-style building dates back only to 1864, the roots of the Presbyterian congregation in Dublin go back to at least 1660, and the current church contains many objects preserved from earlier times. Locals refer to it as Findlater's Church, because it was built with a large donation from Alexander Findlater, a local wine merchant. Opening times vary. Admission: free

Cross over to the footpath beside Parnell Square to the entrance of the **Garden of Remembrance**, a tranquil setting blending flowers, shrubs, statuary, and water. Dedicated to all those who gave their lives in the cause of Irish freedom, it was created in 1966, on the fiftieth anniversary of the Easter Rising. The mosaics on the floor of the central pool depict broken and discarded weapons, as a sign of peace.

Continue to follow Parnell Square southwards to the **Gate Theatre** (tel. 874 4045 or 874 6042), built in 1784–1786 as an assembly room attached to the Rotunda Hospital. It was converted into a 370-seat theatre in 1930 and run by Hilton Edwards and Micheál Mac Liammóir, pioneers in contemporary Irish theatre who achieved an international reputation by reaching beyond Irish shores and introducing a wide array of European works. The Edwards–Mac Liammóir team helped to launch the careers of many fledgling actors, including Orson Welles and James Mason.

Continuing south, take a slight detour by departing Parnell Square at its southeast corner (onto Parnell Street) and walk one full block and take a left to visit the **James Joyce Centre**, 35 North Great George's Street (tel. 878 8547). Joycean fans and scholars from all over the world gather at this literary shrine celebrating the life and writings of James Joyce, one of Dublin's most creative twentieth-century scribes. Housed in a restored 1784 Georgian town house, the museum's exhibits include a 1922 edition of *Ulysses* and the original Leopold Bloom door from number 7 Eccles Street, as well as other Joycean manuscripts, photos, documents, and memorabilia. There is also a literary archive, reference library, and study area. At various intervals throughout the day, Joyce's relatives and other devotees give readings and conduct 45-minute tours of the house and one-hour walks through 'Joyce Country' in the surrounding neighbourhood. Open Monday–Saturday, and Sunday afternoon. Admission: €; Tours: €€

Return to O'Connell Street, and walk southwards on the east side of the street. One block south of the Parnell Monument is the **Gresham Hotel**, a Regency-style building and one of the oldest hotels in the city, founded in 1817 by Thomas Gresham. Although the area around the hotel has had its ups and downs in recent years, the Gresham holds firm as a bastion of style, hospitality and high standards. Step inside the lobby and view the panorama of Georgian elegance, with marble floors, moulded plasterwork, and crystal chandeliers.

In front of the Gresham, in the central mall, is the Father Theobald Mathew statue, a monument erected in honour of a nineteenth-century priest who founded the Pioneer Total Abstinence Movement in Ireland. The 'Pioneers', as they became known, refrain from alcoholic beverages.

Continuing south, detour left onto Cathedral Street to see **St Mary's Pro-Cathedral**, Cathedral and Marlborough Streets (tel. 874 5441). This is the main Catholic parish church of the city centre. It is the equivalent of a cathedral for Dublin's Roman Catholic population, as the two main cathedrals (St Patrick's and Christ Church) both belong to the Church of Ireland (Anglican/Episcopal). Dedicated in 1825, it combines two unique architectural styles for Dublin – a Greek Revival façade with a six-columned portico modelled after the temple of Theseus in Athens, and a Renaissance-style interior reflecting the design of the church of St Phillippe-le-Roule in Paris. Dubliners and visitors alike flock here at 11 o'clock on Sun-

days to hear the church's celebrated Palestrina Choir, a group that gave the world the great Irish tenor John McCormack. Open daily. Admission: free

Return to O'Connell Street, and walk south to the juncture of North Earl Street, distinguished by its bronze street sculpture of **James Joyce**, standing large as life amid the bustle of Dublin pedestrian traffic. Look to the centre median of O'Connell Street for another view of the Spire (mentioned above), Dublin's new skyscraper monument. Continuing southward, the next building of note is **Clery's**, Ireland's largest department store, dating back to 1883. The monument in the central mall is a statue of **Jim Larkin**, champion of the working class and powerful orator, who organised the Irish Transport and General Workers' Union in 1924.

At the next juncture, take a detour to see the **Abbey Theatre**, Lower Abbey Street (tel. 878 7222), the national theatre of Ireland. Synonymous with some of Ireland's greatest writers, the Abbey was founded in 1904 by William Butler Yeats and Lady Augusta Gregory, and over the years has debuted classics such as *The Playboy of the Western World* by John Millington Synge, *Juno and the Paycock* by Seán O'Casey, *Dancing at Lughnasa* by Brian Friel, and *Da* by Hugh Leonard. In recent years, the Abbey has been at the forefront of encouraging works by new Irish writers such as Sebastian Barry, Marina Carr, Michael Harding and Tom Murphy. The original playhouse, destroyed by fire in 1951, was replaced in 1966 by a modern 600-seat building. Although the theatre is not open for tours, the foyer area – with its colourful posters and portraits from past and present – is accessible during box-office hours; reservations are a must.

Continue south along O'Connell Street for one block to Eden Quay. On the left is **Liberty Hall**, the modern sixteen-storey headquarters of the Irish Transport and General Workers' Union. It was the tallest structure in Dublin until the recent rising of the Spire on O'Connell Street.

Straight ahead is one of the city's foremost public buildings, **The Custom House**, on Custom House Quay (tel. 888 2538). Designed by James Gandon and completed in 1791, it adds a masterfully proportioned profile of bright Portland stone to the north-side quays along the Liffey. The centrepiece is a huge copper dome, topped by a 14.8-metre (16-foot) statue of *Commerce*, surrounded and supported by pavilions, arcades, columns and fourteen 'Riverine Heads' or 'River Gods', each representing one of the thirteen rivers in Ireland plus the Atlantic Ocean. Open mid-March–November, Monday–Saturday, and Sunday afternoon; November–mid-March, Wednesday–Friday, and Sunday afternoon. Admission: €

In contrast, continue one block to see the green-tinted glass façade of the **International Financial Services Centre (IFSC)**, a new government-sponsored development and the epitome of urban renewal, bringing new life to an area that stood for many years in dockside decay. It is now the sleek headquarters for an international assortment of banking and financial institutions. As is so often the case, a nest of new enterprises, ranging from a river-view hotel to wharf-side restaurants and shops, have sprung up on the 11-hectare (27-acre) site around the new financial hub.

Retrace your steps westward now, returning to Eden Quay, and back to the tour's starting point at O'Connell Bridge.

Note: If you have more time and energy, consider this detour or take a taxi or a hop-on/hop-off bus to one or more of these more out-of-the-way places:

From O'Connell Bridge, head west along three long quays – Bachelor's Walk, and Lower and Upper Ormond Quays – to Inns Quay and **The Four Courts**, headquarters of the Irish justice system since 1796. Like the Custom House and other notable Dublin buildings of the Georgian era, this distinctive 134-metre (440-foot) long building was designed by James Gandon. To make it stand out on the Dublin skyline, Gandon gave it a massive 19.5 metre (64-foot) lantern-style dome with Corinthian columns flanked by statues of *Justice, Mercy, Wisdom* and *Moses*.

A block further west leads to **St Michan's Church**, Church Street (tel. 872 4154), a seventeenth-century Church of Ireland edifice with several historic claims to fame. Built on the site of an early Danish chapel (dating back to 1095AD), it gives Dublin's north side one of its strongest Viking connections. It also has some very fine woodwork, including an organ dated 1724 and originally housed in a theatre on Fishamble Street. This is the organ on which Handel is reputed to have played his *Messiah*. The most unique feature of this church, however, is the underground burial vaults. Because of the dry atmosphere, bodies have lain for centuries without showing normal signs of decomposition. The skin of these corpses has remained remarkably soft, even though it is brown and leather-like in appearance. It is said that if you 'shake hands' with the figure known as 'The Crusader', you will always have good luck. Open Monday–Saturday. Admission: €

Turn left at Mary's Lane north of St Michan's and the next right will bring you to **Bow Street**, a cobbled passage that is one of the city's oldest thoroughfares. Legend has it that the street follows the line of a trade route known as *Slighe Mhidhluachra*, which was in existence before the foundation of the city. The street later belonged to the Bow Street Distillery, which ceased operations in 1972, but is now the home of **The Old Jameson Distillery**, Smithfield Village (tel. 807 2355), a museum that tells the story of one of Ireland's brands of whiskey (originally known as *uisce beatha* – the 'water of life'). Accessible only by guided tours, the presentation starts with a film that outlines the 1,400-year history of distilling in Ireland, followed by a series of walk-through exhibits and demonstrations that explain how whiskey is made. The tour culminates in the 'Ball O'Malt Bar', a recreation of a 1920s-style pub, with tastings of the products currently produced. Open daily. Admission: €€

Return to the quays and walk beside the River Liffey. Between Lower Ormond Quay and Bachelor's Walk is the **Liffey Boardwalk**, a picturesque walking path on the north side of the river, and two pedestrian bridges over the River Liffey – **The Millennium Bridge**, built in 1999, and **The Ha'penny Bridge**, built in 1816. Originally known as the Wellington Bridge, the latter acquired its current nick-name because all users originally had to pay a toll of a half-penny to cross over from one side to the other. Don't worry about the toll, however – it was discontinued in 1919. For the record, it is also referred to as 'the metal bridge' because of its sturdy cast-iron construction, but its current official name is Liffey Bridge. Ask any Dubliner, however, and you'll hear it identified simply as the Ha'penny Bridge.

Follow Bachelor's Walk back to O'Connell Bridge, the starting point of the tour.

PAT'S PICKS

RESTAURANTS

Dublin has a plentiful supply of restaurants, cafés, coffee bars, juice bars, noodle bars, tea rooms, burger and pizza places, and ethnic restaurants (from French and Italian to Japanese, Indian, Mexican and Nepalese, to name a few). In the short selection below, we will concentrate on restaurants and cafés that are 'don't miss' experiences in Dublin.

BESHOFF, 14 Westmoreland Street (tel. 677 8026). With an informal Edwardian décor, this classic 'fish-and-chip' shop is run by a family that has been in the seafood business in Dublin since 1913. The menu provides the freshest of fish (often as many as 20 varieties) and chips made from potatoes grown on the Beshoff farm. It is located diagonally across from Trinity College. A second branch is at 7 Upper O'Connell Street (tel. 874 3223). Open daily.

BEWLEY'S CAFÉ, 78–79 Grafton Street (tel. 677 6761). Founded by Quaker Joshua Bewley in 1840, this Dublin landmark is 'the place' to go for coffee, a snack or a full meal, from early morning well into the late evening hours. Relax and enjoy the décor of high ceilings, stained glass, and dark woods, or take in a lunchtime play. Open daily.

BUTLER'S CHOCOLATE CAFÉ, 24 Wicklow Street (tel. 671 0591). Just a block from Grafton Street and run by the famous Irish chocolate company of the same name, this café is a perfect stop for a snack or pick-me-up in the midst of shopping. The menu is sheer heaven for chocolate lovers – fudge shakes, cakes, brownies, truffles and dozens of varieties of handmade chocolates. Beverages range from sinfully rich hot chocolate to coffee, tea and cappuccino. Several other branches have been opened around the city including 18 Nassau Street, directly opposite Trinity College and 9 Chatham Street. Open daily.

CAFÉ BELL, Clarendon Street (tel. 671 8466), This 'coffee shop in a church' is situated in the cobbled courtyard of St Teresa's Church, just off Grafton Street. With indoor and outdoor seating, it's an ideal stop for homemade soup, open sandwiches, stuffed baked potatoes, salads, pastries and pies. Open Monday–Saturday.

CHAPTER ONE, 18–19 Parnell Square (tel. 873 2266). A literary theme dominates the décor and art of this elegant restaurant, situated in the basement of the Dublin Writers' Museum. The menu offers modern Irish cuisine with a touch of French classic influence, for both lunch and dinner.

The early evening pre-theatre menu offers excellent value. Open Tuesday–Saturday, except for two weeks at Christmas.

ELEPHANT & CASTLE, 18 Temple Bar (tel. 679 3121), between Bedford Row and Aston Place. With a décor of modern art and statues of elephants and cartoon characters, this fun restaurant offers an eclectic menu of exotic multi-ingredient salads (Caesar salads are a speciality), omelettes and pastas, as well as the house-special 'Elephant Burger', topped with curried sour cream, bacon, scallions, cheddar cheese and tomato. Open daily.

EPICUREAN FOOD HALL, Lower Liffey Street, off Henry Street. Located in the heart of the city's north-side shopping district, this complex holds several cafés and food shops, ideal for a snack or lunch. Three of the most popular outlets are **Itsabagel** (tel. 874 0486), for the best bagels in Dublin; **C-Bar** (tel. 865 6663), a seafood café; and **Miss Sushi** (tel. 617 4820), a Japanese gourmet take-away and café. Open daily, except Sunday morning.

FADÓ, Dawson Street (tel. 676 7200). Situated on a busy street yet within a garden setting, this elegant restaurant (the name means 'long ago' in the Irish language) is next to the Lord Mayor's residence, one of the best locations in town. The menu features a creative mixture of international dishes with Irish ingredients, including many fresh seafood and vegetarian choices. Open for lunch and dinner, Monday– Saturday.

GALLAGHER'S BOXTY HOUSE, 20–21 Temple Bar (tel. 677 2762), between Bedford Row and Aston Place. Crowds line up at this shop-front restaurant to sample the wide array of boxty, a sort of Irish-style crêpe. It's a traditional rolled potato pancake filled to order with meats, seafood, or vegetables, as well as combinations such as bacon-and-cabbage or beef-and-horseradish. Open for lunch and dinner, daily.

KILKENNY RESTAURANT & CAFÉ, 5–6 Nassau Street (tel. 677 7066), on the first floor (upper level) of the Kilkenny shop, overlooking the playing fields of Trinity College. Even though housed in a shop, it draws many non-shoppers because the food is so reliably good. The self-service menu offers modern Irish and traditional Irish cuisine, such as homemade soups, salads, quiches, casseroles, home-baked breads and cakes. Traditional lamb stew is a speciality. Open for breakfast, lunch and snacks, daily.

LORD EDWARD, 23 Christ Church Place (tel. 454 2420). Dating back to 1890, this upstairs dining-room is Dublin's oldest seafood restaurant. At lunchtime, light snacks and pub grub are available in the downstairs bar. It is located in the heart of the old city, opposite Christ Church Cathedral. Open for dinner, Monday– Saturday; lunch, Monday–Friday.

RESTAURANT PATRICK GUILBAUD, 21 Upper Merrion Street (tel. 603 0600), Meriting two Michelin stars, this is Dublin's most famous restaurant. Owner Patrick Guilbaud, who greets guests personally, blends French recipes with Irish influences and the best of Irish ingredients. It may taste like Paris but it fits well into a classic Dublin town-house setting, with Irish art on the walls and overlooking the gardens of the Merrion Hotel. Open for lunch and dinner, Tuesday–Saturday.

TROCADERO, 3 St Andrew Street (tel. 677 5545). A theatrical atmosphere, clientèle, and décor prevail at this long-time-favourite restaurant (est. 1956), known locally as 'The Troc'. It is renowned for its steaks and its reasonably priced early-bird, pre-theatre and post-theatre menus. It is adjacent to the Dublin Tourism Office. Open for dinner only, Monday– Saturday.

THE WINDING STAIR, 40 Lower Ormond Quay (tel. 873 3292), at Ha'penny Bridge. For lunch or a snack in a literary atmosphere, step inside this café/bookshop, with classical music playing in the background and tall windows overlooking the River Liffey. The three floors, connected by an eighteenth-century winding staircase, offer good books and a self-service menu of sandwiches, soups, salads and natural juices. Open Monday–Saturday, and Sunday afternoon.

PUBS

It is said that Dublin has 1,000 pubs. The following 0.1 per cent will get you started:

THE BRAZEN HEAD, 20 Lower Bridge Street, at Merchant's Quay (tel. 679 5186). With a history that goes back to 1198, this spot claims to be Dublin's oldest pub and it is aptly situated in the old section of the city. Walk through the cobbled courtyard and into the lantern-lit rooms to enjoy a drink, snack or light lunch in a memorabilia-filled atmosphere.

DAVY BYRNE'S, 21 Duke Street, off Grafton Street (tel. 677 5217). Dating back to 1873, this pub is a favourite with poets, writers, and yuppies who come for the turn-of-the-century atmosphere and very classy pub grub (from beef in Guinness to oysters and pheasant in season). James Joyce mentioned it in *Ulysses* as 'a moral pub'.

DOHENY & NESBITT, 5 Lower Baggot Street (tel. 676 2945). The locals call this classic Victorian-style pub simply 'Nesbitt's'. Unlike most Dublin pubs emphasising food or music, this place is an oasis for conversation. There are two fine specimens of 'snugs' here (a small cubicle with a sliding door where women were served drink in private in days of old).

MCDAID'S, 3 Harry Street (tel. 679 4395). Established in 1779, this pub has lots of character and literary ambience (it was a favourite haunt of Brendan Behan's).

Popular with a younger crowd, it is very easy to find, in front of the Westbury Hotel, just off Grafton Street.

NEARY'S, 1 Chatham Street (tel. 677 7371). With globe lanterns, gleaming brass trim, a marble bar, and solid mahogany furnishings, this well-established pub is a haven of traditional atmosphere, just off Grafton Street. It is close to the Gaiety Theatre, so is a favourite with stage folk and theatre-goers, before and after performances.

THE OLD STAND, 37 Exchequer Street (tel. 677 7220). Named after the old stand at the Lansdowne Road rugby grounds, this pub has a definitive sports-bar atmosphere. It is also known for serving hearty pub grub, including Irish stews, steaks, omelettes and chips. It is located around the corner from the Dublin Tourism Office.

O'DONOGHUE'S, 15 Merrion Row (tel. 676 2807). With live traditional music every night, this is the grand-daddy of Dublin's music pubs, just off St Stephen's Green near the Shelbourne Hotel. Arrive here early, as it gets very crowded into the evening.

OLIVER ST JOHN GOGARTY, 57 Fleet Street (tel. 671 1822), is in the heart of Temple Bar. Named after one of Ireland's leading literary figures, it is known for Irish traditional music and dancing sessions, as well as good bar food – stews, steaks, seafood and snacks.

O'NEILL'S, 2 Suffolk Street (tel. 679 3656). Located opposite the Dublin Tourism Office, this pub is just a block from Trinity College so it is popular with college students. It has a lovely old-world exterior, complete with vintage clock over the front door, and it has been in the O'Neill family since 1920. It also serves reasonably priced bar food.

THE PORTERHOUSE, 16–18 Parliament Street (tel. 679 8847). Opened in 1996, this is Dublin's first micro-brewery pub, producing ten different beers on the premises, including a red ale and an oyster stout (made with fresh oysters). Visitors are welcome to watch the brewing process as well as to order from the bar. It is located between the old city and Temple Bar.

DIGRESSIONS

BREWERY TOUR: No visit to Dublin is complete without a visit to the Guinness Brewery. Located slightly off the beaten track on the west side near Heuston Station, the brewery is best reached by bus or by taxi. Visitors are channelled into the Guinness Storehouse, built in 1904 as a plant to ferment and store Guinness stout, and recently transformed into a stunning new €30 million visitor centre. Step inside and enter a giant pint-shaped glass atrium. A walk-through 'Guinness Experience' tour explains how the drink is made, from the ingredients (water, hops, barley and yeast) to the processes (milling, mashing, boiling, fermenting, maturing, clarifying, and blending). The tour culminates with a sampling of the famous dark brew in a rooftop pub, with sweeping 360° views of Dublin. Open daily. Information: Guinness Storehouse, St James's Gate (tel. 408 4800 or www.guinness-storehouse.com).

CASTLE CAPER: With a balanced array of turrets and towers, Malahide Castle is everything a castle should be, and well worth the 12.8 km (8-mile) trip north of the city centre. Nestled in a 100-hectare (250-acre) parkland estate, it was built by Richard Talbot in 1185 and was occupied by the Talbot family for nearly 800 years. In 1973, Dublin Tourism restored the castle, adding a comprehensive collection of Irish furniture, dating from the seventeenth through the nineteenth century. The walls are lined with Irish portraits and tableaux. Each painting reflects a segment in the history of the Talbot family, including the family's involvement in the historic Battle of the Boyne in 1690. The estate includes three other attractions – an 8-hectare (20-acre) garden with more than 5,000 species of plants and flowers; a model railway museum; and *Tara's Palace*, an award-winning dolls' house modelled after an eighteenth-century Irish mansion. Castle and grounds open daily; model railway and dolls' house,

April–September, Monday–Saturday, and Sunday afternoon. Information: Malahide Castle, Malahide (tel. 846 2184 or www.visitdublin.com).

CULTURAL QUARTER: When on the south side of the River Liffey, amble into Temple Bar, the hippest ten blocks of Dublin property. Described variously as Dublin's Greenwich Village, Left Bank, or Latin Quarter, Temple Bar is a compact hotchpotch of narrow streets and alleys running between Westmoreland and Fishamble Streets. Buildings are painted in bright primary colours, and loud music blares from new-age shops, coffee houses and pubs. People of all ages stroll the narrow alleys and streets, or browse in second-hand shops and speciality boutiques. Trick-cyclists whizz by, pavement artists chalk up portraits, buskers play music on every corner, and students just 'hang out' at the pavement cafés. Temple Bar is the home of many art, design and photography galleries, music studios and theatres, plus the Irish Film Centre; the Ark Children's Centre; and Meeting House Square, an outdoor festival space. Two markets are held on Saturdays – the Temple Bar Food Market and the Temple Bar Book Market. Information: Temple Bar Properties, 18 Eustace Street (tel. 677 2255 or www.templebar.ie).

TOURS GALORE: Tired of walking? Dublin offers a wide array of hop-on/hop-off and sightseeing tours by bus, spanning 90 minutes to three hours, depending on the scope of the tour. One company, Viking Splash Tours, conducts its tours in an amphibious vehicle, dipping into the Grand Canal for part of the route. Most tours make pick-ups throughout the city, including the Dublin Tourism Office on Suffolk Street. Information: Dublin Bus, 59 Upper O'Connell Street (tel. 873 4222 or www.DublinBus.ie); Irish City Tours, 33–34 Bachelor's Walk (tel. 872 9010 or www.irishcitytours.com); Guide Friday/ Gray Line, 13 South Leinster Street (tel. 676 5377 or www.guidefriday.com); Viking Splash Tours, Bull Alley Street (tel. 855 3000 or www.vikingsplashtours.com).

A WALK IN THE PARK: As the largest urban enclosed park in Europe with a total area of 709 hectares (1,752 acres), the Phoenix Park is a 'must see', about 3.5 km (2 miles) west of the city centre. Traversed by a network of roads and quiet pedestrian paths, this vast expanse of pasturelands, woodlands, nature trails, sports fields and gardens is Dublin's playground. Opened in 1747, it is also the setting for Áras an Uachtaráin, the residence of the President of Ireland (open to the public on Saturdays), as well as the residence of the US ambassador to Ireland, and Dublin Zoo, established in 1830 and the third-oldest public zoo in the world (after London and Paris). The zoo occupies 26.5 hectares (66 acres), providing natural living environments for over 700 species from snow leopards and gorillas to fruit bats. Open daily. Information: Phoenix Park Visitor Centre, Phoenix Park (tel. 677 0095 or www.heritageireland.ie).

4: Counties Meath and Louth – The Boyne River Valley

Meandering in an east–west direction through the rich farming counties of Louth and Meath, the River Boyne has long been a pivotal setting in Irish history. Indeed, if the river could speak, it would reveal many a spellbinding tale!

Follow the flow of the Boyne between Slane and Drogheda. The banks are lined with landmarks from almost every phase of Ireland's past – from the prehistoric passage tombs at Newgrange, to the legendary Hill of Tara, seat of the Irish high kings, as well as monuments from the early days of Christianity.

Above all, this land is remembered as the setting for the infamous Battle of the Boyne in July of 1690 when King William III defeated the exiled King James II for the crown of England – and changed the course of Irish history.

So come to the banks of the Boyne to see history at every turn. While you are here, climb down into Stone Age passage graves older than Stonehenge or the pyramids of Giza, walk the halls of medieval castles, or lend a hand at a working Irish farm. It's all part of a short break in the bucolic Boyne River Valley.

FAST FACTS

Travel Information Offices

BRU NA BOINNE (NEWGRANGE) TOURIST OFFICE, Brú Na Bóinne, Donore, Co. Meath (tel. 041 988 0305). Open all year.

CARLINGFORD TOURIST OFFICE, Dispensary Building, Carlingford, Co. Louth (tel. 042 937 3033). Open all year.

DROGHEDA TOURIST OFFICE, Millmount Complex, Drogheda, Co. Louth (tel. 041 984 5684). Open all year.

DUNDALK TOURIST OFFICE, Jocelyn St, Dundalk, Co. Louth (tel. 042 933 5484). Open all year.

KELLS TOURIST OFFICE, Kells Heritage Centre, The Courthouse, Headfort Place, Kells, Co. Meath (tel. 046 924 7840). Open all year.

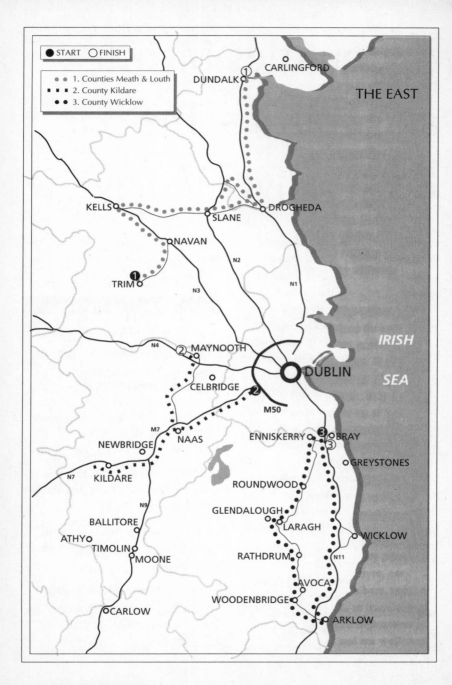

NAVAN TOURIST OFFICE, 21 Ludlow Street, Navan, Co. Meath (tel. 046 907 3426). Open June–September.

TRIM TOURIST OFFICE, Mill Street, Trim, Co. Meath (tel. 046 943 7111). Open May–September.

TRAVEL INFORMATION ONLINE: www.meathtourism.ie and www.louthholidays.com

TELEPHONE AREA CODES: Area codes for counties Meath and Louth include 041, 042, 044 and 046. To avoid confusion, each telephone number will be listed with its area code.

MAJOR EVENTS

LAYTOWN RACES – The small resort of Laytown in eastern County Meath is the home of this annual racing event, the only official beach strand races remaining in Europe. Information: Laytown Races, tel. 041 984 2111 or www.meathtourism.ie. (Mid-June)

SLANE CASTLE ROCK CONCERT – Historic Slane Castle overlooking the River Boyne hosts a huge outdoor rock concert every summer. Past performers have included U2, the Rolling Stones, Queen, Robbie Williams and Bruce Springsteen. Information: Slane Castle, tel. 041 988 4400 or www.slanecastle.ie. (End of August)

BOYNE VALLEY DRIVING TOUR

Duration: Half-day or full-day, depending on stops

The Boyne River Valley is steeped in history. Begin a tour in the southwestern corner of County Meath at **Trim**. This small market town on the banks of the River Boyne has a familiar profile as it was featured in the epic film *Braveheart*.

Much of the film was set at **Trim Castle** (tel. 046 943 8619), a sprawling stone fortress that is recognised as the finest and largest Norman castle in Ireland. Started by Hugh de Lacy in 1173 and completed in the thirteenth century, this structure has scarcely been modified, except for recent restorations before it was opened to the public in 2000. The centrepiece of this site is a massive three-storey keep with a 20-sided tower, cruciform in shape, originally protected by a ditch, moat and curtain wall, some of which still stands. Access is by guided tour only. Open daily, May–October. Admission: €

Just over 11 km (7 miles) northeast of Trim are the remains of **Bective Abbey**, founded in 1146 and entirely rebuilt in the late twelfth or early thirteenth century. It was the second Cistercian monastery founded in Ireland (built after Mellifont in neighbouring County Louth). There is no trace of the original building but the ruins of the twelfth/thirteenth-century chapter house and part of the cruciform church still remain.

Continue towards **Navan**, 9.5 km (6 miles) north, the prosperous chief administrative town of County Meath, at the confluence of the rivers Boyne and Blackwater. About 8 km (5 miles) south of Navan off the main N3 road from Dublin is one of Ireland's most historic sites – the **Hill of Tara** (tel. 046 25903).

Perched 91 metres (300 feet) above the surrounding countryside, this impressive site has been a key element of Irish history and legend since the late Stone Age when a passage tomb was constructed here. Tara is best known, however, as the seat of early Irish high kings and the host of great open-air assemblies in the early centuries just before and after Christ.

Every three years, Tara was the scene of a *feis* (great national assembly), when laws were passed, tribal disputes settled, and matters of peace and defence decided. By the end of the sixth century, the Tara monarchy had become the most powerful in Ireland. Hence the name of Tara, which is derived from the Irish *teamhair*, meaning 'elevated place' or 'assembly hill'. The words to the famous song, 'The harp that once through Tara's halls, the soul of music shed ...' still reverberate today.

Tara's fame was also perpetuated by Ireland's patron saint. St Patrick preached here in the fifth century and used a simple three-leafed shamrock to illustrate the doctrine of the Trinity – and convert High King Laoire and his followers to Christianity. Little remains of Tara's former glory today except grassy mounds and earthworks that were used for ritual and burial purposes. Use your imagination to comprehend the full impact that Tara has had through the ages, or you can watch the audiovisual show called *Tara, Meeting Place of Heroes,* shown continuously in the adjacent visitor centre on the grounds. Guided tours of the site are available on request. Open daily, May–October. Admission to visitor centre: €

A detour just over 17.5 km (11 miles) northwest of Navan leads to **Kells**, a small market town whose Irish name, *Ceanannus Mór*, means 'Great Fort'. It was originally a royal residence in pre-Christian times. It is believed that St Colmcille established a religious settlement at Kells in 550AD. The monks from his far-reaching community on the Scottish island of Iona fled to Kells in 806 to escape Viking raiders. Once relocated at Kells, the monks then completed their illuminated manuscript of the Four Gospels, and hence their work became known as the Book of Kells, one of Ireland's great artistic treasures, now housed at Trinity College, Dublin. This theory is explained in an exhibition on monastic Ireland at the **Kells Heritage Centre**, The Courthouse, Headfort Place (tel. 046 924 7840). A facsimile copy of the Book of Kells is also on display. Open daily, May–September; and Tuesday–Sunday in October–April. Admission: €

The High Cross of Kells, a fine example of a decorative high cross, is on display on the grounds of the heritage centre. The cross depicts scenes from the Old and New Testaments and dates from the ninth or tenth century.

From Kells or Navan, continue eastwards to **Slane**, a small crossroads village. It stands at the intersection of the Dublin/Derry and Drogheda/Navan roads, and is a unique example of an eighteenth-century planned town. The focal point is a group of four almost identical Georgian houses, standing at the four corners of the central intersection. These four houses and the openings to the four roads make the eight sides of an octagon. Though commonly called the 'village square', Slane's octagon is a one-of-a-kind architectural layout in Ireland.

On the west edge of the town is **Slane Castle** (tel. 041 988 4400), dating back to the late-eighteenth and early nineteenth centuries and designed by three of Ireland's most noteworthy architects, James Gandon, James Wyatt and Francis Johnston. Nestled beside the River Boyne, the castle was built for the Conyngham family and was considered one of Ireland's most beautiful inhabited castles until it was almost destroyed by fire in 1991. Happily, it has been carefully restored under the direction of its present occupant, Lord Henry Mountcharles, who has recently reopened the castle to the public for guided tours. At the heart of the house is a Gothic Revival ballroom with ornate plasterwork, saved from the flames.

Other rooms have been carefully restored with internal features reproduced in the spirit and style of the originals, including wall coverings, gilded furniture, heirlooms and gifts from King George IV who stayed here in 1821. To finance the restoration, Lord Mountcharles has been staging huge summer open-air rock concerts on the 9 hectares (22 acres) of grounds in front of the castle, starring a diverse collection of international talent. Tours of the castle are available mid-May to mid-September only, Sunday–Thursday, from noon to 5pm. Admission: €€

After visiting the castle, take a slight detour 1.5 km (1 mile) north of the village to the **Hill of Slane**, a lofty 152.5metre (500-foot) mound where St Patrick is said to have lit the paschal fire in 433 and proclaimed Christianity throughout all of Ireland. It is not as famous or well preserved as Tara, but still it is worth a look.

Slane is also the gateway to the passage-grave site at **Newgrange**, considered one of the finest Stone Age archaeological wonders of Western Europe. Built between 3500BC and 2700BC, it was used as a tomb in which Stone Age men buried the cremated remains of their dead. It is estimated that it took at least 40 years to build – the equivalent of the life's work of a whole generation. Newgrange is 500 years older than the pyramids of Giza, and 1,500 years older than Stonehenge.

To gain access to the site, turn east on the N51 and follow the signposts to **Brú Na Bóinne – The Boyne Valley Visitor Centre**, Donore (tel. 041 988 0300), a spectacular circular rock-trimmed museum built to harmonise with the surroundings. Even the huge parking area is tastefully laid out with trellises and arbours, and stone walkways. For a guided tour of Newgrange, it is necessary to register with the reception-desk personnel, and in the busy summer months, the wait can be up to three hours for a tour (maximum of 25 persons).

However, there is plenty to do at the centre, and some visitors will be satisfied to get their experience of Newgrange indoors and forego the on-site tour (which takes a full hour). The exhibits at the centre, which also take one hour to complete, range from a seven-minute introductory audiovisual to a walk-through replica of Newgrange which includes a simulation of the winter solstice and a thorough explanation of why Newgrange is Ireland's best-known prehistoric monument.

If you choose to tour the Newgrange site itself, you will be transported there from the visitor centre by minibus. As you approach, you will see a huge mound made of quartz and granite – 11 metres (36 feet) tall, with over 200,000 tons of stone including a 6-ton capstone,

and other stones weighing up to 16 tons each. It covers almost half a hectare (one full acre) of ground. The guide will take you down into the site itself, to see remnants of stone implements and fine examples of primitive carved-stone artwork such as tri-spiral designs, as well as chevrons, arcs, radials and diamonds. Two other prehistoric passage graves are nearby – Knowth and Dowth. Knowth is also open for tours, but Dowth is still under excavation. Allow at least a half-day here, if you want to do it all. Newgrange is open all year; Knowth, from May to October. Admission: € to €€

For a totally different experience nearby, follow the signs for the adjacent **Newgrange Farm** (tel. 041 982 4119), a 133-hectare (30-acre) working farm. Willie and Ann Redhouse and their family welcome visitors to join in the daily chores such as milking the cows, feeding the ducks, bottle-feeding the baby lambs and kid goats, checking on the hatching chicks in the incubator house, or grooming a calf.

A walk-around tour takes you through a courtyard to see the hen house, chicken house, rabbit hutch, dove/pigeon loft, and stables with horses, as well as a working forge and a rural life museum with demonstrations of spinning and making rush candlesticks. Step outside to see exotic pheasants, turkeys and other fowl; as well as sows and piglets, and sheep of all sizes being kept in order by working sheepdogs. In addition, there are horse-drawn farm vehicles, vintage farm machines, crop and wool displays, and a herb garden. To cap your visit, Farmer Willie will take you on a narrated tractor ride tour to see the fields of corn, wheat, oats and barley, and other far-flung parts of the farm as it slopes down to the waters of the River Boyne. The tractor ride also provides sweeping 'insider' views of the adjacent Newgrange prehistoric site, not normally seen from the road. Open daily, April–August. Admission: € to €€

After visiting Newgrange, return to the main (N51) road which follows the course of the River Boyne. At Donore, on the south bank of the river, approximately 10 km (6 miles) east of Slane, is the **Oldbridge Estate** (tel. 041 988 4343), the actual site of the Battle of the Boyne, the historic encounter between James II and William of Orange in 1690. Guided tours of the site (30–45 minutes) are available daily, June to early September. Admission: free

From the N51, take a slight detour towards Collon and enter into neighbouring County Louth, to visit two of Ireland's greatest Christian monuments.

Old Mellifont Abbey, Tullyallen, Collon (tel. 041 982 6459) was Ireland's first Cistercian monastery, started in 1142 by St Malachy of Armagh and known then as *Monasterium Fons Mellis*, evolving over the years simply to 'Mellifont'. Nestled in a peaceful setting beside the River Mattock, this foundation grew so extensively that it became known as 'The Big Monastery'. Not too much remains of the abbey today, except for remnants of a fourteenth-century chapter house, several arches of Romanesque design, and an octagonal lavabo (monks' washing-house), dating back to *c.*1200, the most interesting of the surviving structures. A visitor centre houses an exhibit on the work of masons in the Middle Ages. Open daily, June–October. Admission: €

Continue eastward for about 3.5 km (2 miles) until you arrive at the equally impressive site known as **Monasterboice**, off the N1 (Dublin–Belfast Road), near Collon (no phone). Dating back to the early sixth century, Monasterboice was chosen as a monastic site by St Buite, but it is best known as the home of a huge monument, known as **Muiredach's Cross**. One of the most perfect specimens of a high cross in Ireland, this 5-metre (17-foot) tall cross can be traced back to 922. It is ornamented with sculptured panels of biblical scenes from the Old and New Testaments including a Crucifixion on the west face and a Last Judgment on the east face. The latter is one of the earliest surviving representations of the scene, and also has the most figures in a single scene of any of the Irish high crosses. The west face of the shaft still bears a readable inscription asking for a prayer for the person named Muiredach who had the cross made. The grounds also contain a round tower, two early grave-slabs, and an early Irish sundial. Open daily. Admission: free

Return to the main N51 road and drive the remainder of the scenic route into **Drogheda**, an ancient walled town founded by the Danes in 911. A tableau of stone walls, gates, and churches, Drogheda ranked alongside Dublin and Wexford as a Viking trading centre. By the fourteenth century, it was one of the four principal walled towns in Ireland, and Drogheda continued to prosper until Oliver Cromwell took it by storm in 1649 and massacred its 2,000 inhabitants. Happily, the population has grown to ten times that number today, and the town is a thriving port and industrial centre.

To learn more about the area, stop into the **Millmount Museum**, Duleek Street (tel. 041 983 3097), the oldest surviving man-made structure in the town. Set in the courtyard of a twelfth-century fort that later became an eighteenth-century army barracks, this museum presents historical and geological exhibits on Drogheda and the Boyne River Valley. The collections include medieval guild banners, and kitchen items ranging from a traditional dresser to smoothing irons, a pot-oven, bellows and an oil lamp. In addition, there is an industrial room with authentic equipment for spinning and weaving, brewing, shoe- and rope-making, shipbuilding and ironworks. The adjacent Martello tower provides panoramic views over the town and the Boyne

Valley. Open Monday–Saturday, and Sunday afternoon. Admission: €

Just over 32 km (20 miles) north of Drogheda, via the main N1 road, is **Dundalk**, the county town of Louth, and a prosperous manufacturing centre, seaport and market hub. Dundalk derives its name from the Irish *Dún Dealgan*, which refers to a prehistoric fort that early Irish literature treats as the home of the mythical hero Cú Chulainn. In the later Middle Ages, the town was an important border fortress. The history of the area is depicted in a series of interactive exhibits at the **County Museum**, Jocelyn Street (tel. 042 932 7056), a restored eighteenth-century warehouse. Open daily except Sunday mornings and on Mondays from October through April. Admission: €

From Dundalk or Drogheda, follow the main N1 road south into Dublin or north to Belfast, or set out on some of the Digressions (described below).

PAT'S PICKS

RESTAURANTS

BOYLE'S LICENSED TEA ROOMS, Main Street, Slane, Co. Meath (tel. 041 982 4195). Housed in a shop-front setting and operated by the third generation of the Boyle family, this old-world restaurant has kept much of its 1940s charm and décor. Food is served all day but most people gather here for a traditional afternoon tea with all the trimmings. As testimony to its global clientèle, the menu is printed in twelve languages. Open Monday and Wednesday–Saturday.

THE FORGE GALLERY, Collon, Co. Louth (tel. 041 982 6272). Established 20 years ago, this restaurant is housed in a former forge, which has been transformed into a modern restaurant, with local artwork on the walls. The creative menu, which blends French provincial with 'new' Irish cuisine, features local produce, local meats such as Cooley lamb, and seasonal seafood. It is situated on the N2, between Slane and Ardee. Open for dinner only, Tuesday–Saturday.

THE GATEWAY, 15 West Street, Drogheda, Co. Louth (tel. 041 983 2755). Situated within a fifteen-minute walk of the Millmount Museum, this dependable self-service eatery serves a variety of light meals and snacks, including homemade soups, salads and vegetarian dishes. Open Monday–Saturday.

OLD BYRE COFFEE SHOP, Newgrange Farm, Slane, Co. Meath (tel. 041 982 4119). Housed in a converted eighteenth-century coach house on a working farm, this family-run café has a homely atmosphere, with white-washed walls, open fireplace, local art, and assorted memorabilia. The self-service menu offers a wide array of homemade soups, baked goods, and snacks, prepared with ingredients produced on the farm. Open for lunch and snacks, daily, April–August.

THE OLD POST OFFICE, Main Street, Slane, Co. Meath (tel. 041 982 4090). As its name implies, this eighteenth-century Georgian building was originally a post office. It is now a very pleasant family-run restaurant, featuring a variety of home-cooked soups, sandwiches, and casseroles. Open Monday–Saturday.

THE OYSTERCATCHER BISTRO, Market Square, Carlingford, Co. Louth (tel. 042 937 3922). For seafood fans, it's worth a trip to the northern perimeter of County Louth to this small shop-front restaurant, just to indulge in Carlingford oysters, lobsters, crab and other local *fruits de mer*. The menu also offers an assortment of locally sourced organic meat and vegetarian dishes. Open for dinner only, Tuesday–Sunday.

PUBS

MONASTERY INN, Clonard, Co. Meath (tel. 044 75121). In this area rich in monastic settlements and relics, this old-world pub fits right in. The décor features wall-to-wall monastic information in prints, pictures and artefacts, as well as a welcoming open fireplace. Bar food is available all day. It is located southwest of Trim on the main N4 road, on the County Westmeath border.

O'HARE'S, Main Street, Carlingford, Co. Louth (tel. 042 937 3106). Located in the heart of town, this vintage pub hasn't changed much over the years, with hardwood floors, a big open fireplace and a traditional grocery at the front. Carlingford oysters are the speciality on the bar-food menu. Traditional music sessions are on tap on Thursday nights, with jazz on Sunday afternoons.

RYAN'S BAR, 22 Trimgate Street, Navan, Co. Meath (tel. 046 21154). Built on an original town wall, this pub exudes an old-world atmosphere, with dark woods, globe lamps, tin ceiling, wood floors, and old photos on the walls. Bar food, served at lunchtime on weekdays, goes beyond the usual pub grub, with stuffed panini sandwiches, wraps and toasties.

SCANLON'S OF KILBERRY, Kilberry Cross, Navan (tel. 046 902 8330). Situated about a ten-minute drive north of Navan, this thatched-roof Irish pub is a blend of old and new. The original bar is outfitted in traditional style with timber floors and open fireplaces, while a newer section offers big-screen TV for sports fans. Live bands play music at weekends. Food is served throughout the day and evening.

DIGRESSIONS

DESIGNER GARDENS: Unlike many of Ireland's gardens which trace their roots back hundreds of years, Butterstream Gardens at Trim are a modern creation, begun in the 1970s by horticulture expert Jim Reynolds. This natural enclave carefully integrates plants, herbaceous borders and architectural features. The display includes hedges of beech, thorn and yew, as well as wildly refreshing clusters of plant colour schemes – from a white garden with white butterflies to a hot-coloured garden, as well as an old roses garden, a laburnum tunnel and lime alleys. Gardeners from all over the world – including Prince Charles, the Prince of Wales – have come to see this garden for themselves. Open May–September. Information: Butterstream Gardens, Kildalkey Road, Trim, Co. Meath (tel. 046 36017).

DOWN ON THE FARM: Take a day off and lend a hand at the Causey Farm near Navan for a sampling of traditional Irish life. This eight-hour 'cultural day' programme includes a bog trip, a game of hurling, a lesson in bread-making, a *súgán* (straw-rope) demonstration, farm visit and sheepdog demonstrations, céilí dancing and bodhrán classes, culminating in a colcannon supper and a live traditional music session. Operates year-round but schedule varies. Advance booking required. Information: Lily or Angela Murtagh, The Causey Farm, Girley, Fordstown, Navan, Co. Meath (tel. 046 34135 or website www.causeyexperience.com).

GAELTACHT: The smallest of Ireland's Gaeltachts is located in west County Meath in the neighbouring communities of *Rath Cairn* (Rathcairn), northwest of Trim, and *Baile Ghib* (Gibbstown), east of Kells. The families residing here were originally from Gaeltacht areas of Connemara, Mayo and Kerry but settled in Meath in the 1930s after the War of Independence. They brought with them their native Irish language and their great love of Irish music, culture and tradition. If you'd like to brush up on your Irish or hear the language spoken, head to this corner of County Meath and visit the shops and pubs. Information: www.gaelsaoire.ie.

MEDIEVAL TOWN: The northern tip of County Louth is home to the picturesque medieval town of Carlingford, nestled beneath Slieve Foy, the highest peak of the Cooley Mountains, and across the water from the Mountains of Mourne. With its cluster of narrow streets, lanes and historic old stone buildings, including castles, fortified town houses, an abbey, town gate and mint, Carlingford is a delight to walk around. The town's heritage centre, housed in a restored medieval church, traces Carlingford's origins from Norman times. Information: Carlingford Tourist Office, Dispensary Building, Carlingford, Co. Louth (tel. 042 937 3033 or www.carlingford.ie).

OFF THE BEATEN PATH: Not all of Meath's history is beside the Boyne. Northwest County Meath has a wealth of prehistoric sites in and around the Loughcrew Hills, near the town of Oldcastle, with passage graves, megalithic chambers and decorated stones in the same style as Newgrange. One of the hills, built over a prehistoric tomb, is the highest point in County Meath. Here you can also visit Loughcrew

Gardens, restored seventeenth- and nineteenth-century gardens with an ancient yew walk, a lime avenue, flowers, herbaceous borders, trees and shrubs, enhanced by statues, sculptures, grottos, follies, rockeries, woodland walks and waterfalls. Open April–September. Information: Loughcrew Historic Gardens, Oldcastle, Co. Meath (tel. 049 854 1922).

WANDERING WEST: Working your way west from County Meath? Plan a stop at Belvedere House and Gardens, set overlooking Lough Ennell, just under 5 km (3 miles) south of Mullingar. Considered by many to be one of Ireland's finest historic houses, Belvedere was built in 1740 and designed by Richard Castle, the same architect who drew up plans for Leinster House, the Rotunda Hospital, Powerscourt Estate and Russborough House. Admission provides access to the Georgian-era house as well as a heritage centre, walled gardens with many exotic plants, walking trails, and 65 hectares (160 acres) of woods and parkland plus a café, shop, children's pet corner and play area. A tram connects the heritage centre with the various outdoor attractions. The grounds also include one of Ireland's largest man-made follies (a large 'jealous wall' built by the earl of Belvedere). Open daily. Information: Belvedere House, Gardens and Park, Mullingar, Co. Westmeath (tel. 044 49060 or www.belvedere-house.ie).

5: County Kildare – Horse Country

Located inland east of Dublin and bisected by the main M7/N7 road, County Kildare is a convenient getaway from many directions. Not only is it a stone's throw from the Irish capital, but it is also sandwiched in between the Boyne River Valley and the Wicklow Mountains.

The northern part of County Kildare provides a sylvan setting for many historic homes and gardens, such as Castletown and Celbridge, while the southern half of the county offers a mix of unique attractions, ranging from the Moone High Cross to the Quaker settlement at Ballitore.

Above all, with vast panoramas of open grasslands and limestone-enriched soil, County Kildare is the hub of Ireland's horse-breeding and racing country. Stud farms dot the countryside and racing takes place regularly at three Kildare tracks – Punchestown, Naas and the Curragh, home of the annual Irish Derby. Check the Irish newspapers to see if a race is scheduled when you are visiting, or, if you are a horse-rider yourself, make a booking at one of Kildare's dozen riding schools and equestrian centres.

Kildare town is the setting for the Irish National Stud, a benchmark of equine excellence and the best place to learn why Ireland and the horse have always been synonymous.

North County Kildare is also the home of one of Ireland's major learning centres, the National University of Ireland at Maynooth, with an enrolment of over 5,000 students.

(See map p.44)

FAST FACTS

Travel Information Office

COUNTY KILDARE FÁILTE/KILDARE TOURIST OFFICE, 38 South Main Street, Kildare, Co. Kildare (tel. 045 898 888). Open all year.

TRAVEL INFORMATION ONLINE: www.ecoast-midlands.travel.ie and www.kildare.ie

TELEPHONE AREA CODE: The telephone area code for most numbers in County Kildare is 045. A few numbers in the northern part of the county use the 01 code, and in the southern part of the county use 059 – these are clearly indicated in each case.

MAJOR EVENTS

IRISH NATIONAL HUNT FESTIVAL – One of the highlights on the spring racing calendar, this four-day festival blends social events and hurdle racing, with prizes topping €1.4 million. Information: Punchestown Race Course, tel. 897 704 or www.punchestown.com. (Late April/early May)

IRISH DERBY FESTIVAL – This is Ireland's equivalent of the Kentucky Derby or Royal Ascot – a three-day programme of flat racing and entertainment events, topped by the annual race run by Europe's best thoroughbreds. Information: Curragh Racecourse, tel. 441 205 or www.curragh.ie. (Late June)

COUNTY KILDARE DRIVING TOUR

Duration: 3–5 hours plus stops

Starting out from Dublin, head west via the N7/M7, the Naas Road, a modern road that bypasses many small towns. After travelling just over 32 km (20 miles), you will see signs for Naas (pronounced Nay-se), the chief town of County Kildare, and you may wish to get off the main road and take a slight detour through **Naas**. An ancient town that was one of the royal seats of the province of Leinster, Naas takes its name from the Irish *Nás na Ríogh*, meaning 'the assembly place of the kings'. It is said that Naas was the residence of local royalty and a great meeting place until the tenth century. Today, it is a busy market town and little remains from those early glory days. The town's prime claim to fame is that it is home to two racetracks – the **Naas Racecourse** (tel. 897 391), for flat racing, and **Punchestown Racecourse** (tel. 897 704), a steeplechase track famed as the venue for the three-day Irish National Hunt Festival races in late spring (*see* Major Events above).

Continue for 13 km (8 miles) more to the town of **Newbridge**, often referred to in maps and books as *An Droichead Nua*, which literally means 'the new bridge' in the Irish language. Situated at the crossing point of the Naas–Kildare road and the River Liffey, Newbridge is a small manufacturing town best known as the home of **Newbridge Silverware**, Cutlery Road, off the Dublin/Limerick N7 road, (tel. 431 301), one of Ireland's leading manufacturers of silverware for the past 80 years. The showrooms present a display of silver place settings, bowls, candelabras, trays, timepieces, frames, and one-of-a-kind items. There is also a video on silver-making, a craft that has been practised in the area since the time of Ireland's high kings. Open Monday–Saturday, and Sunday afternoon. Admission: free

Continue for almost 6.5 km (4 miles) and suddenly – appearing on both sides of the road – is the vast open spread of grasslands known as **The Curragh**, the largest area of arable land in the country

(2,023.5 hectares/5,000 acres). In 1994, Mel Gibson used this panoramic expanse to stage some of the battle scenes in his movie *Braveheart*. Even though the film was set in Scotland, the Irish scenery proved the perfect backdrop to recreate the sights and sounds of early Scotland.

On the north side of the road, you will see the **Curragh Racecourse** (tel. 441 205), famed as the 'Churchill Downs' of Ireland. It is one of Ireland's largest and most modern racetracks, the home of the annual Irish Derby and many other classic races throughout the year.

In just over 1.5 km (1 mile), you come to the town of **Kildare**, honoured as the birthplace of St Brigid, Ireland's second patron saint, after Patrick. It is said that Brigid, who lived in the fifth or sixth century, made a lasting contribution to 'women's lib' by founding a Kildare monastery that held the unique distinction of being a 'double monastery' – one part for nuns, one part for monks, ruled jointly and equally by an abbess and abbot-bishop. The place name of Kildare comes from the Irish language *Cill Dara*, meaning 'church of the oak' – the traditional location of St Brigid's foundation being in a sacred grove of oak trees.

To acclimatise yourself to the layout and history of Kildare, visit the **Kildare Town Heritage Centre**, 38 South Main Street (tel. 521 240), in the centre of town at the restored eighteenth-century market house. Open daily except for weekends of October–April. Admission: €

Take time to visit **St Brigid's Cathedral**, The Square (tel. 521 229), reputed to be on the site where St Brigid founded her monastery in 480AD. The cathedral itself, dating back over 750 years and completely restored in 1996, has many interesting monuments including a round tower, started in the sixth century and completed in the eleventh century. It is 32 metres (108 feet) high with stone 6 metres (20 feet) in diameter at its base. There are five storeys inside, connected by ladders. Open daily, May–October. Admission to Cathedral: by donation; to Round Tower: €

South of Kildare's main street is a signposted road leading to the **Irish National Stud**, Tully (tel. 521 617), a sprawling horse farm set on 958 acres of prime grasslands. It was established in 1945, to provide a government-sponsored prototype of ideal horse-farm conditions for others to emulate throughout the land. Some of Ireland's most famous horses have been bred and raised on these grounds, and visitors are welcome to watch the horses being exercised and groomed.

A tour, which takes approximately 40 minutes to an hour, includes a visit to the Sun Chariot Yard which houses the mares and foals, the Foaling Unit, the Stallion Paddocks, Saddler Shop, and the Forge. In addition, there are two walks – the

Oak Walk, which runs along the stallion paddocks, and the **Tully Walk** beside the mares' paddocks. From mid-spring to mid-autumn, mares and foals run freely in the verdant grassy enclosures. A converted groom's house serves as the setting for a horse museum, with exhibits on equine pursuits in Ireland from the Bronze Age to the present. There are also displays of horses in transport, racing, steeplechasing, hunting and showjumping, plus the skeleton of Arkle, one of Ireland's most famous equine heroes.

A visit here includes admission to two distinctive gardens. The adjacent **Japanese Gardens**, laid out between 1906 and 1910 by the Japanese gardener Tassa Eida to symbolise the Life of Man in 20 different stages from Oblivion to Eternity, are considered among the finest in Europe. The configuration includes cherry blossoms, bonsai trees and other exotic plantings, as well as a tea house and a miniature Japanese village.

The newer garden, known as **St Fiachra's Garden**, is named in honour of the sixth-century Irish monk who is the patron saint of gardeners. Designed to recreate the serene environment that inspired the spirituality of the sixth- and seventh-century monastic movement in Ireland, this garden is a natural oasis of woodlands, waterfalls and wetlands, with aquatic plants, islands, and greenery of all types. Unique features include a sunken oak forest, filled with 5,000-year-old bog oak from the Bog of Allen; 1,200 tons of

rocks and boulders from the west of Ireland; a splendid statue of St Fiachra seated on a lakeside peninsula; and three replicas of early monastic cells or beehive huts.

Within the main cell is a unique flood-lit subterranean garden, featuring glass-shaped rocks and plants such as ferns and orchids. The crystal pieces were handcrafted by Waterford Crystal. Allow at least an hour to walk and wander, reflect and relish.

Entrance to the National Stud is through a visitor centre built in the style of a Japanese country inn. Facilities include a wide-windowed and sky-lit restaurant that has an outside deck overlooking the gardens. Even if your interest in horses is minimal, it is worth the drive to Kildare just to relax in this serene setting. Open daily, mid-February to mid-November. Admission: €€ (includes entrance to all three attractions).

Depending on time and your interests, you can choose to tour more of County Kildare by retracing your steps back to Naas and then going north. This northward extension tour, primarily a 'house and garden' trail, can also be taken as a stand-alone tour on a separate day.

North from Naas: Take the R407 to Clane and then a right turn onto the R403 for about 13 km (8 miles) to **Castletown House**, Celbridge (tel. 01 628 8252), the largest Palladian-style country house in Ireland. It was built *c*.1722 for the then Speaker of the Irish House of Commons, William Conolly (1662–1729), using the designs of several important architects of the time – Alessandro Galilei, Sir Edward Lovett Pearce, and Sir William Chamber. Distinguishing characteristics include a long gallery, laid out in the Pompeian manner, with Venetian chandeliers; an eighteenth-century print room; a main hall and staircase decorated with elaborate Italian plasterwork; and a fine collection of eighteenth-century furniture and paintings. The house was transferred to the Irish nation in 1994 as a heritage site. Open daily, April–November. Admission: €

Nearby are the **Celbridge Abbey Gardens**, Clane Road, Celbridge (tel. 01 627 5508), a sylvan array of plantings dating back to the seventeenth century, set beside the River Liffey and surrounding an abbey that is now a private home. The gardens, reputedly planted in honour of author Jonathan Swift by the daughter of the original abbey owner, contain various river walks, bridges, an island and a weir. Open Monday–Saturday, and Sunday afternoon. Admission: €

From Celbridge, make a turn onto the R405 and travel 8 km (5 miles) to Maynooth, home of the **National University of Ireland, Maynooth** (tel. 01 628 5222), Ireland's second oldest university. The university traces its origins directly to the foundation in 1795 of St Patrick's College, originally established as a seminary. Over the years, it was expanded and became a fully recognised component of the National University of Ireland. The campus includes Bicentenary Gardens, commissioned to commemorate the two hundredth anniversary of Maynooth in 1995. The gardens are based on a biblical theme from chapters of Genesis, and all plants on display are mentioned in the Bible and come primarily from the Holy Land. The grounds and gardens are open to the public, as is a visitor centre. Open May–September. Admission is free but there is a charge for guided tours: €.

The restored castle at the gates of the university, **Maynooth Castle** (tel. 01 628 6744), dates back to the thirteenth century when it was a centre of political power for the FitzGeralds, the earls of Kildare. The original keep, constructed $c.$1203, was one of the largest of its kind in Ireland, although seventeenth-century remodelling de-emphasised its proportions. Turned over to the Irish nation in 1991 the castle is now a national monument, and recent restorations have made the keep accessible to visitors. Open June–October. Admission: free

From Maynooth, it is less than 16 km (10 miles) northwest via the N4 (or R148) and R125 to **Larchill Arcadian Gardens**, Dunshaughlin Road, Kilcock (tel. 01 628 7354). Larchill is the sole surviving example in Ireland or England of a mid-eighteenth-century-style garden known as a *ferme ornée* (ornamental farm garden). The focus of the garden is a circular walk through landscaped parkland, decorated with ten follies, resting areas, gazebos, beech avenues, a Greek temple and a lake with island fortress. The parkland is stocked with rare and exotic breeds of domestic farm animals. Open May–September. Admission: €

From Kilcock, return to the N4, going east to Dublin or moving on to other parts of Kildare or neighbouring counties.

PAT'S PICKS

RESTAURANTS

BARBERSTOWN CASTLE, Straffan (tel. 01 628 8157). For a special splurge, dine like nobility of another era. This restaurant, housed in the keep of a thirteenth-century castle, offers a seasonal but limited à la carte menu, served in a medieval setting of whitewashed rooms and alcoves, enhanced by candlelight and open fireplaces. Open for dinner, daily, except Christmas and January.

LAWLORS OF NAAS, Poplar Square, Naas (tel. 897 332). A long-time favourite meeting place for trainers, owners, jockeys and racing fans, this restaurant offers a varied menu of snacks, homemade soups, and seafood, including the house special of Lawlors' fish smokies. Open for lunch and dinner, daily.

LES OLIVES, 10 South Main Street, Naas (tel. 894 788). Tucked in a first-floor setting over a pub in the centre of town, this contemporary restaurant is known for its seafood dishes such as prawn kebabs, lobster salad and John Dory sole, as well as exotic meats ranging from ostrich to kangaroo. Open for dinner, Tuesday–Sunday.

THE MANOR INN, Main Street, Naas (tel. 897 332). The racing set gathers often at this restaurant, known for its décor of equestrian pictures and memorabilia. Steaks are a speciality, but the menu also includes a wide array of sandwiches and salads, burgers, meat pies, omelettes, pastas and fish. Open for lunch and dinner, daily.

RED HOUSE INN, Main Street, Newbridge (tel. 431 657). An old-world ambience prevails at this restaurant, serving traditional local favourites such as prime beef and Kildare lamb. For lighter meals, there is also a bistro café with a Mediterranean flair and flavours. Open for dinner, Tuesday–Saturday; and for lunch on Sunday, except two weeks in early January.

YUM YUMS, Tully, Kildare (tel. 521 619). This café is the self-service restaurant at the Irish National Stud, designed in the style of a Japanese Teahouse, amid lush gardens, with indoor and outdoor seating. An ideal place for a snack or full meal, the menu varies each day but includes freshly made soups, salads, sandwiches, hot dishes, and all types of breads, cakes, pies and scones. Open for lunch and snacks, mid-February to mid-November.

PUBS

MOONE HIGH CROSS INN, Moone (tel. 059 862 4112). There's more than a drink waiting at this old inn. Appropriately named after the historic High Cross that sits a mile away, this pub is decorated with a variety of local memorabilia and is surrounded by lovely gardens. Jacob sheep graze in the nearby fields.

SILKEN THOMAS, The Square, Kildare (tel. 522 232). Located in the centre of town and with a décor of dark woods and brass, this historic award-winning pub is named after a famous character in local history – Thomas Fitzgerald, tenth earl of Kildare – who led an unsuccessful rebellion against England. There is a carvery lounge for bar-style meals.

THOMAS FLETCHER, Main Street, Naas, Co. Kildare (tel. 897 328). A local landmark dating back to the 1800s, this pub has been in the Fletcher family since the 1930s. Step inside to enjoy a quiet drink in an authentic atmosphere of wooden floors, mahogany bar, and stained-glass panels.

DIGRESSIONS

FLUTTERING FARM: In the northern half of County Kildare, take a detour a few kilometres south of Celbridge to Straffan, home of Ireland's first live tropical butterfly farm. Founded in 1986, this indoor all-weather centre provides an opportunity to see at close range some of the world's most exotic creatures and observe their interesting life cycles. Open June–August. Information: Straffan Butterfly Farm, Ovidstown (tel. 01 627 1109 or www.straffanbutterflyfarm.com).

QUAKER IRELAND: For insight into Ireland's deep-rooted Quaker traditions, head to the secluded village of Ballitore, off the N9 in southern County Kildare, founded by Quakers from Yorkshire in the 1700s. Explore several buildings that tell the story of the area's Quaker settlement, including the Quaker Museum, the original meeting house for the Society of Friends. It contains memorabilia of interest, including a wedding dress and bonnet worn by a Quaker bride in 1853, and a ledger dated 1807–1810, manuscripts, letters, notebooks and watercolours painted locally in 1809. In addition, a visitor centre has been developed at the adjacent Crookstown Corn Mill (c.1804) on the banks of the River Griese. Information: Quaker Museum, Ballitore (tel. 059 862 3344).

TIMOLIN-MOONE: Considered the oldest inhabited area of County Kildare, the villages of Timolin and Moone are worth a detour (from Kildare town, follow the R145 southeast to the N9 and then south for 8 km/5 miles). One of Ireland's most perfect high crosses – the Moone High Cross – is located in a field off the main road. This unusually slender monument, dated to the ninth century, was found buried in the ground in 1835 and was pieced together and re-erected. The decoration of the cross follows the form of prayer popular at the time, depicting events from the Old and New Testaments.

Three and a half kilometres (2 miles) north is Timolin, founded as a monastic settlement by St Mullins *c*.645, and home to Ireland's oldest pewter mill. Pewter, like bronze, is the oldest of alloys, used to make jewellery, tankards, plates and animal figurines – with various designs, including medieval, Celtic, and early Christian/Book of Kells. Visitors can watch craftsmen casting and fashioning pewter pieces on the premises. The mill also has a Moone High Cross Room, with a display about the monument. Information: Irish Pewtermill, Old Mill Road, Timolin-Moone, Co. Kildare (tel. 059 862 4164 or www.irishpewtermill.com).

6: County Wicklow – The Garden of Ireland

County Wicklow displays nature at its best. Aptly described as 'the Garden of Ireland', it offers a blend of verdant coastal and mountain scenery, quiet country lanes and tree-shaded walking trails, flower-filled glens and meandering rivers, sloping hills and sandy seascapes. In the heart of the county is the Wicklow Mountains National Park, one of six national parks in Ireland.

Even the place names of County Wicklow sound alluring – from Lugnaquilla to Sally Gap, Devil's Punch Bowl, Glenmalure, Glen of the Downs, and Shillelagh.

If the scenery imparts a *déjà-vu* feeling, it is because County Wicklow is the home of Ardmore Studios (at Bray) and has provided background settings for many films including *Braveheart, Excalibur, Michael Collins, Far and Away,* and *Angela's Ashes.* In particular, the small village of Avoca has drawn more than its share of exposure as the location of the recent BBC TV series *Ballykissangel,* and the Irish village setting for some episodes of CBS TV's *Murder She Wrote* in the 1990s.

In addition to its incomparable scenery, County Wicklow presents a host of other sightseeing and cultural attractions, each worth a visit in its own right – from the sixth-century monastic settlement of St Kevin at Glendalough, and historic eighteenth- and nineteenth-century country manors and estates, to the famous Vale of Avoca, literary setting for the poetry of Thomas Moore.

(See map p.44)

FAST FACTS

Travel Information Offices

WICKLOW TOURIST INFORMATION OFFICE, Fitzwilliam Square, Wicklow (tel. 0404 69117). Open all year.

ARKLOW TOURIST INFORMATION OFFICE, Main Street, Arklow (tel. 0402 32484). Open June–September.

GLENDALOUGH TOURIST INFORMATION OFFICE, Glendalough (tel. 0404 45688). Open June–September.

TRAVEL INFORMATION ONLINE: www.wicklow.com, www.wicklow.ie and www.ecoast-midlands.travel.ie/wicklow

TELEPHONE AREA CODES:

The majority of telephone numbers in County Wicklow use the area code '0404'. However, some numbers that are close to Dublin use the '01' area code, and some others use the '0402' code. As there is a mixture of codes, we list each code as appropriate.

MAJOR EVENT

WICKLOW GARDENS FESTIVAL – Forty gardens, large and small, open their gates to the public for this county-wide horticultural display, when flowers are at peak bloom. The programme includes herb luncheons, guided tours, musical recitals and garden parties. Information: Wicklow Gardens Festival, tel. 0404 20100 or www.wicklow.ie. (May–July)

COUNTY WICKLOW DRIVING TOUR

Duration: 3–4 hours plus stops

Take the main road (N11) south from Dublin towards **Bray**, a long-established seaside resort (*c.*1838), often called 'the Brighton of Ireland' because of its busy tempo and Georgian and Victorian architecture. It is favoured by many Dubliners for its 1.6-km (1-mile) long beach and esplanade. The landscape is dominated by Bray Head to the south, rising steeply to 240 metres (790 feet) above the sea. There is a scenic cliff walk on the eastern side of Bray Head that leads to **Greystones**, a pleasant seaside town.

A well-signposted exit puts you on the road to **Enniskerry**, a sheltered little village set in a wooded hollow among the hills. Once you reach Enniskerry, follow the signs for 1.6 km (1 mile) to **Powerscourt House & Gardens** (tel. 01 286 7676). For over 60 years, this 19-hectare (47-acre) garden has been the epitome of County Wicklow's reputation as the home of Ireland's most beautiful and lush greenery. It is a fine example of an aristocratic garden with Italian and Japanese themes, plus herbaceous borders, ornamental lakes, splendid statuary, and decorative ironwork.

The centrepiece of the grounds, an eighteenth-century Georgian house, offers a range of exhibits, guided tours, a dozen shops, and a café with indoor and outdoor seating. In addition, the grounds hold a pet cemetery, a wildlife park, and a waterfall, the highest in Britain and Ireland, which tumbles downward from a 120-metre (400-foot) high cliff. Open daily. Admission: €€

Next, head south via the R755 for 16 km (10 miles) over the mountains to **Roundwood**, reputed to be the highest village in Ireland (over 213 metres/700 feet above sea level). Roundwood is home to a couple of atmospheric seventeenth-century inns, each worth a stop for a meal or light refreshment. On Sunday afternoons, the village hosts the **Roundwood Country Market**, an indoor gathering (in the parish hall) featuring an array of locally made crafts, from sweaters, woollens and crochet-work, to paintings, as well as preserves and baked goods. Open Sunday afternoons, March–December. Admission: free

From Roundwood, continue southward on this winding mountain road, passing Lough Dan and the Wicklow Gap on your right, for 14.5 km (9 miles) to **Laragh**, at the junction of the Annamoe Valley, the Clara Valley and Glendalough, Glendasan, Glenmacnass – a meeting place of roads that traverse some of the most scenic areas of County Wicklow. Follow the signposts for 1.6 km (1 mile) to the most celebrated site within all of these directions, the sixth-century monastic settlement at **Glendalough**.

Nestled in a glaciated valley between two bodies of water (the Upper Lake and the Lower Lake), Glendalough has a well-chosen name. In the Irish language, *Gleann Dá Loch* literally means 'valley of (the) two lakes'. It was here in the sixth century that St Kevin founded a monastery that would become a leading centre of learning for all of Europe, with thousands of students from Ireland, Britain, and the continent. Glendalough flourished until the fifteenth century, when it was plundered by Anglo-Norman invaders.

Although much of the monastic city is in ruins today, the site includes a visitor centre (tel. 0404 45325) with exhibits and an audiovisual that tell the story of St Kevin and his many successor-abbots, including St Lawrence O'Toole. Tours of the grounds will show you a nearly perfect 31-metre (103-foot) round tower, hundreds of hand-carved Celtic crosses and a variety of churches, including St Kevin's own chapel, a fine specimen of an early Irish barrel-vaulted oratory with a miniature round belfry. Open daily. Admission: €

For national-park connoisseurs, a recommended detour begins close to Glendalough's Upper Lake, off the Green Road, at the information point for the **Wicklow Mountains National Park**, about 2.5 km (1.5 miles) from the Glendalough Visitor Centre, near the Upper Lake parking area. This park, which covers much of upland Wicklow, contains 20,000 hectares (49,421 acres) of land, including large areas of mountain blanket bogs and the Glendalough Wood Nature Reserve. The park provides protection for the landscape and wildlife, from rare orchids to the peregrine falcon.

Return to Laragh, and then head southwards via the R755 through the scenic wooded valley known as the **Vale of Clara**. Look west for expansive views of **Lugnaquilla Mountain** (926 metres/3,039 feet), the third highest mountain in Ireland, and the tallest outside County Kerry. For a change of pace or to stretch your legs, stop for a while at **Rathdrum**, a village perched above the Avonmore river. Continue 2.5 km (1.5 miles) south of the village to visit one of County Wicklow's historic houses,

Avondale House and Forest Park, Rathdrum (tel. 0404 46111).

Set beside the Avonmore River, Avondale is the birthplace and former home of Charles Stewart Parnell (1846–1891), one of Ireland's great political leaders, affectionately called 'the uncrowned king of Ireland'. The house, built in 1779, is filled with Parnell memorabilia and furnishings. The main attraction is the surrounding 202-hectare (500-acre) estate, with an internationally acclaimed arboretum, forest walks and signposted nature trails. Developed as a training school for the Irish Forest and Wildlife Service, the park is considered as the catalyst and testing ground of modern Irish forestry. Open daily, March–October. Admission: €

This route continues south via the R752 for 5.5 more kilometres (3.5 more miles), to the point where the Avonmore river meets the Avonbeg river to form the Avoca river – described idyllically by the nineteenth-century poet, Thomas Moore, as **The Meeting of the Waters**. A lone tree, well-picked by souvenir hunters over the years, still stands on the spot where Moore is said to have spent long hours looking for inspiration before he finally penned the oft-sung words: *'There is not in this wide world a valley so sweet, as the vale in whose bosom the bright waters meet ... '* The adjacent pub, known as **The Meetings**, displays an interesting collection of Moore memorabilia, including an 1889 edition of the poet's best works (See Pubs below).

Follow the Avoca River for less than 1.5 km (1 mile) south into the village of **Avoca**, crossing over the bridge to visit **Avoca Handweavers** (tel. 0402 35105), the oldest hand-weaving company in Ireland, dating back to 1723. Housed in a cluster of white-washed stone buildings, this enterprise invites visitors to take a walk-through tour to observe all stages of production – from wool preparation, spinning, carding and dyeing, to the actual weaving process. The adjacent mill shop stocks the results – travel rugs, blankets, bedspreads, cushion covers, stoles, suits, coats, jackets, ponchos and hats. Although all colours are available, the predominant tones of mauve, aqua, teal and heather are much in demand, often perceived as a reflection of the landscape of the surrounding countryside. Open daily. Admission: free

From Avoca, continue approximately 8 km (5 miles) south on the R752 to **Woodenbridge**, home of one of Ireland's oldest hotels (dating back to 1608), and east via the R747 to **Arklow**, a fishing port and seaside resort. Dating back to Viking times and long known for the building of small wooden ships, this busy town is the appropriate setting for the **Arklow Maritime Museum**, St Mary's Road (tel. 0402 32868). The displays include photographs and models of vessels built in Arklow hundreds of years ago. Open Monday–Saturday, April–August. Admission: €

Less than 8 km (5 miles) north of Arklow on the R750 is **Brittas Bay**, one of the finest beaches on Ireland's east coast. Popular with Dubliners, this beach stretches for 3 km (2 miles) with powdery sands and an extensive system of sand dunes. The dunes, which are a designated area of scientific interest, are home to some rare species of wildlife and plants. With the bracing sea breeze, it's an ideal place for a long walk, a swim or bird-watching.

From Arklow, follow the main road (N11) north back to Dublin via **Wicklow**, the chief town of the county and a small seaport and seaside resort at the mouth of the River Vartry. The main attraction of this town is **Wicklow's Historic Gaol** or Jail, (tel. 0404 61599), well signposted on Kilmantin Hill. Built in 1702, this museum depicts the conditions of Irish jails prior to the prison reforms of the late eighteenth century. The displays also illustrate how prisoners, both guilty and innocent, tried and untried, lived their daily lives; the events that led to over 50,000 people being sent as convicts to Australia; and the contributions these Irish people made to their new land. Open daily, April–October. Admission: €€

Less than 6.5 km (4 miles) north of Wicklow town off the N11 is one of the area's great horticultural attractions, **Mount Usher Gardens**, Ashford (tel. 0404 40116). For garden enthusiasts, this is a 'must-stop'. Set on 8 hectares (20 acres) beside the River Vartry, Mount Usher is a paradise of over 5,000 types of plant, tree and shrub from all over the world, blending familiar species such as rhododendrons, magnolias, camellias, eucalyptus and palms, with the exotic, such as Burmese jumpers, Chinese spindles and North American swamp cypress. One of the best examples of a romantic Robinsonian garden, Mount Usher dates back to 1886. Water plays an essential part in the layout, with cascades and bridges visible in just about every section. Open daily, mid-March–October. Admission: €

From **Ashford**, the main N11 road wends its way north via a scenic forested area known as the **Glen of the Downs** on the corridor between two towns with the fanciful tongue-twister names of Newtownmountkennedy and Kilmacanogue. Views of the **Great Sugar Loaf Mountain** (505 metres/1,659 feet) rise on the left. Before completing your tour, you may wish to stop at another of County Wicklow's great houses, **Kilruddery House and Gardens**, just south of Bray (tel. 01 286 2777).

Picturesquely ensconced between Bray Head and the Little Sugar Loaf Mountain (341 metres/1,120 feet), this bucolic setting has been the seat of the earl of Meath since 1818. The original part of the house dates back to 1820, with many additions including a nineteenth-century Victorian conservatory that was modelled after the Crystal

Palace in London. The gardens are even older, dating back to the 1680s, laid out in French style. The core of the garden is a pair of canals that connect the house at one end and an avenue of lime trees at the other. On one side, there is a series of radiating walks flanked by hedges of beech, hornbeam and lime. On the other is a sylvan theatre and a great circular pool enclosed by high hedges. The tableau is completed by an extensive natural rock garden. House open daily in May–June. Gardens open daily in April–September. Admission: €

Turn east on the R767 or R766 for **Bray**, to complete the tour circuit.

PAT'S PICKS

RESTAURANTS

AVOCA CAFÉ, Avoca Handweavers, off the N11, Kilmacanogue (tel. 01 286 7466) and in the village of Avoca (tel. 0402 35105). Although many people come to shop for the colourful Avoca woollens, they end up staying for lunch or a snack. Food is fresh and healthy, using many local ingredients for homemade soups, salads, sandwiches, quiches and casseroles. Farmhouse cheeses and multi-grain breads are also featured. The food is so delicious that customers keep asking for the recipes – and two Avoca Café cookbooks have been the result. Open daily.

FISHERS – THE OLD SCHOOLHOUSE, Main Street, Newtownmountkennedy (tel. 01 281 9404). Situated within a well-known sports-clothing shop, this stylish café is a bit off the beaten track but worth a detour – for a snack (cappuccino or espresso with hot scones or biscuits, laced with butter, cream and jam) or for lunch. The menu offers unusual items such as Caesar salad, oak smoked-chicken or salmon, baked scallop or crab, hot tuna melt, hot chicken pesto, cold honey-baked ham and freshly puréed vegetable soups. Open Monday–Saturday and Sunday afternoons.

HUNTERS' HOTEL, Newrath Bridge, Rathnew (tel. 0404 40106). Old-world charm is the keystone of this restaurant, with antiques, polished brass, heirlooms, vintage prints, open fireplaces and splendid gardens. Specialities include roast Wicklow lamb, prime rib of beef with Yorkshire pudding, stuffed chicken and ham, and fresh wild salmon, served with herbs, vegetables and fruits from the garden. Established over 280 years ago, this creaky coach house has been in the same family for five generations and is popular with the locals. Open for lunch and dinner, daily.

ROUNDWOOD INN, Main Street, Roundwood (tel. 01 281 8107). Antique furnishings, wooden floors and open fireplaces add to the atmosphere of this 1750s coaching inn, known for international cuisine with a German slant. Full meals are served, as is bar food such as Irish stew, seafood platters and salads. Open for lunch, snacks and dinner, daily.

STRAWBERRY TREE, Brooklodge Hotel, Macreddin Village (tel. 0402 36444). For special occasions or big splurges, it's worth the trek to find this award-winning restaurant, nestled in the sylvan setting of a recreated village, just under 5 km (3 miles) outside Aughrim and west of Avoca. Well-known throughout Ireland (and re-located several years ago from Killarney), this romantic mirrored-ceiling dining-room is known for creative 'new Irish' cuisine, using organic produce from local sources. Open for lunch and dinner, daily.

WICKLOW HEATHER RESTAURANT, Main Street, Laragh (tel. 0404 45157). Surrounded by flowering gardens, and a short drive from Glendalough, this family-run eatery is an affordable and reliable choice for snacks and full meals throughout the day. Open daily.

PUBS

CARTOON INN, Main Street, Rathdrum (tel. 0404 46774). Have a laugh or a chuckle as you enjoy a beverage or homemade soups, sandwiches and other light refreshments at this humour-themed pub. The walls are lined with the works of many leading Irish and international cartoonists.

COACH HOUSE, Main Street, Roundwood (tel. 01 281 8157). It's hard to pass this 1790s pub by without a drink or at least a photograph – the Tudor-style façade is adorned with baskets filled with colourful flowers. Antiques and local memorabilia make the interior just as enticing.

THE MEETINGS, at the Vale of Avoca, Avoca (tel. 0402 35226). Situated beside the famous 'Meeting of the Waters' which inspired poet Thomas Moore, this Tudor-style pub is decorated with Moore artefacts and other local treasures. On summer weekends, there is often traditional Irish music or an open-air céilí.

DIGRESSIONS

LIGHTS, CAMERA, ACTION! County Wicklow has long been a setting for major film productions. Parts of the county have been shown on the wide screen in more than a dozen productions including: *Henry V* (Enniskerry, 1944); *The Blue Max* (Kilpedder, 1966); *Zardoz* (Wicklow, 1973), *Excalibur* (Powerscourt Waterfall, Roundwood, Enniskerry, 1981), *The Dead* (Glendalough, 1987), *The Miracle* (Bray Head, 1991), *Into the West* (Kilruddery, 1992), *Braveheart* (Blessington, Sally Gap and Glendalough, 1995), *Michael Collins* (Rathdrum, Avoca, Arklow, 1996) and *Dancing at Lughnasa* (Blessington, 1998), as well as the popular BBC TV and PBS TV series, *Ballykissangel*

(Avoca, 1996–2002). The Wicklow Film Commission has mapped out three different 'film trails' with appropriate signposts. To find the film locations as you drive around County Wicklow, get a copy of 'County Wicklow Film Location Trails' or 'Ireland – Film Locations' from any tourist office. Information: Wicklow Film Commission (tel. 0404 20176 or www.wicklow.ie).

ON THE WILD SIDE: Sally Gap, Lough Tay and other off-the-beaten-track parts of County Wicklow are often overlooked on standard day tours. Wild Coach Tours takes visitors into these remote bog and mountainous areas, as driver/guides provide a light-hearted commentary along the route. Transport is in 26–29-seater Mercedes coaches. Information: Aran Tours Ltd, 14 Lower Albert Road, Sandycove, Co. Dublin (tel. 01 280 1899 or www.wildcoachtours.com).

WEST WICKLOW WANDERINGS: The western half of County Wicklow is dominated by Poulaphuca Reservoir, more commonly known as Blessington Lake, a 2,023-hectare (5,000-acre) man-made lake formed for hydroelectric purposes from the River Liffey. Focal point of the town of Blessington is Russborough House, one of Ireland's finest Palladian-style big houses. Built in 1741–1751 for the earl of Milltown, the house is furnished with European antiques, porcelain, silver and tapestries, with some noteworthy stucco ceilings by the Lafranchini brothers. It is also the home of the Beit art collection, displaying paintings by Vernet, Guardi, Bellotto, Gainsborough, Rubens and Reynolds. Open daily, May–September; Sundays and bank holidays in April and October. Information: Russborough House, Blessington (tel. 045 865 239).

The Southeast

7: Kilkenny – Medieval City

In appearance, authenticity and ambience, Kilkenny is Ireland's medieval city.

Founded in the sixth century by St Canice, Kilkenny takes its name from the Irish *Cill Chainnigh*, which means 'Canice's Church'. Like most Irish cities, Kilkenny fell into Norman hands in the twelfth century, but, thanks to its inland location beside the River Nore, became a prosperous walled medieval city and served as the venue for many parliaments. At one point, from 1642 to 1648, the Confederation of Kilkenny functioned as an independent Irish parliament, and Kilkenny was briefly considered the capital of a united Ireland. Alas, Kilkenny fell into conquering hands in 1650 when Oliver Cromwell's army swept into town. Never again did the city rise above regional prominence, but it has earned great respect in the southeast as a marketing hub and an architectural gem.

Much of Kilkenny's thirteenth/fourteenth-century character and layout remain today. Walk from one end of the city to the other, and encounter a continuous tableau of well-preserved medieval churches, public buildings, narrow streets and arched laneways, many with descriptive names like Pennyfeather Lane, Horseleap Slip, Butter Slip, Pudding Lane and New Building Lane.

One of the most famous natives of Kilkenny was Dame Alice Kyteler (born *c*.1280), a local beauty who was accused of witchcraft but escaped to England. Her servant Petronella was not so lucky – she was burned at the stake in 1324. The legend of Dame Alice lives on at her original house, restored in 1966 and now a tavern.

In addition to its medieval identity, Kilkenny is also known as 'The Marble City' – because fine black marble used to be quarried on the outskirts of town. Up until 1929, some of the streets had marble pavements.

FAST FACTS

Travel Information Office

KILKENNY TOURIST OFFICE, Rose Inn Street, Kilkenny (tel. 056 775 1500). Open all year.

TRAVEL INFORMATION ONLINE:
www.southeastireland.com,
www.kilkennytourism.ie and
www.kilkennycraic.com

TELEPHONE AREA CODE:
The telephone area code for all numbers
is 056, unless indicated otherwise.

MAJOR EVENTS

CAT LAUGHS FESTIVAL – Drawing talent
from all over Ireland, Britain, Europe and
the US, this comedy festival is unique for
two reasons – no television cameras are
allowed into any of the shows, and there
are no competitions, prizes or awards to

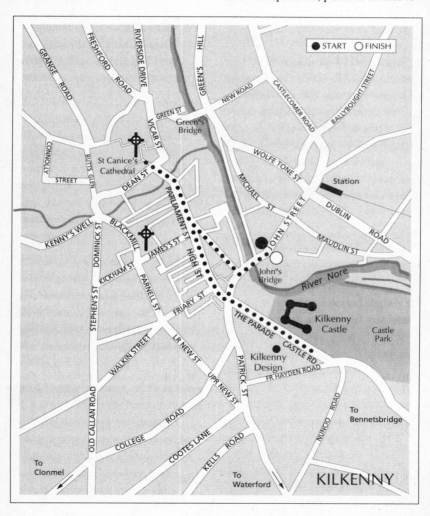

be won except for lots of audience laughter. Information: Cat Laughs Festival, 19 Dean Street, tel. 776 3416 or www.thecatlaughs.com. (Last weekend of May)

KILKENNY ARTS WEEK – Kilkenny is at its best (and busiest) during this annual event, blending classical and traditional music, plays, readings, films, poetry, art exhibitions, outdoor plays and many social events. Information: Kilkenny Arts Festival, 92 High Street, tel. 776 3663 or www.kilkennyarts.ie. (Second week of August)

KILKENNY CITY WALKING TOUR

Duration: 1–2 hours plus stops

Start this tour at **John's Bridge** crossing over the River Nore from **Lower John Street** into the entrance of the medieval city. Cross over the bridge and the street name changes to **Rose Inn Street**. On the right side is the **Shee Alms House**, built in 1582 by Sir Richard Shee to shelter paupers, and now the city's tourist office.

After visiting the tourist office and gathering the latest brochures, step outside, turn right and continue on Rose Inn Street for half a block; to the left, the road opens out onto the wide thoroughfare known as **The Parade**, with a parking area and the grounds of Kilkenny's centrepiece attraction, **Kilkenny Castle** (tel. 772 1450). With a striking façade of huge towers and battlements edging the banks of the River Nore, Kilkenny Castle dominates the southern end of Kilkenny city. It dates back to 1192, when it was built by the Norman leader, Strongbow, who eventually passed it to his son-in-law, but it was acquired in 1391 by the Butlers, the dukes and marquesses of Ormonde. The Butler family remained for over 500 years, in almost uninterrupted occupancy, until 1935. The castle was eventually given to the Irish government in 1967, to be preserved as a national monument.

Interior access is by guided tour only – to see the library, drawing room, bedrooms and sitting rooms, decorated in 1830s style with pieces from the National Furniture Collection of Ireland. In addition, the former servants' quarters have been restored as the Butler Art Gallery, a showcase for changing exhibitions of contemporary art. The grounds include riverside walks and seasonal gardens. Open daily. Admission: €€

Cross the street to visit the former castle stable, built in 1760 and transformed into another local landmark – the **Kilkenny Design Centre**, The Parade (tel. 772 2118). Enter this bustling complex by passing through a unique arched gateway under a copper-domed clock tower. Inside is a world of creativity, a showcase for the best of Irish design and workmanship chosen from over 200 studios and workshops throughout Ireland. Jewellery, pottery, glassware, ceramics, metalwork, porcelain, handknits, candles, art and home furnishings are but a few of the wares for sale. 'Shop till you drop' is easily applicable here. Open daily, April–December; Monday–Saturday in January–March. Admission: free

Behind the Design Centre, continue through the cobbled courtyard to the crescent-shaped cluster of buildings occupied by the **National Craft Gallery** (tel. 776 1804), a permanent museum operated by the Crafts Council of Ireland, with ever-changing exhibits of Irish and international crafts, and frequent appearances by working artisans. Open daily, April–December; Monday–Saturday in January–March. Admission: free

Stroll from the castle grounds to the heart of the city, along **High Street** which becomes **Parliament Street**. On the right side is **The Tholsel**, with an arcaded front and clock tower. Erected in 1761, it served originally as a toll house, city hall, and exchange for local produce, and is now the town hall. It contains municipal archives and charters, including Kilkenny's first book of records, dating back to 1230, as well as the charter of 1609 elevating Kilkenny to the status of a city, official sword (1609) and mace (1677). Open Monday–Friday. Admission: free.

The next right turn is **Butter Slip**, one of the city's many medieval passageways. It is a narrow covered lane with steps built in 1616 to accommodate people seeking a short cut between the raised ground of High Street and the lower level of St Kieran Street. Its name came about when a local woman used the lane as a market place to set up a stall and sell butter. If you follow the slip to St Kieran Street, you can visit **Kyteler's Inn**, a fourteenth-century tavern that was reputedly the home of a witch (*see* Pubs below).

Moving along to the point where the street changes its name to Parliament, on the left side is **Rothe House**, Parliament Street (tel. 772 2893). Identified as one of Kilkenny's oldest houses, this museum is a fine example of a Tudor-style middle-class home, built in 1594 by a local merchant, John Rothe. It is actually three restored buildings, joined by cobbled courtyards. A tour includes a reception room with splendid hand-carved oak furniture and a collection of costumes, as well as a large common kitchen, bakery and brewery. Throughout the house, there is an interesting panorama of pictures and artefacts of Kilkenny's past. Open Monday–Saturday and Sunday afternoons, March–October; and afternoons only, November–February. Admission: €

Walk one block and take a left down a narrow medieval street, passing through **Black Ferren Gate**, the last remaining gate of the original walls of the town. Continue for a few hundred yards to see one of the city's best preserved and restored churches, the **Black Abbey**, Abbey Street (tel. 772 1279). Founded in 1225 by William Marshall, earl of Pembroke, this abbey was formed as the Dominican Friary of the Most Holy Trinity. It was suppressed 300 years later, and all of the property was confiscated for Henry VIII. Subsequently, it was used as a courthouse until 1650 when Cromwell's troops reduced the abbey to a roofless ruin. In 1816, the local people revived it as a house of worship, and gradually began to restore it. A new nave had been constructed by 1866 and the entire building had been restored by 1979. The abbey derives its name from the fact that the Dominicans wore a black *cappa* over their white habit.

Items of note include stone coffins from the thirteenth century at the entrance; the great east window (1892), measuring 46.5 square metres (500 square feet) and depicting the fifteen mysteries of the rosary; a sculpture of the Holy Trinity, *c.*1400, carved from alabaster, on view in a glass case near the altar; and a pre-Reformation Irish oak statue of St Dominic, believed to be the oldest of its kind in the world. Open daily. Admission: free

Another ecclesiastical landmark, **St Francis Abbey**, built in 1234, sits directly across Parliament Street, to the right. Although this abbey no longer operates as a church, its walls and belfry tower live on as part of the façade of **Smithwick's Brewery**, Parliament Street (tel. 772 1014). The brewery, which was founded at this site by John Smithwick in 1710, now brews Budweiser for Irish markets, as well as the original Smithwick's brand. Open for tours, conducted May–September (phone for schedule). Admission: free

Next on the right is the **Watergate Theatre**, Parliament Street (tel. 776 1674), one of Ireland's newest theatres (1993). It presents a variety of shows in a contemporary setting.

Follow the street to the end, over the bridge at Irishtown, and you will arrive at the place that gave Kilkenny its name – **St Canice's Cathedral**, St Canice's Place, Coach Road (tel. 776 4971). St Canice founded a monastery on this site in the sixth century. The Irish for Kilkenny – *Cill Chainnigh* – means St Canice's Church. The present Gothic-style church was built mostly in the thirteenth century, but has been expanded over the centuries. It is the second longest of Ireland's medieval cathedrals, at 64.5 metres (212 feet) in length.

An equally imposing structure on the exterior and the interior, St Canice's has over 100 of the finest six-teenth-century funerary and sepulchral monuments of Ireland. Relatively modern highlights include a hammer-barn roof that dates back to 1863, made from Canadian red pine timber; an organ dating back to 1854 and still in use; and a marble floor composed of the four marbles of Ireland. The grounds include steps that were constructed in 1614, and a massive 31-metre (101-foot) high round tower, believed to have survived from St Canice's time, also open to the public. Open daily except Sunday mornings when services are on. Admission: €

Complete this tour by retracing your steps and strolling back along Parliament, High and Rose Inn Streets, taking the opportunity this time to branch off into the various lanes and slips, or to note the many decorative shopfronts along the way.

PAT'S PICKS

RESTAURANTS

CAFÉ SOL, William Street (tel. 776 4987). Located on a narrow lane off High Street, this trendy restaurant presents creative cuisine for snacks or lunch (and dinners on summer weekends). The menu changes often but usually includes made-from-scratch soups (such as curried parsnip and apple soup) or exotic salads (such as salad of monkfish, salmon and pine kernels) as well as unusual sandwiches and casseroles, and freshly made breads and scones. Open Monday–Saturday.

CROTTY'S, St Kieran Street (tel. 776 4877). For morning coffee, afternoon tea or lunch, this family-run coffee shop is a favourite with the locals. The selection includes freshly made soups and made-to-order sandwiches, as well as cakes, breads, pastries and scones baked on the premises. Homemade apple tart is a speciality. Open Monday–Saturday.

KILKENNY DESIGN CENTRE RESTAURANT, The Parade (tel. 772 2118). Housed in the original coach house of Kilkenny Castle, this self-service café offers an ever-changing lunch/snack menu of freshly made soups, salads, casseroles, pastries and breads, and other local goodies, all presented in a welcoming atmosphere of whitewashed walls, handcrafted furnishings and local art. Open daily, April–December; Monday–Saturday in January–March.

LACKEN HOUSE, Dublin Road (tel. 776 1085). Ideal for a big splurge, this award-winning restaurant is the centrepiece of an elegant Georgian guesthouse, nestled in a residential area about 1.6 km (1 mile) from the centre of town. The cuisine is a blend of Irish and international, with emphasis on locally raised meats, just-caught fish, and organic vegetables and fruit. Open for dinner only, Tuesday–Saturday, except most of January.

LAUTREC'S BISTRO, 9 St Kieran Street (tel. 776 2720), is a small, old-world-style bistro with a décor of beamed ceilings, stone walls, hanging wine casks and a potbelly stove. The menu offers modern international favourites, from pastas and pizzas to chargrilled meats, salads, and stuffed baked potatoes. Open for lunch and dinner, daily.

PARIS TEXAS, 92 High Street (tel. 776 1822). As its name implies, this café-bar delivers more fiery flavours and exotic ingredients than the usual Irish fare – it's a fusion of Tex-Mex and French cuisine. Open for lunch, snacks and dinner, daily.

PORDYLO'S, Butterslip Lane, off High Street (tel. 777 0660). The location of this restaurant is part of the attraction – nestled in a restored sixteenth-century building on one of the city's smallest and oldest thoroughfares. The menu entices, too, with specialities of fresh coastal shellfish and other local seafood, as well as seasonal wild game. Open for dinner, daily.

RISTORANTE RINUCCINI, 1 The Parade (tel. 776 1575). If you crave Italian food, it's hard to top this Irish/Italian restaurant run by the Cavaliere family. Specialities include a variety of chicken, beef and veal dishes, plus shrimp scampi and homemade pastas such as the house speciality of spaghettini with fresh lobster. Open for lunch and dinner, daily.

PUBS

CAISLEÁN UÍ CUAIN – THE CASTLE INN, Castle Street (tel. 776 5406), at the corner of High Street. Founded in 1734 as a stagecoach inn, this pub exudes old-world charm, with lots of memorabilia on display. Traditional music is on tap many nights, and the Irish language is often spoken by patrons and staff alike.

JOHN CLEERE, 28 Parliament Street (tel. 776 2573). Sitting in the heart of Kilkenny's main thoroughfare, with a distinctive old-style shopfront façade, this pub is known for Irish traditional music sessions every Monday night. In addition to the main pub, there is a small 100-seat theatre at the back of the premises, offering an eclectic mix of music, comedy and drama in intimate surroundings.

KYTELER'S INN, St Kieran Street (tel. 772 1064). This stone-faced pub is a fine example of a medieval tavern, dating back to the fourteenth century. Wander through the interior of caverns and arches, oak-beamed ceilings and wooden floors, and warm yourself by the huge open fireplace. Order a beverage or snack and settle in to examine the memorabilia associated with Dame Alice Kyteler who was accused of being a witch.

TYNAN'S BRIDGE HOUSE, 2 Horseleap Slip (tel. 772 1291), next to John's Bridge. Established in 1861, this classic pub is the oldest original bar in Kilkenny. It once doubled as a grocery store and pharmacy, so the authentic horseshoe-shaped bar is surrounded by décor of wide drawers marked 'mace', 'citron' and 'sago', as well as seventeenth-century weighing scales, shaving mugs, teapots and vintage books, including a time-worn copy of Chaucer's *Canterbury Tales*.

DIGRESSIONS

CIRCLING THE CITY: Not all tours of Kilkenny are on foot. City Sightseeing Tours operates one-hour open-top double-decker bus tours that circle the entire city, stopping at thirteen sites, including Kilkenny Castle, St Canice's Cathedral, Black Abbey and Rothe House.

Best of all, you can hop off the bus at one attraction and hop back on another bus later, saving both time and shoe leather. One fare provides unlimited on and off privileges all day, mid-May to mid-September. Information: City Sightseeing Tours (tel. 01 872 9010 or www.city-sightseeing.com).

EXPLORING BELOW THE SURFACE: If you want to get to the bottom of things, head out from the city via the Castlecomer Road about 11 km (7 miles) to Dunmore Cave, an authentic underground cave system formed millions of years ago. It consists of a series of chambers with some of the finest calcite formations found in Ireland. First mentioned in the ninth-century Irish triads, the cave has been enhanced in recent times by catwalks and lighting for safe exploring, but it is accessible only by guided tours. Open daily, March–October; Saturday and Sunday, November–February. Information: Dunmore Cave, Ballyfoyle (tel. 056 776 7726 or www.heritageireland.ie).

MEDIEVAL KILKENNY WALKS: For a tour of Kilkenny city with emphasis on its medieval streets, laneways and landmarks, join award-winning local guide Pat Tynan on one of his one-hour strolls. You'll learn not only history, but a host of trivia as well, and fun-filled facts abut Kilkenny. Tours depart daily from the Shee Alms House/Tourist Office, mid-March–October; and Tuesday– Saturday, November–mid-March. Information: Tynan Tours (tel. 087 265 1745 or www.tynantours.com).

8: Nore and Barrow River Valleys

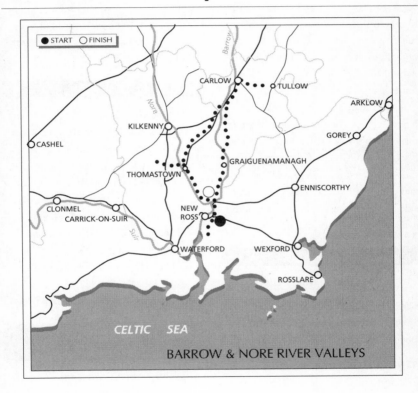

BARROW & NORE RIVER VALLEYS

The Barrow and the Nore are two of Ireland's most picturesque rivers, meandering through four adjacent southeastern counties – Kilkenny, Carlow, Waterford and Wexford – and bordered on the east by the Blackstairs Mountains.In the midst of an ever-changing landscape of fertile farm country, the Barrow and Nore both travel in a north–south direction, weaving along beside some lovely 'undiscovered' towns with lyrical, distinctive names like Bennettsbridge, Graiguenamanagh, Inistioge and Mooncoin.

The two rivers are widely known for salmon and trout fishing, yet their bucolic banks are less travelled by tourists than are many other parts of Ireland.

From Kilkenny city, Waterford city, or Wexford town, it's an easy drive to take in the best of the Barrow and the Nore. But be forewarned – much of this tour is 'off the beaten track' at best – not too many restaurants, pubs, man-made attractions or festivals, just beautiful natural river-valley vistas and non-touristy towns.

As is true of many scenic settings, however, creative inspiration and artistry thrive in this area, particularly along the back roads of County Kilkenny. The studios of potters, weavers, glass-makers and other craft workers dot the countryside. A 'Craft Trail' brochure is readily available from the local tourist offices.

FAST FACTS

Travel Information Offices

KILKENNY TOURIST OFFICE, Rose Inn Street, Kilkenny (tel. 056 775 1500). Open all year.

WATERFORD TOURIST OFFICE, The Granary, The Quay, Waterford (tel. 051 875 823). Open all year.

WEXFORD TOURIST OFFICE, Crescent Quay, Wexford (tel. 053 23111). Open all year.

CARLOW TOURIST OFFICE, Tullow Street, Carlow (tel. 059 913 1554). Open all year.

NEW ROSS TOURIST OFFICE, The Quay, New Ross, Co. Wexford (tel. 051 421 857). Open all year.

TRAVEL INFORMATION ONLINE:
www.southeastireland.com

TELEPHONE AREA CODES:
As this tour covers parts of four counties (Waterford, Wexford, Carlow and Kilkenny), area codes are specified with each listing.

MAJOR EVENT:

THE DUNBRODY FESTIVAL – The *Dunbrody* ship – docked at New Ross on the River Barrow – is the focal point of this three-day festival which includes an array of free musical entertainment, pub music trails, exhibitions, street theatre, a craft fair, helicopter trips, hot-air balloons, fishing competitions and a symposium. Information: Dunbrody Festival Committee, The Quay, New Ross, Co. Wexford, tel. 051 421 857 or www.jfkdunbrodyfestival.com. (Mid-July)

NORE AND BARROW RIVER VALLEYS DRIVING TOUR

Suggested driving time – 3–5 hours plus stops

Although the starting point for this tour can be Waterford, Kilkenny or Wexford, this suggested route departs from the city of Waterford, heading east on the N25 road toward **New Ross**, a busy port town on the joint estuary of the Barrow and the

Nore. In medieval times, New Ross rivalled Waterford as a seaport, positioned on the water at the western edge of County Wexford.

In the mid-nineteenth century, the port was a departure point for many Irish emigrants including the great-grandfather of President John Fitzgerald Kennedy, 35th president of the United States. To learn more about this phase of Irish history, walk along the Quay and step aboard **The Dunbrody** (tel. 051 425 239), an impressive three-masted barque that is a full-scale recreation of an actual timber-built ship that brought Irish famine emigrants across the Atlantic to New York. Although the original was built in Canada in 1845, this replica was constructed at New Ross by a team of local craftsmen and trainees, aided by funds from the JFK Trust.

Climb down the steep wooden staircase below deck and step back into the mid-nineteenth century – experience the sights, smells and sounds of a wooden sailing ship. Costumed actors narrate the story of the *Dunbrody* and its many passengers, including the forebears of President Kennedy. The ship's modern equipment includes a computer database of over 2 million individual passenger records, so it also serves as a genealogical centre. Open daily. Admission: €€

If time allows, take a short detour 7 km (4.5 miles) south via the R733, to track down other aspects of the Kennedy ancestral homeland at the **John F**

Kennedy Arboretum, Dunganstown (tel. 051 388 171), a 243-hectare (600-acre) memorial park, located near a hill known as **Slieve Coillte**. Opened in 1968 as a gift from the US to the Irish people, it is laid out and landscaped to provide for leisure, education and research, with a lake and 200 forest plots, as well as over 4,500 species and varieties of trees, plants and shrubs, from five continents. Thanks to Wexford's mild climate, it is expected that the number will eventually reach 6,000. Visitor facilities include a picnic area, self-guided walking trails, an information centre with an audiovisual show, and a hilltop observation point that presents sweeping views of at least four Irish counties – Wexford, Waterford, Kilkenny and Tipperary. Open daily. Admission: €

Signposted nearby is the **Kennedy Homestead**, Dunganstown (tel. 051 388 264), the original thatched farm home of President Kennedy's great-grandfather who emigrated to Boston. President Kennedy made a special point of visiting his cousins here in 1963 during his historic visit to Ireland. The site now includes a visitor centre with an audiovisual and a collection of memorabilia covering five generations of Kennedys. Open mid-May–September. Admission: €

Return to the main road and follow signs for the N30 and then take a left turn into a local road, R705, which runs along the west bank of the Barrow in

County Kilkenny. The drive is particularly scenic, with panoramic farmland landscapes, bordered by Brandon Hill to the left and the Blackstairs Mountains to the right. On the right is a look-out point over the valley, known as **Saint Mullins**. This was the setting for an ecclesiastical village of the same name founded by St Moling in the seventh century. The ruins contain parts of the monastery and a round tower. It is well worth a stop here for the panoramic view of the valley.

After 16 km (10 miles), this road curves into the village of **Graiguenamanagh** (pronounced *Gray-ge-na-maan-ah*), a name that means 'village of the monks'. Sitting beside the River Barrow, this little town derives its name from the monks who founded, worked and prayed at **Duiske Abbey**, Main Street (tel. 059 972 4238), from the year 1204.

Duiske (pronounced *Doo-shkaa*) Abbey is named after a small local river (*dubh uisce* or 'black water') that rushes down from Brandon Hill into the River Barrow. It took 40 years to build and was considered a fine example of the style of architecture known as 'Early English', as well as being the largest of the Irish Cistercian monastery churches (with a nave over 60 metres/200 feet in length). It became a hub of ecclesiastic and scholastic activity in the Middle Ages, only to be suppressed in 1536 and eventually fall into ruin. It was fully restored in the 1970s, thanks to the efforts of the local community who pooled their talents and once again made the abbey the focal point of the area.

Highlights from the thirteenth century include part of the original tiled floor and stone carvings on windows, doorways and arches, as well as rugged stone-faced walls, lime-washed in the original manner. The great oak roof, although new, was constructed exactly as a medieval roof, with dowels and wedges and not a single nail. Celtic crosses in the grounds are believed to pre-date the foundation of the abbey, dating as far back as the ninth century. A nearby visitor centre offers a display of Christian art and artefacts. Open daily. Admission: free

For craft-seekers, there are two enterprises of note in the town, both located in the High Street, Old Road area. **Cushendale Woollen Mills** (tel. 059 972 4118), originally part of the thirteenth-century Duiske Abbey foundation, carries on a great tradition of woollen crafts. This small mill shop offers a range of products in Irish wool, mohair, lamb's wool, and Merino wool – all reflecting the soft colours of the surrounding countryside. Open Monday–Friday, and Saturday morning. Admission: free

Duiske Glass (tel. 059 972 4174) takes its name from the local river and abbey. Founded in 1974 by the O'Shea family, this company uses the traditional intaglio method of engraving to produce unique glassware. Open Monday–Friday, and Saturday morning. Admission: free

When departing the town, take note of the stone bridge crossing the River Barrow to the County Carlow side. Built in 1767, it is the second bridge on this site and is considered to be one of the most aesthetically pleasing bridges in all of Ireland.

From Graiguenamanagh, continue north to follow the R705 along the River Barrow via Borris and Muine Bheag (Bagenalstown), and then via the N9 into **Carlow**, the chief town of County Carlow, and the largest market centre of the Barrow Valley.

The surrounding area is often called 'Dolmen Country' because it is rich in archaeological sites, particularly the **Brownshill Dolmen**, also known as the Mount Browne Dolmen, just under 5 km (3 miles) east of town on the Hacketstown Road. Dating from 2,500BC, this monument is a fine example of a portal-tomb or *cromlech*, thought to be the burial place of a significant prehistoric prince. Topped by a capstone that weighs over 100 tons, it is considered the largest of its kind in Ireland and perhaps in Europe.

A 16 km (10-mile) detour east via the R725 leads to the prime attraction of County Carlow – **Altamount Gardens**, Tullow (tel. 059 915 9444), signposted between Tullow and Ballon off the convergence of the N80 and N81. Originally a private estate, these nineteenth-century gardens contain a brilliant array of flowers, shrubs and trees, all laid out to surround a man-made lake. There is particular emphasis on rare trees, a profusion of roses and herbaceous plants that scent the air. Open daily except weekends in winter. Admission: €

Return to the main road, N9, from Carlow, heading south via Leighlinbridge, Royal Oak, Whitehall, and Gowran, following a sign to the right for **Bennettsbridge**, on the banks of the River Nore, and back into County Kilkenny. Originally known as St Benet's Bridge, this small town sits beside a bridge over the Nore, on a route that was the medieval highway from Dublin to the south of Ireland. Because of its secluded yet convenient location – 8 km (5 miles) southeast of the city of Kilkenny – in recent years the town has drawn a number of artisans and craftspeople who have taken up residence and opened studios and craft shops that welcome visitors, with no admission charges. Hours of business vary, so phone in advance.

The oldest of these is **Nicholas Mosse Pottery** (tel. 056 772 7105), an enterprise that produces brightly coloured earthenware made from Irish clay, decorated with traditional motifs. The pottery is housed in a former flour mill beside the River Nore, and has been owned by the Mosse family for eleven generations. Visitors can watch potters at work, or stroll through a small museum displaying the antique Irish pottery known as spongeware.

Other craft studios in Bennettsbridge are **The Bridge Pottery** (tel. 056 772 7077), **Chesneau Leather Goods** (tel.

772 7456), **Dyed in the Wool Knitwear Studio** (tel. 882 7684) and **Stoneware Jackson Pottery** (tel. 772 7175). Still another craft enterprise is located about 8 km (5 miles) west and south of Bennettsbridge, via the main N10 road – the **Jerpoint Glass Studio** (tel. 056 772 4350), Stoneyford. Glass-blowing demonstrations are given on weekdays only, but the shop is open daily.

From **Stoneyford**, you can take a short detour, about 3 km (2 miles) west, to **Kells**, the only complete walled medieval town in Ireland, founded in 1193 as an Augustinian priory. Although largely in ruins, the extensive curtain walls, seven towers, and some monastic buildings have been preserved.

Returning to Stoneyford, continue about 3 km (2 miles) east along a rural stretch of farming countryside when the road suddenly curves to reveal an imposing monument of long ago – **Jerpoint Abbey**, Thomastown (tel. 056 772 4623).

In many ways, Jerpoint Abbey is a kind of ghost town. Founded as a Cistercian Monastery in 1160, it became a thriving town, with infirmary, granary, stables, watermills, gardens and various houses and buildings, flourishing well into the fifteenth century. Like most Irish religious foundations, it was suppressed in the sixteenth century and eventually fell into ruin in the seventeenth century. Highlights include original twelfth-century Romanesque pillars, a medieval chancel, a four-teenth- century window with elaborate tracery, and one of the most decorative cloister arcades of any Irish church, partially reconstructed in 1953. The carvings are of great interest, ranging from human figures such as a bishop, a knight and his lady, to small unexpected figures in corners or on bases. There is also a remarkable collection of medieval glazed earthenware tiles, generally dated to the fourteenth and fifteenth centuries, with four design patterns – a lion rampant, fleur-de-lys, a naturalistic design on a cusped frame, and a border tile with a running vine-scroll motif. Open March–November. Admission: €

About 3 km (2 miles) eastward is **Thomastown**, a small market town situated at the head of the Nore river valley. It is named after Thomas FitzAnthony who founded the town in the thirteenth century. In the Middle Ages it was a walled town, but only the ruins of its walls and castles remain. The centrepiece today is Mount Juliet, originally a private estate and now a holiday resort with an eighteen-hole championship Jack Nicklaus-designed golf course, horse stud farm and other sports facilities, including Ireland's oldest cricket club.

Follow the R700 south of Thomastown for about 8 km (5 miles), along a scenic and verdant tree-shaded section of the River Nore valley to **Inistioge** (pronounced *Innish-teague*), a name derived from the Irish *Inis Tiog*, meaning 'Teoc's riverside meadow'. Aptly named, this beautiful little village is situated on the banks of the River Nore, crossed over by a romantic eighteenth-century stone bridge of nine arches. A well-landscaped square sits in the middle of the village, with a fountain erected in 1879.

It is no wonder that Inistioge's idyllic setting has often been recognised as a splendid location for films – including *Circle of Friends*, based on the Maeve Binchy novel, and *Widow's Peak*, starring Mia Farrow.

From Inistioge, follow the scenic riverside route along the Nore for 16 km (10 miles), returning to New Ross and the starting point of this tour.

PAT'S PICKS

RESTAURANTS

LORD BAGENAL INN, Main Street, Leighlinbridge, Co. Carlow (tel. 059 972 1668). Situated on the banks of the Barrow off the N9, this old-world inn has long been a mecca for good food in a cosy atmosphere, with open fireplaces and local memorabilia. The menu features steaks, game and Dunmore East seafood, as well as lighter fare including hearty soups and local farmhouse cheeses. Open for lunch and dinner, daily.

MOSSES' MILL CAFÉ, Bennettsbridge, Co. Kilkenny (tel. 056 772 7505). Nestled beside the River Nore on the first floor of an old mill, this restaurant makes good use of Nicholas Mosse's pottery, with a décor of local art. The innovative lunch/snack menu changes daily, but always includes home-baked breads and scones (made with the local Mosses' flour), and soups, sandwiches and salads. Open for lunch and snacks, daily.

RATHWOOD, Rath, Tullow, Co. Carlow (tel. 059 915 6285). Flowers and plants provide a relaxing background to this café which is part of a garden centre/craft complex, situated on a back road amid sheep-filled fields. The menu offers freshly made soups, casseroles and salads, as well as made-to-order sandwiches and home-baked pastries and breads, all served on local pottery, with seating indoors or outdoors, under cover or in the open air. Open for lunch and snacks, daily.

The Watergarden, Ladywell Street, Thomastown, Co. Kilkenny (tel. 056 24690). Surrounded by lush gardens, this coffee shop sits beside a small tributary of the River Nore. It is run by the Camphill Community, a voluntary organisation that helps people with disabilities. The menu specialises in freshly prepared and home-baked food, made with all organic ingredients, most of which are grown in the gardens or nearby farms. Open Tuesday–Friday and Sunday.

WATERSIDE, The Quay, Graiguenamanagh, Co. Kilkenny (tel. 059 972 4246). Housed in a nineteenth-century granary with authentic dark wood-beam ceilings, leaded windows, and an imposing granite façade, this homely restaurant sits beside the River Barrow at the foot of Brandon Hill. The menu offers modern Irish cuisine with local touches, such as smoked eels from a nearby fishery, salmon from the river, and farm-sourced meats, produce and cheeses, all topped by homemade ice cream. Open for dinner only, and for Sunday lunch.

PUBS

CASTLE INN, Inistioge, Co. Kilkenny (tel. 056 775 8483). Nestled in the heart of an idyllic village near the River Nore, this cosy country pub has lots of atmosphere and, on Sunday nights, traditional Irish music sessions.

CORCORAN'S, Irishtown, New Ross, Co. Wexford (tel. 051 425 920). One of the oldest pubs in the area, this stone-faced hostelry has been in the same family for five generations. Step inside to savour the old-world ambience, and enjoy some pub grub, or a quiet drink, music session or card game. For sunny days, there is a beer garden outside.

LONG MAN OF KILFANE, Dublin Road, Thomastown, Co. Kilkenny (tel. 056 772 4774). Named after a landmark effigy of a long-legged fourteenth-century knight, which is part of a nearby church, this pub is a local favourite. Besides its folkloric theme, it is noted for its bar food, beer garden and weekend traditional Irish music sessions.

DIGRESSIONS

BARGING ALONG: Cruise the river waters of the 'Three Sisters' rivers (Nore, Barrow and Suir) on a double-deck barge, while enjoying a narrated tour with lunch, afternoon tea, dinner or cruise-only option. These relaxing trips last from one to three hours, depending on time of day, April–October. Information: Galley River Cruises, Bridge Quay, New Ross, Co. Wexford (tel. 051 421 723 or www.rivercruises.ie).

DOWN ON THE FARM: Roll up your sleeves, put on the wellies, and visit a farm – it's an enriching experience for kids and parents alike. For a first-hand look at tillage and sheep-raising, head to 81-hectare (200-acre) Ballylane Farm in western County Wexford, just over 3 km (2 miles) east of New Ross, for a 90-minute self-guided tour encompassing fields of crops, woodlands, boglands, ponds, farm buildings and all the animals along the way. Open May–September. Information: Pat Hickey, Ballylane Farm, New Ross (tel. 051 21315). Nore Valley Park Open Farm near Bennettsbridge invites kids of all ages to feed the lambs and goats or handle the rabbits and chicks. Farm trailer rides are also available, as is a children's playground sandpit, straw-bounce, picnic area, 3-km (2-mile) river walk and more. Open Monday–Saturday, March– September. Information: Nore Valley Park Open Farm, Annamult, Bennettsbridge (tel. 056 772 7748).

9: Waterford City

Mention the word 'Waterford' and many people automatically say 'glass'. Without doubt, the city's beautiful hand-cut crystal, produced since 1783 at the Waterford Crystal factory, is known and treasured around the world. But the word 'Waterford' symbolises a lot more than glass – it is the name of one of Ireland's most notable maritime cities. With a population of 50,000, Waterford is the main seaport of the southeast coast.

Stretching for almost a kilometre (over half a mile) along the southern bank of the River Suir (pronounced *Shure*), the city of Waterford sits at the point where the river opens into the estuary of Waterford Harbour. The city's name dates back to the ninth century, when it was an important Danish settlement known as *Vadrefjord*. A still earlier name for it in the Irish language was *Cuan na Gréine*, or 'harbour of the sun'. The city's present Irish name, which you'll often see on buses and official government signs, is *Port Láirge*, which means 'Láirge's Landing Place'.

Not surprisingly, Waterford has been a favourite landing place throughout the years, first for the Vikings who are credited with founding a settlement here in the tenth century, later for the Normans and the English, and still more recently for tourists from all over the world who come via a variety of modes of transport, including cruise ships, buses and cars.

FAST FACTS

Travel Information Offices

WATERFORD TOURIST OFFICE/SOUTH EAST TOURISM, The Granary, The Quay, Waterford (tel. 051 875 823). Open all year.

WATERFORD CRYSTAL VISITOR CENTRE TOURIST OFFICE, Cork Road, Waterford (tel. 051 358 397). Open all year.

ARDMORE TOURIST OFFICE, Sea Front, Ardmore (tel. 024 94444). Open June–September.

DUNGARVAN TOURIST OFFICE, The Courthouse, Bridge Street, Dungarvan (tel. 058 41741). Open all year.

LISMORE TOURIST OFFICE, Heritage Centre, Lismore (tel. 058 54975). Open June–September.

TRAMORE TOURIST OFFICE, Railway Square, Tramore (tel. 051 381 572). Open June–September.

TRAVEL INFORMATION ONLINE:
www.waterfordtourism.org and
www.southeastireland.com

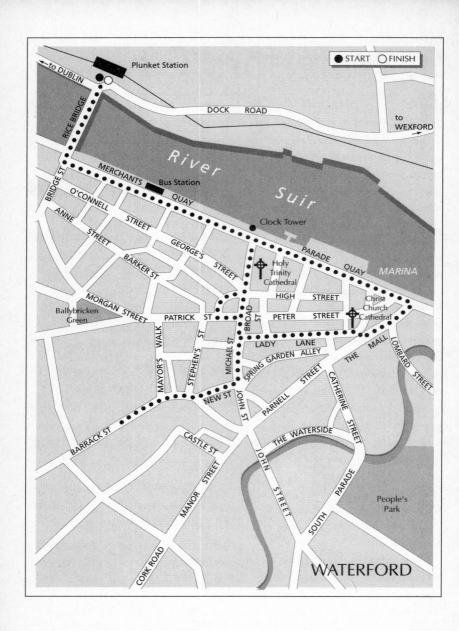

TELEPHONE AREA CODES:
The telephone area code for all numbers is 051, unless indicated otherwise.

MAJOR EVENTS

WATERFORD SPRAOI – Celebrated over the August Bank Holiday weekend, this three-day festival is billed as Ireland's largest outdoor summer event, with international music, street theatre and street spectacle throughout Waterford city centre. Information: Spraoi, The Glen, tel. 051 841 808 or www.spraoi.com. (First weekend of August)

WATERFORD LIGHT OPERA FESTIVAL – This annual gathering includes two weeks of competitions for amateur musical societies from all over Ireland, Britain and beyond. Information: Waterford Festival, Theatre Royal, The Mall, tel. 051 375 437 or www.waterfordfestival.com. (Late September into early October)

WATERFORD CITY WALKING TOUR

Duration: 2–3 hours plus stops

Start your tour at the bus and rail depot, Plunkett Station, on the north bank of the River Suir. Cross over the **Edmund Ignatius Rice Bridge**, named after one of the city's great altruistic citizens who devoted his life to the poor and is currently a candidate for sainthood (*see* Barrack Street below).

The south bank of the river is the city's main feature, known simply as **The Quay**, although it is, in fact, four quays (Grattan Quay, Merchant's Quay, Meagher Quay and Parade Quay), stretching for ten blocks or about a kilo-metre (half a mile). Do as the Water-forders do – turn left and stroll along the Quay at a leisurely pace, looking at the distinctive shop windows and pub façades en route.

Proceed in an eastward direction, along Merchant's Quay to Hanover Street, and you will see the main entrance to the **Waterford Tourist Office** at the Granary (*see* above). Turn right to visit the **Museum of Treasures**, Hanover Street (tel. 304 500). Housed in a restored nineteenth-century six-storey granary building, this new museum is the ideal way to get to know a lot about Waterford in a short time. It presents a one-stop rendezvous with some of Waterford's greatest people, places, and things, dating from Viking times to the present. All of the city's 'treasures' (for-merly housed at several smaller loca-tions) are now united under this one roof – from Viking jewellery to medieval gold, bronze and silver artefacts, as well as the city's original charter roll, civic regalia and specimens of rare old Water-ford glass.

Using a sound-guide headphone (available in adults' and children's ver-sions), you can also step back in time to enjoy a simulated eight-minute sea voyage on a Viking ship, observe the twelfth-century wedding of Strongbow and Aoife, and savour the atmosphere of a Georgian society ball. The tour takes about one hour, but you are free to set your own pace. In addition, there is a twelve-minute audiovisual and an art gallery displaying works of local artists. Open daily. Admission: €

Return to the Quay area and continue to **Meagher Quay**. On the right is the **Granville Hotel**, a focal point of the city, incorporating several buildings that were once private Georgian-era residences, including the birthplace of Waterford patriot Thomas Francis Meagher. The site was later purchased for use as a coaching inn by Carlo Bianconi, who started the first public transport system in Ireland using a horse-drawn fleet of vehicles called *Bians*.

At the next intersection, **Barron-strand Street**, is the **Clock Tower**, a Victorian Gothic landmark of local cut stone which helped sea captains keep their ships on schedule. Built in 1861, it once had troughs of water at its base for horses to drink from, and was often referred to as the Fountain Clock. The original structure, with its troughs, was replaced with the present clock in 1954.

Providing a backdrop for the clock is the **William Vincent Wallace Plaza**, a wide promenade area along the marina, named after a Waterford-born opera composer. With wooden benches and nautically themed sculpture, this plaza is a pleasant open-air resting place and also serves as a venue for public events such as summer musical concerts.

At this point, take a short detour for half a block to the right to see the **Cathedral of the Most Holy Trinity**, Barronstrand Street (tel. 874 757). Dating back to 1793, it was designed by Waterford-born architect John Roberts, with an austere Ionic-style façade. The interior, however, is rich and decorative, with a high vaulted roof, Corinthian pillars, carved oak pulpit, and a magnificent set of Waterford Crystal chandeliers donated by Waterford Crystal in 1979 after the church was renovated. Open daily. Admission: free

Continue along the Quay for five short blocks, passing the General Post Office and an assortment of shops, pubs and department stores.

A sign indicates a lane to the right which is known as Greyfriars Street, site of the Grey Friars ecclesiastical ruins, originally a Franciscan Abbey (founded in 1240). After it was disbanded by Henry VIII, the friary was used in turn as a hospital, a burial place and a parish church for French Huguenot refuges; hence the site is usually referred to by locals as **French Church**. Today it consists of the ruins of the nave, chancel, choir and tower of the monastic church, a chapel, and many centuries-old tombs, such as that of John Roberts, the Waterford architect who is responsible for most of the city's fine buildings, including its two cathedrals.

Turn the corner and see Waterford's most impressive Viking monument –

Reginald's Tower, The Quay (tel. 304 220). Built in 1003 by a Viking governor named Reginald, this 21.5-metre (70-foot) circular fortress gives Waterford its unmistakable Viking ambience, with 3-metre (10-foot) thick walls and a huge conical roof. It dominates the east end of the Quay, at the juncture of the Mall, and is considered the oldest urban civic building in Ireland, and possibly the oldest tower of mortared stone in Europe. As the historic centrepiece of Waterford, it served first as a fortress, then a prison, military depot, mint and air-raid shelter, and is now a museum of Waterford history. Open daily, April–October; Saturday and Sunday during rest of year. Admission: €

After visiting the tower, turn right onto **The Mall**, Waterford's wide ceremonial street. In the centre of the street is a statue of Luke Wadding, a local man who spent most of his life in Rome as a Franciscan priest and scholar, the only Irishman ever to be a candidate for the papacy. Half a block to the right is **City Hall**, the Mall (tel. 860 856), headquarters of the Waterford city council. An impressive eighteenth-century building designed by Waterford-born architect John Roberts, it houses a comprehensive collection of local art; a permanent exhibit of the battle flags, uniforms and swords of local patriot-turned-Civil War commander Thomas Francis Meagher; some priceless antique Waterford crystal display pieces; and the ornate

Victorian-style **Theatre Royal**. Open Monday–Friday. Admission: free

After City Hall, turn right at the next street to see **Christ Church Cathedral**, Cathedral Square (tel. 874 119). Built in 1770–79 to the specifications of John Roberts, who also designed City Hall, the Catholic Cathedral of the Most Holy Trinity and other notable Waterford landmarks, it occupies the site of an old Viking cathedral and its medieval successor which lasted until 1770. The present cathedral, which belongs to the Church of Ireland, still has some medieval monuments on view, including a small crypt and fifteenth- and sixteenth-century tombs. Open daily for tours except during services. Admission is free but donations are encouraged.

To the right is **Lady Lane**, a narrow passage that is considered to be Waterford's best example of a surviving medieval street. It still serves as a through-street, wending its way beside the modern City Square Shopping Centre, of 1990s vintage.

Follow Lady Lane to **Michael Street**, famed in the nineteenth century as the headquarters of Waterford's guild of weavers, and today a busy main commercial strip. At this point, you may wish to detour to the left to New Street, for two blocks past Convent Hill, to visit the **Edmund Rice Centre**, Mount Sion, Barrack Street (tel. 874 390). Housed at the Christian Brothers School, this museum focuses on the life of Waterford's spiritual hero, Edmund Ignatius Rice (1762–1844), a local man who sold all his possessions to help the poor. Founder of the teaching order of the Irish Christian Brothers, he was beatified (declared blessed) by Pope John Paul II in 1996. A visit includes a multi-image audiovisual presentation and a tour of the chapel where his tomb is located. Opening times vary; phone in advance to check. Admission: free

Returning to **Michael Street** at the corner of Lady Lane, turn right and walk in a northerly direction, as Michael Street changes its name to Broad Street. Make a left at **Broad Street**, beside the Broad Street Shopping Centre, another 1990s commercial addition to the city.

Go on up **Patrick Street** and **Little Patrick Street** to the **Waterford Heritage Genealogical Centre**, Jenkins Lane (tel. 876 123). If you have Waterford family ancestry, this is the place for you. It contains a vast collection of Waterford records, and staff are trained in helping visitors to find their roots. Open Monday– Friday. Admission is free, but fees are charged for genealogical searches.

Even if you don't have Waterford connections, this centre is an interesting attraction, as it is housed at **St Patrick's Church**, Waterford's oldest church. Although its exact date of origin is unknown, it began as a Penal chapel in a corn store and was identified on a 1764 map as a 'Mass House'. Highlights include an eighteenth-century arch and bell tower, and a unique U-shaped gallery inside. Open daily. Admission: free

Follow Little Patrick Street to George's Street, a pedestrian shopping street. To the left is the **Chamber of Commerce Building** (tel. 872 639), a fine example of eighteenth-century Georgian architecture, designed by the ubiquitous John Roberts and open during normal business hours. At the intersection of Gladstone Street, George's Street becomes O'Connell Street. Coming up on the left is the **Garter Lane Arts Centre**, 5 O'Connell Street (tel. 855 038), a contemporary art gallery and craft centre. Open Monday–Saturday. Admission: free

One block further is the **Garter Lane Theatre**, 22a O'Connell Street (tel. 855 038), a 170-seat performing arts venue. It is housed in the former Friends Meeting House.

Walk three more blocks on O'Connell Street to Bridge Street and turn right to return to the Edmund Ignatius Rice Bridge and the Quay, the starting point of the tour.

But your tour is not over yet – the best is yet to come. From the Quay, take a bus or taxi, or drive to the final highlight of a visit to Waterford city – the **Waterford Crystal Visitor Centre**, Kilbarry (tel. 332 500), about 3 km (2 miles) south of the city-centre area on the Cork Road (N25).

Founded in 1783, Waterford Crystal is the *grand-dame* of all Irish craft enterprises and one of the world's best-known names in genuine handmade decorative glass production. A visit includes a seventeen-minute audiovisual and a walk-through tour of the factory to see the whole magical process – from the master blowers, shapers, and cutters to the engravers, including an interactive exchange and time to ask questions. A visit also provides an opportunity to browse in the Waterford Crystal Gallery, the most comprehensive display of this glassware in the world, from stemware to trophies, globes and chandeliers. Tours are available daily, March–October; Monday–Friday, November–February. Admission: €€

Return to Waterford city or continue on to a new destination.

PAT'S PICKS

RESTAURANTS

DWYER'S RESTAURANT, 8 Mary Street (tel. 877 478), off Bridge Street. Chef-owner Martin Dwyer has transformed an unlikely setting – a former barracks building on a back street – into a cosy haven of innovative international cuisine, featuring local seafood and produce, enhanced by time-tested family recipes. Open for dinner, Monday–Saturday.

JADE PALACE, 3–4 The Mall (tel. 855 611), two doors from Reginald's Tower. This upstairs restaurant is one of Waterford's most surprising finds – top-class Chinese food served in an elegant atmosphere of fine linens, antique furnishings, Waterford Crystal accessories and silver cutlery (or chopsticks, if you prefer). Open for lunch and dinner, daily.

HARICOT'S WHOLEFOOD, 11 O'Connell Street (tel. 841 299). Established in 1986 by Breda and Elaine Ryan and named after the haricot bean, this restaurant specialises in fresh and unprocessed foods, with emphasis on vegetarian dishes, but also including locally sourced meat, poultry and seafood selections. Menus also cater to vegan, gluten-free and diabetic diets. Open for lunch and snacks, Monday–Saturday.

MCALPIN'S COTTAGE BISTRO, Cheekpoint Village (tel. 380 854). For a change of pace, it's well worth an 11-km (7-mile) drive east of Waterford city to this family-run restaurant near the harbour where three rivers meet (Suir, Nore and Barrow). The menu presents the best of locally sourced seafood, meat and produce, served in a cosy seventeenth-century maritime-themed cottage atmosphere. Open for dinner, Monday–Saturday, May–September; Tuesday–Saturday, October–April; except closed January and last week of September.

THE REGINALD, The Mall (tel. 855 087), next to Reginald's Tower. Taking its name from the famous adjacent landmark, this pub-restaurant has a décor reminiscent of Viking times, including alcoves, arches and part of an old city wall (c.850). The menu offers burgers, steaks, prime ribs and seafood, as well as sandwiches and pub grub. Open for lunch and dinner, daily.

THE WINE VAULTS, High Street (tel. 853 444). This restaurant is housed in a fifteenth-century building, formerly the home of the mayor, on one of Waterford's oldest streets. With such an atmospheric setting, it's no wonder that it is a favoured spot for a special meal. The menu features seafood, pastas, chargrilled meats, game and vegetarian dishes, accompanied by a wine-bar choice of over 300 labels. Open for lunch and dinner, Monday–Saturday.

PUBS

JACK MEADE'S PUB, Cheekpoint Road (tel. 873 187). Off the beaten track, this pub is located under a bridge in a sheltered valley 6.5 km (4 miles) south of Waterford city. It dates back to1705 and has been in the same family for almost 150 years. Enjoy old pictures, antiques and open fireplaces inside, and a beer garden and walking trails in the grounds outside.

THE MUNSTER, The Mall (tel. 874 656). Sitting in the heart of Waterford, this pub is outfitted with etched mirrors, antique Waterford-glass sconces, and dark-wood walls, some of which came from timber recycled from the original Waterford toll bridge. 'The Men's Bar' is a classic remnant of a different age.

THE OLDE STAND, 45 Michael Street (tel. 879 488), at the corner of Lady Lane. A Victorian atmosphere prevails at this vintage pub, with a décor of paintings and maps of old Waterford. Pub-grub snacks and carvery-style lunches are available each day.

T & H DOOLAN'S, 32 George's Street (tel. 841 504). Dating back over 200 years and claiming to be Waterford's oldest pub, this place was originally a stagecoach stop. It has a Tudor façade and a lantern-lit interior of great charm. It's a good stop for a drink, snacks or evening sessions of traditional music.

DIGRESSIONS

AN GAELTACHT: Just over 53 km (33 miles) southwest of Waterford city is Ring (An Rinn), a small coastal Gaeltacht overlooking Dungarvan Harbour. Spend an afternoon here to brush up on your Irish, enjoy panoramic views from Helvick Head (70 metres/230 feet) or just to bask in the hospitable old-world atmosphere of the pubs and shops. In the summer months, language-learning courses and a summer camp are held here. Information: An Rinn (tel. 058 46128).

CAR FERRY: For a delightful excursion through Waterford Harbour (or to save time and mileage between Waterford and Wexford), drive aboard the continuous car ferry, departing from Passage East, 16 km (10 miles) east of Waterford. Crossing time is five minutes and service is from 7am (Mondays–Saturdays) or 9.30am (Sundays) until 8pm (October–March) or 10pm (April–September). On the Wexford side, the terminal is at Ballyhack, approximately 32 km (20 miles) southwest of Wexford town. No reservations necessary; pay on board. Information: Passage East Car Ferry (tel. 382 480 or www.passageferry.com).

HERITAGE TOWN: Dating back to the seventh century, Lismore sits beside the River Blackwater in the shadow of the Knockmealdown Mountains, 65 km (40 miles) west of Waterford city. It is a pleasant town of eighteenth- and nineteenth-century buildings and a sixteenth-century cathedral, as well as Lismore Castle Gardens (open April–September). Guided tours of the town are conducted from April through October. Information: Heritage Centre (tel. 058 54975).

VINTAGE RAIL TRIPS: For a nostalgic train trip, climb aboard the Waterford and Suir Valley Railway. This narrow-gauge train follows part of the original rail route along the banks of the River Suir between Waterford city and Kilmeadan. The route extends for approximately 6.5 km (4 miles) with views of the Suir, mountains, farms, and parklands. Operates July–August; schedule varies. Information: Business Development Manager, Chamber of Commerce, George's Street, Waterford (tel. 872 639 or www.wsvrailway.ie).

WALKING TOURS OF HISTORIC WATERFORD

For a tour of Waterford city with emphasis on history, join award-winning local guide Jack Burtchaell on one of his one-hour strolls. You'll learn not only history but a host of trivia as well (for example, the first frog in Ireland was released in Waterford; the modern method of bacon curing was developed in Waterford; and Waterford is the only city in Europe whose Roman Catholic and Protestant cathedrals were designed and built by the same person). Tours depart daily, March–October, from the Waterford Treasures Museum. Information: Waterford Walking Tours (tel. 873 711).

10: Wexford Town

Wexford and history are synonymous. A town of narrow streets, hidden laneways, crumbling stone walls, and ancient abbey ruins, Wexford is one of Ireland's oldest settlements. Ideal for walking and meandering, it is situated on a sheltered inlet where the River Slaney, once known as the River Garma, meets Wexford Harbour.

The first reference to Wexford goes back to the second century when Ptolemy's maps marked the site as a place called *Menapia*, after a Belgic tribe which is believed to have settled here in prehistoric times. The area was later named in Irish as *Loch Garman*, which literally means 'lake of the river Garma', but that name is so old that its origin was disputed even in pre-Christian times.

Vikings, who founded a trading settlement in the area in the ninth century, called it *Waesfjord*, which means 'esker fort' or, literally, 'inland by the sandbank'. Three centuries after the Viking sea-rovers had claimed the land, the Normans followed and took control, anglicising the name to its current spelling. By the fourteenth century, they had added a new towered wall with five gates to the town layout, but it did not provide invincibility.

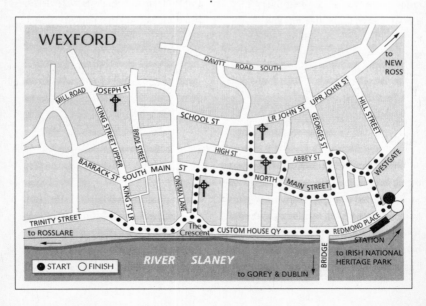

Like the rest of Ireland, Wexford struggled under English rule for many centuries, in 1649 suffering a massacre by Cromwell's forces. Wexford's shining moment in Irish history came in 1798 when a group of local men rallied to lead a full-scale rebellion to protest at the oppressive penal laws of the eighteenth century. The insurgents were mostly farmers, armed only with their enthusiasm and pikes in hand. Eventually called the 'Pikemen', these brave rebels met with success at first but were finally defeated. Their glory lives on, as evidenced by many memorials and statues throughout the town and county of Wexford.

It's no wonder that a walk along the streets of Wexford today reveals history every step of the way.

FAST FACTS

Travel Information Offices

WEXFORD TOWN TOURIST OFFICE, Crescent Quay, Wexford (tel. 053 23111). Open all year.

ENNISCORTHY TOURIST OFFICE, Castle Hill, Enniscorthy (tel. 054 34699). Open mid-June–August.

ROSSLARE HARBOUR TOURIST OFFICE, Kilrane, Rosslare Harbour (tel. 053 33232). Open May–September.

TRAVEL INFORMATION ONLINE:
www.southeasttourism.com,
www.wexfordtourism.com and
www.wexfordweb.com

TELEPHONE AREA CODE:
The telephone area code for all numbers is 053, unless indicated otherwise.

MAJOR EVENTS

STRAWBERRY FAIR FESTIVAL –
'Strawberries and Cream' is the theme of this nine-day annual fruit feast at Enniscorthy in the heart of strawberry country. The programme offers many opportunities to enjoy the local crop, as well as street entertainment, marching bands, pub sessions and a craft fair. Information: Strawberry Fair Office, tel. 054 33256. (Late June or early July)

WEXFORD FESTIVAL OPERA –
Internationally acclaimed, this is a two-week programme of world-class operas and many other musical and artistic fringe events. Information: Festival Office, tel. 053 22144 or www.wexfordopera.com. (End of October and early November)

WEXFORD TOWN WALKING TOUR

Duration: 2–3 hours plus stops

Start your tour at the O'Hanrahan Station at **Redmond Square**, the bus/rail depot on the north side of the town. This square commemorates a prominent nineteenth-century Wexford family. Walk one block west from the station along Slaney Street to **Westgate Street**, site of the original western walls and west gate of the city, dating back to Viking/Norman times and currently home to local government offices and the **Westgate Heritage Centre** (tel. 46506), an art gallery and exhibition space. From the walls, bear right onto **Temperance Row** and at the end of the street, on the right, are the ruins of the thirteenth-century church of the Augustinian Priory of Saints Peter and Paul, commonly called **Selskar Abbey** (that is, Abbey of the Holy Sepulchre). This ruined abbey is believed to be the oldest place of worship in County Wexford. The first Anglo-Irish treaty was signed here in 1169, and it is said that Henry II spent the Lent of 1172 here, doing penance for having Thomas à Becket beheaded.

Continue via George's Street to North Main Street. **Main Street**, both north and south, is the principal shopping thoroughfare of Wexford. It is narrow and irregular, having evolved over the centuries from a Viking market trail into a street. It embodies the friendly and close-knit atmosphere of this ancient town.

On the right is **White's Hotel**, an old coaching inn dating back to 1779 but renovated and enlarged over the years. The layout incorporates many former private houses and buildings, including the family home of Robert McClure, who is credited with discovering the Northwest Passage. Continue walking southward for two blocks until you come to the **Bull Ring**, a market square in the centre of town. It dates back to 1621 when the local butchers' guild introduced the sport of bull-baiting for the amusement of the resident Norman nobles. Over the centuries, it evolved into a place of public assembly, and is still remembered as the place where, in 1798, Wexford's local freedom fighters, the 'Pikemen', boldly put forward Ireland's first declaration as a Republic. Today a statue in memory of the 'Pikemen' stands in the centre of the Bull Ring, which is now used primarily for a weekly outdoor market.

Now take a right and go one block to the **Cornmarket**, once the central marketplace of the town. Although it lost some of its prominence in the nineteenth and twentieth centuries, it is slowly coming back through urban renewal, once more humming as a commercial centre. The focal point is the market house, built in 1775, and now the **Wexford Arts Centre** (tel. 23764), a venue for art exhibitions and events. Over the years, this building served as a dance hall, concert venue, town hall, and municipal offices, before it was given new life as an arts milieu. Open Monday–Saturday. Admission: free

The Cornmarket is also home of the **Thomas Moore Tavern**, originally known as 'The Ark', the house where poet and songwriter Thomas Moore's mother was born.

From the Cornmarket, follow High Street one block to **Rowe Street**, to see the Church of the Immaculate Conception, known as one of Wexford's **Twin Churches**. The other, five blocks away on **Bride Street**, is the Church of the Assumption. Both churches were built in 1851–58 to the designs of the same architect, Robert Pierce, a pupil of Augustus Pugin. Their spires are an identical 70.1 metres (230 feet) in height.

Follow Rowe Street back to High Street. On the right-hand corner is the **Theatre Royal**, opened in 1832, and current headquarters of the Wexford Festival Opera. Continue one block back to North Main Street and directly ahead is **St Iberius Church** (tel. 22936), standing on an ecclesiastical site that dates back to St Patrick's time (fifth century). It is dedicated to a local saint whose name is used in various forms such as St Ibar and St Iver. Built in 1660, this church blends an elegant Georgian interior with a late nineteenth-century Venetian Renaissance façade. Open daily except during Sunday services. Admission: free

Continue along Main Street, passing Anne Street on the left. In the past, it was a street used for meat markets, and was consequently referred to as the 'Flesh Market' and the 'Shambles'. Anne Street marks the changeover from North Main Street to South Main Street. Coming up on the left is **Keyser's Lane**, one of the narrowest and the oldest thoroughfares in Wexford, dating back to Viking times. **Slegg's Lane**, across Main Street, is the inland continuation of this route. To the right is Allen Street, first paved in 1793.

Take a left to the river at Henrietta Street, once lined by sawmills and timber yards. Here is **Crescent Quay**, a half-moon-shaped riverbank, and setting for the **John Barry Monument**, a modern statue of Commodore John Barry, born at nearby Ballysampson, 16 km (10 miles) south of Wexford town. Barry left Wexford in his teens and volunteered in the cause of the American Revolution. One of the US Navy's first commissioned officers, he became the captain of the *Lexington*. In 1797, George Washington appointed him Commander-in-Chief of the US Navy, and thus he has been considered ever since as the 'Father of the United States Navy'. The statue, which faces out towards the sea, was a gift from the American people in 1956. Behind the monument is the **Wexford Tourist Office**.

If you wish to see the **Talbot Hotel**, long a fixture on the Wexford riverfront and originally a schoolhouse, detour two blocks south along Paul Quay, and then return to Crescent Quay.

From Crescent Quay, walk northward along the marina via the two remaining quays (Custom House Quay and Commercial Quay), returning to Redmond Square, the starting point of this walking tour.

To complete the tour of Wexford, go now by car or taxi 3 km (2 miles) north of the town to visit the **Irish National Heritage Park**, Ferrycarrig (tel. 20733), a 12-hectare (30-acre) outdoor walk-around museum of interest to all ages.

You can walk through 9,000 years of Irish history at this park, starting with a campsite dating from the Mesolithic Period (7000BC). The exhibits also depict an early Irish farmstead and a portal dolmen from the Neolithic Period (2500BC), a cist burial site and stone circle from the Bronze Age (2000BC), as well as dwellings, vessels and tools from the Celtic, Early Christian and Early Norman periods. Meander into a tenth-century monastery, cross over a Celtic crannóg, explore a Viking boat-yard, or climb into a Norman fort. To add to the ambience, there are demon-strations of age-old crafts, from pole lathing and weaving to pottery. Open daily. Admission: €€

PAT'S PICKS

RESTAURANTS

LA CUISINE, 80 North Main Street (tel. 24986). For a packed lunch or a light meal of freshly made soups or salads, this self-service delicatessen/coffee shop is a real find. Try locally made chocolates and cheeses or the speciality items of brown bread and coleslaw. Open Monday–Saturday.

FULACHT FIADH, Irish National Heritage Park, Ferrycarrig (tel. 20733). Taking its name from the old Irish words meaning 'ancient cooking place', this bright and wide-windowed restaurant overlooks a crannóg and lake. The menu features

Irish fare ranging from traditional stew to beef and mushroom pie, or roast leg of lamb, as well as vegetarian lasagne, stuffed wild mushrooms, salads and chowders. Open for lunch, daily; dinner, Thursday–Saturday.

LA RIVA, 2 Henrietta Street (tel. 24330), off Crescent Quay. With windows looking out onto Wexford Harbour and the River Slaney, this upstairs bistro offers some of the best dining views in town. The menu has a Mediterranean/ Italian flair, with a wide choice of homemade pastas and pizza, as well as steaks and seafood. Open for dinner, daily, except two weeks in January.

LOBSTER POT, Carne (tel. 31110). Situated about 16 km (10 miles) south of Wexford town, this cottage-style restaurant is known for its rustic, nautical atmosphere and fresh seafood – from wild salmon, Dover sole, local crab and Kilmore scallops, to lobsters or oysters from the tank. Steaks, chicken and duckling are also available. Lighter items, ideal for lunch, include seafood salads, platters and chowders. No reservations accepted. Open daily, June–August; Tuesday–Sunday, September–December and February–May; closed January.

MICHAEL'S RESTAURANT, 94 North Main Street (tel. 42196). A favourite with the locals, this dependable mid-town place specialises in Irish stew, casseroles and other comfort foods. Open for lunch, snacks and dinner, daily.

PUBS

CON MACKEN'S – THE CAPE OF GOOD HOPE, The Bull Ring (tel. 22949) off North Main Street. The sign outside this pub tells of three services all under one roof: 'Bar–Undertaker–Groceries'. Step inside, pass by the funeral wreaths, and enjoy a drink amid an intriguing Old Wexford atmosphere. Long a favourite meeting place for local patriots and politicians, it is chock full of rebel souvenirs, weapons, and plaques.

OAK TAVERN, Ferrycarrig Bridge, Ferrycarrig Road (tel. 20922). Originally a tollhouse, this 150-year-old tavern overlooks the River Slaney, with seating indoors and on a riverside patio. Bar food is served throughout the day and evening. It is 3 km (2 miles) north of Wexford town, adjacent to the Irish National Heritage Park.

TIM'S TAVERN, 51 South Main Street (tel. 23861). In the heart of town, this pub is known for wholesome bar food in hearty portions, from burgers and casseroles to steaks and seafood. Sunday brunch is a feature here, along with traditional music sessions.

THE WEST GATE TAVERN, Westgate (tel. 22086). Dating back to 1761, this vintage pub was originally part of a traditional grocery shop and was frequented by dealers who attended fairs and markets held on the street outside. Now the premises caters to locals and visitors, with activities ranging from folk and ballad music sessions to quizzes and dart competitions. Step inside and join the fun.

DIGRESSIONS

CAR FERRY: For a delightful waterside excursion (or to save time and mileage between Wexford and Waterford), drive aboard the continuous car ferry, departing from Ballyhack, approximately 32 km (20 miles) southwest of Wexford town. Crossing time is five minutes and service is from 7am (Mondays–Saturdays) or 9.30am (Sundays) until 8pm (October–March) or 10pm (April–September). On the Waterford side, the terminal is at Passage East, 16 km (10 miles) east of Waterford. No reservations necessary; pay on board. Information: Passage East Car Ferry (tel. 051 382 480 or www.passageferry.com).

GUIDING LIGHT: Climb the 115 steps to the parapet of Hook Lighthouse to enjoy wide vistas of counties Wexford and Waterford and the open sea. Situated at the tip of the Hook Peninsula (56.4 km/35 miles southwest of Wexford town) and built by the earl of Pembroke in the thirteenth century, this lighthouse is the only remaining example in Ireland of a medieval circular tower or 'juliette', and is the oldest operational lighthouse in Ireland or Britain. It consists of three stone-vaulted chambers, with a spiral stairway ascending through the thickness of the wall. Open daily but guided tour schedule is limited from November–February. Information: Hook Lighthouse, Hook Head, Fethard-on-Sea (tel. 051 397 055 or www.thehook-wexford.com).

HISTORY ON A HILL: Step back into Irish history at the National 1798 Visitor Centre, on a hill overlooking the River Slaney at Enniscorthy, 24 km (15 miles) north of Wexford town. This modern museum commemorates the heroic undertakings of the United Irishmen of the 1798 Rebellion, one of the key events of the Irish struggle for independence. Through a series of exhibits and a walk-through tour, the saga of 1798 is relived – young Irish people are shown fighting brave battles with pikes and hay forks against artillery at Enniscorthy, New Ross, Vinegar Hill and Oulart. Open daily. Information: National 1798 Visitor Centre, Millpark Road, Enniscorthy (tel. 054 37596 or www.1798centre.com).

The Southwest

11: Cork City and Blarney

In the south of Ireland, it seems that all roads lead to Cork, a busy and burgeoning city with a history going back to the sixth century when St Finbarr founded a monastery on this site. Sitting between two channels of the River Lee, Cork is a city of many river-front quays and no fewer than 25 bridges.

Like other parts of Ireland, Cork experienced long periods of domination by outside forces, from Viking raids in the eighth and ninth centuries, to Anglo-Norman invasions in the twelfth century, and English suppression for hundreds of years afterwards. Cork was granted a charter as a city in 1188 by Prince John of England, and remained under English rule until the twentieth century.

The name Cork, which has nothing to do with bottles or drinking, dates back to earliest times. It is derived from the Irish language word *corcach*, which means 'marsh'. The sixth-century monastic settlement of St Finbarr was built on the edge of a marsh, and until the eighteenth century, major thoroughfares, like St Patrick's Street and the Grand Parade, were built over steep stretches of muddy streams.

During Ireland's long struggle for independence, it was usually the Corkonians who led the way in self-reliance and spunk, earning the title of 'Rebel Cork' for the city and county. County Cork men were at the forefront of Ireland's modern political forma-tion, from local heroes Thomas Mac-Curtain and Terence MacSwiney, to charismatic national leaders like Michael Collins, recently immortalised in a major Hollywood movie bearing his name.

As the third largest city in Ireland (after Dublin and Belfast), with a popu-lation of 160,000, Cork is an important seaport and manufacturing centre, while equally recognised in the cultural sphere (European Capital of Culture in 2005). Of particular interest to visitors, Cork is also a congenial city with a 'hometown' atmosphere. Corkonians are a friendly people with a delightful way of speaking that is all their own. The Cork accent is fast-paced and almost sing-song in style. It may take you a few hours to 'tune in' your ears, but you'll be glad you did.

Travel Information Offices

CORK TOURIST OFFICE, Grand Parade, Cork (tel. 021 425 5100). Open all year.

BLARNEY TOURIST OFFICE, Main Street, Blarney, Co. Cork (tel. 021 438 1624). Open all year.

TRAVEL INFORMATION ONLINE:
www.corkkerry.ie and
www.blarneytourism.com

TELEPHONE AREA CODE:
The telephone area code for all numbers in Cork city is 021 unless indicated otherwise.

MAJOR EVENTS

CORK INTERNATIONAL CHORAL FESTIVAL – The streets of Cork are alive with the sound of music during this annual singing competition for school, youth and adult choirs from all over the world. The programme includes premières of specially commissioned works by noted composers, and seminars given by composers. Performances take place in concert halls, theatres, public buildings, cathedrals, churches, shops and on the street. Information: Cork International Choral Festival, tel. 430 8308 or www.corkchoral.ie. (Early May)

CORK INTERNATIONAL FILM FESTIVAL – Established in 1956, this annual gathering is Ireland's oldest and biggest film event. The one-week programme showcases Irish and international feature films, documentaries, animation, short films, experimental and student work, in an atmosphere of plenty of film-world camaraderie. Information: Cork International Film Festival, tel. 427 1711 or www.corkfilmfest.org. (Mid-October)

GUINNESS CORK JAZZ FESTIVAL – Hailed as one of the top three jazz festivals in the world, this annual three-day event attracts over 40,000 visitors to hear 1,000 musicians from 25 countries perform non-stop jazz in concerts, clubs and pubs from afternoon to late evening. Information: Guinness Cork Jazz Festival, tel. 427 8979 or www.corkjazzfestival.com. (Last weekend of October)

CORK CITY WALKING TOUR

Duration: 2–3 hours plus stops

Cork is a big city, divided into three parts – the **South Bank** and the **North Bank** of the River Lee, and the main island or city-centre area, usually referred to as the **Flat of the City**. The best place to start a tour is in the flat of the city at the **Cork Tourist Office** on the Grand Parade, a prime source for basic local information, maps and brochures.

Take time to stroll the **Grand Parade**, a wide thoroughfare that blends the remains of the old city walls and eighteenth-century bow-fronted houses with modern offices, shops and the **Bishop Lucy Park**, a welcome

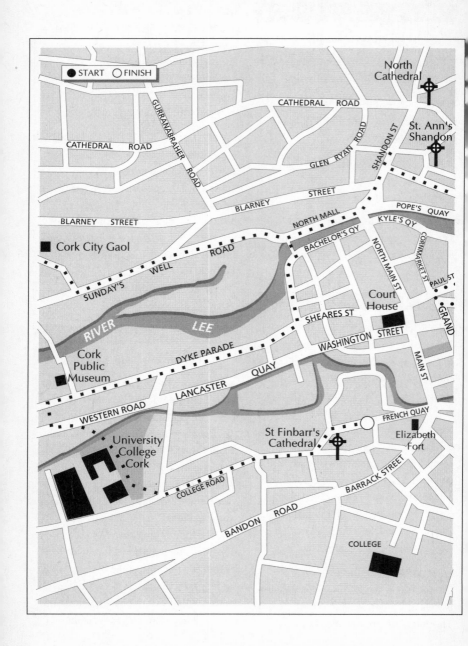

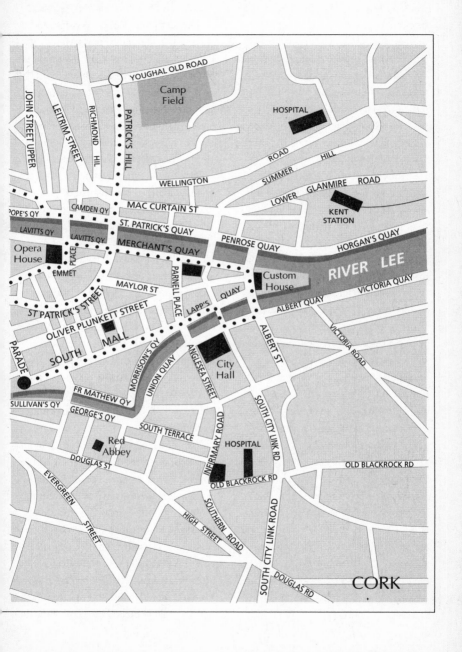

patch of greenery, with benches, sculptures and a fountain, named for a local prelate. Parts of the old city walls can still be seen on the perimeter of the park.

On the south end of the Parade is the junction with the **South Mall**, the fiscal hub of the city, with many well-preserved Georgian buildings now occupied by banks, stockbrokers, and other financial institutions.

Follow the South Mall to **Lapp's Quay** along the South Channel of the River Lee. On the opposite side of the river is the classical domed façade of **City Hall**, on Albert Quay, Cork's chief administrative centre. Dating back only to 1936, it was built on the site of a previous structure that was burned down during the Irish War of Independence in 1921. In 1852, the earlier building had been the setting of the first-ever national Industrial Exhibition in Ireland, modelled after a similar event held at the Crystal Palace in London. The interior of the present building houses a 2,000-seat concert hall, a popular venue for major shows and events.

Continue along Lapp's Quay to **Custom House Quay** and the **Custom House**, on **Albert Street**, now the Harbour Board Office, a classical structure (built 1814–18) that many people consider to be Cork's finest building. The defining features of its exterior include a pale grey limestone façade, Palladian windows, and the Cork coat of arms.

Follow Albert Street north for one block to **Michael Collins Bridge**, and make a left, walking west to Merchant's Quay. On the left is the Bus Éireann Central Bus Station. The next block is devoted to Merchant's Quay Shopping Centre, a two-storey enclosed shopping mall housing over 20 Irish and international shops. Straight ahead is **St Patrick's Street Bridge**, opened in 1859.

Take a left onto **St Patrick's Street**, known locally as **Patrick Street**, or colloquially 'Pana', the city's main street. This broad avenue was formed in 1789 when an open channel of the river was filled in on the marshy land. In the centre of the street is one of Cork's best-known landmarks, the **Fr Theobald Mathew Statue**, a monument to a nineteenth-century priest who led a crusade against alcoholic drink, and is fondly called 'the apostle of temperance'. The statue, stands at the juncture of Patrick Street and Patrick Bridge, considered the city's central point, and a favourite meeting place for Corkonians.

Not known particularly for great monuments or museums, St Patrick's Street is unabashedly a shopping street – sometimes called the Regent Street or Fifth Avenue of Cork. Stroll along the street, looking at the great variety of department stores and speciality shops. Make a left on **Prince's Street** into one of Patrick's Street great institutions – the **Old English Market**, more recently known as the City Market, a huge indoor marketplace dating back to 1610, although the current building dates only to 1786. Browse amid the colourful stands, brimming with vegetables, fish, and fruit, as well as traditional Cork foods, such as tripe (animal stomach), crubeens (pigs' feet) and drisheen (local blood sausage).

Return to Patrick's Street, crossing over to the right onto **Cornmarket Street**. On Saturdays only, this is the scene of **Coal Quay Market**, Cork's original outdoor street market beside the River Lee. Rejuvenated in recent years as part of an urban renewal project, the Coal Quay Market is a colourful and aromatic shopping experience, overflowing with delicacies such as sun-dried tomatoes, smoked fish, olives with anchovies, and stuffed vine leaves, mustards, relishes, farmhouse cheeses and herb oils. It isn't a place to find the usual souvenirs, but it is the ideal spot to rub shoulders with Corkonians, bask in the local ambience, and perhaps get a great photo.

From Cornmarket Street, make a right onto **Paul Street**, in the heart of Cork's Huguenot Quarter, originally populated by French Huguenot merchants and craftsmen. Today the Huguenots are gone, but their cobbled streets and tiny shop fronts remain. This is now Cork's newest 'in' place to shop, a solid block of craft, fashion, and souvenir enterprises. It is also a veritable 'bookshop row', with a branch of the international Waterstone's chain as well as speciality book stores such as Mainly Murder, 2a Paul Street, a storehouse of Irish and international mysteries and curious tales ideal for rainy days. A half-block away is Mercier Press, French Church Street, Ireland's oldest independent publishing house, and a prime source for hard-to-find Irish history and folklore titles.

Paul's Lane, a narrow off-shoot to the left, is lined with a handful of antique shops, and recognised as Cork's 'antique row'.

At the end of Paul Street is Emmet Place, home of two of Cork's main cultural keystones. To the left is the **Crawford Municipal Art Gallery** (tel. 427 3377). With a striking classical façade of red brick dressed with limestone, this impressive building was erected in 1724 as the Custom House, but less than 100 years later, as the port of Cork expanded, the Custom House was moved to its present location, and the art gallery was born. The collections include paintings by some of Ireland's finest masters, from Jack B Yeats to Nathaniel Grogan, James Barry, William Orpen and Daniel Maclise, and sculptures by John Hogan. In addition, there are casts from antique sculptures from the Vatican Galleries, given to Cork in 1818; as well as handcrafted silver and antique glass pieces. Open Monday–Saturday. Admission: free

The adjacent building is the **Opera House**, Emmet Place (tel. 427 0022), a relatively new addition (1963–65) to the Cork scene, and the major venue in the southwest for opera, drama, musicals, concerts and more. Reservations are a must.

From Emmet Place, make a left onto Lavitt's Quay and walk one block to **St Patrick's Bridge**, crossing over the River Lee to the **North Bank** of the city. Opened in 1859, the bridge leads to the north side of the city, a hilly and terraced section where the continuation of St Patrick's Street is called Bridge Street and then **St Patrick's Hill**. This hill has an incline so steep that it is often compared to the hills of San Francisco. Climb the stepped sidewalks of St Patrick's Hill for incomparable views of the Cork skyline.

At this point of the tour, it is best to take a taxi, open-top sightseeing bus or public bus to the **South Bank** of the city for the second part of the tour, which explores some of the more far-flung attractions, and involves more extensive walking. Start at a structure that has come to be symbolic of Cork – **St Finbarr's Cathedral**, Bishop Street (tel. 496 3387). Named after the saint who is credited with founding Cork, this impressive Church of Ireland cathedral is of fairly recent vintage (1867–79), but it stands on ground that is said to be the site of St Finbarr's monastic settlement (c.650). In the eighth and ninth centuries, it was a focal point during Ireland's period as 'the isle of saints and scholars', as students from all parts of Europe gathered here to immerse themselves in Christian scholarship. Ever since the Reformation, the church has been the seat of the bishopric of the Church of Ireland. The present structure is a multi-spired early French Gothic edifice, known for its elaborate scriptural carvings, mosaic pavements and great rose window. The graveyard outside holds many interesting hand-carved monuments. Open Monday–Saturday. Admission: €

Make a right turn onto **Gill Abbey Street**, which then becomes **College Road** and visit **University College Cork**, Western Road (tel. 490 3098). Dating back to 1845, this college is a component of Ireland's National University, and intellectually nurtures over 7,000 students. It is set in a riverside quadrangle, with several interesting Gothic revival-style buildings, as well as the **Honan Chapel**, added in 1915 and modelled after Cormac's Chapel at the Rock of Cashel. It contains a splendid collection of stained-glass windows, including works by Harry Clarke and Sarah Purser. Outside there is an area known as the 'Stone Corridor', a collection of stones inscribed with the ogham style of writing, an early form of the written Irish language. Walking tours of the campus can be arranged by contacting the Office of Public Affairs. Open for tours, June–September. Admission: free

From the Western Road, cross over to the **Mardyke Walk**. Here you can stroll through **Fitzgerald Park**, a 7-hectare (18-acre) site named after Edward Fitzgerald, former Lord Mayor of Cork. On the grounds of the park, visit the **Cork Public Museum**, Fitzgerald Park (tel. 427 0679). An elegant Georgian house serves as the setting for this museum, opened in 1945. The collections provide insight into the city's colourful political and social history, with artefacts from recent excavations within the city, and an archive of photographs and documents relating to Cork-born Irish patriots Terence MacSwiney, Thomas MacCurtain and Michael Collins. In addition, there are noteworthy collections of civic regalia, as well as Cork silver, glass, needlepoint lace, and other crafts practised locally during the nineteenth and twentieth centuries. Modern Irish sculptures are displayed outside, including works by Oisín Kelly and other noted sculptors. Open Monday–Friday, and Sunday afternoon. Admission: free; except on Sunday: €

From the Park, take **Dyke Parade** east, crossing over the Lee between Grenville Place and Bachelor's Quay to the **North Bank** to Sunday's Well Road, and an area of the city known simply as **Sunday's Well**. Turn right and walk for one block to the **Cork City Gaol** (Jail), Convent Avenue (tel. 430 5022). In spite of its castle-like facade, this impressive nineteenth-century prison building treated its occupants more wretchedly than royally. Indeed, many a Cork patriot served

time within these walls under miserable conditions in the cause of Irish freedom. The layout includes furnished cells, life-like animated figures, sound effects, and an audiovisual show, all of which recreate prison life in Cork. Open daily, March–October; and Monday–Friday in November–February. Admission: €

Also within the Gaol's complex, in the former jail governor's house, is the **Radio Museum Experience**, a museum that spotlights the impact of radio on all of our lives, with various exhibits on the early days of Irish international radio broadcasting. Open daily. Admission: €

Ramble back toward the city along the North Bank of the river, following Sunday's Well Road to the North Mall. Take a left at **Shandon Street** and follow it into one of the city's oldest residential areas, north of Pope's Quay. The centrepiece is **St Ann's Shandon Church**, Church Street (tel. 450 5906). Dating back to 1722, this Church of Ireland edifice is the North Bank's prime landmark, synonymous with the Cork skyline. From almost anywhere in the city centre, you can see the church's tower, a giant pepper-pot steeple, two sides of which are made of limestone and two of sandstone, with a top crowned by a gilt ball and a 3.4-metre (11-foot) salmon-shaped weathervane. Each side of the steeple also boasts a clock. Most of all, this church is known for its eight melodious bells that echo throughout the city. Visitors are encouraged to climb up to the belfry and play a tune, or at least enjoy panoramic views of the city. Corkonians are always raising their heads up toward Shandon, if not to hear the bells, then to set their watches by one of the clocks, or to check the fish weathervane for a weather forecast. Open Monday–Saturday. Admission: €

Directly opposite the church is a unique museum known as the **Cork Butter Market**, O'Connell Square (tel. 430 0600). Housed in the original Cork Butter Exchange building, this museum tells the story of Cork's eminence in the eighteenth and nineteenth centuries as a major producer of butter. In its day, the Cork market was the largest market of its type in the world.

The exhibition traces the history of butter production in Ireland, from the origins of dairying and the Irish practice of preserving butter in bogs, to the importance of 'milch cows' in medieval Ireland and the development of 'butter roads'. One whole floor of the museum is devoted to displays of butter-making equipment, and there is also an audiovisual that explores the butter industry in modern times. Open May–September, Monday–Friday and Sunday. Admission: €

Make a right and follow **John Redmond Street** back to the quays and walk eastward along **Camden Quay**, which leads to St Patrick's Bridge. Cross over to Patrick Street, back to the heart of Cork, to complete your tour.

Detour: A trip to Cork city invariably also means a detour to the nearby village of **Blarney**, about five miles northwest of the city centre (the easiest route is to take the N20 north to the Blarney exit). You'll need to drive yourself or take a local bus or taxi to reach Blarney.

Designed in the Tudor style, around a village green, Blarney sits on the edge of the River Martin, surrounded by wooded countryside and quiet country lanes. It was planned as a water-powered linen and wool-processing centre, the latter of which crafts still flourishes today at the Blarney Woollen Mills, a local enterprise that produces and stocks knitwear of all kinds plus a wide range of souvenirs and gifts. Although historical details on the origins of Blarney are a little sketchy, legend and tradition have filled in the gaps.

For this reason, **Blarney Castle** (tel. 438 5252) is to Ireland what Big Ben is to Britain, the Statue of Liberty to the US, or the Eiffel Tower to France. Just about everyone in the western world has heard of the castle's **Blarney Stone** and identifies it with the Emerald Isle. It is just an ordinary grey stone, yet people believe that a quick kiss on the old cold rock will impart magical powers and particularly the gift of eloquence or 'the gift of the gab'.

As the centrepiece of the village of Blarney, this famous castle was built *c.*1446. Originally the stronghold of the MacCarthys, the castle is long since gone, except for its massive square keep, a tower with a battlemented parapet rising over 25 metres (83 feet) in height. The fabled Blarney Stone is wedged underneath the battlements, and, in order to kiss it, visitors must lie down on the ground and bend backwards into a trench where the stone awaits. It sounds awkward, but the area is fully protected, and a trained guide supervises all the kissing. The hardest part of the whole experience is climbing up more than 100 ancient curved stone steps to the parapet.

The legend of the Blarney Stone goes back to the days of Queen Elizabeth I, when the castle and lands of Blarney belonged to a local Irish family, the MacCarthys. The head of the clan, Cormac MacDermott MacCarthy, the Lord of Blarney, did not want to swear allegiance to the queen, but he also did not want to lose his land. He was completely evasive when asked by the queen's deputy, to renounce the traditional systems and take the tenure of his lands from the Crown. While seeming to agree to the proposal, he put off fulfilling his promise from day to day with 'fair words and soft speech'. The queen is reputed to have declared finally, 'This is all Blarney – what he says, he never means!' And thus the word 'Blarney' came to mean pleasant talk intended to deceive without offending, and in its modern interpretation, as a clever and intense form of flattery. Somewhere over the centuries, the tradition evolved that anyone who kisses the Blarney Stone will obtain the everlasting eloquence of Cormac MacDermott MacCarthy. Open daily. Admission: €€

Return to Cork city or continue on to your next destination.

PAT'S PICKS

RESTAURANTS

Cork is known for several traditional foods, such as tripe (animal stomach), crubeens (pigs' feet) and drisheen (local blood sausage). If any of these don't appeal to you, you can always try one of the local beers, Beamish and Murphy's. For tea-drinkers, Cork is the home base of Barry's Tea, blended here since 1901.

BULLY'S, 40 Paul Street (tel. 427 3555). Wedged in the heart of a busy shopping street, this bistro offers a tasty selection of international fare at moderate prices, from chargrilled steaks and burgers, to pastas, omelettes and a dozen varieties of pizza made on a wood-burning stove. Open for breakfast, lunch and dinner, daily.

CAFÉ PARADISO, 16 Lancaster Quay, Western Road (tel. 427 7939). A small shop-front restaurant situated opposite Jury's Hotel, this place has made a name for itself as a totally vegetarian restaurant, using seasonal organic produce in creative and tasty ways. The menu offers dishes such as goat's cheese, pine-nut and oven-roasted tomato charlotte; vegetable sushi; cauliflower and aubergine tempura; and broad bean salad. Open for lunch and dinner, Tuesday–Saturday (except closed two weeks in late August).

CRAWFORD GALLERY CAFÉ, Emmet Place (tel. 427 4415), next to the Opera House. An artistic atmosphere prevails at this café, nestled on the ground floor of Cork's leading art gallery. The cuisine, provided by the Allen family of Ballymaloe Cooking School fame, is best described as 'Cork country cooking', with choices such as chicken pie, Scotch eggs, stuffed fillet of pork, spinach and mushroom pancakes, and Ballycotton Bay seafood. All breads and baked goods come from the Ballymaloe kitchens. Open for breakfast, snacks and lunch, Monday–Saturday.

FARMGATE CAFÉ, Old English Market, Prince's Street (tel. 427 8134). After you've enjoyed the sights and aromas of Cork's prime indoor marketplace, savour the tastes at this restaurant upstairs. The ever-changing menu uses only the freshest produce, meats, seafood and cheeses from the market stalls below. Open for lunch and snacks, Monday–Saturday.

FENN'S QUAY RESTAURANT, 5 Fenn's Quay, Sheares Street (tel. 427 9527). Nestled one block around the corner from Cork's courthouse, this shop-front bistro has a simple décor, with square tables and lots of mirrors, enhanced by modern art. But the menu is the star attraction, making full use of fresh local ingredients and creative recipes, such as roast chicken breast with confit of root vegetables and Cashel blue cheese; marinated pork steak filled with vegetables; lamb noisettes with aubergines; and cherry tomato and shallot tart. Open for lunch and dinner, Monday–Saturday.

ISAAC'S, 48 MacCurtain Street (tel. 450 3805). Housed in a former eighteenth-century warehouse, this restaurant presents fine food at modest prices in a traditional setting of high ceilings, stone arches and brick walls. The menu offers creative Mediterranean-style salads, such as warm squid and almond salad, as well as pastas, seafood chowders and unique items like salmon and potato cakes. Open for lunch Monday–Saturday; and dinner, daily.

JACOB'S ON THE MALL, 30a South Mall (tel. 425 1530). One of Cork's top restaurants, it is known for creative European cuisine using the best of local ingredients. The menu features dishes such as onion and cider soup, grilled polenta with flat mushrooms, smoked chicken with walnut and parsley pesto, roast haddock with champ, bacon, and thyme – all accompanied by homemade breads. Open for lunch and dinner, Monday–Saturday.

JACQUES, 9 Phoenix Street (tel. 427 7387), located just off the South Mall. One of Cork's most successful restaurants for many years, this restaurant is run by two members of the Barry family, famous for Cork's signature brand of tea. But the menu offers a lot more than tea – it is a blend of old Irish recipes, fresh local produce and creative new ideas, all at moderate prices. Open for lunch, Monday– Friday, and dinner, Tuesday– Saturday.

TABLE 8, 8–9 Carey's Lane (tel. 427 0725). This chic contemporary bistro is located on a small pedestrian lane between Patrick and Paul streets. Prices are moderate, and food is creative, fresh and fun – from roast cod with prawn colcannon or chargrilled chicken with mushrooms to linguini with mussels, tomato, ginger and chilli. All the breads are baked on the premises. Open for lunch and dinner, Monday–Saturday.

PUBS

DAN LOWERY'S TAVERN, 13 MacCurtain Street (tel. 450 5071). A standout on the North Bank of the city, this pub blends an authentic décor of stained-glass windows, mahogany bar and brass fixtures with a friendly atmosphere and good pub food, including many seafood choices.

FRANCISCAN WELL BREWERY, 14B North Mall (tel. 421 0130). As Cork's original brewery pub, this place produces three beverages on the premises – Blarney Blonde, Rebel Red Ale and Shandon Stout – as well as serving all the usual libations. Traditional music sessions are held on Monday night.

THE LONG VALLEY, Winthrop Street (tel. 450 8122). Located opposite the main post office, this vintage pub has been a Cork favourite since 1842. Live music is on tap each Friday and Saturday.

MUTTON LANE INN, 3 Mutton Lane (tel. 427 3471, off St Patrick's Street. Step into this pub for a dose of Old Cork. Named after the adjacent laneway which was developed as a path for sheep going to market, it was opened as a public house in 1787 and still looks the same, with lantern lights, panelled walls, beamed ceilings and lots of local memorabilia. The pub grub is hearty and standard – stews, soups and sandwiches.

REIDY'S WINE VAULTS, Lancaster Quay, Western Road (tel. 427 5751). Transformed from an old wine warehouse, this pub has an atmospheric décor of vaulted ceilings, traditional tiles, a massive mahogany bar, bevelled mirrors, stained-glass windows and a gallery of antiques. The bar food features soups, meat pies, seafood platters and savoury pancakes, plus breads and quiches baked daily on the premises.

BREWERY TOUR: No visit to Cork is complete without sampling the local stouts made by Beamish and Murphy's. Any of Cork's pubs will happily oblige. If you'd like to see the actual brewing process, only the Beamish & Crawford brewery is currently open for tours. Beamish has been a mainstay of the Cork beverage industry since 1792. A walk-through tour explains how the drink is made, from the ingredients (pure Cork water, barley, hops) to the processes (malting, mashing, boiling, fermenting, cooling, maturing), and ending with a tasting. Tours are conducted May–September on Tuesday and Thursday; October–May on Thursday. Information: Beamish & Crawford Brewery, South Main Street (tel. 491 1100 or www.beamish.ie).

CASTLE CAPER: Step back in time and explore a castle at Carrigtwohill, between Cork city and Cobh. Barryscourt Castle dates back to the twelfth century, and for over 500 years was the seat of the Barrys, one of Cork's leading families to this day (founders of Barry's Tea). The present castle, with a largely intact bawn and corner towers, is a fine example of a fifteenth-century tower house with sixteenth-century additions. Extensively restored, both the Main Hall and the Great Hall are now open to the public. Open daily, June–September; and Friday–Wednesday in October–May. Information: Barryscourt Castle, Carrigtwohill (tel. 488 2218 or www.heritageireland.ie).

CIRCLING THE CITY: Not all tours of Cork are on foot. City Sightseeing Tours operates 70-minute open-top double-decker bus tours that circle the entire city, stopping at thirteen sites including the Grand Parade, St Finbarr's Cathedral, Patrick Street, Cork City Gaol and Western Road. Best of all, you can hop off the bus at one attraction and hop back on another bus later, saving both time and shoe leather. One fare provides unlimited on and off privileges all day, mid-April–October. Information: City Sightseeing Tours (tel. 01 872 9010 or www.city-sightseeing.com). Alternatively, you can opt for a three-hour continuous tour of Cork city combined with Blarney, available June–September. Information: Bus Éireann, Parnell Place (tel. 021 450 8188 or www.buseireann.ie).

12: East County Cork – From Youghal to Cobh

Stretching from the County Waterford border to the outer limits of Cork city, east County Cork is often overlooked as visitors drive in an east–west direction on the wide and straight N25 road.

East Cork is the home of Cobh, Ireland's chief port and departure point for millions of emigrants before air travel, and main port of call for transatlantic liners today. It is also the location of Fota Island, a delightful harbour-side wildlife park and arboretum.

The main towns are Midleton, the hub of Ireland's whiskey-distilling industry; Shanagarry, once the home of William Penn and now the setting for Ireland's premier cooking school; and Youghal, a scenic, walled fishing port, immortalised in the movie *Moby Dick* and Irish home of Sir Walter Raleigh who introduced both tobacco and the potato to Ireland.

East Cork is bordered by the waters of Cork Harbour, Youghal Bay and Ballycotton Bay, with many coastal fishing

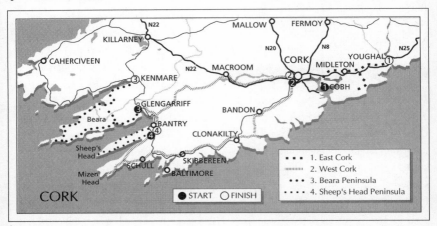

villages, cliff walks and award-winning beaches along the route.

Although it is positioned on the main corridor between the cities of Cork and Waterford, East Cork is a destination in its own right – a refreshing contrast to the big cities. Plan to spend a few days here and you won't want to leave.

FAST FACTS

Travel Information Offices

CORK TOURIST OFFICE, Grand Parade, Cork (tel. 021 425 5100). Open all year.

EAST CORK TOURISM, Market Square, Youghal (tel. 024 92592). Open June–September.

TRAVEL INFORMATION ONLINE:
www.corkkerry.ie,
www.cobhharbourchamber.ie and
http://homepage.eircom.net/~Youghal

TELEPHONE AREA CODES:
The telephone area codes for numbers in this area are 021 and 024. To avoid confusion, the code is shown for each telephone number.

MAJOR EVENTS

COBH CARILLON RECITALS – For more than 75 years, the 49-bell carillon of St Colman's Cathedral has been rung in hour-long recitals on most Sundays in summer. Information: St Colman's Cathedral, tel. 021 481 1219. (May–September)

YOUGHAL MARITIME WEEKEND – This annual three-day event focuses on all types of sea activity on Youghal Bay – rowing, sailing, raft racing, sand-castle contests, and maritime art competitions. Information: Youghal Maritime Weekend, tel. 024 92447 or www.youghalfestivals.com. (End July)

EAST CORK DRIVING TOUR

Duration: 2–3 hours plus stops

Start a tour on the eastern edge of County Cork, at **Youghal** (pronounced *Yawl*), East Cork's major coastal town, situated on the County Waterford border at the mouth of the River Blackwater.

Youghal, a town known for its yew trees, takes its name from the Irish word *Eochaill*, meaning 'yew wood'. A leading beach resort, Youghal is loosely identified with Sir Walter Raleigh, who was the mayor of the town from 1588–89. According to local lore, it was here that Raleigh, fresh from a visit to Virginia, smoked the first tobacco in Ireland and grew the first potatoes in Ireland. His house, 'Myrtle Grove', dating back to 1462, is still occupied today, but is not open to the public. Historically, very little is known about Youghal until the thirteenth century, when the Anglo-Normans founded a baronial town that evolved into a busy walled port.

Follow the signs to the strand or promenade and park your car along **Strand Street** or **The Mall**, in the public parking area. Then take a left turn and walk one block up to **Main Street**, a long and narrow one-way thoroughfare, to see the **Clock Gate**, a five-storey, arched red-sandstone building spanning over South Main Street. Erected in 1777 to replace an earlier medieval iron gate, it served as the town jail until 1837.

Around the corner on **Market Square** is the Moby Dick Pub, the last visible reminder that in 1954 the town of Youghal served as the setting for the Hollywood-produced movie *Moby Dick*, starring Gregory Peck. Market Square is also home to the **Youghal Heritage Centre**, Market Square (tel. 024 92447), an exhibit that depicts the story of the development of Youghal from earliest days. Guided walking tours of the town depart from this centre during June–September. Open daily. Admission: €

On the north end of Main Street is **St Mary's Church**, erected about 1250 and restored in the mid-nineteenth century. It is a cruciform structure, with an aisled nave of five bays, massive bell-tower, candle-snuffer roof, and a fascinating collection of tombs and monuments including fourteenth- and fifteenth-century effigies. Just off North Main Street are portions of the original city walls.

End your walk at Strand Street or the Mall and take a seaside stroll along the promenade to enjoy views of Youghal's wide and sandy 6.5-km (4-mile) beach.

From Youghal, take the main N25 road back west towards Cork, for 16 km (10 miles) to **Castlemartyr**, a small market town. At this point, if you are interested in a culinary detour, take a right, following the signposts for 8 km (5 miles) to **Ballymaloe House**, Ballycotton Road, Shanagarry (tel. 021 464 2531). A founding member of the Irish Country Houses & Restaurants Association, Ballymaloe has been a prime mover in the emergence of top-class Irish country cuisine. Relying on local seafood and produce, accompanied by fresh vegetables from the garden, the Allen family has drawn connoisseurs of fine food from all parts of the world to this remote spot near Ballycotton Bay.

The success of the Ballymaloe restaurant has spawned the trend-setting **Ballymaloe Cookery School** (021 464 6785), offering more than 35 different courses a year, ranging from one day to twelve weeks in duration. Designed for amateur and professional chefs of all levels of proficiency, the courses cover topics such as bread-making, weekend entertaining, hors d'oeuvres, seafood, vegetarian food, family food, barbecue food, mushroom cookery and Christmas recipes. It is also possible to join in an afternoon demonstration session – phone in advance to enquire what's on during your stay in the East Cork area. If you don't have time to take a course, the Ballymaloe shop offers a wide range of cookbooks by members of the Allen family, as well as an array of cooking utensils, accessories, preserves, condiments and other foods.

Take time to stroll in the adjacent **Ballymaloe Cookery School Gardens**, the epitome of a cooking-school plantation, with an extensive herb garden and a *potager* or vegetable garden laid out on a strict geometric pattern with many traditional and exotic vegetables. There is also a formal fruit garden, with apples, pears, plums, peaches and cherries, many cultivated in arches. A rose garden, herbaceous borders, specimen trees and shrubs, and a small lake complete the setting. Open daily, April–September. Admission: €€

While in **Shanagarry**, visit the **Stephen Pearce Pottery** (tel. 021 464 6807). A native of this area, Pearce is one of Ireland's master ceramic craftsmen, distinguished for his earth-toned tableware and furnishings. This huge sky-lit factory/showroom is a retail outlet and demonstration centre for this well-known potter's work. Open daily. Admission: free

Before leaving Shanagarry, it is of interest to know that William Penn, founding father of the state of Pennsylvania, made his home for a time in the 1660s at **Shanagarry House** on the Cloyne Road. His father, Admiral Sir William Penn, had been granted the lands of east Cork and sent his son to administer his estates. Descendants of Admiral Penn held the Shanagarry estate until 1903.

Return to the main N25 road and continue westward for 9.5 km (6 miles) to **Midleton**. The origins of this historic town go back to 1180AD when the Cistercian monks established a monastery here on the banks of the Owenacurra river. The location of Midleton on rich agricultural land resulted in the development of related industrial activity – the distilling of Irish whiskey, first produced here in 1825 when the Murphy family opened a distillery.

To learn more about the history of whiskey-making in this town and indeed in Ireland, make a right and follow the signs for a visit to the **Old Midleton Distillery** (tel. 021 461 3594). A tour provides close-up views of the mill building, maltings, corn stores, still houses, warehouses, kilns, water wheel and copper stills, including the largest pot still in the world, with a capacity of 143,871.8 litres (31,648 gallons). To illustrate the step-by-step whiskey-making process, there is an audiovisual presentation, as well as demonstrations and working models. Afterwards, enjoy a sampling of the various brands of whiskey produced at this facility (John Jameson, John Power, Tullamore Dew and others). Open daily. Admission: €€

From Midleton, return to the main N25 road and drive for 13 km (8 miles) to **Carrigtwohill**, and make a left turn onto local road R624. Continue for 1.6 km (1 mile) south and cross over the causeway onto **Fota Island**, home of the Fota Island Golf Club (host to the Irish Open tournament for two consecutive years, 2000 and 2001).

Attractions on the island include **Fota Arboretum and Gardens** (tel. 021 481 2728) which present a showcase of magnificent nineteenth-century trees, most of them planted by the Smith-Barry family who originally owned this property. The plantings include a fine collection of Victorian conifers (huge redwoods and wellingtonias), flowering acacias and mature magnolias. In 1975, the estate was acquired by University College Cork, and eventually transferred to the Irish State in 1996. Since then, there has been ongoing restoration, regeneration and general upgrading, including the conversion of an old fruit and vegetable garden into a formal rose garden. It contains themed borders of monocot, shade and South American plants, as well as a large selection of climbers and a collection of Irish-bred daffodils. Tours are available by appointment. Open daily. Admission is free but a nominal parking charge applies: €

The centrepiece of the estate is **Fota House** (tel. 021 481 5543), a 74-room Regency-style house built in the early to mid-nineteenth century by John Smith Barry. It was acquired by University College, Cork, in 1975 and opened to the public in 1983, but was closed in the early 1990s because of structural defects. It is now in the hands of Fota Trust, which embarked on a major €3 million restoration in 2001–2002. Open daily. Admission: €€

Fota Island is also home to the **Fota Wildlife Park** (tel. 021 481 2678), an island zoological paradise where conservation and ecology are the buzz words. Established in 1983, this park is considered one of the most modern of its kind in Europe. It provides a habitat for more than 90 species of exotic animals and birds in open natural surroundings with no obvious barriers. Giraffes, ostrich and antelope roam together in 16 hectares (40 acres) of grasslands, similar to the setting of an African savannah. Monkeys swing through trees, while kangaroos, macaws and lemurs pass nearby. Only the cheetahs are secluded by a fence. Open daily, Mid-March–October; Saturday–Sunday in November–mid-March. Admission: €€

From Fota, continue southward via the R624 and onto another island, known as **Great Island**, the largest island in Cork Harbour. It is less than 6.5 km (4 miles) to Ireland's chief transatlantic port of **Cobh** (pronounced *Cove*), a word that means 'haven' in the Irish language. In its earliest days, the town was referred to as 'the Cove of Cork', but in 1849 the name was changed to Queenstown in honour of Queen Victoria.

For many years, Queenstown was a British naval station, and during the First World War it was used by the US navy as its principal base in European waters. The town's name was restored to Cobh in 1922 after the Irish achieved independence from Britain.

In the days before airline travel, Cobh was Ireland's chief port of entry or exit, with up to three or four transatlantic liners calling here each week. Records show that from 1848 to 1950 more than 2.5 million people emigrated from the port of Cobh. For many who left in poverty during the famine years and the early part of the twentieth century, Cobh was the last glimpse of Ireland they would ever see.

For an overview of Cobh's heydays as a transatlantic port and emigration depot, follow the signs to the town's main heritage centre/museum – **Cobh – The Queenstown Story** (tel. 021 481 3591). Housed in Cobh's former railway station, this heritage centre focuses on the town's role as a major seaport and emigration centre. Step inside and take a 'walk-through' tour of Ireland in the mid-nineteenth century, when people were forced to starve or leave home for a better life in a new country. The life-size exhibits and tableaux include scenes of dockside departures and prototypes of emigrant cabins aboard the crowded ships. Cobh's role as a major port for luxury ships is also presented, with recreations of interiors of great ocean liners, and scenes from historic events in the waters nearby, including Cobh's connections to the ill-fated *Titanic* which sank in Atlantic waters on her maiden voyage in 1912, and Cobh's rescue efforts during the sinking of the *Lusitania* off Cork Harbour during the First World War.

For anyone with an Irish name or Irish roots, this centre also houses a genealogy record-finder search service, designed for people interested in tracing their ancestors but who have no knowledge of genealogical records. Based on a limited amount of information, they can provide (for a fee) a custom-made analysis of all Irish records relevant to researching a particular ancestor. Open daily, February–December; Monday– Friday in January. Admission: €€

Once in Cobh, take time to explore the town, starting at the top – **St Colman's Cathedral**, Cathedral Place (tel. 021 481 3222), a nineteenth-century French-Gothic-style building set high on a hill overlooking all of Cobh. Designed in the shape of a cross, it took 47 years to build (1868–1915). Take particular note of its tall spire, clock, and carillon, the largest in Britain and Ireland, consisting of 49 bells. Regular recitals of religious and secular music are scheduled in the summer months. Open daily. Admission: free

Return to the harbour front to see an assortment of other noteworthy sites including **The Promenade**, a waterside public park; the **Sirius Art Centre** (tel. 021 481 3790), a contemporary art gallery housed in a building that was formerly the home of the Royal Cork Yacht Club (1854–1969); and memorials to the victims of the *Lusitania* and the *Titanic*.

Return to the main N25 road, turn left and continue into Cork city or other points west.

PAT'S PICKS

RESTAURANTS

AHERNE'S SEAFOOD RESTAURANT, 163 North Main Street, Youghal (tel. 024 92424.). Situated in the heart of town, this old-world inn has no sea views, but the best of the local catch (straight from the fishing boats of Youghal Harbour) is always on the menu – from lobsters and oysters out of the tank, to crab claws and giant prawn tails, as well as seafood chowders, pies and salads. Open for lunch and dinner, daily.

BALLYMALOE HOUSE, Shanagarry (tel. 021 465 2531). Housed in a Georgian country house in an off-the-beaten-path setting, this restaurant is known for top-class cuisine, using the freshest produce from its own farm, gardens, and nearby waters. The food is so good that it has inspired an on-premises cooking school and half-a- dozen cookbooks. Reservations are a must. Open for lunch and dinner, daily.

FARMGATE RESTAURANT, Coolbawn, Midleton (tel. 021 863 2771). Fresh locally produced foods are the mainstay of this cosy restaurant. Specialities include free-range poultry, meats and fresh local fish, as well as farmhouse cheeses. If you prefer a picnic, there is also a deli on the premises. Open for lunch and snacks, Monday–Saturday; and dinner, Thursday–Saturday.

JACOB'S LADDER RESTAURANT, Harbour front, Cobh (tel. 021 481 5566). Housed in the Watersedge Hotel, this restaurant has a maritime atmosphere, capped with wide-window views of the water. The menu features local fresh seafood – from Rossmore oysters to Shanagarry smoked salmon, as well as a good selection of meats and vegetarian dishes. Open for lunch and dinner, daily.

STEPHEN PEARCE CAFÉ, at the Stephen Pearce Pottery, Shanagarry (tel. 021 464 6807). Surrounded by pottery and the latest in Ireland's ceramic creations, this self-service restaurant offers seating indoors and on an outdoor patio. The menu changes daily but includes homemade soups, pies and traditional dishes, as well as salads. Open for snacks and light meals, daily.

PUBS

MANSWORTH BAR, 4 Midleton Street, Cobh (tel. 021 481 1965). Established in 1895, this family-run enterprise is reputed to be the oldest established bar in Cobh – and the walls are appropriately lined with artefacts and seafaring memorabilia. It is situated in the hilly part of town, above the cathedral. Tea, coffee and bar food are served.

TRACEY'S THE NOOK BAR, 20 Main Street, Youghal (tel. 024 92225). Run by the Treacy family since 1901, this traditional shop-front pub sits in the heart of Youghal. Step inside and enjoy the old-world atmosphere. Traditional music is on tap many nights in the summer season.

THE OLD THATCH, Killeagh (tel. 024 95116). Situated on the main N25 road between Youghal and Midleton, this white-washed and thatched pub is an eye-catcher. Claiming to be the oldest licensed premises in the south of Ireland (and in the same family since 1695), it offers an authentic old-world ambience and bar food all day.

DIGRESSIONS

CAR FERRY: For an excursion on Cork Harbour (or to bypass Cork city and save time and mileage between Cobh and the Kinsale/Carrigaline area), drive aboard the continuous car ferry, departing from Carrigaloe on the outskirts of Cobh. Crossing time is five minutes, and service is from 7.15am to 12.45am daily, year-round. On the Kinsale/Carrigaline side, the terminal is at Glenbrook, about 19 km (12 miles) northeast of Kinsale. No reservations necessary; pay on board. Information: Cross River Ferries, Atlantic Quay, Cobh (tel. 021 481 1223).

HISTORIC FOOTSTEPS: Guided walking tours are conducted by local historians in both Cobh and Youghal. In Cobh, there are two different themed tours – the 'Titanic Trail', taking in nineteen different sites or buildings connected

with the ill-fated ship, and the 'Ghost Walk', visiting the town's 'haunted' places. Information: Michael Martin (tel. 021 481 5211 or www.titantic-trail.com). In Youghal, local guides escort visitors on walking tours of historic landmarks, including the town's thirteenth-century lighthouse and walls, and eighteenth-century Clock Gate. Information: Youghal Walking Tours (tel. 024 92447).

MEDIEVAL MEMORIES: Close to East Cork is Ardmore, County Waterford, less than 13 km (8 miles) east of Youghal. Tucked between Youghal Bay and Ardmore Bay, this historic town is said to be the oldest Christian settlement in Ireland. It was settled by St Declan, who lived in the period 350–450AD and Christianised this area before the coming of St Patrick. St Declan's monastery flourished in medieval times, and many fine structures remain, including a beautifully proportioned twelfth-century round tower and many Romanesque sculptures, dating from the ninth and twelfth centuries, and arranged in a series of arcades that depict scenes from the Old and New Testaments. From this site, long-distance walkers can also embark on 'St Declan's Way', a walking trail based on a series of ancient pilgrimage routes from Ardmore to the Rock of Cashel in County Tipperary. Information: Ardmore Tourist Office (tel. 024 9444).

13: West Cork

Stretching from Kinsale west to Mizen Head, and then up along the coast to Bantry Bay, the west coast of Cork is a happy mix of bays and coves, inlets and islands. The landscape presents a rainbow of constantly changing colours, warmed by Gulf breezes and fanned by palm trees and lush subtropical foliage. It's a magical place, attractive to fishermen, yachtsmen, tourists, retirees, artists, craftspeople and weekenders from Cork and other Irish cities.

Unlike the more travelled parts of Ireland, there are relatively few 'must-see' man-made attractions in West Cork. It's simply a place for incomparable 'wide-open-spaces' scenery, 'let's get away from it all' country lanes, new discoveries at every turn, and a surprising cornucopia of great food, from locally caught seafood and organically grown vegetables to farmhouse cheeses.

(See map p.117)

FAST FACTS

Travel Information Offices

BANTRY TOURIST OFFICE, Old Courthouse, Bantry (tel. 027 50229). Open May–September.

CLONAKILTY TOURIST OFFICE, Ashe Street, Clonakilty (tel. 023 33226). Open all year.

GLENGARRIFF TOURIST OFFICE, Town Centre, Glengarriff (tel. 027 63084). Open June–September.

SKIBBEREEN TOURIST OFFICE, North Street, Skibbereen (tel. 028 21766). Open all year.

TRAVEL INFORMATION ONLINE: www.corkkerry.ie, www.westcork.ie and www.bearatourism.com

TELEPHONE AREA CODES: As there are at least three area codes operable in this area (023, 027 and 028), all numbers will be preceded by their area code, to avoid confusion.

MAJOR EVENTS

BANTRY INTERNATIONAL MUSSEL FAIR – Celebrating one of the area's prime seafood products, this three-day festival is timed to coincide with the harvesting of mussels in Bantry Bay. Mussels are available at all bars and restaurants throughout the weekend. Information: Bantry International Mussel Fair, tel. 027 50360 or www.bantrymusselfair.ie. (Second weekend of May)

WEST CORK GARDEN TRAIL – This annual event gives an opportunity to view sixteen diverse gardens of West Cork, some of which are not ordinarily open to the public. Information: Phemie Rose, Kilravock Garden, Durrus, tel. 027 61111 or www.westcorkgardentrail.com. (Last two weeks of June)

CAPE CLEAR INTERNATIONAL STORYTELLING FESTIVAL – If you have a story to tell, this festival is made to order. Irish and international storytellers participate in storytelling concerts, discussions, sessions by the fireside, bilingual storytelling, workshops and story swapping. Information: Cape Clear International Storytelling Festival, tel. 028 39116 or http://indigo.ie/~stories. (First weekend of September)

WEST CORK DRIVING TOUR

Duration: 4–6 hours plus stops

Depart Cork city on the main N71 road, heading south via the local villages of Ballinhassig, Halfway and Inishannon, to Bandon, a small market town dating back to the early seventeenth century. About 1.6 km (1 mile) outside Bandon, you may wish to take a left and detour on local road R602 to **Timoleague**, a small village that takes its name from the Irish language words *Tigh Molaige*, meaning 'St Molaga's house'. A monastery was founded here in the sixth century by St Molaga, a disciple of St David of Wales. It was replaced in the thirteenth century by a new monastery, built for the Franciscans, which became one of the largest and most important religious houses of Ireland in medieval times.

Continue for 4.8 km (3 miles) to **Courtmacsherry**, an attractive fishing village on Courtmacsherry Bay, with lovely cliff-side walks, including an area of seven indentations, known as **The Seven Heads**. This place name has nothing to do with sherry, but is instead derived from the Irish language *Cúirt Mhic Shéafraidh*, meaning 'residence of the sons of Geoffrey', apparently an Anglo-Norman family who settled the area long ago.

From Timoleague, continue on local road R600 for 8 km (5 miles) to link up with the main N71 road and arrive in **Clonakilty**, a busy and colourful market town dating back to the thirteenth century, with a place name derived from the Irish *Cloch na Coillte*, meaning 'stone (fort) of the woods'.

Clonakilty is a delight to the senses – a series of narrow streets, overflowing with flowers in hanging baskets and on stanchions, and lined with traditional hand-painted shopfronts, many displaying signage in Gaelic lettering. Local planning authorities have encouraged the use of older buildings for twenty-first-century purposes – a nineteenth-century mill has been adapted for use as the town library; a small Presbyterian church has been 'born again' as the post office; a disused linen hall dating back to 1819 now serves as a bakery; and the former Methodist National School is now the home of the West Cork Regional Museum.

In addition, the defunct West Cork Railway station on the edge of town has been imaginatively transformed into the **West Cork Model Railway Village**, Inchydoney Road (tel. 023 33224). A special delight for children, this is a miniature walk-around version of six West Cork towns – Clonakilty, Kinsale, Bandon, Dunmanway, Bantry and Skibbereen – as they appeared in the 1940s, and connected by a miniature railway based on the long-closed West Cork Railway. Open daily, February–October. Admission: €

From Clonakilty, wend your way westward. Woodfield, 6.5 km (4 miles) down the road, is the birthplace of Michael Collins (1890–1922), recently immortalised in the movie of the same name. One of Ireland's great political heroes during the 1916–22 period of rebellion, Collins was a General of the Free State Army, and his powerful personality made him a legend in his own time. There is a memorial to his memory at Sam's Cross, Woodfield.

From this point, the route becomes more rugged, with the sea carving deep inlets and bays as it rolls in from the Atlantic. For the next 24 km (15 miles), the route passes through a series of picturesque harbour villages with melodic and curious names – Rosscarbery, Glandore, Leap and Union Hall. Take time to get off the main road and explore one or two of these little treasures.

The next major town is **Skibbereen**, fondly referred to as the 'capital of West Cork'. Its place name is probably derived from the Irish *An Sciobairín*, meaning 'the place of the little boats'. Sitting on the banks of the River Ilen near Roaringwater Bay, Skibbereen is a popular hub for fishermen and yachtsmen. It is also the home of the **West Cork Arts Centre**, North Street (tel. 028 22090), a showcase for artists and craftspeople from all parts of rural Ireland.

A lively market centre, Skibbereen is the gateway to several more remote towns and attractions. Take local road R596 to **Castletownsend**, a place whose name commemorates a castle built by an English settler, Colonel Richard Townsend. The castle is now in ruins, but the town has survived very well, thanks to the prominence it received as the home of Edith Somerville and 'Martin' (Violet Mary) Ross, the nineteenth-century writing team who penned *The Experiences of an Irish R.M.*, a classic book adapted for an award-winning television series in the 1980s.

The small fishing and sailing port of **Baltimore** is 11 km (7 miles) southwest of Skibbereen, and well worth a short detour. It is generally acknowledged that the place name derives from the Irish language, *Baile na Tighe Mór*, meaning 'townland of the big house'. The big house, in this case, belonged to Lord Calvert whose family seat was the barony here. The American city of Baltimore derives its name from this Irish place. From Baltimore, boat trips are available to the islands of Cape Clear and Sherkin.

Heading west from Skibbereen, the N71 passes through an open scenic stretch for 13 km (8 miles), with various inlets of Roaringwater Bay on the left and Mount Gabriel rising on the right (347 metres/1,339 feet). The next spectacle is man-made – a beautiful twelve-arch bridge leading into **Ballydehob**, a cheery village of brightly coloured shopfronts, each one trying to outdo the next. Many of the shops and pubs have murals and wall art on their façades. It is not surprising that this remote village is a popular retreat for artists, poets and writers who have come to live among the farming community. Ballydehob's artisans often exhibit their works in the local craft shops and galleries, as well as museums in Dublin, London, the US and throughout Europe. The curious-sounding place name is derived from the Irish *Béal an Dá Chab*, meaning 'entrance of the two mouths', usually interpreted as Ballydehob's position on the shores of the bay and base of the mountain.

Although Ballydehob will probably win your heart, this tour is not yet over, but our use of the N71 is for a while. Switch now to local roads R592 and R591, continuing along the rim of Roaringwater Bay for 8 km (5 miles), to **Schull** (pronounced *skull*), from the Irish word *An Scoil*, meaning 'the school', and relating to an early school founded by monks at this site. It is one of the most popular resorts on the West Cork coast for yachting. The island of Cape Clear, as mentioned above under Baltimore, lies across the bay, while at the west of the harbour's mouth are Long Island, Horse Island and Castle Island, all thriving centres of the fishing industry of long ago, and now almost deserted. In the summer months, all types of water-sports activities and boating trips are available from Schull Harbour and nearby Colla Pier, including a coastal ferry service between Schull and Baltimore.

For a slight diversion with a celestial theme, make a left from **Main Street**, onto **Colla Road**. Three blocks down the road beside the bay is the **Schull Planetarium**, Schull Community College (tel. 028 28552). Touted as the only planetarium in southern Ireland, this star-gazing centre invites visitors to view the heavens under optimum conditions. At least once a day (schedule varies), there are 'star shows' lasting approximately 45 minutes. Open Tuesday–Saturday in July–August; Tuesday, Friday and Saturday in June; and Sunday in March–May. Admission: €

From Schull, it is just over 11 km (7 miles) to the remote resorts of Toormore, Goleen, Crookhaven and Barleycove, the latter of which is known for its golden beaches, and finally to land's end – **Mizen Head**, the most southerly point on the island of Ireland.

Above: Dublin is famous for its colourful Georgian doorways –
this one is on Merrion Square near the National Gallery.

Left (top): On Dublin's north side, the Moore Street Market is a traditional open-air gathering place for the sale of fresh fruits, vegetables, fish and more. Stop and listen to the lyrical Dublin accents.

Left (middle): Dublin's Temple Bar Market on the south side is a haven for gourmet foods and freshly baked breads.

Below: Young musicians, known as 'buskers', play on Dublin's Grafton Street as shoppers stroll by.

Above: Powerscourt House, an eighteenth-century Georgian mansion, sits amid forty-seven acres of glorious gardens in the heart of County Wicklow.

Right: Nestled in the shadows of the prehistoric Newgrange passage graves, Newgrange Farm is a 330-acre working farm in County Meath that welcomes visitors to join in the daily chores, like feeding the ducks.

Above: The well-named Antique Tavern is a favourite meeting place in Enniscorthy, County Wexford, on the main road to Dublin.

Left: Ardmore, County Waterford, is said to be the oldest Christian settlement in Ireland. It was founded by St. Declan (350-450AD), who christianised the area before the coming of St. Patrick.

Above: Sailboats and yachts of every size and description moor along the marina at Kinsale, County Cork.

Below: Many visitors are surprised to see that palm trees grow all over Ireland. These are flourishing at Parknasilla, on the Ring of Kerry.

Above: A 'one-man band' plying his trade in Patrick Street, Cork City.
Below: Sheep graze on a hill overlooking Slea Head in County Kerry.

Above: Ladies View, a high vantage point in Killarney National Park, looks out on the three Killarney Lakes and the spectacular MacGillycuddy Reeks.

Below: Muckross House, overlooking Killarney's Middle Lake, is often called the 'jewel of Killarney'. Built in 1843, this twenty-room Victorian mansion has sixty-two chimneys.

Above: Dating back to 1425, Bunratty Castle at Bunratty, County Clare, is open for guided tours and for nightly medieval banquets.

Below: Using reeds, a local thatcher repairs the roof of a farmer's cottage in Bunratty Folk Park, adjacent to Bunratty Castle. This restored nineteenth-century village includes shops, a school, a church, a blacksmith's forge and more.

Walkers and hikers will particularly enjoy the trek out to this wind-swept outpost. Park your car at the end of the R591 and embark on a tour of **Mizen Vision/The Mizen Head Signal Station Visitor Centre**, Harbour Road (tel. 028 35115). Walk (for approximately 20–30 minutes) along the well-fenced coastal precipice, passing over a suspension bridge and going down a cliff for 99 steps, to gain access to the signal station. Once you have arrived, you can use telescopes outside to look far out to sea and to distant views of the **Fastnet Lighthouse**, standing on a rock 11 km (7 miles) off the coast. Take coastal pictures to your heart's content, or examine the various indoor displays set up within the lighthouse. The return trip retraces your steps, although there is a graded walkway back up, if you prefer not to climb up the 99 steps. Dress warmly, wear comfortable shoes, be prepared for brisk and bracing ocean breezes at every turn, and you'll have a once-in-a-lifetime experience. Open daily, mid-March–October; Saturday–Sunday in November–mid-March. Admission: €

Now that you have 'gone to the end of the world', as the locals call it, there is only one way to go – back to mainland County Cork. Retrace your steps in an easterly direction via local road R591 and back to the main N71, and head north for approximately 8 km (5 miles) to the town of **Bantry**, with the waters of Bantry Bay visible on the left.

In a county known for its beautiful bays, Bantry is the benchmark of Cork's waters. Nestled off the Atlantic between the Beara and Sheep's Head peninsulas, Bantry Bay displays nature at its best – glistening and pure waters bordered by lush and colourful foliage. Time after time, it inspires an artist's best impression or a photographer's finest frame. It provides the perfect backdrop for a scenic tour or a romantic rendezvous.

The Irish-language place name for Bantry, *Beanntraighe*, describes it very well, meaning 'headland of the shore'. Historically, Bantry Bay played an important role in Ireland's struggles to gain independence from Britain. French fleets, in support of the Irish, twice entered Bantry Bay. In 1689, they came to help James II in his unsuccessful campaign against William of Orange, and in 1796 the 'French Armada' returned to aid Wolfe Tone and his United Irishmen in their abortive efforts to overthrow the British.

The name Bantry also belongs to the adjacent market town, distinguished as the home of the earls of Bantry since 1739. At the south end of the town is **Bantry House** (tel. 027 50047), one of Ireland's grandest eighteenth-century houses. Built *c*.1740 for the earls of Bantry, with a mostly Georgian façade with Victorian additions, this house contains many items of furniture and *objets d'art* from all over Europe, collected by the earls of Bantry, including four panels of Aubusson tapestry made for Marie-Antoinette, and wainscoting of seventeenth-century Spanish leather, chests from the Indies, and urns from the Orient. Note: At time of going to press, the house is undergoing a substantial maintenance and refurbishment programme and is closed to the public. The intention is to reopen in 2004, but this has not been confirmed, so phone ahead to confirm before visiting.

Even while the house is closed, visitors are welcome to visit the adjacent stables which contain the **1796 Bantry Exhibit** (tel. 027 51796), commemorating the 1796 visit of the French Armada into Bantry Bay. This historical vignette is recalled by a walk-through tour, and enhanced by music and sound effects, scale models and interactive displays, all depicting life in Bantry over 200 years ago. Visitors are also invited to tour the extensive gardens, with subtropical plants and shrubs, original statuary and several walking paths. Climb the steps behind the house for a panoramic view of the house, gardens and Bantry Bay. Both exhibit and gardens are open daily, March–October. Admission: €

For still more views of Bantry Bay, drive northwards via Ballylickey for 16 km (10 miles) along the main N71 road, amid a profusion of tall and shady trees and lush greenery, to **Glengarriff**, a place name derived from the Irish language, *An Gleann Garbh*, meaning 'the rugged valley'.

As its name implies, Glengariff is a village in a beautiful glen – thickly wooded with oak, elm, pine, yew, holly and palm trees, bordered by the bay and sea coast. The mild climate, influenced directly by the warm breezes of the Gulf Stream, favours the growth of luxuriant Mediterranean flora, such as arbutus, eucalyptus, rhododendron, fuchsia and blue-eyed grass. The unbridled beauty of the area has always attracted visitors from near and far, including artists, writers and show-business folk.

Offshore lies Inacullin, known more commonly as **Garinish Island** (tel. 027 63040). The 15-hectare (37-acre) island is home to an Italian garden of rare and tender tropical plants, not usually seen in Ireland or northern Europe. It was here that George Bernard Shaw is reputed to have written his play *St Joan*. The paths around the gardens, ideal for strolling, include ponds and pedimented gateways, a Martello tower and a Grecian temple overlooking the sea. You can easily spend a morning or afternoon here. Open daily, March–October. Admission: €

Access to the island is via boat (a 30-minute trip) from the pier. Blue Pool Ferries (tel. 027 63333) operates the boats, and a separate fee is charged. Boat fare: €

From Glengarriff, continue northward on the N71 to Kenmare in County Kerry, a scenic and twisty drive via the eastern end of the Caha Mountains, passing through remote boglands, steep hillsides and tunnels hewn from solid rock. It takes about one hour to drive although it is less than 26 km (16 miles).

Alternatively, you can return to Cork city via an inland route. If you select the latter, retrace your steps to Ballylickey and take the R584 over the Shehy Mountains, travelling northeast as the road ascends via **Keimaneigh Pass** (which means 'The Pass of the Deer's Step') and the **Ouvane Valley**. After 13 km (8 miles), make a left turn to follow the signs for **Gougane Barra**, a national park and the source of the River Lee. Legend has it that St Finbarr, the founder of Cork city, also had a hermitage here in the sixth century, and hence its Irish-language name, *Guagán Barra*, which means 'Finbarr's rocky cave'. It's a beautiful spot, a glistening clear-blue lake, enhanced by cascades from the cliff sides, and surrounded by mountains, ancient trees, and lush flora.

Return to the R584 and begin a scenic drive through the West Cork Gaeltacht – an Irish or Gaelic-speaking area – where the signs indicate place names in Irish first, and then in English, if at all.

Next, after 5 km (3 miles), is *Béal Átha an Ghaorthaidh* (**Ballingeary**), a name that means 'ford-mouth of the wooded valley'. It is a popular place for students to come in the summer to immerse themselves in the Irish language.

After 8 km (5 miles) more, with Lough Allua on the right side, the village of **Inse Geimhleach (Inchigeelagh)** appears. The place name is so old that it is rarely given an English translation.

The next place of interest, as the R584 meets the main N22 road, is **Macroom**, a busy market town at the confluence of three rivers – the Lee, Laney and Sullane. In the centre of the town stand the remains of **Macroom Castle**, a thirteenth-century fortress that was granted in 1654 by Oliver Cromwell to Sir Admiral William Penn, father of the founder of Pennsylvania. It is said that young William spent much of his childhood here, before he left to study at Oxford in 1660. Over the years, the castle has endured many pillages and was burned for the final time during the Irish Civil War in the early 1920s. The ruins have been declared a national monument, and the entrance gateway has been restored.

From Macroom, via the main N22 road, head east, following the path of the River Lee for 37 km (23 miles) back to Cork city.

Note: If you have an extra day or more, add on one or both of these peninsula detours:

BEARA PENINSULA

Locally referred to as the Ring of Beara Drive, this is the largest of Cork's three finger-like peninsulas (Beara, Sheep's Head and Mizen Head), jutting into the Atlantic Ocean. The full circuit is over 145 km (90 miles), but it can be cut in half, by following the Tim Healy Pass through the Caha Mountains for a total drive of about 80 km (50 miles).

The Ring of Beara covers some of the most remote and undiscovered scenery in Ireland. From Glengarriff, make a left turn onto local road R572 at the north end of town. Follow the shores of Bantry Bay for 17.5 km (11 miles), with the Caha Mountains rising on the right, to **Adrigole**, a small village famous for its nearby mountain, **Hungry Hill** (686 metres/2,251 feet), a reminder of the famine of 1845. The highest peak in the Caha range, this mountain gave its name to the Daphne du Maurier novel about local copper-mining barons of the nineteenth century.

Continue west for 14.5 km (9 miles) to **Castletownbeare**, the principal town of this peninsula and home of Ireland's largest whitefish port. Often referred to as Castletown Bearhaven, the town takes its name from the Irish language, *Baile Chaisleáin Bhéarra*, meaning 'the town of (the) castle of Bear'. Bear (or Bere) Island, formerly a fortified anchorage for the British Atlantic fleet, sits off the coast sheltering the town.

Choices in routing arise now. If you are fond of the wilderness, continue 17.5 km (11 miles) west on the R572 to the very tip of the peninsula, to the remote village of **Allihies**, surrounded by copper mines that have existed here for over 3,000 years. The peninsula ends with the remote outposts of Dursey Island, Crow Head and Cod Head.

Alternatively, turn right onto the R571 which leads to **Eyeries**, a village of gaily painted houses that served as a setting for the French film *The Purple Taxi*, shot on location here in 1975. The third routing is the most popular for visitors in search of a scenic drive. It requires going back to Adrigole, for a turn north onto local road R574 to follow the **Tim Healy Pass** through the Caha Mountains. It is a spectacular route with Glanmore Lake below, and great chasms and ravines opening on either side. Reaching a height of 330.5 metres (1,084 feet), the road is named after Tim Healy, a one-time governor-general of the Irish Free State and a native of Bantry.

The route descends gradually to Lauragh and the County Kerry border, joining local road R571. Make a right and follow this winding and twisty road as it wends its way along a scenic stretch of the Kenmare River Estuary, with the Ring of Kerry in the distance, into Kenmare. At this point, you can travel onward in County Kerry or to other parts of Ireland, or return to Cork using the local road R569 via Kilgarvan to link up with the main N22 road east via Macroom.

SHEEP'S HEAD PENINSULA

From Bantry, you can take a short 48-km (30-mile) detour around the **Sheep's Head Peninsula**, a thin strip of land wedged between Bantry and Dunmanus bays. This is the least travelled of all the southwestern peninsulas in either Cork or Kerry. Remote and undeveloped, it is a haven for those who appreciate superb seascapes and mountain scenery.

Follow the road west to **Ahakista**, a unique name derived from the Irish language *Áthan Chiste*, meaning 'ford of the treasure'. No one knows where the treasure is today, but this small village does have a memorial walled garden and sundial by Cork sculptor Ken Thompson. The garden leads down to the water's edge.

The last village on the peninsula is **Kilcrohane**, and then the road ends. If you are fond of hiking, walk out along the pathway to the tip of the peninsula, known locally as 'the edge of the known world', with only the ocean below and beyond.

Continue the drive by making a right turn back towards Bantry on the road that runs along the north coast of the peninsula – a route known as the **Goat's Pass**. It's a scenic secondary road that rises gently and then plunges steeply down the other side, opening to views of Bantry Bay and the Caha Mountains in the distance. Continue eastward through the village of Gerahies, and, on the approach to the town of Bantry, look left for views of **Whiddy Island**, a small parcel of land floating in the bay west of Bantry town. Return to Bantry and continue back to Cork city or onward to County Kerry.

PAT'S PICKS

RESTAURANTS

ADÈLE'S, Main Street, Schull (tel. 028 28459). The creative cookery of Adèle O'Connor is the big draw at this shop-front café, for a snack or light meal in the heart of Schull. The menu changes daily but often includes homemade soups, salads, quiches, fish pies, chilli and pastas. All breads and desserts are made on the premises, including chocolate squiggle flapjacks and cherry buns. Open for snacks, lunch and dinner, daily, April–October.

ANNIE'S, Main Street, Ballydehob (tel. 028 37292). For over 20 years, this little shop-front restaurant of Annie Barry's has been a mainstay of this vibrant and creative village. The menu features flavourful home cooking, freshly baked breads, farmhouse cheeses and local produce, with choices such as seafood salads, steak and kidney pie, and lamb kidneys in pastry. Open for dinner, Tuesday–Saturday, in January–September, and part of December.

BLAIR'S COVE, Durrus (tel. 027 61127). For fine food in a romantic setting, it's hard to beat this long-established culinary outpost overlooking Dunmanus Bay. This Belgian-owned restaurant is housed in a restored and modernised 250-year-old stone barn. The menu is international, with emphasis on meats and fish cooked slowly and succulently on an open wood fireplace. Open for dinner, Monday –Saturday, July–August; Tuesday–Saturday in mid-March–June and September–October.

CHEZ YOUEN, The Pier, Baltimore (tel. 028 21036). Shellfish is the star of this little restaurant overlooking the harbour. Brittany-born Youen Jacob, chef-owner since 1979, adds a touch of France to every dish. 'Seafood in the shell' is the house speciality, including lobster from local waters, Dublin Bay prawns, Baltimore shrimp and velvet crab. Open for dinner, daily, except November and February.

HERON'S COVE, Goleen Harbour (tel. 028 35355). With wide-windowed water views, this restaurant offers hearty soups, homemade breads, farmhouse cheeses and other snacks by day, while in the evening it serves full dinners in romantic candlelit surroundings. The menu emphasises fresh local produce; lobsters and oysters from a seawater tank; prawns, crab, and fish from the Goleen fleet; plus homemade desserts and ice cream. Open for dinner, daily, and lunch on Sunday, June–September; in October–May, it is open only according to demand.

SEA VIEW HOUSE, Ballylickey (tel. 027 50462). Set overlooking Bantry Bay amid its own lush gardens, this Georgian-style country inn has won many awards for its creative cookery, using the best of local seafood and produce. Even the ice creams for dessert are homemade. Enjoy freshly made soups, salads and sandwiches by day in the bar, or a full five-course dinner in the antique-filled formal Georgian-era dining room at night. Open daily, mid-March to mid-November.

PUBS

AULD TRIANGLE, Main Street, Macroom (tel. 026 41940). For over 300 years, this stone-faced pub has been a favourite with the locals and as a stopping place on the main road between Cork city and West Cork. Bar food, from soups and salads to sandwiches, is served all day.

JOHNNY BARRY'S BAR, Main Street, Glengarriff (tel. 027 63315). This friendly pub offers a relaxing old-world setting and hefty portions of bar food all day, from soups and sandwiches to seafood platters and steaks. There is music at night from May to October.

BUSHE'S BAR, The Square, Baltimore (tel. 028 20125). Long a fixture in the town, this family-run bar is rich in maritime traditions and décor, with a fascinating collection of lanterns, ships' clocks, compasses, tide tables and pennants. Members of the second generation of Bushes provide a welcoming ambience, with home-cooked food including a speciality of open crab sandwiches on home-baked brown bread. In fine weather there is seating outside, overlooking the harbour.

CASEY'S, Baltimore (tel. 028 20197). Great views of the bay are part of the atmosphere at this traditional pub, with a nautical theme and open fireplaces. Quite fittingly, the bar menu offers the best of the local seafood catch. Traditional music sessions are held on most weekends.

MARY ANN'S, Castletownsend (028 36146). Situated in the heart of a remote village and just up the hill from the quay, this old-world pub dates back to 1844. The décor and furnishings reflect its longevity and a nautical ambience is created by ships' wheels and lanterns, and seafaring memorabilia.

DIGRESSIONS

CLIMB UP IN A LITTLE CABLE CAR: Driving around the Beara Peninsula? If you venture out to the point where the road ends at the far end of the peninsula, it is not necessarily the end of your touring. A cable-car service (the only one of its kind in Ireland) connects the end of the mainland to the little island of Dursey out in the Atlantic Ocean. The cabin capacity is six persons or one person and a cow. (Note that cows take precedence over humans in order of transport priority.) A mere 304.5 hectares (753 acres) in size, Dursey is the most westerly of West Cork's inhabited islands. It provides the visitor with some lovely walks and views of the nearby West Cork coastline, plus a close-up look at many rare birds. Information: Beara Tourism and Development Association, The Square, Castletownbeare, Co. Cork (tel. 027 70054 or www.bearatourism.com).

ISLAND-HOPPING: West Cork offers many opportunities to visit offshore islands by boat or car ferry. Here is a summary to help you plan your island adventures:

BERE ISLAND: Nestled in Bantry Bay 3 km (2 miles) off the coast of Castletownbeare on the Beara Peninsula, Bere Island is a small and hilly island, facing the open Atlantic to the south and southwest, and offering spectacular views in all directions. The following companies provide car and passenger transport year-round between Castletownbeare and the island: Bere Island Ferries (tel. 027 75009); and Murphy's Ferry Service (tel. 027 75014 or www.murphysferry.com).

CAPE CLEAR ISLAND/OILEÁN CLÉIRE: Accessible by boat from Baltimore or Schull, Cape Clear is Ireland's most southerly island, just under 5 km (3 miles) long and 2.5 km (1.5 miles) wide. This Irish-speaking island is home to around 120 inhabitants. A paradise for bird-watchers, the island is the home of Ireland's only manned bird observatory. Five kilometres (3 miles) further out in the Atlantic stands the Fastnet Rock Lighthouse, the largest off the Irish coast. The following companies operate passenger ferry services to Cape Clear Island and Fastnet Rock Lighthouse from May to September: Karycraft

Cruises, Skeagh, Schull (tel. 028 28278); and West Cork Coastal Cruises, Baltimore (tel. 028 39153 or www.westcorkcoastalcruises.com).

SHERKIN ISLAND: Perched off the tip of Baltimore, this tiny island sits in Roaringwater Bay, providing a 'get away from it all' atmosphere, with its wealth of cliffs, strands, rocky bays and coastal views. The following companies provide passenger ferry services to Sherkin Island from May to September: Baltimore & Sherkin Island Ferry, Baltimore (tel. 028 20218); and Karycraft Cruises, Skeagh, Schull (tel. 028 28278).

14: Kinsale

Sitting on the gentle slope of Compass Hill, beside the Bandon Estuary, Kinsale is a picturesque seaport with a wide, sheltered harbour. Less than 23 km (20 miles) from Cork city, this little town of 2,000 residents is a favourite haunt for Corkonians and international visitors alike, especially those who have a penchant for boating, fishing or just strolling along the wide marina. The place name of Kinsale is indeed fitting, derived from the Irish *Cionn tSáile*, meaning 'head of (the) sea'.

Historically, Kinsale traces its origins back to 1177 when the Anglo-Normans founded a town in a small walled area close to the water. The town received its first royal charter from King Edward II in 1335. Almost 300 years passed before Kinsale achieved its moment of fame in the long struggle for Irish freedom. In September of 1601, an Iberian fleet of masted warships, known as the 'Spanish Armada', pulled into Kinsale Harbour to help the Irish chieftains O'Neill and O'Donnell from Ulster in their quest to win the town from the English. Unfortunately, the Spanish–Irish alliance was betrayed from within and attacked at the Battle of Kinsale, turning the joint effort into defeat. Afterwards, Kinsale became an important British naval base.

Rather than submit to the Crown, many of the Irish clan leaders fled to the Continent, signalling the end of the old Gaelic order in Ireland. Their escape from Ireland, which is referred to variously as 'The Flight of the Earls' or 'The Flight of the Wild Geese', provided mainland Europe with many legacies, including the establishment of Irish colleges and regiments in France, Italy and Spain, and development of the wine and spirits industry in Europe. Few have not heard of Hennessy brandy, but there are also Irish names on some of France's best wines, such as Château McCarthy, Château Dillon, Château Barton, Château Kirwan, Château Phelan, Château Lynch and Château Clarke. In time, Kinsale benefited from these connections, becoming one of Ireland's principal wine ports in the seventeenth and eighteenth centuries.

Kinsale's other significant rendezvous with history was more recent. In 1915, just off the coast of Kinsale, the *Lusitania* was sunk by a German submarine, with the loss of over 1,500 lives. Many of the dead were buried in a local cemetery.

Today, Kinsale is best known for its well-maintained waterside setting, consistently winning national and international awards for the quality of its environment, and use of trees and flowers. Thanks to the abundance of fresh seafood on its doorstep, Kinsale has also made a big name for itself as the 'gourmet capital' of Ireland. Home to more than a dozen award-winning restaurants and pubs, Kinsale draws lovers of good food year-round, and particularly each October when it hosts a three-day gastronomic festival.

FAST FACTS

Travel Information Office

KINSALE TOURIST OFFICE, Pier Road at Emmet Street (tel. 021 477 2234). Open all year.

TRAVEL INFORMATION ONLINE: www.corkkerry.ie, www.kinsale.ie

TELEPHONE AREA CODE:
The telephone area code for all numbers is 021, unless indicated otherwise.

MAJOR EVENTS

KINSALE REGATTA – Sea-faring enthusiasts from near and far gather to see boats and yachts of all sizes and styles rally in Kinsale Harbour for three days of outdoor activities along the marina. Information: Dermot Ryan, Kinsale Regatta, tel. 477 2729 or www.kinsale.ie. (First weekend of August)

KINSALE ARTS FESTIVAL – This eleven-day event presents the best of Irish arts – from classical music performances to piano and violin recitals, readings by contemporary authors, lectures and films to dance music and one-act plays. Information: Kinsale Arts Festival, The Gallery, The Glen, tel. 477 4558 or www.kinsalearts.com. (Mid-September)

KINSALE INTERNATIONAL FESTIVAL OF FINE FOOD – Originally known as the Kinsale Gourmet Festival, this three-day event features the best of local cuisine, presented at the town's many fine restaurants and pubs, as well as street entertainment, music, parades, walking tours, harbour cruises, horse racing and wine-tasting. Information: Denis Kieran, Festival Office, tel. 477 2382 or www.kinsale.ie. (Second weekend of October)

KINSALE WALKING TOUR

Duration: 2–3 hours plus stops

Start a tour at the tourist office, on **Pier Road** at Emmet Street, also known as **Emmet Place**. The town's original Water Gate stood here, as part of the original city walls built by the Normans. To the left is the **Temperance Hall**, the first building of its kind to be built for the purpose of discouraging drink among the local folk.

Turn right and walk along **The Pier**, built in 1890, with Kinsale's vast marina and harbour front on the left. On the right are rows of lovely Georgian houses and gardens, some now serving as hotels and guesthouses. Make a right

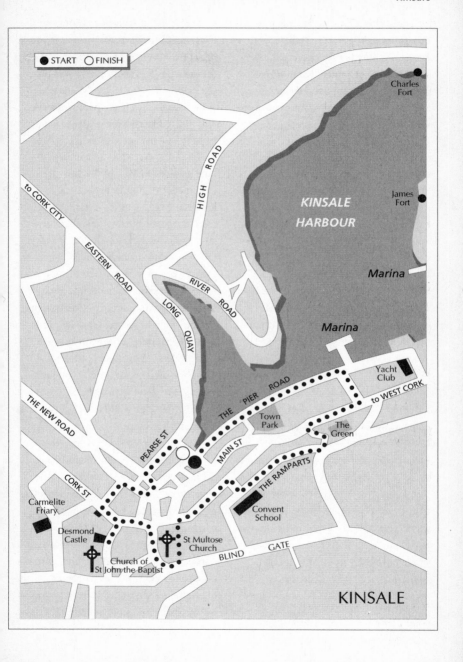

KINSALE

at **Denis Quay**, one of fifteen original quays that served the harbour front before the Pier was added. In the seventeenth and nineteenth centuries, these quays not only served as moorings for huge cargo ships, but also provided workshops for fish coopering and net-repairing, sail-making and other nautical trades. Denis Quay, like the others, is now a road.

Cross over **Lower O'Connell Street**, a busy thoroughfare now housing an assortment of restaurants, guesthouses and shops, and turn left, and then a quick right, to climb **St John's Hill**. On the right is the Bowling Green, now known simply as **The Green**, used as a place of social gatherings and assemblies in the eighteenth century. It is said that William Penn visited and that John Wesley preached about Methodism here.

Continue to **The Mall** and make a left turn onto **Compass Hill**, the highest point on this walk, with sweeping views of the houses and harbour below. Return to the Mall, which was the fashionable walkway of eighteenth-century Kinsale. Stroll along the Mall, passing the old **Municipal Hall** on the right, and some seventeenth-century almshouses, known locally as the **Gift Houses**, on the left. These have been restored in recent years. This walkway then changes its name to **The Rampart** because it is on the site of the upper wall of the old walled town.

Take a left at **Rampart Lane** and then a left at **Blind Gate**. The gate derived its name from having been walled or 'blinded' up in 1695 when it was proving convenient for smugglers. Blind Gate merges into **Rose Abbey Street** and then **Church Street**. Here to the right is **St Multose Church**, Church Street (tel. 477 2200), a Church of Ireland edifice and one of the two significant medieval buildings still left in Kinsale. Built in 1190, it has changed over the years, but still retains many of its original features, including black letter inscriptions in Norman French, an Easter sepulchre, carved memorials and reredos, and a wooden coat of arms.

Follow Church Street to **Cork Street**, making a left to see the **Church of St John the Baptist**, Friars Street (tel. 477 2138). This Classical-style Catholic church is of more recent vintage, built shortly after the Catholic Emancipation Act of 1829. The walls were built of local shale and limestone.

Returning to Cork Street, you will see on the left Kinsale's other significant medieval building – **Desmond Castle**, Cork Street (tel. 477 4855), replete with mullioned windows and stepped battlements. Built by the earl of Desmond, *c.*1500, this castle has had a long and colourful history. It served first as a customs house for wine, wool and tobacco. During the Battle of Kinsale in 1601, it was used by the Spanish to store ammunition. In the mid-eighteenth century, it became a prison for Frenchmen captured during the Napoleonic wars, and was known locally as 'French Prison'. Declared a national monument in 1938, it has now been adapted as an international wine museum. The displays depict Kinsale's days as a leading wine port. Ireland's connections to the 'Wine Geese' – the families named Dillon, Kirwan, McCarthy, Lynch, Clarke, Barton and Phelan – who fled to Europe, the Americas and Australia are also explained in a series of colourful exhibits. Open daily, mid-June to early-October; Tuesday–Sunday, mid-April to mid-June. Admission: €

Turn right and follow **Chairman's Lane** down the hill to **Market Square**, the heart of Kinsale. The centrepiece of this commercial square is **Market House**, erected *c*.1600 as a traditional two-storey building with arches on all four sides, and a brick façade with Dutch gables, a clock, bell cote and turrets. There were offices upstairs and markets below. In 1706, the building gained a new dimension as the town courthouse and official meeting rooms. More recently, the building was 'born again' as the **Kinsale Regional Museum**, Market Square (tel. 477 2044). The museum has a display of old Kinsale craftwork and other memorabilia, including an exhibit on the legendary Kinsale Giant. He was Patrick Cotter O'Brien, reputed to have been over 2.4 metres (8 feet) tall. Open daily. Admission: €

Bear left onto **Pearse Street**, originally part of Long Quay and lined with merchants' residences and warehouses. On the left is the **Blue Haven**, originally the Old Fish Market and now an inn. The street was renamed in honour of the Irish patriot Padraic Pearse after the Easter Rising of 1916.

From Pearse Street, take a right onto **Emmet Street**, named after another Irish patriot, Robert Emmet, and you have completed the walking portion of the tour.

The remainder of Kinsale is best covered with the help of a car or taxi. Two forts are worth exploring, each situated on one side of the harbour entrance. Both forts, now in ruins, were built by the British to protect their interests in Kinsale, and remained in British hands until 1922. First, follow Long Quay and the High Road to **Charles Fort**, Summer Cove (tel. 477 2263), a unique star-shaped fort, built *c*.1677. Across the harbour, via the Pier Road, is **James Fort**, built in 1602. Both are fine examples of seventeenth-century military architecture, offering sweeping views of the harbour, the town, and each other. Only Charles Fort is fully accessible to the public. Open daily, mid-March–October; Saturday–Sunday in November–mid-March. Admission: €

Return to the heart of Kinsale and complete your tour by strolling along **Main Street**, lined with local craft shops, or return to the **Pier Road**, to watch the fishing boats with the fishermen unloading their daily catch, or the sail boats gliding into the marina.

RESTAURANTS

BLUE HAVEN, 3 Pearse Street (tel. 477 2209). In the centre of town, this old inn offers bar food all day, with emphasis on seafood, such as fish chowders and plates of mussels and smoked salmon. There is outdoor seating in an enclosed courtyard during the summer. Open for lunch and dinner, daily.

COTTAGE LOFT, 6 Main Street (tel. 477 2803). As its name implies, this little restaurant has a cottage-style ambience, housed as it is in a 200-year-old building, with a décor of antiques, cane chairs and beamed ceilings. The menu, prepared by a Euro Toque chef, offers a mix of Irish and international dishes, from local seafood to farmyard duck and rack of lamb. Open for dinner, daily (except some Mondays in off season).

CRACKPOTS, 3 Cork Street (tel. 477 2847). Looking for something different? This attractive restaurant is also a working pottery studio, so if you fancy the colourful ceramic plates and dishes, you can buy them. The menu is international, with emphasis on fresh Kinsale seafood, salads and vegetarian dishes. The wine list features labels from the Wine Geese, as depicted at the wine museum just up the street. Open for dinner, daily.

FISHY FISHY CAFÉ, Guardwell (tel. 477 4453). Operating as a combined fish shop, delicatessen and restaurant, this place is a haven for seafood enthusiasts. The menu changes with the catch of the day but often includes smoked salmon, prawns, lobster, crayfish and crab – and you can pick out your own fish and have it cooked to your liking. Open for lunch, daily, April–September; Monday–Saturday, October–March.

MAN FRIDAY, Scilly (tel. 477 2260). Set on a hill overlooking the town, this tree-shaded restaurant is one of Kinsale's longest-established eateries, with a tropical atmosphere including a garden terrace. The menu offers traditional choices, such as steak, lamb and duck, but emphasises seafood, with specialities such as crab au gratin or Kinsale seafood platter. Open for dinner, Monday–Saturday.

MAX'S, 48 Main Street (tel. 477 2443). Nestled in a cosy shop-front setting with stone walls, this little wine bar offers light and healthy meals, with emphasis on fresh seafood and vegetarian dishes, as well as a house special of roast rack of lamb in lavender sauce. Open for lunch and dinner, Wednesday–Monday, March–October.

PUBS

THE BULMAN, Summercove (tel. 477 2131). Situated in Summercove, on the eastern side of the harbour en route to Charles Fort, this 200-year-old pub takes its name from the Bulman Buoy, a well-known nautical landmark, pointing the way for boats to enter the harbour safely. The interior has open log fires and maritime memorabilia, but the real fun of this pub is sitting outside beside the quay on a summer's day and watching the boats glide by.

THE HOLE IN THE WALL, The Glen (tel. 477 2939). One of Kinsale's liveliest entertainment pubs, this place features DJs and live music. For sports fans, there is also a big-screen TV for all the sporting events. In addition, there are computers for e-mail and internet access.

JIM EDWARDS, Market Quay, off Emmet Place (tel. 477 2541). Since 1971, this pub has earned a reputation for an authentic nautical atmosphere and an extensive bar-food menu, featuring seafood including lobster and oysters from the tank, as well as the best of the local catch and a variety of steaks, poultry and lamb dishes. Don't miss the distinctive clock at the entrance. Instead of numbers, the time is shown in letters that spell out the owner's name.

LORD KINGSALE, 4 Main Street (tel. 477 2371). No, this pub name is not misspelt – it is the old English spelling of the town, dating back to medieval days. The pub itself is not quite so old, but has served the town for 250 years, having been first leased for one penny per year. It has retained much of its old-world trappings, from its Tudor-style façade and stone walls to a custom-made fireplace, old fan bellows, horse brasses and a variety of lamp lighting. Entertainment includes Thursday evening sessions of Irish songs, music and poetry.

SPANIARD INN, Scilly (tel. 477 2436). Set high above the harbour en route to an area known as Summercove, this pub exudes an early-seventeenth-century atmosphere, harking back to the days of the Spanish Armada, with low-beamed ceilings, stone floors and lots of seafaring memorabilia. The food is simple pub grub, from soups, salads and sandwiches to Irish stew. There are traditional music sessions on many nights.

DIGRESSIONS

BREWERY TOUR: The brewing of beer has long been a tradition in Kinsale, starting with the Landers Malt House in the 1700s and followed by the Williams Brewery & Beer Cellars in the 1800s. Although both of those enterprises faded away into history, today the new Kinsale Brewing Company operates on the same site, around the corner from Pearse Street.

Visitors are welcome to see the brewing process and sample the finished product. Tours are available daily, but phone in advance for schedule. Information: Kinsale Brewery, The Glen (tel. 470 2124 or www.kinsalebrewing.com).

CAR FERRY: For an excursion on Cork Harbour (or to bypass Cork city and save time and mileage between the Kinsale/Carrigaline area and East Cork), drive aboard the continuous car ferry, departing from Glenbrook, about 19 km (12 miles) northeast of Kinsale. Crossing time is five minutes, and service is from 7.15am to 12.45am daily, year-round. On the Cobh side, the terminal is at Carrigaloe on the outskirts of Cobh. No reservations necessary; pay on board. Information: Cross River Ferries, Atlantic Quay, Cobh (tel. 481 1223).

CRUISING ALONG: See Kinsale from the water as you cruise the harbour and up the Bandon River on board the 50-passenger *Spirit of Kinsale*. The excursion includes a commentary about the area, along with music. The lower deck is enclosed, while the upper deck offers open-air seating. Trips last from one to three hours, depending on time of day. Boats depart from the Kinsale Marina, Pier Road, April–October. Information: Kinsale Harbour Cruises, Summercove (tel. 477 3188 or www.kinsaleharbourcruises.com).

HISTORIC FOOTSTEPS: With many historic landmarks, winding streets, a long marina path and coastal trails, Kinsale is ideal for walking tours. There are several different types of local guided walks, to suit every interest. Departure points and days of operation vary; check at the tourist office for latest schedules. Information: Herlihy Walking Tours, one-hour walks around the historic sections of Kinsale (tel. 477 2873); Coastal Walking Tours, mountain and hill climbing (tel. 477 2642), and Ghost Tours of 'haunted' places (tel. 477 2240).

15: Killarney Town

Mention Killarney and people automatically conjure up images of glistening lakes, cascading waterfalls, majestic mountains, legendary islands, ancient trees, lush foliage and romantic nature trails. Poets have strained to find adequate words to describe it, lamenting that even 'Heaven's Reflex' or 'Beauty's Home' fail to convey the grandeur of Killarney.

The good news is that all of this is true. Killarney is a natural treasure. There may not be gold in the hills but there certainly are unparalleled peace and pristine beauty. The bad news is that all of this is no secret – Killarney is popular and usually crowded except in the depths of winter.

Killarney is divided into two parts – a compact little town and an expansive national park. The town is rather ordinary, with no outstanding landmarks other than a fine cathedral. Its streets are lined by hotels, guesthouses, restaurants and shops, all geared to the buoyant tourist trade. The adjacent national park, in striking contrast, is a spectacularly scenic 65-km-square (25-mile-square) area, a magnet for artists, photographers, poets, and tourists.

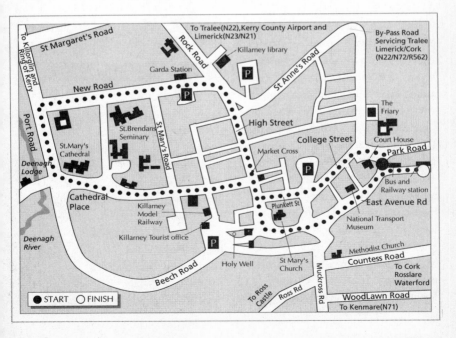

Like many Irish towns, Killarney probably has its origins in or before the ninth century as a religious site. Its name in the Irish language, *Cill Áirne*, literally means 'the church of the sloe', and there were many sloe woods in the area. It is not known exactly when Killarney began, but the growth and development of the town were tied closely to the fortunes of the local landlord, the earl of Kenmare, Sir Valentine Browne. In 1588, he was granted 2,655 hectares (6,560 acres) of land by the earl of Glencar. Browne also purchased much land and added greatly to his estate. The family lived at Ross Castle until 1721 when they moved to a new home near what is now Killarney town. Surveys conducted prior to this time did not mention a town or village called Killarney.

By 1747, however, a survey showed that a small town had been born, consisting of the earl's mansion, four slated houses, and 100 thatched cabins. Within a short seven-year period, a new street with a large inn was added, and visitors were warmly welcomed. At this stage, Lord Kenmare realised that a tourist industry could be profitable, and he encouraged building more inns and a series of colourful laneways. (For this reason, the two-year period 2004–05 is heralded as the 250th anniversary of tourism in Killarney).

As tourism began to become viable, even Queen Victoria was Killarney-bound. When she visited the town with a large entourage in 1861, she made Killarney instantly fashionable, and it has been a thriving destination ever since.

Although most of Killarney's charms lie on the outskirts of town in the National Park district, the town itself is well worth a walk, for at least an hour or two.

FAST FACTS

Travel Information Office

KILLARNEY TOURIST OFFICE, Beech Road, Killarney (tel. 064 31633) off New Street. Open all year.

TRAVEL INFORMATION ONLINE:
www.corkkerry.ie,
www.killarneywelcomes.com

TELEPHONE AREA CODE:
The telephone area code for all numbers in Killarney town is 064 unless indicated otherwise.

MAJOR EVENTS

KILLARNEY SUMMERFEST – This ten-day summer family festival is packed with all kinds of outdoor activities, from open-air concerts by top international artists, street entertainment and a teddy-bear picnic, to cycling, a regatta and guided walks, as well as an arts programme featuring puppet theatre and workshops in dance, drumming, painting and unusual crafts. Information: Marion Gowran, Killarney SummerFest, tel. 71560 or www.killarneysummerfest.com. (Last week of June and first week of July)

KILLARNEY 250 – Experience life in Killarney as it was in 1754 – that's the aim of this two-year festival celebrating the 250th anniversary of Killarney as a tourist destination. It comprises a continuous schedule of parades, garden parties, walking events, sports, music, street entertainment and exhibits on Killarney's history, heritage, folklore, scenic wonders and more. Information: Jerry O'Grady, Killarney 250 Ltd, Beech Road, tel. 36622 or www.killarney250.com. (17 March 2004 to 31 October 2005)

KILLARNEY TOWN WALKING TOUR

Duration: 2 hours plus stops

Start your tour at the **Railway Station** on the eastern edge of the town. The rail depot is one of Killarney's oldest buildings. Dating back to 1853 and made of local stone, it was built as the terminus for the Killarney Junction Railway. It was the first railway company in Ireland to own and operate its own hotel, **The Great Southern**, which opened in 1854 as the Killarney Railway Hotel. Step into the hotel and sample some of its nineteenth-century atmosphere, particularly in the grand lobby with its marble columns, ornate ceilings, and warming open fireplace.

From the grounds of the Great Southern, turn left onto **East Avenue Road**. On the right is Killarney's only purpose-built museum, the **Museum of Irish Transport** (tel. 32638). An ideal place for a rainy day, this museum presents a unique collection of Irish veteran, vintage and classic cars, as well as bicycles, motorcycles, carriages and fire engines. The exhibits include the rarest car in the world – a 1907 Silver Stream, the only model ever built; a 1910 car driven by William Butler Yeats; and a DeLorean. The walls are lined with early motoring and cycling periodicals and licence plates from all over the world. Open daily, April–October. Admission: €

Return to East Avenue Road, and coming up on the right is **Brewery Lane**, one of Killarney's many colourful and often still-cobbled eighteenth- and nineteenth-century laneways. As its name implies, it was the site of at least one brewery over 100 years ago. The locals say that hops continued to grow all along the wall until a few years ago. This lane also earned fame in 1936 as the setting for a locally produced film, *The Dawn*.

Continue towards town and look to the left. At this juncture, **Kenmare Place**, intersected by **Muckross Road**, is one of the town's main jaunting-car stations. During all daylight hours, there is usually a fleet of horse-driven jaunting cars assembled here, at the ready to take tourists on trips around the National Park area. The 'jarveys' (drivers) can be a little aggressive in soliciting business, but will always accept a polite 'No, thank you', if you wish to walk by and continue on your way.

Next on the right is the town's prime historical landmark, **St Mary's Church**, Church Place (tel. 31832). This building is revered not for what it is, but where it is. Standing on the site of the original *Cill Áirne* (the church of the sloe woods), this small Church of Ireland edifice is the latest of a number of churches built on this hallowed ground since the ninth century. This neo-Gothic structure, which dates back to 1870, has an interior that includes a nineteenth-century organ and a mural commemorating Rev. Arthur Hyde, vicar of Killarney in 1808 and great-grandfather of the first President of Ireland, Douglas Hyde. Open Sundays and other days according to season (check the sign at entrance). Admission: free

Opposite the church is the **Town Hall**, seat of the Urban Council. Although the building itself is not very notable, there is an old stone-covered well at the rear. For many years, this 'holy well' was a centre of local devotion, particularly because it was so near to the church. The name of the street now becomes Main Street.

Continue on **Main Street** for one block, passing a variety of shops and fast-food eateries, to the intersection of New and High streets. This is the centre of town, known as **Market Cross**. Many different kinds of market were originally held here, selling everything from butter to turf. On the right is the **Old Town Hall**, a red-brick building erected by Lord Kenmare with bricks left over from his mansion.

Take a left and walk down **New Street**, Killarney's youngest thoroughfare, as its name implies. On the left is the post office and the entrance to **Bridewell Lane**, considered Killarney's most beautiful lane, and the only lane where all of the houses are still occupied. The focal point is the **Frank Lewis Gallery**, 6 Bridewell Lane (tel. 34843). Set in a restored artisan's dwelling, this gallery presents an ever-changing display of paintings, photographs and sculptures by leading and emerging Irish artists. Open Monday–Saturday. Admission: free

Return to New Street and continue in a westward direction to the end of the street to see **St Mary's Cathedral**, Cathedral Place (tel. 31014). This is Killarney town's centrepiece, considered as one of the most beautiful Gothic-revival cathedrals in Europe. Built of limestone and designed by the noted architect Augustus Pugin, the building is cruciform in shape. Although construction started in 1842, it was interrupted by the Great Famine, and the building was used as a hospital during the famine years. A great redwood tree near the western doorway marks a children's mass famine grave. Eventually completed in 1855, the cathedral is officially known as the Catholic Church of St Mary of the Assumption. Highlights include a giant spire reaching almost 87 metres (285 feet) high, which was added in 1912; lovely rose windows over the north and south transepts; and other stained-glass windows that tell stories from the Bible and illustrate the lives of Irish saints. Open daily. Admission: free

Directly opposite the cathedral, across the River Deenagh, is the entrance to the **Knockreer Estate**, Cathedral Place (tel. 31440), an easily accessible part of the National Park grounds and ideal for long nature walks. Once part of Lord Kenmare's home, the estate has a turn-of-the-century house, now used as a field-study centre (not open to the public), a pathway along the River Deenagh, and gardens with 200-year-old trees and flowering shrubs. Opened to the public relatively recently (1986), this stretch of parkland offers lovely views of Killarney's Lower Lake. Open daily. Admission: free

Returning to Cathedral Place, follow **Port Road** north for one long block along the extensive cathedral grounds to **New Road**, lined with lovely lime trees, and make a right. This area is known as Killarney's educational district, as it is the home of St Brendan's College, Killarney Community College, Presentation Monastery and Mercy Convent Schools. Take a right at **Bishop's Path** to see the bishop's house and more schools, including the Presentation Convent which dates from 1793, and was the hub of Killarney's lace-industry for many years. *Note*:

These buildings, not open to the public, can be viewed only from the outside.

Continue on New Road for one block. To the right is **St Mary's Road**, also known as St Mary's Terrace, the setting for a row of houses with colourful gardens, known as the Castlerosse Cottages. These houses, originally built by Lord Kenmare for the workers on his estate, have been well preserved and enlarged by the current owners.

Continue on New Road to the traffic lights and turn right onto **High Street**, one of Killarney's busiest commercial thoroughfares, with a variety of shops, many of which have fine examples of scroll-work fascias and late ninth-century traditional carvings. High Street also has eleven laneways, the greatest number of any Killarney street – Dodd's, Pawn Office, Barry's, Fleming's, Bower's, Brasby's, Huggard's, Ball Alley, Duckett's, Hogan's and New Market. Many are named after sub-landlords who received use of the lanes from Lord Kenmare. Ball Alley Lane was the local site for handball games.

High Street leads back into Main Street. Continue for one block and then make a left onto **Plunkett Street**, originally known as Henn Street, the narrowest street in town. Take a sharp left to see some more of the town's original commercial lanes, with names ranging from Old Market Lane to Glebe Place. They were the early settings for the local post office and the shops of craftsmen, such as cart-makers, bakers, harness-makers, coopers, flour and grain merchants, and tweed suppliers. The old Milk Market was also held here.

Plunkett Street leads to **College Street**, so named because it was the site for colleges run by the Franciscans, Mercy Sisters and Presentation Brothers, operated at one time or another up until 1850. At the far end of the street, on the right, is the local **Court House**.

As College Street merges into Park Road, this area is known as **Fair Hill**. It was originally known as Martyr's Hill, because it was a place of execution in the seventeenth century. On the left side of the street is the **Franciscan Church and Friary** (tel. 31066). This church is relatively new, dating back only to 1860, although the tradition of Franciscan service in Killarney goes back to 1440 when friars made a foundation at Muckross Abbey. Officially known as the Church of the Most Holy Trinity, this building is attributed to Eugene Pugin, eldest son of the famous Augustus Pugin who designed the cathedral. It is simple in style, with a lofty arched ceiling and oak panelling. Highlights of the interior include a beautifully hand-carved wooden altar and a stained-glass window over the entrance, designed by the famous Irish artist Harry Clarke. Open daily. Admission: free

Opposite the church grounds, overlooking the left side of the road, is a local landmark – the statue known as the **Spéir Bean** (spirit woman), representing the spirit of Ireland. It commemorates the four Kerry poets of the Irish language, Pierce Ferriter (1616–53), Geoffrey O'Donoghue (1620–90), Aogán Ó Raithile (1670–1726), and Eoghan Rua Ó Súilleabháin (1748–84).

Directly to the left are the Killarney Outlet Centre and the Railway Station, where this tour began. At this point you might like to get your car or take local transport to see some of the surrounding areas of the Killarney National Park and beyond.

PAT'S PICKS

RESTAURANTS

BRICÍN, 26 High Street (tel. 34902). Named after a local bridge, this rustic enclave is housed in one of the town's oldest buildings, dating back to the 1830s, with original stone walls, pine furniture and turf fireplaces. It is a combination restaurant-craft shop, inviting guests to dine amid a creative selection of Celtic art work, pottery and books. The menu presents traditional Kerry boxty dishes (potato pancakes with various meat and vegetable fillings), as well as a variety of seafood choices, Irish stew and a house speciality of chicken Bricín (breast of chicken in red currant and raspberry sauce). Open for dinner, Monday–Saturday, March–November.

GABY'S, 27 High Street (tel. 32519). When it comes to seafood, this nautically themed restaurant is the benchmark, and well worth a big splurge, particularly for the Kerry shellfish platter, a cornucopia of fresh prawns, scallops, mussels, lobster and oysters, or the house speciality of 'Lobster Gaby', served grilled in a sauce of cognac, wine, cream and spices. Open for dinner, Monday–Saturday, except last week of December and mid-February to mid-March.

OLD PRESBYTERY, Cathedral Place (tel. 30555). Sitting opposite Killarney's cathedral, this elegant three-storey Georgian house with a unique copper roof was once a home for the clergy. Today it is a restaurant in the quieter part of town, with seating on two floors. The cuisine combines local Irish ingredients and international recipes, along with home-baked breads. There is soft live piano music in the background. Open for dinner, Wednesday–Sunday.

PANIS ANGELICUS, 15 New Street (tel. 39648). This shop-front restaurant-bakery takes its name from an old Latin phrase meaning 'bread of angels'. And it is well named. The menu offers a tempting selection of freshly baked breads, cakes and pastries, with all styles of international coffees and teas, as well as creative salads, soups, sandwiches, meat

and seafood dishes, Irish farm cheeses and speciality potato cakes, all served throughout the day. Open for lunch and snacks, daily; and for dinner, Thursday–Monday in May–September.

ROBERTINO'S, 9 High Street (tel. 34966). Operatic arias and a Mediterranean-style décor convey the ambience of Italy at this mid-town restaurant with five separate dining areas. The menu features a variety of pastas plus veal saltimbocca, roast rib of lamb flamed in Marsala wine sauce, and local seafood. Open for dinner and lunch, daily, May– September.

PUBS

BUCKLEY'S, 2 College Street (tel. 31037). Established in 1926, this is Killarney's sports bar, a hang-out for followers of the Kerry football team. As might be expected, the décor has a decidedly sporting theme – Kerry football trophies, uniforms and team photos. Irish traditional music is often on tap on summer evenings.

THE DANNY MANN TRADITIONAL PUB, Eviston House Hotel, New Street (tel. 31640). For more than 30 years, this large pub in the heart of town, run by the Eviston family, has gained a reputation as a gathering spot for traditional Irish ballad music sessions. Different bands play every night of the week in summer and at weekends during the rest of the year.

THE LAURELS, Main Street at Market Cross (tel. 31149). Founded by Thado O'Leary in 1917 and now carried on by the third generation of O'Learys, this pub displays lots of memorabilia, including a rare collection of old water jugs that has attracted visitors from around the world. This place is best known, however, for its evening sessions of music, ranging from Irish ballads and step-dancing to a collection of international favourite tunes, as well as sing-alongs.

MURPHY'S BAR, College Street (tel. 31294). A Killarney favourite since 1955, this pub displays information about the Murphy surname, originally known as Ó Murchadha from the sixth century and later anglicised to O'Murchoe. The current owner, Seán Murphy, is a grandson of the famous cyclist, Pat Murphy, whose prize trophy, the 'Macgillicuddy Cup', won in 1899, is proudly displayed in the bar. Over the years, this pub has won several awards and has built up a strong following for its traditional music sessions on summer nights.

JIMMY O'BRIEN, College Street (tel. 31786). Small and simply furnished, this cosy pub is a haven for those who eschew the touristy, and instead seek a quiet drink in an 'Old Killarney' atmosphere. Amble in and chat with the ever-present publican of the same name, or listen in as truly 'spontaneous' Irish traditional music sessions invariably erupt.

DIGRESSIONS

AROUND TOWN IN THE TRADITIONAL WAY: The number-one way to see Killarney is by traditional horse-drawn jaunting car (an open side-cart), with the driver (known as a 'jarvey') providing a commentary of folklore, humour and occasional song as well. Jaunting-car rides are available from various points throughout Killarney, such as Kenmare Place or in front of major hotels. No reservations are needed – first come, first served. Information: Tangney Tours (tel. 33358 or mobile 087 253 2770; and Deros Tours, Main Street (tel. 31251 or www.derostours.com).

BUSSING BY: Not all tours of Killarney are on foot or via horse-drawn jaunting car. Several companies operate two- or three-hour narrated bus tours of the town area, year-round, depending on demand; departure times vary. Reservations are recommended (call one day in advance). Information: Deros Tours, Main Street (tel. 31251 or www.derostours.com); Corcoran's Tours, 8 College Street (tel. 36666); and Gap of Dunloe Tours, 7 High Street (tel. 30200 or www.castlelough-tours.com).

CASTLE CAPER: Step back in time and explore Ross Castle, a fifteenth-century fortress less than 3.5 km (2 miles) from the centre of town. Once the home of the earl of Kenmare who built Killarney town, this castle was probably built by one of the chieftains of the local O'Donoghue clan.

Overlooking the Lower Lake, it is surrounded by a fortified bawn, with curtain walls and two circular towers. The interior, enhanced with fifteenth- and seventeenth-century furniture, has a stone staircase leading to upper chambers including a minstrels' gallery. Climb to the parapets to enjoy sweeping views of the lake and surrounding countryside. Open daily, May– September; Tuesday– Sunday in October. Information: Ross Castle, Ross Road, off Kenmare Road (tel. 35851 or www.heritageireland.ie).

KILLARNEY LAKES CRUISES: Spend an hour cruising around Killarney's Lower Lake on board a glass-enclosed boat. The one-hour cruises include a live commentary and close-up views of special sights, including Innisfallen, an 8.5-hectare (21-acre) island floating 1.6 km (1 mile) from shore in the midst of the lake. St Fallen founded a monastery here in the seventh century and it flourished for 1,000 years. From 950 to 1320, the *Annals of Innisfallen*, a chronicle of early world and Irish history, was written in Irish and in Latin on this island by a succession of 39 monastic scribes. Cruises depart from the Ross Castle pier daily, April–October, or according to demand; schedules vary. Information: *Lily of Killarney* Watercoach, Deros Tours, Main Street (tel. 31251 or www.derostours.com); or MV *Pride of the Lakes* Waterbus, Destination Killarney, East Avenue Road (tel. 32638 or www.gleneaglehotel.com/lakes.htm).

16: Killarney National Park

'How can you buy Killarney?' That's the question the old song asks. The answer is simple. You can't. In fact, no one can buy Killarney – it belongs to the people of Ireland, as the country's leading national park. Fortunately, the owners are very willing to share their treasure with visitors.

The Killarney National Park consists of a 65 km-square (25 miles-square) area of unspoiled and unpolluted lakes, mountains and woodlands – a 'green zone' in the truest sense. The Lakes of Killarney, as the district is collectively known, are carefully protected by the government, which means no billboards, no fast-food chains, no rows of condominiums, no commercial developments, and no motorised traffic within parklands and along the lakeshores.

The layout includes three major lakes, surrounded by Ireland's highest range of mountains, Macgillicuddy's Reeks. Nearest the town is the Lower Lake (also known as Lough Leane, from the Irish for 'lake of learning'). It is the largest lake (2,023 hectares/5,000 acres) with about 30 islands. On the eastern shore of the Lower Lake are two popular historic sites, Muckross Abbey and Ross Castle.

The wooded peninsula of Muckross separates the Lower Lake from the Middle Lake (275 hectares/680 acres), sometimes called Muckross Lake. On the eastern shore are Muckross House and Torc Waterfall.

A narrow strait known as the Long Range leads to the third lake, the slender and finger-like Upper Lake (174 hectares/430 acres) which is almost embedded in the mountains. The Upper Lake is the smallest lake but often deemed the most beautiful of the Killarney trio. In addition, there are many smaller lakes in the folds of the mountains, as well as numerous waterfalls and cascades.

Plant and animal life enhances Killarney's landscape. The woodlands thrive with a luxuriant medley of oak, birch, yew, ash, cedar and juniper. The smaller flora include holly, fern, rhododendron and arbutus (the strawberry tree), Killarney's native plant. Red deer, black Kerry cattle and other animals roam freely, while over 100 species of bird fly in this wide natural expanse. For the human species, there are at least four signposted nature trails and countless garden-edged paths and walks. Quite simply, this park really is a paradise.

(See map p.162)

Travel Information Office

KILLARNEY TOURIST OFFICE, Beech Road, Killarney (tel. 064 31633) off New Street. Open all year.

TRAVEL INFORMATION ONLINE:
www.corkkerry.ie,
www.killarneywelcomes.com and
http://homepage.eircom.net/~knp
(Killarney National Park)

TELEPHONE AREA CODE:
The telephone area code for all numbers in Killarney town is 064 unless indicated otherwise.

MAJOR EVENTS

FÉILE CHULTÚIR CHIARRAÍ/KERRY'S FESTIVAL OF CULTURE – Held at Muckross Traditional Farms within the national park, this annual spring event is geared to participation by children, with vintage coach rides, farm tours and demonstrations of baking over an open fire, butter-making, harnessing horses and traditional music workshops.
Information: Kerry's Festival of Culture, Muckross House, tel. 31440 or
http://homepage.eircom.net/~knp.
(Mid-April or May)

KILLARNEY 250 – Although this festival has its headquarters in the town (see Killarney, Chapter 15), many events will take place in the national park, including walking trails, garden tours, wildlife walks and talks, boat trips, balloon rides and more. Information: Jerry O'Grady, Killarney 250 Ltd, Beech Road, tel. 36622 or www.killarney250.com.
(March 2004–October 2005)

KILLARNEY NATIONAL PARK DRIVING AND WALKING TOUR

Duration: half-day or full-day

Access to Killarney National Park is available via several entrances along the Killarney–Kenmare Road (N71). In every case, you'll have to park your car and do your touring on foot, bicycle or via horse-drawn jaunting car. No motorised traffic is allowed within the park grounds and along the lakes.

Start a tour at the entrance to the Friary of Muckross, popularly known as **Muckross Abbey**, Muckross Estate (tel. 33926), a well-preserved ruin on the shores of the **Lower Lake**. Founded in the 1440s by the Franciscans, this abbey flourished for more than 300 years, until it was suppressed by the Penal Laws. The remains include a church with a wide belfry tower and an intact vaulted cloister, with an arched arcade, surrounding a square courtyard. The centrepiece of the courtyard is an ancient yew tree, said to be as old as the abbey. Through the years, the abbey property and grounds have served as a burial place for local chieftains and also for four of Kerry's famous Gaelic-language poets – Pierce Ferriter (1616–53), Geoffrey O'Donoghue

(1620–90), Aogán Ó Raithile (1670–1726) and Eoghan Rua Ó Súilleabháin (1748–84) – who are also commemorated by the statue in Killarney town. A visit to the abbey is a favourite stop on the jaunting-car route. Open daily. A guide is on duty from June to September. Admission: free

Return to the main road and continue for 2.5 km (1.5 miles) to the entrance to one of the premier focal points of the lakeshore on the **Middle Lake – Muckross House & Gardens** (tel. 31440). Often called 'the jewel of Killarney', this splendid 20-room Victorian mansion, built in 1843, provides a glimpse of the lifestyle of the landed gentry of Killarney in the nineteenth century.

The house features elaborate architecture, from mullioned and stepped windows to its 62 chimneys, and is decorated with locally made period furniture and needlework, as well as imported treasures such as Oriental screens, Venetian mirrors, Chippendale chairs, curtains woven in Brussels, and Turkish carpets. The display areas also comprise a folk museum, with exhibits of County Kerry folk life, history, cartography, geography, geology, flora and fauna. In addition, the well-manicured gardens outside are renowned worldwide for their collections of azalea and rhododendron. Open daily. Admission: €€

Next to the house is the **Killarney National Park Visitor Centre** (tel. 31440), a separate building that serves as an orientation point for exploring the surrounding parklands. There are continuous showings of an audiovisual, *Mountain, Wood, Water*, and exhibits, visual histories and scale models on the trees, birds and wildlife. Open daily, mid-March–October. Admission: free

Twenty-eight hectares (70 acres) of adjacent land are devoted to the **Muckross Traditional Open Farms** (tel. 31440). This is a real working farm, although different from many of the other modern 'open farms' in Ireland today. On this site, farming is done in the style of the 1930s, with horse-drawn equipment and pre-electrification methods. Visitors can watch sowing and harvesting or potato-picking and haymaking, depending on the season. Farmers tend the livestock, while the blacksmith, carpenter and wheelwright ply their trades. It is necessary to walk from farmhouse to farmhouse, and among the various cottages, outbuildings, and workshops, along a 1.6-km (1-mile) long boreen (unsurfaced country road) that has some steep hills, so this tour is best done in good weather by those with a lot of time, stamina and energy. Touring requires several hours, but it is well worth taking the time to explore, especially for families. (*Note:* for seniors or the physically challenged, vintage coach transfers are provided from building to building). Open daily, May–September; Saturday–Sunday in mid-March–April and October. Admission: €€

Returning to the main Kenmare road, continue for another 1.6 km (1 mile) to the signs for **Torc Waterfall**, one of the area's natural wonders and among the finest waterfalls in Ireland. Surrounded by tall shady trees, a footpath winds its way up beside 18 metres (60 feet) of cascading waters, affording magnificent views of the lake district from the upper end. The area is well signposted and has its own car park.

Go back to the main Kenmare road. On the right, along the lakeshore, is an area known as the **Meeting of the Waters**, the point where the waters of the Upper Lake meet those of the other two lakes, the Middle (or Muckross) Lake and the Lower Lake (Lough Leane). It is spanned by the **Old Weir Bridge**, known for its swirling rapids.

Continue for another 11 km (7 miles) to an area known as **Ladies' View**. From this high vantage point, all three lakes can be viewed in one sweeping panorama, as well as part of the **Macgillicuddy's Reeks**, including **Carrantuohill**, Ireland's highest mountain. The area derives its curious name from the time of Queen Victoria's visit to Killarney over 140 years ago. It is said that, as the royal entourage approached Killarney, the queen's ladies-in-waiting called out for the coaches to stop so that they could admire the view. Hence it has since been known as Ladies' View. Today it is still an ideal spot for a picture.

From this point, retrace your steps through Killarney to take in more of the lakeland vistas. After passing through the town, follow the signs for the Killorglin road for 6.5 km (4 miles) to Beaufort, and then take a left at the sign for the **Gap of Dunloe**. A natural mountain wonder, this 11-km (7-mile) glacial breach valley requires the better part of a day to explore fully (see 'Digressions' below). The route passes beside **Black Lake**, otherwise known as Serpent Lake, where St Patrick is reputed to have drowned the last snake in Ireland. Then it's on via **Cushvalley** and **Augur Lakes**, with the **Tomies** and **Purple Mountains** on the left and **Macgillicuddy's Reeks** on the right. The trail ends on the shore of the Upper Lake at **Gearhameen**. Here you can walk back to Killarney town, turn around and walk back up the Gap, or take a boat on the Upper Lake, through the Long Range to the Meeting of the Waters under **Brickeen Bridge**. Here you shoot the rapids and go through Lough Leane to **Ross Castle**, and back to Killarney.

From the Gap, return to the Killorglin road and take the first turn to Aghadoe. Continue for 2.5 km (1.5 miles) to **Aghadoe Hill**, at 122 metres (400 feet), one of the highest points in the Killarney lake district, affording one of most sweeping views of the whole area, with a panorama of mountains and lakes. From here, it is 4 km (2.5 miles) back to Killarney town.

RESTAURANTS

FREDRICK'S, Aghadoe Heights Hotel, Aghadoe (tel. 31766). For sweeping views of the Killarney lakes, mountains and golf courses, this upstairs restaurant cannot be beaten. It offers a wide array of classic French dishes using Irish ingredients, such as Châteaubriand, Kerry rack of lamb, and local seafood. A pianist adds to the atmosphere at dinner but the mainstay is always the incomparable view. Open for dinner, daily; and lunch on Sunday.

THE GARDEN, Mucros Craft Centre, Muckross House (tel. 31440). Overlooking a Victorian walled garden and the Torc and Mangerton Mountains, this restaurant offers a huge buffet selection, ranging from snacks, soups and salads to creative hot entrées and freshly baked pastries and cakes. Vegetarian, vegan and gluten-free options are also available. Seating is available in a glass conservatory or on an outdoor deck, and the adjacent shop presents the best of Kerry crafts, including a working pottery and weaving centre. Open for snacks and lunch, daily.

PANORAMA RESTAURANT, Hotel Europe, Fossa (tel. 31900). Aptly named, this large hotel restaurant enjoys one of the best locations in Killarney, overlooking the lakes and mountains in an uninterrupted panorama. The menu offers the best of local Kerry lamb and seafood, with a German/European twist (such as Westphalian ham, with rosti potatoes or freshly made coleslaw). It's not cheap but the view is priceless. Open for lunch and dinner, daily, mid-March to mid-November.

PUBS

KATE KEARNEY'S COTTAGE, Beaufort (tel. 44146). Perched at the entrance to the Gap of Dunloe, this remote old pub is named for a local resident who used to run a speakeasy selling *poitín* (the local potato brew) on this site. With over 150 years of history, it has a lot of atmosphere and local memorabilia. Snacks are served throughout the day, and Irish coffee is a speciality. Traditional music is on tap from May through September on Wednesday, Friday and Saturday.

DIY GOLF PUB, Killeen House Hotel, Aghadoe (tel. 31711). Golfer or not, don't miss this pub at a small hotel overlooking the lakes. Its walls are decorated with thousands of golf balls from all over the world – and the barman actually accepts golf balls as legal tender! Service can be minimal at times, so guests follow the honour system and are actively encouraged to DIY (do it yourself). Open April–October.

MOLLY DARCY'S PUB, Muckross Road, Muckross Village (tel. 31938). Situated across from the entrance to Muckross House, this traditional thatched-roof pub offers a genuine country atmosphere, with stone walls, oak-beamed ceilings, open fireplaces, alcoves, snugs and local memorabilia. In the summer, there is musical entertainment, Wednesday–Sunday.

DIGRESSIONS

GUIDED WALKS: With a profusion of trees, trails, flowers and lakeside scenery, the Killarney National Park is ideal for walking. But many people ask where to start and where to go. To get your bearings and an overview of all the walking opportunities, take a two-hour guided walk. The pace is leisurely, suitable for all ages. Tours are conducted daily at 11am, May–September, and at other times by appointment. Departures are from the Shell petrol station on New Street, Killarney (opposite St Mary's Cathedral). Information: Killarney Safari (tel. 33471).

JAUNTING AROUND: Although you can easily drive from one attraction to the next in Killarney National Park, many people prefer to move around in the old fashioned way – by traditional horse-drawn jaunting car (an open side-cart). The jaunting cars, which travel on designated off-road paths, are to Killarney what cable cars are to San Francisco or subways to New York. The driver, known as a jarvey, is both a guide and storyteller. Jaunting-car rides are available from various points throughout Killarney and within the park, such as Muckross House, Muckross Abbey and Ross Castle. Information: Tangney Tours (tel. 33358 or mobile 087 253 2770; and Deros Tours, Main Street (tel. 31251 or www.derostours.com).

NATURE TRAILS: Rain or shine, step into nature at its best. Walk amid the wildflowers, beside the lakes, under leafy old trees, and in the freshest of air in the Killarney National Park. Four signposted nature trails are provided: Old Boathouse Trail, less than 1.6 km (1 mile), 45 minutes in duration, begins at a nineteenth-century boathouse below Muckross Gardens; Arthur Young Nature Trail, 4.8 km (3 miles), 1.5 hours in duration, begins and ends near Muckross House; Blue Pool Nature Trail, 2.5 km (1.5 miles), one hour in duration, begins at Muckross village and meanders to a secluded horseshoe-shaped lake; Cloghereen Nature Trail, the first nature trail in Ireland for the visually impaired, marked with a guide rope, with emphasis on touch, sound and scent. Information: Killarney National Park Visitor Centre (tel. 31440 or http://homepage.eircom.net/~knp).

THROUGH THE GAP AND OVER THE LAKES:
The legendary Gap of Dunloe excursion
is unique to Killarney. It is an all-day
outdoor activity trip, starting with an
11-km (7-mile) trek through the scenic
glacial valley known as the 'Gap of
Dunloe'. No cars or buses are allowed –
travel by walking, cycling, riding on a
pony or taking a seat as a passenger in a
horse-drawn cart. The route passes by
three lakes (Black, Cushvalley and
Augur) and three sets of mountains
(Purples, Tomies and Macgillicuddy's
Reeks). The trail ends at Lord Brandon's
Cottage where a picnic lunch is
customary, followed by a row-boat trip
across the three lakes of Killarney. It's
an exhilarating way to see Killarney,
requiring six to seven hours. Operates
daily, April–October. Information: Gap
of Dunloe Tours, 7 High Street (tel.
30200 or www.castlelough-tours.com);
Deros Tours, Main Street (tel. 31251 or
www.derostours.com); Corcoran's
Tours, 8 College Street (tel. 36666);
O'Donoghue Brothers, Muckross Road
(tel. 31068); and O'Connor's Tours,
Ardross, Ross Road (tel. 31052).

17: The Ring of Kerry

Extending westward from Killarney, the Iveragh Peninsula – or the Ring of Kerry as it is commonly known – is assuredly Ireland's most popular scenic drive. It is an ever-changing panorama of sea coast, bogland, mountain and lakeside vistas. Not only does the Ring start with the glistening waters of the Lakes of Killarney and reach out beyond boglands and beaches to the splashing surf of the Atlantic, but it also includes the profiles of Ireland's four highest mountains – Carrantuohill, rising to a height of 1,040 metres (3,414 feet), followed by Beenkeragh (1,010 metres/3,314 feet), Caher (975 metres/3,200 feet), and an unnamed peak southwest of Carrantuohill (957 metres/3,141 feet).

The Ring of Kerry drive can be undertaken in either direction, but the normal route is in a counter-clockwise pattern. The duration can be anything from four or five hours to a full day, depending on how many stops you make for exploring heritage centres and attractions, taking pictures and videos, visiting pubs and cafés, chatting with the local farmers and turf-cutters, beach-walking, hill-climbing, shopping and craft-hunting, and detouring down the side roads. Plan to cover 32 km (20 miles) an hour or less. This is a drive to be relished, not rushed.

Although a little rain or passing showers should not deter you from doing this drive, it is best not to set out in heavy sea mist, fog or heavy rain. If the clouds are moving, however, that usually means that a good day on the Ring will follow.

Unlike in some parts of Ireland, there are no great museums or man-made landmarks along the Ring of Kerry, although there are heritage centres that are well worth visiting. Primarily, the Ring is a continuous 177-km (110-mile) circuit of natural wonders and views. The drive itself is the attraction.

FAST FACTS

Travel Information Offices

KILLARNEY TOURIST OFFICE, Beech Road, Killarney (tel. 064 31633). Open all year.

CAHIRCIVEEN TOURIST OFFICE, Church Street, Cahirciveen (tel. 066 947 2589). Open June–September.

KENMARE TOURIST OFFICE, The Square, Kenmare (tel. 064 41233). Open April–September.

WATERVILLE TOURIST OFFICE, Town Centre, Waterville (tel. 066 947 9474). Open May–September.

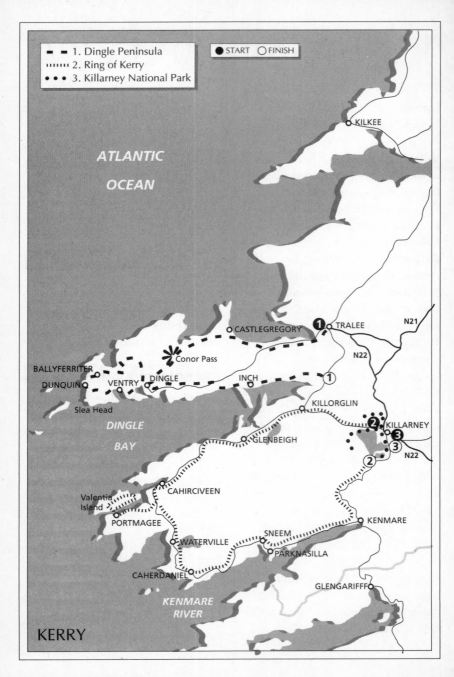

TRAVEL INFORMATION ONLINE:
www.corkkerry.ie

TELEPHONE AREA CODES:
There are two area codes used for telephone numbers on the Ring of Kerry – 064 and 066 – so each number that follows includes its area code.

MAJOR EVENTS

KENMARE WALKING FESTIVAL – Drawing thousands of people together from all over the world, this annual event invites participants to walk side-by-side in the town of Kenmare and its many scenic surroundings, including the Kerry hills and Carrantuohill, Ireland's highest mountain. Information: John Skilling, Kerry Walking Festival, tel. 064 42639 or www.kenmare.com/walking. (Last week of May)

CAHIRCIVEEN CELTIC MUSIC FESTIVAL – Celtic music in all its forms is heard throughout this bustling town on the western end of the Ring of Kerry – from traditional concerts, sessions, set dancing, busking competitions and a street pageant, to pipe-band playing. There are also art and music workshops, guided walks through the countryside, and a treasure trail. Information: Shane O'Driscoll, Cahirciveen Celtic Music Festival, Church Street, tel. 087 222 4166 or www.celticmusicfestival.com. (First weekend of August)

PUCK FAIR – One of Ireland's oldest festivals, this annual three-day summer gathering at Killorglin includes traditional cattle and horse fairs, as well as the coronation and dethronement of a goat. There is also an array of free family entertainment ranging from busking, parades, fireworks and concerts, to morris dancing and Irish dancing. Information: Puck Fair Committee, tel. 066 976 2366 or www.puckfair.ie. (Second week of August)

RING OF KERRY DRIVING TOUR

Duration: 5 hours or more, plus stops

The Ring of Kerry is splendidly signposted. You can set out from Killarney or Kenmare in either direction, and follow 'The Ring of Kerry' signs without ever having to know the names of the towns, or distances. A map adds to the enjoyment, but it is not necessary. The routing is well marked.

Assuming that you are setting out in a counter-clockwise direction from Killarney, you depart via the main N72 road for 24 km (15 miles) as you head out onto the Ring. This route presents lovely views of the **River Laune** to the left, as you approach the small marketing town of **Killorglin**, a name derived from the Irish *Cill Orglan*, meaning 'Orgla's church'. No evidence is left of the namesake, but instead this town is celebrated today as the home of the annual **Puck Fair**, a mid-August horse, sheep and cattle fair that is presided over by a wild goat (see Major Events). The animal, captured from the nearby mountains by the local folk, is enshrined in the centre of town as a catalyst for three days of festivities. Depart Killorglin and link up with the main Ring of Kerry road (N70).

As you drive westward on the N70, the road soon presents vistas of **Dingle Bay** on the right and **Carrantuohill**, Ireland's tallest mountain (1381.5 metres/3,414 feet) on the left. Vast open expanses of open bog land also come into view. Bogs, which cover much of the Kerry landscape, are an important source of fuel for the farm families who live on the Ring. Local residents spend much of the summer digging up pieces of 'turf' (dried brick-like wedges of peat), to burn in their fireplaces for warmth. These boglands, formed thousands of years ago, consist mainly of decayed trees and foliage. Because of uneven surfaces, the roads built over the bogs tend to be bumpy and hard on cars. Take caution when driving over bog roads.

In addition to the bogs, the Ring of Kerry landscape winds around cliffs and the edges of mountains, with nothing but the sea below. The countryside is also dotted with the remains of many abandoned cottages, dating from the famine years of the mid-1840s, when the Irish potato crop failed and millions of people either starved or were forced to emigrate. This peninsula lost three-quarters of its population during the famine and emigration era.

One of the best ways to revisit what the Ring of Kerry was like in the nineteenth century is at the **Kerry Bog Village Museum**, Ballycleave, Glenbeigh (tel. 066 976 9184) – a cluster of thatched buildings, including a turf-cutter's house, working forge, labourer's cottage and thatcher's home, plus a stable, dairy house and hen house. Visitors are encouraged to walk through the interiors of each building to see authentic furnishings, household implements and farming tools. Turf fires burn in the small hearths, and piles of turf are stacked at the entrance to the village. Open daily, March–November. Admission: €

The road leads next to the village of **Glenbeigh**, a tree-lined fishing resort, with a lovely dune-filled beach called **Rossbeigh Strand**. The name Glenbeigh comes from the Irish language, *Gleann Beithe*, meaning 'the glen of the birch trees'. You may wish to stop here or continue for 27 km (17 miles) more, via the wide sweep through the mountains and along the sea's edge. On clear days, the horizon to the right reveals spectacular views of the **Dingle Peninsula** and the **Blasket Islands**.

The road now merges with the main street of **Cahirciveen**, also spelt Cahersiveen. Either way, it is derived from the Irish words *Cathair Saidhbhín*, meaning 'little Sabina (Sadhbh/Sive)'s dwelling place'. Not too much is known about

Sabina or her fort today, but the town is particularly colourful and well-kept, consisting of one long main street.

Off the coast of Cahirciveen, you can often see the **Skellig Islands** – Skellig Michael and Small (or Little) Skellig – sitting almost 13 km (8 miles) out in the Atlantic Ocean. In the sixth century, St Fionan founded a monastery on these rocky outposts. Considered among the best-preserved early Christian sites of its kind in the world, the Skelligs contain six corbelled-stone beehive huts and two boat-shaped oratories, plus stone-built terraces, retaining walls and stairways. Today, the Skelligs are home to rare colonies of sea birds.

To learn more about these famous islands, take a slight detour to **Portmagee** and follow the signs over the bridge to the **Skellig Heritage Centre**, Valentia Island (tel. 066 947 6306).

With a stark stone façade framed by grassy mounds, this modern interpretative centre blends in with the local landscape. Through a series of interactive displays and a sixteen-minute audiovisual, it conveys 'The Skellig Experience' – what life has been like on the Skellig Islands through the ages, from scholarly pursuits at St Fionan's sixth-century cliff-top monastery until today when the islands serve as a habitat for seabirds. In addition, exhibits cover underwater life around the islands and the history of local lighthouses and their crews. For a supplementary fee, visitors can take a 90-minute boat cruise from Valentia to circle the rocks and get close-up views – a chance to see, hear and smell the Skellig world as it sits peacefully in the midst of the roaring seas (see 'Digressions' below). Open daily, April–November. Admission: €

While here, spend some time exploring **Valentia Island**, 11 km (7 miles) long, and one of the most westerly points of Europe. Connected to the mainland by a bridge at Portmagee, this island was the site of the first telegraph cable laid across the Atlantic in 1866. In addition, Valentia Harbour was infamous in the eighteenth and nineteenth centuries as a refuge for smugglers and privateers. It is said that US naval commander John Paul Jones, noted for his part in the American War of Independence, also often anchored here.

Returning to the main N70 road, it is almost 18 km (11 miles) to **Waterville**, a narrow strip of land on **Ballinskelligs Bay** between the Atlantic and Lough Currane. For many years, this town was a favourite summer hideaway for Charlie Chaplin who helped to popularise it as a beach, golfing and fishing resort.

After departing from Waterville, the road then passes through **Coomakista Pass**, the crest of which looks out onto beautiful views of the Kenmare river, and Scariff and the Deenish Islands. After travelling 11 km (7 miles), you will see signs pointing to the entrance of **Derrynane National Historic Park**, Caherdaniel (tel. 066 947 5113). Set on

121 hectares (300 acres) of wooded and dune-filled lands along Derrynane Bay, this is the ancestral home of Daniel O'Connell, lawyer, politician, statesman, and one of Ireland's major leaders of the nineteenth century, known as 'The Liberator'. With a unique façade of turreted slate and stone, the house is laid out as it was in O'Connell's time, including the family portraits and silver, and an assortment of Victorian furnishings. The most unique room is the chapel, complete with altar, confessional, pews, coloured-glass windows, and a variety of ecclesiastical vessels and vestments. A tour includes a 25-minute audiovisual profile of O'Connell, *Be You Perfectly Peaceable*. In addition, the coach house displays O'Connell's triumphal chariot, while the grounds include extensive gardens with rare plant collections, plus a ringfort and a variety of self-guided beach and nature trails. Open daily, May–September; Tuesday–Sunday in April and October; and Saturday–Sunday in November–March. Admission: €

A little over 1.6 km (1 mile) to the east is the hamlet of **Caherdaniel**. Although some people assume that it was named in honour of Daniel O'Connell, the Daniel in question is actually a much earlier one. The place name is derived from the Irish language *Cathair Dónal*, meaning 'Dónal (or Daniel)'s fort', and the fort of the same name is beside the road just under a kilometre (about half a mile) west of the village. Not too much is known about this old stone fort except that it was probably built by a man named Dónal as far back as 600BC.

A little beyond Caherdaniel are the sandy beaches of **Westcove** and **Castlecove**, and beyond these is the signposted left turn for **Staigue Fort**, a large circular stone structure, reputed to date back to 1000BC. Although little is certain about its origins, Staigue is one of the largest and best-preserved forts of its kind in Ireland, a fine example of dry-stone construction (no mortar is used). The area enclosed is a massive 27.5 metres (90 feet) in diameter, with walls as high as 5.5 metres (18 feet), a base that is almost 4 metres (13 feet) thick, and a set of steps up to what was once a rampart. The fort, which sits on private land, is accessible at the discretion of the owner. Open daily. Admission: €

Return to the Ring road and continue to the village of **Sneem**, a name derived from the Irish word *An tSnaidhm*, meaning 'the knot' or 'the juncture'. It is thought that Sneem earned this name because it sits at the head of an inlet where the Kenmare river meets the Sneem and Ardsheelhane rivers. Sneem is a colourful little hamlet with twin parklets and houses painted in vibrant shades of blue, pink, yellow, purple and orange, almost like a Mediterranean cluster. Because this area is a good fishing spot, the local church sports a salmon-shaped weather vane on its steeple. There is a sculpture park in town, featuring a collection of international works such as the *Peaceful Panda* (a white marble statue from China); *Metal Tree* (a stainless-steel sculpture from Israel); *Angry Christ* (from Singapore); and *The Goddess Isis* (from Egypt).

Continue in an eastward direction on the main road. The foliage becomes richer and more extensive, thanks to the warming waters and winds of the Gulf Stream. When you begin to see a profusion of palm trees and other subtropical vegetation, you'll know that you are in **Parknasilla**, one of Ireland's lushest resorts. The exotic-sounding place name is actually derived from the Irish language, *Páirc na Saileach*, meaning 'field of the willows'. It has long been a favoured resort of the rich and famous, with princely and regal, presidential and political visitors coming seeking sheltered seclusion. George Bernard Shaw is reputed to have written his play *St Joan* here. Take time to visit the **Great Southern Hotel**, nestled amid 121 hectares (300 acres) of lush foliage, palms, and flowering shrubs in one of the loveliest seascape settings in Ireland.

From Parknasilla, follow the main road, which runs on the north shore of the Kenmare river, for 22.5 km (14 miles) into **Kenmare**, the final town on the Ring of Kerry circuit, and by far the most captivating. The place name in the Irish language is *Neidín*, meaning 'little nest'.

Kenmare is indeed a little nest. Founded in 1760 by Sir William Petty, it is a well-maintained town amid lush foliage, nestled between the River Kenmare and the River Roughty. The town streets are laid out in an intriguing X-shaped pattern, with a central **Market Place** and **Fair Green**, a park for markets and fairs, in the heart of the town. In the mid-nineteenth century, Kenmare also became a hub of Irish lace-making, thanks to a local nun who set up a thriving industry by training local women in fine needlepoint work. Samples of Kenmare lace have been exhibited at the Victoria and Albert Museum in London and the National Gallery in Washington.

The many facets of Kenmare history and enterprise are portrayed graphically at the **Kenmare Heritage Centre**, The Square (tel. 064 41233), using a walk-through display, with individual cassette commentaries. The centre also includes an exhibit and demonstrations on the art of lace-making (upstairs). In addition, beautiful lace tablecloths, place settings and decorative items are on view and for sale. Open Monday–Saturday, April–September. Admission: free

From Kenmare, it is just 32 km (20 miles) back to Killarney, but the journey averages at least an hour. The route is particularly scenic, beginning with panoramas of wild heather, followed by winding mountain turns. The road swings northeast around **Peekeen Mountain**, and then the lake-filled vistas of Killarney come into view at **Moll's Gap**, a high look-out point. From the Gap, the road descends to **Ladies' View**, **Torc Waterfall** and **Muckross**, and the heart of the Killarney lake district.

RESTAURANTS

FIONAN'S KITCHEN, Skellig Heritage Centre, Valentia Island (tel. 066 947 6306). With a rustic décor of súgán chairs, pine tables and stone floors, this self-service eatery is an ideal spot for sandwiches, soups, salads, pastas, Irish stew and quiche, all enhanced by stunning floor-to-ceiling views of the Portmagee Harbour. Open for lunch and snacks, daily, April–November.

THE HUNTSMAN, The Strand, Waterville (tel. 066 947 4124). With floor -to-ceiling windows facing Ballinskellig Bay, this restaurant really makes the most of its waterfront location. The menu offers the best of the local catch, including Skellig lobster and Kenmare Bay prawns, as well as Irish stew, rack of lamb and seasonal game. Daytime snacks include burgers, omelettes, pastas and seafood salads. Open for lunch and dinner, daily, April–October.

LIME TREE, Shelbourne Road, Kenmare (tel. 064 42225). Innovative 'new Irish' cuisine, presented in a charming setting, is the secret of success at this restaurant, housed in a former schoolhouse dating back to 1821, with a lime tree out front. The ever-changing menu offers choices such as warm salad with prawns, Kenmare seafood *en papillote*, oak-planked Kenmare salmon, and roast herb-crusted Kerry lamb, all accompanied by a basket of barbecued bread with olive-oil spread. Open for dinner only, April–October.

PACKIE'S, Henry Street, Kenmare (tel. 064 41508). With a traditional décor enhanced by colourful Irish art, this shop-front bistro is known for its creative menu, making use of herbs and organic produce from its own garden. Irish stew, rack of lamb, braised beef in Guinness, crab cakes, and gratin of crab and prawns are house specials. Open for dinner only, Tuesday–Saturday, mid-March to mid-November.

THE PARK HOTEL, off Shelbourne Road, Kenmare (tel. 064 41200). A tour of the Ring is not complete without a meal or a drink at this luxury Victorian château-style hotel, dating back to 1897. Consistently deemed to be among the finest hotels in Ireland, it has an award-winning restaurant with a romantic setting overlooking palm-tree-lined gardens and the Kenmare Estuary. The menu is as dazzling as the setting – Kenmare Bay lobster, rack of Kerry lamb and local Skeaghanore duck are specialities. Finish with a selection of local cheese served with walnut bread. Open for lunch and dinner, daily, April–December.

THE QUARRY RESTAURANT, above Pat's Shop and Post Office, Kells (tel. 066 947 7601). Panoramic views are the big draw of this second-floor restaurant-in-the-round. The self-service menu offers an international selection of dishes, ranging from Greek salads and moussaka, to quiches, pastas, curries and Irish stew. It is situated midway between Glenbeigh and Cahirciveen. Open for lunch and snacks, daily, April–October.

SMUGGLER'S INN, Cliff Road, Waterville (tel. 066 947 4330). Located 1.6 km (1 mile) east of town, overlooking Ballinskelligs Beach, this converted farmhouse restaurant is a favourite with golfers (it sits opposite the Waterville Golf Course). The décor and menu favour the nautical, offering lobsters from the tank, local seafood, and fish brochettes, as well as steaks. Open daily, March–October.

THE THATCH, Strandsend, Cahirciveen (tel. 066 947 2316). Home-baking is a speciality at this authentic thatched-roofed cottage, set on its own grounds along the main Ring of Kerry road. The menu is self-service, offering soups, salads, sandwiches, traditional casseroles, pastries, scones and pies. Seating is also available at picnic tables outside. Open for lunch and snacks, daily, April–October.

PUBS

MICKEY NED'S, The Square, Kenmare (tel. 064 40200). Housed in a building dating back to 1795, this pub is now the domain of Mickey Ned O'Sullivan, an All-Ireland Kerry football star, and his wife, Marian. Surprisingly, the décor of this spacious pub is not sporty but contemporary, with a mixture of white walls, dark woods, mirrors, cubed seats, leather sofas and modern art. Music (traditional or jazz) is provided on weekend nights.

THE MOORINGS BRIDGE BAR, Main Street, Portmagee (tel. 066 947 7108). Set beside the harbour, this family-run pub is a hub of village life. In the evenings, locals gather for sessions of traditional Irish music and set dances with audience participation and dance lessons, particularly on Tuesday (June–August only), Friday and Sunday. Open April–October.

O'NEILL'S 'THE POINT' BAR, Renard Point, Cahirciveen (tel. 066 947 2165). Operated by the same family for over 150 years, this vintage pub sits on the harbour looking out towards Valentia Island. The interior conveys a nautical theme, mixed with family memorabilia. Bar food is served during the day, April–October.

PURPLE HEATHER, Henry Street, Kenmare (tel. 064 41016). Situated in the heart of town, this small and homely pub has a long bar, an assortment of small tables and a huge open fireplace. It is a popular stop for a quick drink, snack or lunch with a gourmet flair.

RED FOX INN, Ballycleave, Glenbeigh (tel. 066 976 9184). With open turf fireplaces, old family pictures on the walls, and local memorabilia, this pub has a Kerry-cottage atmosphere. Snacks are served all day in the bar, and music is provided on many summer nights. In warm weather, customers head outside to picnic tables.

SCARIFF INN, Caherdaniel (tel. 066 947 5132). Perched on a cliff overlooking the Atlantic, this pub-restaurant is known for its picture-window views over the Atlantic, and good pub grub.

DIGRESSIONS

CAR FERRY: Heading to Valentia Island? Instead of driving the full route from Cahirciveen to the island by land and bridge, you can save time and mileage by taking a car/passenger shuttle ferry from Renard Point near Cahirciveen to Knightstown on Valentia Island. This service operates daily from early morning to late evening, April– September, on a drive-on/drive-off basis. The trip takes just five minutes. Information: Valentia Island Ferry (tel. 066 947 6141).

ISLAND HOPPING: With the Skellig Rocks providing fascination for many visitors, several local boat operators provide trips to Skellig Michael from mainland ports in the summer months (April or May to September or October, depending on weather and sea conditions). Boat rides average an hour in duration each way, with two or three hours allowed on the island. Information: Des Lavelle, Skellig Island Passenger Boat Service, Valentia Island (tel. 066 947 6124 or http://indigo.ie/~lavelles); Brendan Casey, Skellig Boats, Cahirciveen (tel. 066 947 2437 or www.skelligislands.com); and Seán Feehan, Ballinskelligs Watersports, Dungegan, Ballinskelligs (tel. 066 947 9182 or www.skelligboats.com).

NARRATED BUS TOURS: If you prefer to sit back, relax and leave the driving to someone else, there is a good choice of escorted sightseeing tours, covering the full circuit around the Ring of Kerry (Iveragh Peninsula). Duration averages seven hours, starting out and returning to Killarney. Tours operate year-round, depending on demand (unless specified otherwise). Information: Bus Éireann, The Travel Centre, Killarney (tel. 064 30011or www.buseireann.ie), available June–September only; Corcoran's Tours, 8 College Street, Killarney (tel. 064 36666); Cronin's Tours, College Street, Killarney (tel. 064 31521); Deros Tours, Main Street, Killarney (tel. 064 31251 or www.derostours.com);

and O'Connor's Tours, Ardross, Ross
Road, Killarney (tel. 064 31052).

SEAL-WATCHING CRUISES: View Kenmare
and the surrounding waters on board a
seal-watching and eco-nature cruise. The
19.5-metre (64-foot) boat covers 16 km
(10 miles) in two hours, with an
informative commentary on the history of
the area and close-up views of tropical
plants nurtured by the Gulf Stream, bird
life, and Ireland's largest seal colony,
where 300 or more seals make their
home. Operates daily, May–September;
schedule varies. Departs from the pier,
Kenmare. Information: Kenmare Seafari
(tel. 064 83171 or www.seafariireland.com).

18: Dingle Peninsula

Long before Ireland was fashionable as a film setting, the Dingle Peninsula was flashed across the silver screen throughout the world in the David Lean film *Ryan's Daughter*. Although the film itself might be largely forgotten, the seascapes of Dingle have long lived on in memory and tourist promotional blurbs. The rustic cottages, the endless beaches and the romantic mist-laced mountains of Dingle, with the rhythmic cadence of the native Irish language, are all part of what is still fondly referred to today as '*Ryan's Daughter* country'. Until its cinematic fame, the Dingle Peninsula was relatively undiscovered, compared to its neighbouring peninsula, the Ring of Kerry. Now, over 30 years later, Dingle is decidedly one of Ireland's 'in' places – and it can get downright crowded in the peak of summer.

Reaching out from Tralee like a thumb plunging into the Atlantic, the Dingle Peninsula (sometimes called 'The Ring of Dingle') is less than 65 km (40 miles) long, but it seems much larger because there is so much to see and do.

Like the Ring of Kerry, Dingle is rich in seacoast vistas and mountain passes. It is surrounded by water on three sides (the Atlantic, Tralee Bay and Dingle Bay), and overshadowed by the Slieve Mish Moun-

tains and Mount Brandon, the fifth highest mountain in Ireland (953 metres/3,127 feet). Named after St Brendan who had an oratory here in the sixth century, Mount Brandon is the highest peak in Ireland outside of the Macgillicuddy's Reeks, the range to the south.

The western tip of the Dingle Peninsula is also home to the West Kerry Gaeltacht, an area known as *Corca Dhuibhne* where the Irish language (Gaelic) is readily spoken in everyday communication. Along with the language, native Irish traditions, folklore, crafts and music flourish throughout the Dingle Peninsula.

Without a doubt, the peninsula's most famous 'personality' in recent years has been Fungie, an adult male bottlenose dolphin who swam solo into the waters of Dingle Harbour in 1984, and has thoroughly endeared himself to local residents and visitors alike.

(See map p.162)

FAST FACTS

Travel Information Offices

DINGLE TOURIST OFFICE, The Quay, Dingle (tel. 066 915 1188). Open all year.

TRALEE TOURIST OFFICE, Ashe Memorial Hall, Denny Street, Tralee (tel. 066 912 1288). Open all year.

TRAVEL INFORMATION ONLINE:
www.corkkerry.ie or
www.dingle-peninsula.ie

TELEPHONE AREA CODES:
Area codes for all telephone numbers are
066, unless indicated otherwise.

MAJOR EVENTS

FÉILE NA BEALTAINE ARTS FESTIVAL –
Celebrated over May Day weekend each
year, this festival signals the official
start to the summer in Dingle, according
to the Celtic calendar. The programme is
a unique blend of local, national and
international topics at a political
symposium, as well as a medley of the
arts (drama, dance, music, literature, art,
film and street theatre). It is held
primarily in Dingle but events are placed
all over the peninsula. Information:
Trish Hendrick, tel. 915 1082 or
www.feilenabealtaine.ie. (First weekend
of May)

ROSE OF TRALEE INTERNATIONAL FESTIVAL –
This six-day event is a sort of Irish Mardi
Gras, with all kinds of street
entertainment, free outdoor concerts,
parades, fireworks and horse races, as well
as an international beauty pageant
competition to select an annual 'Rose' to
reign over the festivities. More than
100,000 people converge on the town, so
don't come without advance reservations.
Information: Siobhán Hanley, tel. 712
1322 or www.roseoftralee.ie. (Last week
of August)

DINGLE PENINSULA TOUR

Duration: 4–6 hours plus stops

Driving tours of the Dingle Peninsula
usually start at **Tralee**, the gateway
and chief town of County Kerry. It
seems that many people who approach
the town of Tralee automatically start
to hum the lilting melody of 'The Rose
of Tralee'. Although there isn't always
music in the air, Tralee is a town that
owes much of its fame to music. The
signature song, written by local
resident William Mulchinock over a
century ago, was composed in honour
of a young woman named Mary who
had won his heart, and every time it is
played throughout the world
(especially around St Patrick's Day), it
conjures up idyllic images of Tralee.

Even if there were no Rose, Tralee
would still be an alluring town to visit. It
sits at the head of **Tralee Bay** and the
northeast corner of the Dingle Peninsula.
The place name, Tralee – in the Irish language *Trá Lí*, which means 'strand or
beach of the River Lee' – comes from the
River Lee which flows into Tralee Bay.

Historically, the town grew up around a
castle built in 1243 by John Fitzthomas
Fitzgerald, one of the many earls of Desmond. Much of the present town of Tralee
dates from the eighteenth and nineteenth
centuries, and the streetscapes have a distinctive Georgian flavour.

Stop at **Denny Street**, one of the principal streets of the town, constructed in

1826 and named after a family that was prominent in the town for over 300 years. It is said that the Great Castle of the Geraldines stood on this site in medieval times. Unfortunately, almost all traces of the castle have disappeared.

Bordered by well-preserved eighteenth- and nineteenth-century Georgian terraces and townhouses, Denny Street leads to the 30-hectare (75-acre) **Town Park**. It is a haven for outdoor activity, with a series of leisure walks, rose gardens, and a fountain commemorating William Mulchinock who composed the song 'The Rose of Tralee'. Open daily. Admission: free

At the end of Denny Street is **Ashe Memorial Hall**, an impressive three-storey Georgian public building. It is home to **Kerry the Kingdom** (tel. 712 7777), the main visitor hub of the town. Ideal for a rainy-day indoor visit, this building presents three different attractions that tell the story of County Kerry history and lifestyle, all under one roof. The first section is devoted to 'Kerry in Colour', a multi-image audiovisual display on County Kerry's scenery, historic monuments, and traditions. The second part is the 'Kerry County Museum', an interactive exhibition tracing human history in Kerry from 5000BC to the present, featuring archaeological displays from the National Museum of Ireland, as well as slide presentations, scale models and audio and visual gadgets. A 'Kerry Today' section has live link-ups with Radio Kerry and the Irish-language station, Raidió na Gaeltachta. The final stage is 'Geraldine Tralee – The Irish Medieval Experience', an action-packed time-car ride through Tralee as it looked, smelt and sounded in the Middle Ages. Open daily, except the last ten days of December. Admission: €€

Depart the town via **Prince's Street,** following signs for the N86 and Blennerville. Straight ahead on the left is the **Tralee Aqua Dome**, Dan Spring Road (tel. 712 8899), an ideal place to bring the kids, with indoor swimming pool, water slides, waves, rapids, whirlpools and more. Open daily. Admission: €€

Adjacent is the boarding station for the **Tralee–Blennerville Steam Railway** (tel. 712 1064). This vintage train uses equipment and tracks that once comprised the Tralee and Dingle Light Railway (1891–1953), one of the world's most famous narrow gauge railways in its heyday. The trip takes 20 minutes and runs along a scenic nineteenth-century canal route, going from Tralee to Blennerville, about 3 km (2 miles) west. Trains depart every hour on the hour; return trip from Blennerville runs every hour on the half-hour. Open daily, May–October (except second Monday–Tuesday of each month for maintenance). Admission: €

Whether you take the train or drive a car to Blennerville, your eyes will immediately be drawn to the **Blennerville**

Windmill (tel. 712 1064). At first glance, it looks like something from the Netherlands, but this 18-metre (60-foot) high tower-mill has been a fixture on the Tralee horizon since 1800. Reputed to be the largest working windmill in Ireland or Britain, it produces 5 tons of ground wholemeal flour per week. Take a guided tour of the inside of the windmill and join in 'hands-on' demonstrations of the wind-driven milling process, or watch an audiovisual on the history of milling. In addition, since the Tralee-Blennerville area was once a leading port along the Kerry coast, there are exhibitions on nineteenth-century emigration. Open daily, April–October. Admission: €

Among the ships that set sail several times to cross the Atlantic from Tralee was the *Jeanie Johnston* (1847–58), a triple-masted 200-passenger barque that carried thousands of emigrant passengers to Baltimore, New York and Quebec. This ship had a remarkable safety record and never lost a passenger to disease or the sea. To commemorate this phase of history, a replica of the ship was built on the quay at Blennerville (1996–2002) and set sail across the Atlantic in early 2003 to recreate the original *Jeanie Johnston* voyages. When not on the high seas, the ship is a floating museum in Tralee Bay.

From Blennerville, head westward out onto the Dingle Peninsula, and the scenic drive starts to unfold immediately – with Tralee Bay on the right and the Slieve Mish Mountains rising on the left. Ahead on the right is a golden stretch of sandy beaches as you approach the village of **Camp**. The un-Irish-sounding name has nothing to do with outdoor living, but is instead derived from the Irish language *An Com*, meaning 'the hollow' of 'the mountain recess'. You'll understand that it is aptly named as you drive through this pleasant area with wild fuchsia bushes growing on either side of the road. From Camp, the road branches right and left. The left route (N86) goes through the mountains into **Annascaul**, while the right road leads to **Connor Pass**. Unless it is raining heavily or deeply misted, opt for the latter route which is by far the more scenic and challenging for a driver, often described as a rugged 'stairway to heaven'. This route, local road R560, swings westward and hugs the shore on high ground, overlooking the beachside village of **Castlegregory**, named after a sixteenth-century castle built on the site by a man named Gregory Hoare. The village is at the neck of a narrow spit of land that separates Tralee Bay from Brandon Bay.

Just over 3 km (2 miles) further on, turn left at Kilcummin to start the ascent up **Connor Pass** (also spelt Conor Pass), cutting through the mountains between the north and south sides of the peninsula. The place name comes from the Irish *An Chonair*, literally meaning 'the path'. And what a path it is!

A winding and twisting route rising to 457 metres (1,500 feet) above the bog lands and beaches, Connor is the highest mountain pass in Ireland. It requires cautious driving, but is well worth the effort. On a clear day, the views are spectacular – from Tralee Bay and Mount Brandon to North Kerry and the mouth of the River Shannon. Rising steeply, this road curves and twists, dips and rises, presenting constantly changing panoramas of rocky mountain slopes and cliffs, including one point named *Faill na Seamróg*, meaning 'shamrock hill'. At the summit, there is a car park that affords sweeping views of both sides of the peninsula.

The final descent brings you to the sheltered fishing port of **Dingle**, the main town of the peninsula, and the most westerly town in Europe. It is a picturesque fishing port, an attraction in itself. The place name derives from the Irish language *An Daingean*, meaning 'the fortress'. Historically, not too much is known about Dingle except that it was the principal harbour in County Kerry during medieval times and it became a borough at the end of the sixteenth century.

Follow signs for the pier, and leave your car in one of the designated parking areas. Dingle town is best explored on foot. Take time to walk along the marina area and see the large fleet of fishing and sporting craft.

To learn more about local waters, visit Dingle's prime indoor attraction, **Mara Beo/Oceanworld**, Strand Street (tel. 915 2111). Housed in a modern complex overlooking Dingle Harbour, this new aquarium tells the story of mariculture and fish farming along the west coast of Ireland. Using a unique walk-through undersea tunnel for up-close views of fish and other sea creatures, visitors can see more than 100 species of fish, both rare and common, including the only red lobster in Ireland, 'vampire' fish (lampreys), box crab and blue mouth, a type of redfish living in deep waters. In addition, the 37 tanks hold sea cucumber, cuttlefish, conger eels, starfish and the freshwater Arctic char. Exhibits also profile the life and voyages of St Brendan, 'The Navigator', who is said to have lived in the area in the sixth century, and set sail from Dingle waters to cross the Atlantic and discover America. Open daily. Admission: €€

Surprisingly, the town's main claim to maritime fame, Fungie, an adult male bottlenose dolphin, does not reside at the aquarium, but frolics freely in Dingle Harbour. Fungie swam solo into local waters over 20 years ago and took up residence, although no one knows where he came from, exactly how old he is, or how long he will stay. He is a born exhibitionist and swims regularly almost on cue beside local boats. Like most dolphins, Fungie is sensitive and gentle, and eagerly interacts with people in the water. Several local companies offer boat trips to see Fungie (see 'Digressions' below), and usually give refunds if the dolphin does not appear.

Take a left off Strand Street onto **Green Street** and **Main Street** to see some of Dingle's many craft shops and restaurants.

After returning to your car, head west out of town on local road R559, signposted for Ventry and Dunquin. For a look at some of the area's signature crafts, turn right into **Ceardlann Na Coille – The Dingle Craft Centre**, The Wood (tel. 915 1797). Laid out in a circular cluster of traditional cottages, these workshops present emerging local artisans at work on crafts such as knitwear, pottery, felt work, leather goods, hand-weaving, wood-turning and making musical instruments. Open daily, March– October. Admission: free

Continue on the R559 for almost 5 km (3 miles). To see yet another of Dingle's speciality craftworkers, take a left for **Holden Leathergoods**, Burnham (tel. 915 1796). Remotely set in an old schoolhouse beside Dingle Bay, this is one of the area's newest enterprises, established in 1989 by Conor Holden, one of the few Irish-born leather artisans in the country. Conor and his staff take the best of local hides and skins to hand-cut and stitch luggage, briefcases, bags, belts and more. Open daily, June–September; Monday–Saturday in March–May and October–November; and Monday–Friday in December–February. Admission: free

Returning to the R559 puts you on a slow and scenic drive of less than 16 km (10 miles) to the edge of the peninsula. En route you will pass **Ventry**, a lovely harbour-side village whose Irish name, *Ceann Trá*, means 'head of (the) strand', a graphic reference to its position overlooking the beach. To the west of Ventry Harbour rises **Mount Eagle** (*Sliabh an Iolair*), to 516.5 metres (1,695 feet). This area is rich in early Christian monuments, most of which date back to about the sixth century. There are good examples of standing stones, beehive huts (called *clocháns*), churches, stone crosses and forts of various sizes and types.

As the road continues westward around Mount Eagle, vast panoramas reveal the gentle profile of **Slea Head**, sweeping down to the sea. This dramatic mountain and seascape is one of the most photographed scenes in Ireland. The road then follows the curved **Dunmore Head** on the way to Dunquin. This is said to be the most westerly point on mainland Ireland.

Next stop is **Dunquin**, a townland that is known in the Irish language as *Dún Chaoin*, meaning 'pleasant fort'. In the summer, the many homes of the area play host to students who come to learn the Irish language. Dunquin's main claim to fame, however, is that it was for many years the chief port for crossings to the **Blasket Islands**, a cluster of seven offshore islands that resemble giant rocks lying over 3 km (2 miles) out on the horizon of the Atlantic. There are four big islands – Inishmore, also know as the Great Blasket, Inishvickillane, Inishtooskert and Inish na Bró; and three smaller ones – Beginish, Young's Island

and Illaunboy. A great sea rock, Tearaght, and a multitude of lesser rocks and reefs also form part of the group. It is hard to imagine that anyone lived on these remote and rocky outposts, but historians believe that monks probably inhabited them in the fifth or sixth centuries, and the Vikings may also have used the islands as jumping-off points for mainland raids in the ninth and tenth centuries. More recently, the largest of the islands, the Great Blasket, was occupied by a hardy assortment of fishing families, until the population was reduced to 22 and they were forced to abandon the island in 1953.

Not surprisingly, the solitude and setting of the island produced several notable poets and writers of the Irish language. The lives of these island people are chronicled in a creative and informative way at **Ionad an Bhlascaoid Mhóir – The Blasket Centre**, Dunquin (tel. 715 6371). This contemporary T-shaped museum provides an insight into life on the Blaskets, through a series of exhibits and an introspective 22-minute audiovisual. Perched on the edge of the Atlantic with unobstructed views of the Blasket Islands, this extensive interpretative centre explores all the dimensions of island living, from the land, the sea and the language, to the weather and the seasons, as well as the distinctive character of the Blasket Islanders. In addition, there are reviews of the far-reaching achievements of the Island writers, along with capsule biographies and moving descriptions of island life, in their own words. To augment the cultural theme, contemporary artworks depicting the harshness and joys of island life have been incorporated into the building and grounds. In the entrance area is a work in stained glass that is reputed to be the largest secular work of its kind in Ireland. Statues, photographs and paintings complete the layout. Open daily, Easter–October. Admission: €

Beyond Dunquin is the dramatic protrusion known as **Clogher Head**, where brisk winds churn up the seas in a constant splash. For a look at the most westerly craft enterprise in Ireland, stop at **Louis Mulcahy Pottery** (tel. 915 6229). This pottery and studio produces a range of creations, using local clay and glazes devised at the shop. The finished wares range from vases and teapots to platters. Open daily. Admission: free

Just over 3 km (2 miles) northeast is **Ballyferriter**, whose name simply means 'Ferriter's townland', from the Irish language, *Baile an Fheirtéaraigh*. It is named after the Irish poet-soldier Pierce Ferriter (1616–53) who was born near here.

Continue on the R559 for 6.5 km (4 miles) to one of the best-preserved early Christian church buildings in Ireland, **Gallarus Oratory**, a beehive hut, built of unmortared stone and dating from about the eighth century. Although the exact date of its foundation is unknown, it has remained watertight for more than 1,000 years. The adjacent **Gallarus Visitor Centre** (tel. 915 5333) depicts the history and significance of the oratory, using an audiovisual and exhibits. Open daily. Admission: €

To the left rises **Mount Brandon**, at 953 metres (3,127 feet) the tallest peak on the peninsula and the fifth highest mountain in Ireland. It is named after St Brendan, and it is said that Brendan had a religious settlement here in the sixth century and set forth on his transatlantic voyage in a leather boat from Brandon Point. Continue on the R559 road back to Dingle.

From Dingle town take the main road, N86, as far as the town of **Lispole**, and then along the coast road, R561, from Annascaul to Castlemaine. The highlight of this 32-km (20-mile) stretch of road is **Inch Strand**, well signposted on the right. Featured prominently in the film *Ryan's Daughter*, Inch has also caught the imagination of other film-makers (*Playboy of the Western World*, and the more recent Tom Cruise epic *Far and Away*), and countless postcard-makers and photographers. Stop and take a picture or just admire the vast 6.5-km (4-mile) expanse of sandy beach. It is one of Dingle's – and Ireland's – most beautiful seascapes.

The final stop on this peninsula route is **Castlemaine**, a small town on the River Maine. It was here that the famous Australian outlaw known as the 'Wild Colonial Boy' was born. From here, it is just over 16 km (10 miles) to either Tralee or Killarney.

PAT'S PICKS

RESTAURANTS

AN CAFÉ LITEARTHA, Dykegate Street, Dingle (tel. 915 2204). With a name that literally means 'the literary café', this place is a combination bookshop/restaurant. The front section offers shelves of books, particularly on Dingle and Kerry topics. The café at the rear features freshly baked goods, salads, seafood and traditional dishes such as Irish stew. Open Monday–Saturday.

BEGINISH, Green Street, Dingle (tel. 915 1321). With a stone façade, arched windows and colourfully painted doorway, this restaurant exudes a Georgian townhouse atmosphere. Named after one of the Blasket Islands, it offers seating in an elegant dining room with seascape paintings, or in a sky-lit conservatory overlooking the back garden. The menu features seafood, with house specials such as poached Dingle Bay lobster, Kerry mountain lamb, honey-glazed duck and vegetarian dishes. Open for dinner, Tuesday– Sunday.

THE CHART HOUSE, Mail Road, Dingle (tel. 915 2255). This award-winning restaurant sits at the east entrance to Dingle town, beside the harbour. Proprietor Jim McCarthy, who has built up a reputation throughout Ireland, blends innovative modern Irish cooking and attentive service. The menu features fresh Dingle Bay seafood, plus free-range beef, pork and lamb, and vegetarian dishes, as well as local specialities such as Annascaul grilled black pudding with baked apples and bacon. Open for dinner, Wednesday–Monday, mid-February to early January.

DOYLE'S SEAFOOD RESTAURANT, 4 John Street, Dingle (tel. 915 1174). In this town of great restaurants, this nautically themed spot has long been a benchmark. With walls and floors of stone, pine furnishings, shellfish tanks and 'old Dingle' art, it has a homely atmosphere. The small kitchen produces an amazing array of dishes, using ingredients from the sea and nearby farms and gardens. Specialities include lobster from the tank and Atlantic shellfish platters, as well as a few token meat dishes such as Kerry rack of lamb, and beef in Guinness stew. Open for dinner, Monday– Saturday, mid-February to mid-November.

HALF DOOR, 3 John Street, Dingle (tel. 915 1600). Carrying on the welcoming Irish tradition of a partly opened doorway, this restaurant conveys a country-cottage atmosphere, with exposed stone walls, copper pots and original tilework. Lobster and salmon dishes are featured, but the menu also includes prawns, scallops, crab claws and mussels. Open for dinner, Monday– Saturday, except late December.

OLD SMOKEHOUSE, Main Street, Dingle (tel. 915 1147). For snacks and light meals throughout the day, this shop-front café is a local favourite. Nestled in the centre of town beside a flowing stream, it is housed in an old stone building, with country-kitchen décor and an outdoor patio. The menu offers made-to-order salads and sandwiches, as well as soups and hot dishes. Open Monday–Saturday.

THE TANKARD, Kilfenora, Fenit, Tralee (tel. 713 6164). Panoramic views of Tralee Bay are the main attractions at this contemporary waterside restaurant, located 8 km (5 miles) northwest of Tralee. In good weather, there is also seating outside on a patio deck. The menu offers fresh local shellfish and seafood, as well as steaks, game and rack of lamb. Open for dinner, daily; and for lunch on Sunday.

WATERSIDE, Strand Street, Dingle (tel. 915 1458). Views of the marina give this restaurant a seafront charm. Seating is available on an outside terrace or in a conservatory-style dining room. Snacks are available by day, and full-service dinners by night. The selection includes cockles and mussels sandwiches, shellfish salads, soups, quiches, crêpes and pastries. Open daily, Easter–October.

PUBS

AN DROICHEAD BEAG/THE SMALL BRIDGE, Lower Main Street, Dingle (tel. 915 1723). Sitting beside a bridge leading to the Connor Pass, this pub has an Old Dingle atmosphere. It is known for its 'mighty' sessions of Irish traditional music, scheduled every night of the year, usually commencing at 9.30 or 10pm.

DICK MACK'S, Green Street, Dingle (tel. 915 1960). Named after leather-craftsman Richard MacDonnell (the current owner's father), this family pub carries on a cobbler's tradition, with a small leather shop still on the premises, and an array of handcrafted leather boots, belts and key fobs still on display. The walls are lined with family memorabilia, old pictures and books. The bar area is small and includes an old-fashioned snug.

JAMES FLAHIVE, The Quay, Dingle (tel. 915 1634). A tailor's shop for over a century, this old pub has put away the needles and threads but it still displays many of the trappings of the trade. The walls also show pictures of many favourite customers over the years, as well as photos of Fungie, the town's resident dolphin. There's no food or music here, just good company and a good pint.

KRUGER'S PUB, Ballinaraha, Dunquin (tel. 915 6127). Located on the westerly reaches of the peninsula, this rural pub is a favourite with locals and visitors alike. It is named after Muiris 'Kruger' Kavanagh, a local lad who was known to pick a fight at school so he was dubbed 'Kruger' after Paulus Kruger, a famous Boer leader. He emigrated to the US where he worked at various jobs, from bodyguard and nurse to PR man for a New York City theatre. After sixteen years, he returned to Ireland and set up this pub, to which he drew many friends from Broadway. Although Kruger passed on, his pub continues to be an entertainment hub, with weekend performances of *sean-nós* singing (an old Irish unaccompanied style) and step dancing.

KIRBY'S, Rock Street, Tralee (tel. 712 3357). With a barn-like façade and interior, this long-standing pub offers an old-world atmosphere, with rushwork furnishings, agricultural implements and a collection of Tralee memorabilia on the walls. Traditional music is often played in the summer.

LORD BAKER'S, Main Street, Dingle (tel. 915 1277). Claiming to be the oldest pub in Dingle, this local landmark is named after Tom Baker, who purchased the premises in 1890 and turned it into a hive of activity, selling wine and spirits, tea, flour, wool and general farm supplies. An elected member of the Kerry County Council, he also worked as an auctioneer and wrote poetry in the Irish language. His legacy lives on in the atmosphere of the bar. Good bar food is served throughout the day.

O'FLAHERTY'S, Strand Street, Dingle (tel. 915 1461). In the heart of Dingle, this vintage pub is known for its rustic atmosphere and great sessions of Irish traditional music. Enter from Strand Street or from the musically themed back gate along the harbour front.

OYSTER TAVERN, Fenit Road, Spa, Tralee (tel. 713 6102). Sit indoors or outdoors at this rustic roadside pub to enjoy a drink overlooking Tralee Bay. The views cannot be beaten, so it is very popular in good weather, especially at weekends.

DIGRESSIONS

CROSS OVER TO CLARE: To save time and mileage when travelling between Kerry and West Clare, head to Tarbert in North County Kerry (about 64 km/40 miles north of Tralee via the N69), departure point for the Shannon Ferry – a continuous car-ferry service across the Shannon Estuary from Tarbert, County Kerry to Killimer, County Clare. Crossing time is just 20 minutes, and ferries depart on a drive-on/drive-off basis every hour on the half-hour from the Tarbert side, starting at 7.30 a.m. Monday–Saturday and from 9.30 a.m. on Sunday. Information: Shannon Ferry Ltd, Killimer, Co. Clare (tel. 905 3124 or www.shannonferries.com).

DINGLE BAY CRUISES: See the Dingle Peninsula from Dingle Bay on board a 15-metre (50-foot) passenger boat, with a commentary on the archaeology, geology, history, birdlife, wildlife and local folklore. The route passes Ventry Harbour, Dunbeg Fort, Blasket Islands, Bull's Head and Minard Castle, as well as a variety of cliffs and sand dunes. Departing from Dingle Pier, the two-hour cruises operate daily, April–October, subject to weather conditions. Advance reservations are suggested. Information: Dingle Marine Eco Tours, The Pier, Dingle (tel. 086 285 8802).

EXPLORING BELOW THE SURFACE: If you want to get to the bottom of things, head out on the N21 road from Tralee for about 19 km (12 miles) via Castleisland to Crag Cave, a natural limestone fossil cave system. Discovered in 1983 and thought to be over one million years old, it consists of a series of chambers with some of the finest stalagmite and stalactite formations found in Ireland. Guided tours of the well-lit passageways are provided, enhanced by dramatic sound and lighting effects. Open daily, mid-March–November. Information: Crag Cave, Castleisland (tel. 066 714 1244 or www.cragcave.com).

FOLLOWING FUNGIE: Ever since 1984, when Fungie, the bottlenose dolphin, first appeared in Dingle Bay, the Dingle Boatmen's Association has been offering one-hour boat trips to see the frolicking and friendly dolphin up close. Longer two-hour trips are also available early each morning (departing at 8am), allowing passengers to 'swim with Fungie'. Trips operate daily, but schedules vary (depending on weather and demand). Information: Dingle Boatmen's Association, Unit 2, The Pier, Dingle (tel. 066 915 2626).

GUIDED WALKS AND BUS TOURS: For an escorted tour of Dingle, there is a good choice of sightseeing tours, covering the full circuit around the peninsula, visiting main points of interest including Slea Head, Gallarus Oratory, Connor Pass, Mount Brandon, Ventry, Coumeenole (filming location for *Ryan's Daughter*) and Graigue (location for *Far and Away*). All tours, which depart and return to Dingle town, average two or three hours in duration, and usually operate daily, May/June–September. More information: Dingle Guided Tours, c/o The Mountain Man, Strand Street, Dingle (tel. 066 915 2400); Moran's Slea Head Tours (tel. 066 915 1155 or www.dingle-peninsula-tours.com); and O'Connor's Slea Head Tours (tel. 087 248 0008).

ISLAND-HOPPING: The remote Blasket Islands, touted as the most westerly land in Europe, and abandoned in 1953, make a memorable one-day getaway. Enjoy a cruise around or a landing on the famous islands, viewing the scenery, birds, and marine life. Cruises operate daily, June–September, but schedules vary according to weather. Boats depart from Dunquin Pier, 16 km (10 miles) west of Dingle town. Information: Blasket Island Adventure Tours, Dunquin Quay (tel. 915 6533); and Blasket Island Boatmen, Dunquin Quay (tel. 915 6422).

MUSEUM OF THE BOG: Driving between Tralee and Listowel on the N69 road? Watch out for 'A Day in the Bog', a thatched-roof bogland museum. The walk-around exhibits are informative – illustrating the ABCs of bogs, from bog formation and types of bogs to the uses of turf and bog cotton, as well as the flora, fauna and findings in the bogs. Turf-cutting machines and equipment are on display outside, as is a collection of farm animals (goats, hens, geese, pigs, rabbits and more), always appealing to younger visitors. Open daily. Information: 'A Day in the Bog', Leam, Kilflynn, Tralee (tel. 066 713 2555).

TELLING TALES: The great storytelling traditions of North County Kerry are celebrated at the Seanchaí, a museum of words in the heart of Listowel, about 27 km (17 miles) north of Tralee. Housed in a nineteenth-century Georgian building, it traces the history of oral storytelling and how it evolved into a form of writing (thanks to the seanchaí – pronounced shan-a-key – or local storyteller). The centre spotlights more than 100 local writers including John B Keane (1928–2002), Bryan MacMahon (1909–98) and Brendan Kennelly. Open daily, April–September; Monday–Friday, October–March. Information: Seanchaí – Kerry Literary and Cultural Centre, 24 The Square, Listowel (tel. 068 22212 or www.seanchai-klcc.com).

Shannon Region

19: County Clare's Castles

It has been said that Ireland has more than 1,000 castles. Some are in ruins or fragments, to be sure, but many have been saved and preserved, restored and opened to the public. There is something magical about castles. Castles conjure up images of long ago – a fairytale place, a mighty fortress, a seat of power, a romantic haven.

The wide and traffic-filled main corridor (N18) between the cities of Limerick and Galway is often considered as the 'castle corridor' of Ireland. It is a gateway to more than half-a-dozen genuine castles that were not only important in Ireland's past, but also play a vital role today as heritage sites, hotels, banquet halls and literary landmarks. One of these, Bunratty Castle, is the most popular attraction in Ireland, outside Dublin.

So, don't rush by on the Limerick–Galway road; plan to make a few stops. This road may be only 100 km (65 miles) in length, but it is packed with all the makings of a day's drive truly fit for a king or queen.

biddy boys and strawboys, all blending together for concerts, *céilithe*, music, song and dancing workshops, street entertainment and pageants/parades. Information: Frank Whelan, tel. 086 826 0300 or www.fleadhnua.com. (Last week of May)

CLARENBRIDGE OYSTER FESTIVAL – Held in a small village by the shores of Galway Bay, this festival celebrates the start of a new oyster season. In addition to inviting you to consume huge quantities of oysters, the activities include a traditional market day, yacht race, hurling game, art and photographic exhibit, as well as a parade and continuous musical entertainment. Information: Bob D'Silva, tel. 091 796 359 or www.clarenbridge.com. (First weekend of September)

ENNIS TRAD FESTIVAL – This five-day off-season event is attended by those who love to hear (or play) Irish traditional music, bringing together the very best musicians in a relaxed and informal atmosphere. Information: John Rynne, tel. 065 684 4522 or www.ennistradfestival.com. (First weekend of November)

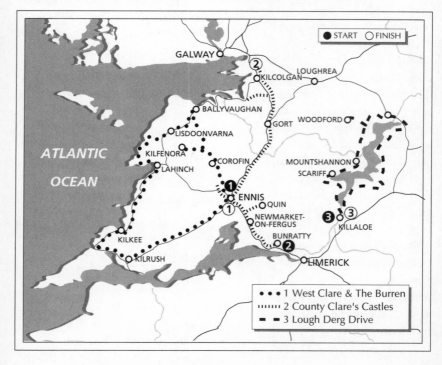

COUNTY CLARE'S CASTLES DRIVING TOUR

Duration: half-day or full day plus stops

The first stop along this route is invariably Bunratty, whether the tour is started in Limerick, 13 km (8 miles) away, or Shannon Airport, 8 km (5 miles) away. Just follow the signs for the Bunratty exit off the N18.

The small village of **Bunratty** takes its name from the Irish language, *Bun Raite*, meaning 'mouth of the River Ratty'. Although the River Ratty has always been important to the town, the focal point is the splendid castle beside the river, **Bunratty Castle** (tel. 061 360 788). No matter from which direction you are coming, on the horizon you readily see the turrets and battlements of this mighty fortress, the most complete and authentic medieval castle in Ireland. Built in 1425 and plundered often, it was long a stronghold of the powerful O'Brien clan. In 1954, it was fully restored, with authentic furnishings, armorial stained glass, tapestries and works of art reflecting the décor and atmosphere of the fifteenth century. By day, the building's inner chambers are open for public tours; at night, the castle's **Great Hall** becomes a candlelit setting for medieval banquets and entertainment.

In addition, the castle is flanked by **Bunratty Folk Park**, an 8-hectare (20-acre) site, laid out to recreate a typical nineteenth-century Irish village. Step inside – and step back in time. Experience an insider's tour of authentic thatched-roof cottages, eight different farmhouses, a watermill and a working blacksmith's forge. Stroll along a typical village street with post office, grocery store, doctor's surgery, print shop, school, drapery shop, pawn shop and village hotel and pub. On the hill is **Bunratty House**, a 'big house' built in 1804 on these grounds and restored and furnished in typical Victorian style. See craftspeople at work, from knitting and weaving, to candle-making, pottery and basketry; farmers working in a traditional hay barn; and women baking fresh breads and scones in fireplace ovens.

Some of the newer features of the park are **Ardcroney Church**, originally built in 1824 in County Tipperary and transferred here; the **Bunratty Walled Gardens**, modelled on the nineteenth-century gardens that supplied fruit, vegetables and flowers to the main house; and **Hazelbrook House**, built in 1898 and home to the Hughes Brothers who started a dairy industry and later produced HB ice cream, a popular brand to this day. Learn about the evolution of ice cream-making, from domestic dairy to the modern production plant. Castle and park open daily. Admission: €€

Returning to the main N18 road, the next stop is **Newmarket-on-Fergus**, a picturesque village that sits beside the River Fergus – hence its descriptive, but basically English, place name. Almost 5 km (3 miles) north of the village, on the right side of the road, is the entrance to the verdant and undulating estate of **Dromoland Castle**, the seat of Lord Inchiquin and the O'Briens until 1962, and then refurbished and expanded into a luxury hotel resort. Although the O'Briens moved to this walled fairytale setting in the seventeenth century, the present baronial-style castle was not built until 1826. With an idyllic array of turrets and towers, it sits beside the River Rine, amid 162 hectares (400 acres) of parkland and gardens and an eighteen-hole golf course. Dromoland is a hotel, open to the public for meals or overnight stays, but not for general visits.

From Dromoland, make a right turn, following signs for **Knappogue Castle**, Quin (tel. 061 360 788), another castle with medieval roots. Built in 1467, this castle was the home of the MacNamara clan who dominated the area for over 1,000 years. The name Knappogue comes from the Irish-language, *An Chnapóg*, meaning 'the little lump' or 'the hillock', undoubtedly a reference to the castle's setting on a sequestered embankment. The original Norman structure has been enhanced by elaborate late-Georgian and Regency wings added in the mid-nineteenth century. Fully restored, it is furnished with authentic fifteenth-century pieces, and, like Bunratty, it provides a setting for medieval banquets at night. Open daily, May–September. Admission: €

While passing through **Quin**, stop to take a break and walk around. No castles here, but in the centre of the village are the ruins of the Franciscan **Quin Abbey**, a national monument. Dating back to 1433, it is a fine example of the architecture and arrangement of a medieval friary. Lovely gardens of wild flowers surround the site.

If Ireland's Bronze Age history is of interest to you, visit nearby **Craggaunowen** (tel. 061 360 788), a 20-hectare (50-acre) prehistoric park. Instead of a castle, the centrepiece of this historic site is an authentically reconstructed Irish *crannóg*. Although it looks like something 'out of Africa', it is a replica of a Limerick-area Bronze Age lake dwelling, constructed of wattles, reeds and mud. Other highlights include a ringfort from the early Christian period, a *fulachta fiadha* (ancient cooking place), a souterrain (underground chamber used as an early refrigerator), one of Ireland's oldest dug-out canoes, and an original wooden roadway from the Celtic Iron Age. The Craggaunowen grounds also shelter the history-making hide boat, the *Brendan*. This is the vessel in which explorer/author Tim Severin sailed across the Atlantic in 1976 from County Kerry to Boston, to prove that St Brendan could have 'discovered' America in the sixth century, long before Columbus. Open daily, May–October. Admission: €€

The next major town along the main N18 road is **Ennis**, the county town of County Clare and a thriving market town. The place name comes from the Irish word *Inis* which means 'island' or 'riverside meadow'. As it sits beside the River Fergus, the latter description seems to fit Ennis best.

Close to the bridge over the river is the town's prime national monument, **Ennis Friary**, Abbey Street (tel. 065 682 9100). Founded *c*.1250 for the Franciscans, this friary quickly grew into one of western Europe's major seats of learning in medieval times, making Ennis a focal point for many years. Records show that it buzzed with scholarly activity in 1375, with at least 350 friars and 600 students gathered at the site. Although it was suppressed in 1692 and fell into ruin, it still shelters many unique features, such as a huge five-panelled window which held blue painted glass, a vaulted sacristy, and intricately carved figures, including the apostles. Open daily, June to mid-September; and Tuesday–Sunday in mid-September– May. Admission: €

From Ennis, continue in a northerly direction. For a short detour, turn left onto local road R476 for about 8 km (5 miles) to one of the area's most intriguing castles in an off-the-beaten-track area – **Dysert O'Dea Castle**, Corofin (tel. 065 683 7401). Built on a rocky outcrop of land in 1480 by Diarmaid O'Dea, this tower house is now an archaeology centre and museum, depicting the history of the area. In addition, the castle serves as a starting point for touring a cluster of other historical and archaeological ruins, all within a 3-km (2-mile) radius. The sites include a round tower, church, holy well and high cross, all estimated to date back to the period 800–1200AD, as well as a fourteenth-century battlefield and an Iron Age stone fort. Open daily, May–September. Admission: €

Return to the main N18 road, which then passes through a 32-km (20-mile) stretch of farmland and grazing fields, interrupted only by two small villages, **Barefield** and **Crusheen**. You will cross over from County Clare to County Galway before reaching **Gort**, a small market town which takes its name from the Irish, *An Gort*, meaning 'the field'.

Just over 3 km (2 miles) north of town, on the left, is **Coole Park** (tel. 091 631 804). This lush and rambling national forest park once sheltered the summer home of Lady Augusta Gregory (1852–1932), dramatist, folklorist, leading force in the twentieth-century Irish literary revival, and co-founder of the Abbey Theatre, along with WB Yeats and Edward Martyn. Although her house was demolished in 1941, her spirit lives on in the beautiful gardens and ancient trees, including an avenue of cedars and a huge copper beech, fondly called 'The Autograph Tree'. Lady Gregory and many of her literary companions, including Yeats, Shaw, and O'Casey, carved their initials on the tree, still readable today. The restored courtyard building houses a visitor centre which presents exhibits on Lady Gregory and her literary friends and an audiovisual on the flora and fauna of the park. Open daily, mid-April–October. Admission: €

Continue on the main road north and watch for a signpost on the right to **Thoor Ballylee** (tel. 091 631 436), a castle with a literary theme. Once a part of Lady Gregory's estate at Coole, and known then as Ballylee Castle, this sixteenth-century Norman tower was purchased in 1916 by Nobel Prize-winning poet William Butler Yeats for £35. The castle, which Yeats restored for himself, his wife, George, and their two children, became his summer retreat and inspiration for much of his poetry, including *The Winding Stair* and *The Tower* collection. In 1992 he re-christened the building 'Thoor Ballylee,' using the word *thoor* which is the phonetic version of the Irish word for 'tower' (*túr*). The castle now houses a Yeatsean museum with exhibits and an audiovisual on the poet's life and works, as well as push-button narrations in each room. Open Monday–Saturday, June–September. Admission: €

The main N18 road continues north for 32 km (20 miles) more, passing stone walls and farmlands via the hamlet of **Ardrahan**, a hilly area. Its place name, *Ard Raithin*, means 'height of the ferns'. For yet another castle, take a detour to the left, for 8 km (5 miles) via the R347 to Kinvara to visit **Dún Guaire Castle** (tel. 091 637 108). Dramatically situated overlooking Galway Bay, this castle consists of a tower house and bawn dating back to the sixteenth century. It sits on the site of an earlier seventh-century castle that was the royal seat of King Guaire of Connacht. In the early part of the twentieth century, it was the country retreat of Oliver St John Gogarty (1878–1957), noted Irish surgeon, author, poet and wit. Displays in the castle now give an insight into the lifestyles of the people who lived there over the centuries. Like Bunratty and Knappogue in County Clare, this castle is also the scene of nightly medieval banquets. Open daily, May to mid-October. Admission: €

Return to the main N18 road, and continue to the next two towns, **Kilcolgan** and **Clarenbridge**, both of which have close access to **Galway Bay** and are considered the heart of 'oyster country'. Many of the events of the annual Clarenbridge Oyster Festival each September are held here, and the local pubs are known for serving hearty platters of the briny bivalves. Follow the main N18 road for less than 16 km (10 miles) into Galway city for the completion of this tour.

RESTAURANTS

BUNRATTY VILLAGE MILLS RESTAURANT

Main Street, Bunratty (tel. 061 364 321). This self-service restaurant is a good place to know along the busy N18 corridor, whether coming from a flight at Shannon Airport or visiting Bunratty Castle (across the street). It offers a continual hot and cold buffet throughout the day, from early morning to late afternoon, as well as a snack and coffee bar. The menu includes freshly made soups, salads, made-to-order sandwiches and main courses. Open for breakfast, lunch and snacks, daily.

GALLAGHER'S, Main Street, Bunratty (tel. 061 363 363). Step inside the cheery red half-door entrance of this restaurant, and enjoy dining in a thatched-roof cottage atmosphere – with open fireplaces, whitewashed walls, lanterns, nautical trappings and local memorabilia. Although the setting is traditional, the menu is very up-to-date – sun-dried tomato bread, farm-raised chicken, chargrilled meats, and an array of fresh seafood, from lobsters, oysters and prawns to seared salmon and baked sole on the bone. Open for dinner, Monday–Saturday.

HAL PINO'S, 7 High Street, Ennis (tel. 065 684 0011). Located just off the main town square, this trendy contemporary restaurant is not named after a Mexican pepper but instead for its owner/chef, Derek Halpin. The menu is an eclectic blend of international dishes with Mediterranean and Eastern influences, using meats from a local butcher, fish from the waters off Carrigaholt, and Clare- grown potatoes. Open for dinner, Tuesday–Sunday.

ROSALEEN'S, The Square, Kinvara (tel. 091 637 503). On the southeast shore of Galway Bay, Rosaleen Tanham presents surprisingly creative cuisine at this bistro-style bakery/restaurant. The menu offers dishes such as chicken wantons, citrus-roast whole trout, salmon *en papillote*, prime Irish Hereford beef steaks, rosettes of lamb, seafood platters and smoked salmon, trout, mackerel, prawns and mussels, with a vegetarian option of lentil and polenta cakes. Open for lunch and dinner, daily, mid-March–September; and as a bakery/coffee house in November–January.

THE OLD SCHOOL HOUSE, Clarinbridge (tel. 091 796 898). Situated along the N18 corridor, this former schoolhouse sits back from the road amid lovely gardens, including an organic vegetable and herb garden that supplies produce for the kitchen. The menu emphasises local seafood, such as Galway Bay oysters and black sole, but also offers some traditional meat dishes such as stuffed pork or breast of corn-fed chicken, as well as vegetarian choices.

With tall windows, live piano music and charming décor, a meal at school was never so good as this. Open for dinner, Tuesday–Sunday, and lunch on Sunday, mid-February– December.

PUBS

CRUISE'S, Abbey Street, Ennis (tel. 065 684 1800). With beamed ceilings, lantern lights, flagstone floors, open fireplaces, and local memorabilia, this homely pub occupies a restored building that dates back to 1647. It sits in the middle of town, adjacent to the old Franciscan friary. Traditional Irish music sessions are scheduled on most nights.

DURTY NELLY'S, Main Street, Bunratty (tel. 061 364 861). Nestled next to Bunratty Castle, this rustic mustard-coloured premises just may be the most popular pub in Ireland. For over 375 years, it has been a tradition in the area, starting out as a watering hole for the castle guards, and now a 'must do' on most tourists' lists. It is always crowded in the summer months, with seating both indoors and outside on picnic tables.

KATHLEEN'S IRISH PUB, Bunratty Castle Hotel, Main Street, Bunratty (tel. 061 707 034). This hotel pub is best known for 'Kathleen's Irish Céilí' evenings, a fun-filled blend of traditional music, song and dance. Clap your hands, sing along, and don't be surprised if you are enticed from your chair to play the spoons or dance to 'The Siege of Ennis'. Audience participation is contagious – you even get a free songbook with all the words of familiar Irish sing-along tunes. Pub is open daily but the *céilí* schedule is May–October or according to demand.

MONKS WELL INN, Main Street, Quin (tel. 065 682 5055). Situated in the heart of a charming village, opposite a fifteenth-century national monument, this family-run pub has an equestrian theme, with horsey pictures and trophies won by a jockey in the family. In the evenings, there are music sessions and occasional pub quizzes.

MORAN'S OYSTER COTTAGE, The Weir, Kilcolgan (tel. 091 796 113). Watching the sun go down on Galway Bay is part of the fun at this 250-year-old thatched-cottage pub, situated on a country lane overlooking the water. It is run by the sixth generation of the Moran family, with seating in homely little rooms, including the original kitchen and snugs. The bar-food speciality is oysters, harvested in September–April from the Morans' own oyster beds.

PADDY BURKE'S, Clarenbridge (tel. 091 796 226). With a thatched roof and a history going back to 1650, this legendary cottage-style tavern on the main road (N18) is known for its nautical décor and seafood bar meals, especially oysters. This is not surprising as the pub is the headquarters for the annual Clarenbridge Oyster Festival.

PREACHER'S BAR, The Square, Ennis (tel. 061 682 3300). Once part of a chapel, this bar is furnished with many items from former churches, including old pews, dark-wood benches, and stained-glass windows, as well as 'old Ennis' pictures and memorabilia. It is now part of the Temple Gate Hotel (itself a former convent), so it exudes old-world charm. A carvery-style pub-food counter operates during the day, and Irish music sessions are held on many nights.

DIGRESSIONS

LEANING TOWER OF IRELAND: Southwest of Gort on the border of County Clare and County Galway are the ruins of Kilmacduagh Monastic Settlement. Although it does not contain any castles, it does present a varied display of early Christian buildings, including a well-preserved eleventh/twelfth-century round tower, standing almost 34 metres (111 feet) tall. The tower is interesting in that it tilts, much like its more famous counterpart in Pisa, Italy. Below the tower are the ruins of a small cathedral. Information: Galway East Tourism (tel. 091 850 687 or www.galwayeast.com).

MEDIEVAL FEASTS – Three castles in this area – Bunratty at Bunratty, Knappogue at Quin, and Dún Guaire at Kinvara – are the settings for medieval-style banquets each evening, with authentic music, song and merriment. Seated at long tables in the castles' magnificent baronial halls, guests feast on ancient recipes using modern Irish ingredients – all served in medieval style. For refreshment, there's mulled wine, claret and jugs of mead (a traditional honey-based spirit). Bunratty is open daily all year, while Knappogue and Dún Guaire operate May–October. Information: Shannon Heritage (tel. 061 361 511 or www.shannonheritage.com).

20: West Clare and The Burren

Contrast is the buzz word for the western half of County Clare.

Facing the churning waves of the Atlantic and edged by the gentle waters of Galway Bay and the Shannon Estuary, this region is naturally diverse. It is rural and rugged, yet it provides a nurturing habitat for rare flora and fauna. Wide stretches of beach and mighty cliffs border the coast, while 'The Burren', a rock-strewn limestone plain, dominates the interior. The roar of jets fills the sky as the silent aura of ancient prehistoric monuments pervades the countryside below. Craftsmen and artists rub shoulders with matchmakers and musicians, and underground caves are as popular as coastal marinas. The Corkscrew Road is as challenging as the championship Lahinch golf courses.

At the back door of Shannon International Airport, this western half of County Clare is often the first or last glimpse of Ireland that transatlantic visitors see. And indeed it is a fitting introduction or finale – small and easy to tour, West Clare provides a kaleidoscopic experience of all that is best in the Emerald Isle.

(See map p.186)

FAST FACTS

Travel Information Offices

SHANNON AIRPORT TOURIST OFFICE, Arrivals Hall, Shannon (tel. 061 471 664). Open all year.

ENNIS TOURIST OFFICE, Arthur's Row (off O'Connell Street), Town Centre, Ennis (tel. 065 682 8366). Open all year.

CLIFFS OF MOHER TOURIST OFFICE, Cliffs Visitor Centre (tel. 065 708 1171). Open April–October.

KILKEE TOURIST OFFICE, O'Connell Square, Kilkee, (tel. 065 905 6112). Open late May to early September.

KILRUSH TOURIST OFFICE, The Square, Kilrush (tel. 065 905 1577). Open June–early September.

TRAVEL INFORMATION ONLINE: www.shannon-dev.ie/tourism and www.tourclare.com

TELEPHONE AREA CODES: Telephone numbers in the west County Clare area use the 065 area code, unless indicated otherwise.

MAJOR EVENTS

WILLIE CLANCY SUMMER SCHOOL – In the past 30 years, this nine-day festival has become the largest international summer school for Irish traditional music worldwide, with over 250 tutors teaching more than 2,000 students from over 40 countries, in various West Clare locations. Information: Harry Hughes, Miltown Malbay, tel. 708 4148. (Early July)

LISDOONVARNA MATCHMAKING FESTIVAL – Music, dancing day and night, matchmaking and lots of *craic* are the keynotes of this annual six-week festival, geared to bachelors and bachelorettes. Information: Marcus White, Lisdoonvarna, tel. 707 4696, www.matchmakerireland.com. (September into early October)

WEST CLARE AND THE BURRENDRIVING TOUR

Duration: 4–5 hours plus stops

From Shannon Airport or Limerick city, drive north on national road N18 as far as **Ennis** (See Chapter 19: County Clare's Castles Tour), and then turn left onto the N85 for about 5 km (3 miles), breaking off to the right at local road R476, for just over 8 km (5 miles) into **Corofin**, a small market village near **Lake Inchiquin**. The place name Corofin comes from the Irish *Cora Finne*, meaning 'Finne's weir'.

In the centre of the town is the **Clare Heritage Centre**, Church Street (tel. 683 7955). Housed in the former St Catherine's Church of Ireland church, dating back to 1718, this centre is an ideal place to stop and learn some background about the area. Its main display, 'Ireland West 1800–1860', portrays the traumatic period of Irish famine, emigration and struggles over land tenure. In addition, there are exhibits on Clare farming, industry, commerce, education, forestry, language and music, all designed to portray life in this area over the past 300 years. Open daily, May–October. Admission: €

The adjacent **Clare Genealogical Centre**, Church Street (tel. 683 7955), contains a comprehensive research library to help visitors trace and identify their Clare ancestry. The material includes indexed records for the 47 parishes of County Clare, with data on more than 500,000 people born in the county during the nineteenth century, plus civil records, maps, property records, census returns and other sources. Open Monday–Friday. Admission: free, but fees are charged for research.

After passing through Corofin, you have now officially entered **The Burren**, sometimes referred to as Ireland's 'rock desert'. It is an amazing 259-km-square (100-mile-square) area, a barren, lunar-like landscape. It is not surprising that the Irish language word for Burren is *Boirinn*, meaning 'rocky place'. Massive sheets of rock, craggy boulders and potholes are visible for miles in an almost moonscape-style pattern, yet this area is also a setting for pocket lakes and streams, set amid hills, turloughs, valleys and mountains, as well as an amazing assemblage of wildlife and greenery.

Experts say that there is always something in bloom here, even in winter, from ferns and moss to orchids, rock roses, milkworts, wild thyme, geraniums, violets and fuchsia. This area is also famous for its 33 species of butterfly. Animals such as the pine marten, stoat and badger, not often seen in the rest of Ireland, are common here.

The story of the Burren began millions of years ago, when layers of shells and sediment were deposited under a tropical sea, only to be thrust above this surface years later, and left exposed to the erosive power of Irish rain and weather, producing the limestone landscape that appears today.

As the locals will tell you, however, the word 'Burren' should not be confused with barren. As early as the Stone Age, man has settled in this curious area. Evidence of human habitation is all around – massive dolmens and wedge tombs, and hundreds of stone forts, known as *cahers*, which were the homesteads of farmers long ago. The area is also rich in Christian ruins – round towers, churches, high crosses, monasteries and holy wells. In recent years, the Burren area has been designated as a national park.

As you progress on the R476, on the right-hand side of the road you will see the impressive ruins of **Lemanagh Castle**, a combination of a fifteenth-century fortified tower and a Tudor mansion, and a favourite local landmark.

Continue on the R476 north for 8 km (5 miles) more, and then make a right to the R480 which goes north. The R476 turns westward at this point. You may wish to take a slight detour by continuing instead on the R476 as it goes west for about 5 km (3 miles), to see the **Burren Centre**, Kilfenora (tel. 708 8030), to learn more about the amazing facets of the Burren. Established in 1975 as a community-development co-operative, this small museum presents 'A Walk Through Time', a multi-dimensional exhibition using a series of vignettes, models, slides and information panels to impart an overview of the Burren's geology, flora and fauna, history, and landscape. The on-premises shop features crafts that are native to the area. Open daily, March–October. Admission: €

Return eastward to the start of the R480. A kilometre and a half (1 mile) down the road there is a right turn for **Carron**, a small hamlet lying on the edge of some of the Burren's best karsts. The place name comes from the Irish An Cairn, meaning 'the mound' or 'the cairn'.

If you take the turn-off for Carron, you will come to the **Burren Perfumery and Floral Centre** (tel. 708 9102), Ireland's first perfumery, set up over 30 years ago. The complex includes a laboratory, gardens and a visitor centre that enables visitors to follow the perfume-making process. See natural essential oils being extracted from the Alpine and Arctic flowers of the Burren, blended with pure Irish water using the traditional still, and then hand-bottled, filtered and packaged as perfumes, bath oils, soaps and bubble baths. A photographic exhibit and an audiovisual presentation also explain the process. Open daily, except Christmas week. Admission: free

Continue via the R480 for the remainder of this drive through the heart of the Burren. Approximately 8 km (5 miles) north of Ballyvaughan, off to the right in a private field is the much-photographed **Poulnabrone Dolmen**, a portal dolmen, signposted and visible from the main road.

Just outside Ballyvaughan, there is a sign for a right turn to one of the area's great natural wonders – **Aillwee Cave** (tel. 707 7036). Formed hundreds of centuries ago yet discovered only in the past 70 years, this cave is one of Ireland's oldest underground sites. The cave has over 1,036 metres (3,400 feet) of passages and hollows running straight into the heart of a mountain. Highlights include subterranean rivers, bridged chasms, deep caverns, a frozen waterfall and an assortment of stalactites and stalagmites, some of which have been given descriptive names such as the 'Praying Hands' or 'Bunch of Carrots'.

In addition, many bones, including those of bears, horses, pigs and badgers, have been found inside, showing that the cave provided a refuge for man and animal over the centuries. Unique features include the bear pits – hollows that were scraped out by the brown bear, one of the cave's many inhabitants. This explains why Aillwee uses a silhouette of a bear as its mascot on signage and literature. Guided tours, lasting about half an hour, are conducted continually, except in November–February when the schedule is more limited. Open daily. Admission: €€

At the entrance to the cave, there is a small, local cheese-making enterprise/shop known as Burren Gold. Stop inside to sample local cheeses and honeys.

Return to the main road, bearing right, and straight ahead is **Ballyvaughan**, a small village and port on the southern shore of **Galway Bay**. The place name, which in the Irish language is *Baile Uí Bheacháin*, means 'townland of the descendants of Behan'. It is a popular village today for all names and nationalities.

A kilometre and a half (1 mile) east of the village, on the N67, is **The Burren Exposure** (tel. 707 7277), a unique narrated walk-through indoor museum depicting the Burren landscape, with three separate sight-and-sound presentations on the rocks, flowers and wildlife of the region. Open daily, March–November. Admission: €

Retrace your steps to Ballyvaughan, and depart in a southwesterly direction on the main N67 road to encounter the

Corkscrew Road, a stretch of road appropriately named because it literally twists and turns like a corkscrew as it wends its way up the hillside from Ballyvaughan. At its highest point, the road has panoramic views of the Burren and Galway Bay in the distance.

In less than 16 km (10 miles), the N67 road leads into **Lisdoonvarna**, a popular resort town that sits at a height of 122 metres (400 feet) above sea level, unusual for this area. 'Lisdoon', as it is called by the locals, has been famed since the eighteenth century for its Victorian-style spa complex, sheltering a natural mineral spring of sulphur, magnesium and iron. Each summer, thousands of people come to bathe in the therapeutic waters.

Adjacent to the spa is the **Burren Smokehouse** (tel. 707 4432), a local fish-smoking enterprise. Step inside and watch an audiovisual and hands-on demonstrations that illustrate how fresh Atlantic salmon is slowly cold-smoked over oak chips to produce one of Ireland's tastiest delicacies. Open daily March–October. Admission: free

Lisdoonvarna, which promotes itself as a matchmaking centre, is the setting each September for Europe's largest 'singles' matchmaking festival. The fanciful place name comes from the Irish language *Lios Din Bhearna*, which means 'ringfort of the gapped fort'. The particular fort in question is the ruin on the right as you enter Lisdoonvarna from Ballyvaughan.

Eight kilometres (5 miles) southwest is **Doolin**, a remote and rambling fishing village that meanders for almost 5 km (3 miles) along the coast. It is famed as a haunt for Irish traditional musicians year-round, at its three well-established pubs (Gus O'Connor's, McGann's and McDermott's), and as a gathering place for backpackers in the summer months.

Departing Doolin, head south on the R478. On the right is **The Clare Jam Company**, Coast Road (tel. 707 4778), a small cottage industry run by the Muir family. They produce over 25 homemade jams, jellies and marmalades, including the popular favourites (strawberry, raspberry, gooseberry and blackcurrant jam, and orange marmalade) as well as more unique concoctions such as three-fruit citrus marmalade, red tomato chutney, strawberry champagne jam and Connemara whiskey marmalade. Open Monday–Friday. Admission: free

Return to the R478, travel 3 km (2 miles) and follow signs for the area's signature scenic attraction – The **Cliffs of Moher**. Acclaimed as one of Ireland's greatest natural wonders, these dramatic cliffs rise to a height of 203 metres (668 feet) above the Atlantic Ocean, stretching for 8 km (5 miles) along the windswept open coastline. The visitor centre (tel. 708 1171) provides basic information and background, and then it's necessary to climb a steep but graded hill up to the edge of the cliffs to enjoy sweeping views of the coastline. Surprisingly, some of the cliff-side terrain is not protectively fenced in, so it's necessary to be careful and cautious, as pavement or grass can be slippery, especially after rain. For the highest perspective, follow the signs to **O'Brien's Tower**, a Victorian-style viewing point erected in the nineteenth century. *Note*: wear comfortable shoes for walking up the hill to the viewing areas. It can also be extra cool and windy along the edge of the cliffs, so wear adequate clothing and be cautious as you walk.

Return to the R478 and travel almost 5 km (3 miles) to **Liscannor**, a small fishing village overlooking **Liscannor Bay**. Its main claim to fame is that is was the birthplace of John Holland (1841–1914), inventor of the submarine. The road then leads to **Lahinch**, a dune-filled beach resort that is home to one of Ireland's most challenging golf courses. There are actually two eighteen-hole courses here, but the longer championship links course is the one that has given Lahinch its far-reaching reputation. The course elevations, such as the ninth and thirteenth holes, reveal open vistas of sky, land and sea; they also make the winds an integral part of the game.

At Lahinch you can join the main N85 road and follow it for 32 km (20 miles) back to Ennis to complete your tour. Alternatively, if you are fond of beaches, and time allows, continue south on the N67, passing some beautiful coastal scenery to the right, via the resort towns of **Miltown Malbay**, **Quilty** and **Kilkee**.

Almost 13 km (8 miles) southeast via the main N67 road is **Kilrush**, fondly called the 'capital' of West Clare. The focal point is the **Town Hall**, built in 1808 as the market house. It burned to the ground in 1922 and was reconstructed in its original style in 1931. Today, it houses the **Kilrush Heritage Centre**, Market Square, off Henry Street (tel. 905 1577), a hub of information on historical and cultural developments in the area. An audiovisual, 'Kilrush in Landlord Times', tells of the struggles of the tenant farmers of West Clare during the eighteenth and nineteenth centuries, particularly during the famine years. Open daily, June–August. Admission: €

On the southern edge of Kilrush is the **Vandeleur Walled Garden** (tel. 905 1760), an eighteenth-century walled garden, featuring subtropical and southern-hemisphere plants. The layout includes a horizontal maze, arboretum, shrub borders and 170 hectares (420 acres) of woodlands. Open daily. Admission: €

From Kilrush, take the main N68 road back for 32 km (20 miles) through the rocky West Clare farmlands to Ennis, or on to Shannon or Limerick; or take the Shannon Estuary ferry from Killimer over to County Kerry (*See* 'Digressions' below).

BRUACH NA HÁILLE, Roadford, Doolin (tel. 707 4120). Bearing a name that means 'bridge over the River Áille', this cosy cottage-style restaurant sits beside the river. The menu has a Continental flair, with dishes such as fillet of sole in cider with shellfish cream; ragoût of seasonal fish; and seafood au gratin. Open for dinner, March–December.

CULLINAN'S, Roadford, Doolin (tel. 707 4183). This restaurant bases its success on using many locally sourced ingredients – Burren smoked salmon, Doolin crab, Aran scallops, Burren lamb and Inagh goat's cheese, as well as home-churned ice creams. Open for dinner, daily, except Wednesday in October–April.

LINNANE'S LOBSTER BAR, New Quay, The Burren (tel. 707 8120). Sitting on the shores of Galway Bay, off the main N67 road east of Ballyvaughan, this well-signposted restaurant is a haven for seafood lovers. As its name implies, lobster is a speciality, as are fresh crab and homemade chowder. Open daily, May–September; weekends, October–April.

MRS O'BRIEN'S KITCHEN, Main Street, Lahinch (tel. 708 1020). Providing the homely atmosphere of a country kitchen in the heart of golf country, this place offers freshly made soups, salads and sandwiches, as well as seafood platters and traditional Irish stew. Open for lunch and snacks, daily.

WHITETHORN, Ballyvaughan (tel. 707 7044). This restaurant is situated under a kilometre (half a mile) east of the village on the N67. If location is everything, this restaurant, sitting right on the southern edge of Galway Bay, scores a 10, especially at sunset and on sunny days. With an all-rock, Burren-inspired exterior, except for floor-to-ceiling picture windows, this contemporary self-service eatery offers freshly made soups, salads, pastas, meat casseroles, wholemeal crêpes and yummy home-baked scones. Open for snacks and lunch, daily, March–October.

BIDDY EARLY BREWERY, Inagh (tel. 683 6742). Named after a Clare folk hero of the 1800s, who was renowned for her magical powers, this pub claims to be Ireland's first microbrewery. Visitors can sample the brews that are produced here and also watch how they are made. It is located in the heart of the Burren on the main road (N85) between Ennis and Lahinch.

GUS O'CONNOR'S, Pier Road, Doolin (tel. 707 4168). Sitting amid a row of fishermen's cottages less than 2 km (1 mile) from the roaring waters of the Atlantic, this historic (c.1832) pub offers daytime snacks and evening sessions of Irish traditional music in the best of the old West Clare style.

MONKS' PUB, The Pier, Ballyvaughan (tel. 707 7059). Hugging the harbour, this old fishermen's pub offers a briny atmosphere and great seafood, with indoor or outdoor seating, and views of the water. House specialities are fresh mussels, seafood chowder, oysters, fish cakes, smoked salmon and fresh crab.

VAUGHAN'S, Main Street, Kilfenora (tel. 708 8004). This pub has been in the same family since 1800, preserving its old-world atmosphere through the centuries. In addition to holding a reputation for excellent pub grub (bacon and cabbage, beef and Guinness casserole), Vaughan's is a mecca for traditional Irish music and set dancing.

DIGRESSIONS

ARAN ISLANDS: Although Galway and Rossaveal are the usual departure points for ferries to the Aran Islands, you can also board a ferry for the islands from Doolin Pier. These ferries operate daily crossings from late April through September. Information: Doolin Ferries, The Pier, Doolin (tel. 707 4455 or www.doolinferries.com).

CROSS OVER TO KERRY: To save time and mileage when travelling between Clare and Kerry, head to Killimer, departure point for the Shannon Ferry – a continuous car-ferry service across the Shannon Estuary from Killimer, County Clare to Tarbert, County Kerry. Crossing time is just 20 minutes and ferries depart on a drive-on/drive-off basis every hour on the hour from the Killimer side, starting at 7am Monday– Saturday, and from 9am on Sunday. Information: Shannon Ferry Ltd, Killimer (tel. 905 3124 or www.shannonferries.com).

DOLPHIN-WATCHING: The Shannon Estuary is home to over a hundred bottlenose dolphins which frolic in the sheltered waters of lower County Clare. Two different companies provide dolphin-watching boat cruises, daily from April to October. Information: Dolphinwatch, The Pier, Carrigaholt (tel. 905 8516 or www.dolphinwatch.ie); and Dolphin Watching on the Shannon, Kilrush Creek Marina, Kilrush (tel. 905 1327 or www.shannondolphins.ie).

MONASTIC ISLAND: Get away from it all! From Kilrush Creek Marina, you can board a boat for a 20-minute cruise to Scattery Island, to see the ruins of St Senan's sixth-century monastic settlement. Operates daily, June– September. Information: Scattery Island Ferries, Kilrush Creek Marina, Kilrush (tel. 905 1327).

OFF-THE-BEATEN TRACK WALKS: Explore the nooks and crannies, archaeology and botany, flora and fauna of the Burren region with local guide Shane Connolly. Walks are available year-round, and duration is two hours or more. Advance reservations are suggested (at least 24 hours before). Contact: Burren Hill Walks, Corkscrew Hill, Ballyvaughan (tel. 707 7168).

21: Lough Derg Drive

Lough Derg is one of Ireland's best-kept secrets – scenically splendid and commercially unspoiled, yet rarely crowded. A body of water that is bigger than most cities, it is the River Shannon's largest lake, 40 km (25 miles) long and almost 16 km (10 miles) wide.

Often referred to as an inland sea, Lough Derg is touted as 'Ireland's pleasure lake', because of all the recreational and sporting opportunities it provides – boating, fishing, hiking, waterskiing, kayaking, windsurfing, canoeing, tubing and jet-skiing.

For walkers and motorists, Lough Derg is a three-county experience, blending the best of the riverside back roads of Clare, Tipperary and Galway. The road that borders the lake, appropriately dubbed the 'Lough Derg Drive', presents ever-changing views at every turn. The silvery blue waters of the Shannon are framed by a rolling patchwork of green fields, dotted by colourful fields of wildflowers and white-washed farmhouses, while the Slieve Aughty and Arra mountains and Slieve Bernagh slope in the background. It is one uninterrupted natural panorama – no billboards, no neon signs, no fast-food chains, no apartment blocks, no tacky amusement parks. Just the Shannon at its best.

Many of the most idyllic spots are designated as 'lay-bys' or 'lookout points' (scenic off-road areas with car-parking space) for visitors to stop and relax, with picnic tables and benches. Linger for a while and drink in the scenery, or bring a picnic and feast amid the rolling green lawns with the Shannon ever in view. The resident birds provide a chorus of harmonious music, interrupted only by the buzz of a bee, the bleat of grazing sheep, the gentle splash of waves as boats cruise by, or perhaps another tourist or two.

The roads that border the lake, a perimeter of 153 km (95 miles), comprise a well signposted circuit. In addition to the riverside scenery, the Lough Derg Drive is replete with well-kept marina towns and harbour-side villages, craft centres, monuments and castles, and a fair share of beguiling pubs.

The origin of the name Lough Derg is uncertain. It is believed to be derived from the Irish language words, *Loch Deirgeirt*, meaning 'lake of (the) red eye'. Some place-name experts maintain that the 'red eye' refers to the colour of a deep point or whirlpool somewhere in the water. For most visitors, the mystery of the name just adds to the magic of the lake.

(See map p.186)

FAST FACTS

Travel Information Offices

SHANNON AIRPORT TOURIST OFFICE, Arrivals Hall, Shannon (tel. 061 471 664). Open all year.

ENNIS TOURIST OFFICE, Arthur's Row (off O'Connell Street), Town Centre, Ennis (tel. 065 682 8366). Open all year.

KILLALOE TOURIST OFFICE, The Bridge, Killaloe (tel. 061 376 866). Open May–September.

PORTUMNA TOURIST OFFICE, Gate Lodge at Portumna Castle, Portumna, (tel. 090 974 1644). Open June–August.

TRAVEL INFORMATION ONLINE:
www.shannon-dev.ie/tourism,
www.killaloe.ie and
www.galway-southeast-tourism.ie

TELEPHONE AREA CODES:
There are at least four area codes for telephone numbers in the Lough Derg area, so area codes will be specified for each number, to avoid confusion.

MAJOR EVENTS

KILLALOE MUSIC FESTIVAL – This five-day feast of classical music features national and international musicians performing lunchtime, evening and late-night candlelight concerts with the Irish Chamber Orchestra. Many new Irish works have been premièred at the festival, set in the historic St Flannan's Cathedral – one of Ireland's oldest cathedrals. Information: Imelda Dervin, University of Limerick, tel. 061 202 620 or www.icorch.com. (Last weekend of July)

FEAKLE INTERNATIONAL TRADITIONAL MUSIC FESTIVAL – Held in the varied pubs of the small village of Feakle, this five-day event focuses on Irish traditional music, song and dance, with workshops, lectures, concerts, *céilithe* and sessions. Information: Gary Pepper, Pepper's Pub, tel. 061 924 322 or www.iol.ie/~feakle. (First week of August)

LOUGH DERG DRIVING AND WALKING TOUR

Duration: 3–5 hours plus stops

Start the tour at **Killaloe**, the historic marina town on the southern shore of Lough Derg, 21 km (13 miles) northeast of Limerick, about half-an-hour's drive. Few towns in Ireland can rival Killaloe for its picture-postcard River Shannon setting. But, as the old saying goes, Killaloe is more than just a pretty face. It is also a historic town that forthrightly claims to have been the capital of Ireland during 1002–14 when Brian Ború reigned as high king of Ireland. Legend has it that Brian made Killaloe one of his chief bases of operations and built a palace on high ground here called Kincora. Even before Brian Ború, Killaloe was making history – and a name – for itself.

Earliest records of the area say that St

Lua founded a monastery here in the sixth century. Hence the name Killaloe or *Cill Dalua*, which means 'Dalua's church'. *Dalua* is sometimes spelled *Do-Lua* or *Mo-Lua* or simply *Lua*. The oratory that he built was originally on Friars' Island, in the middle of the lake, but it was moved to Killaloe's mainland many centuries later.

Surprisingly, the patron of Killaloe is not St Lua but St Flannan, a seventh-century prince and bishop of the church, for whom the cathedral of the town is named.

Because of its enviable position on Lough Derg, Killaloe also gained prominence in the eighteenth and nineteenth centuries, when canal and river commercial traffic was at its height. Killaloe was then considered a key point on the main inland waterway trading route between Dublin and Limerick. In recent years, thanks to its wide and well-maintained marina, it has achieved favour as a boating and fishing centre.

The focal point of Killaloe is its stone bridge, a handsome and symmetrical stone viaduct with thirteen arches. Although there is evidence that a wooden bridge existed here as early as the eleventh century, the present stone bridge had its origins in the seventeenth century, and had nineteen arches. The west end of the bridge was altered in the late eighteenth century, with some arches being removed when a canal was built. The most significant alteration was made in 1929 when a metal navigation arch was inserted to allow vessels to travel under the bridge. Cross over the bridge and you are technically no longer in Killaloe, but in Ballina, County Tipperary.

Ballina, which offers dramatic views of Killaloe from its riverside banks, derives its place name from its position on the water – *Béal an Átha*, its Irish-language name, meaning '(place at the) mouth of the ford'. Because they sit side-by-side on opposite sides of the river as one intertwined community, it is hard to distinguish the difference between the two towns, so they have adopted a 'twin town' approach, calling themselves Killaloe/Ballina, and have been jointly designated as a 'heritage town'.

Beside the bridge is a canal, opened in 1799 to bypass the rapids on the river. For over a century, it provided a vital link in the navigation route between Limerick and other ports on the Shannon. In 1929, the canal fell into disuse when a hydroelectric station was opened at Ardnacrusha, 19.5 km (12 miles) downstream, and the water level of the river was raised over the rapids. Beside the canal is the lock, which controlled the water levels and allowed passing craft to move from one level to another.

For a bit of history, stop into the **Killaloe Heritage Centre**, The Bridge (tel. 061 360 789), originally the lockkeeper's house. Through a series of walk-through exhibits, this centre tells the story of Killaloe from its earliest days of St Lua and Brian Ború to the town's heyday as a hub of inland-waterway activity in the eighteenth and nineteenth centuries. One section, designed to rec-reate the inside of a canal boat, conveys the sights and sounds along the canal waters, using a port-hole-shaped audio-visual. You can also 'step out' onto a lakeside veranda and imagine yourself visiting the local hotel during its early days. Pick up a vintage telephone and listen to local lore. Open daily, May–September. Admission: €

The town's chief landmarks are ecclesiastical buildings. Overlooking the town on the Green, **St Flannan's Church** (tel. 061 376 137 or 061 376 633) is relatively new, built in 1836–37, but the site on which it sits is one of Killaloe's oldest places. Local lore says that, on this high ground once stood Kincora, the eleventh-century palace of Brian Ború. It was totally destroyed in 1119. Open daily. Admission: free

To the right of the church entrance is Killaloe's oldest standing monument – **St Lua's Oratory**, a small stone chapel built in honour of the sixth-century founder and namesake of Killaloe. The oratory, which originally stood on Friars' Island in the Shannon, was moved and rebuilt here in 1929 when the local hydroelectric scheme that raised the water level of the river flooded the island. The nave can be verified as mostly ninth-century work, while the stone-roofed chancel is thought to be a tenth-century replacement of an earlier timber roof. Open daily. Admission: free

In front of the church grounds is an area known as **Market Square**. For centuries, it has been the scene of local markets and exchanges, for produce, animals and other goods.

Walk down the steep hill of **Main Street** to **Church Street**. Straight ahead is **St Flannan's Cathedral – Church of Ireland**, Royal Parade (tel. 061 376 687). Like the landmark cathedrals at Limerick, Cashel and Holycross, this cathedral was built in the twelfth century by King Dónal Mór O'Brien, one of the great benefactors of the church, but unlike the others, it has been in continuous use as a church ever since – first as Catholic and now as Church of Ireland (Anglican/Episcopal). It is named after St Flannan, who became the first bishop of Killaloe in 639. Built in a simple cruciform style, it is designed with an aisle-less nave. Decorative features include an elaborate Romanesque doorway; a medieval font and a twelfth-century high cross, transferred from Kilfenora in 1821, with engravings in ogham and other ancient writings. To the right of the cathedral is **St Flannán's Oratory**, a well-preserved stone-roofed chapel of Romanesque design, also dating back to the twelfth century. Both sites are open daily. Admission: free

Head out of town in a northerly direction. A simple sign on the right-hand side of the road points to **Brian's Ború's Fort**, a site that is strongly associated with Brian Ború, Ireland's high king and chieftain of this area. Cars are not allowed beyond this point, so park your car on the side of the road. Walk along the path until you see a massive earthen ring-work. This mound is said to cover an earlier ringfort, reputed to have been built in the eleventh century by Brian Ború.

Continue to drive north, beside the western shore of the lake, via local road R463. After you exit the well-forested town limits of Killaloe, the road hugs the shore and reveals a continuous tableau of lakeshore scenery on the right.

Just over 3 km (2 miles) north of town is the **University of Limerick Activity Centre**, Twomilegate (tel. 061 376 622), a water-sports enthusiast's haven. Join the locals for boating, fishing, tubing, waterskiing, windsurfing, canoeing and other water-based sports. Open daily, May–September. No admission charge to the grounds but there are rental charges for most sporting equipment.

The route passes through the small hamlet of **Ogonnelloe**, a place of particularly scenic views, and then turns inland for several kilometres until you reach **Tuamgraney**, a small tree-shaded village that is well worth a stop. On the left is the **East Clare Heritage Centre** (tel. 061 921 351), housed in one of Ireland's oldest churches. It was built in the

year 930, reputedly on the site of a monastery founded by St Cronan in the sixth century, and has been in continuous use ever since, although not always as a church. Through a series of exhibits, the centre illustrates the history of this area. Open daily, June–September and according to demand. Admission: €

On the right is a turn off the road for **Raheen Oakwoods** (tel. 061 923 010), an ancient forest that is part of a 202-hectare (500-acre) estate on the shores of the lake. Recognised as one of the last primeval woods in Ireland, this estate was once the home of the late Edward MacLysaght (1887–1986), a leading authority on Irish names, and author of *Surnames of Ireland*. The setting includes all types of tree, from oak, holly and ash, to hazel, birch and alder, blending with a carpet of mosses, ferns and wildflowers. The centrepiece is the **Brian Ború Oak**, Ireland's oldest documented tree, estimated to be 1,000 years old, with a massive 9.75 metres (32-foot) circumference at its base. Legend has it that the tree was sown by the high king of Ireland who ruled from his nearby fort at Killaloe. Open daily, July–September. Admission: €

Continue into the town and follow the bend of the road to the right. On the left-hand side of the road is a colourfully illustrated sign beckoning visitors to **McKernan – Handweavers** (tel. 061 921 527). Housed in a former police barracks, this family-run weaving workshop hums as a husband–wife weaving team, working on looms of various sizes, produce a colourful array of tweed scarves, jackets, vests and blankets. Many items are one-of-a-kind or made-to-order. Open daily, May–September; and hours vary, October–April. If the sign is out, visitors are welcome. Admission: free

From Tuamgraney, the road number changes to R352. Just over 3 km (2 miles) north is the town of **Scariff**, a small market town perched on a hill above Lough Derg. Literary enthusiasts often make a slight detour here, driving 9.5 km (6 miles) inland to the town of **Feakle** in the remote southern foothills of the **Slieve Aughty Mountains**. The full-time teacher and sometime poet Brian Merriman (*c*.1740–1805) is buried in the local churchyard, although no monument marks the spot. Instead a plaque outside the graveyard celebrates the poet and his great opus, *The Midnight Court*, a single poem of 1,206 lines written in the Irish language. Merriman was a teacher at a nearby school.

Return to Scariff, and continue north as the road wends its way along the lakeside to the village of **Mountshannon**, known for its lovely public gardens and picturesque harbour. Take a right at the sign for 'Marina' and follow the road to the water's edge. Park your car and enjoy the walks and flower gardens that encircle the marina.

From Mountshannon, the road continues north via a well-forested area, with the Slieve Aughty Mountains rising on the left. At the next town, **Whitegate**, a popular base for boat cruises, the road forks to the left and continues northward, entering County Galway. At **Clonco Bridge**, take a slight detour for **Woodford**, a well-forested inland town on the River Woodford. The meadows beside the river banks are known for several rare kinds of flora, including blue-eyed grass, a species that flowers in July, with a pale blue colour. Although historical records show that Woodford as a town dates back to the latter half of the seventeenth century, some archaeological sites can be traced to 1200BC. A very musical town, Woodford is a mecca for Irish traditional music in its pubs. From Woodford, a local road leads to Lough Atorik, a sylvan and deserted lake hidden in the Slieve Aughty Mountains.

From Woodford, it is 14.5 km (9 miles) northeast to **Portumna**, the chief town at the northern head of Lough Derg. As you approach the town, the R352 merges to become part of the N65. With a wide and busy bridge crossing over the Shannon, Portumna is a popular berthing place for cabin cruisers plying the waters of the Shannon. The place name Portumna, which comes from the Irish language words *Port Omna*, means 'landing place of (the) oak tree'. And it's a very appropriate name as the town's signature attraction is **Portumna Forest Park**, offering 567 hectares (1,400 acres) of nature trails and signposted walks, amid lush riverside woodlands and foliage. Open daily. Admission: free

For lovely views of Lough Derg, take a right off the N65 onto the marina road to visit **Portumna Castle** (tel. 090 974 1658), built before 1618 by Richard Burke, fourth earl of Clanricard, and recently restored. It is one of the finest seventeenth-century manor houses ever constructed in Ireland, with rows of stone-mullioned windows and Dutch-style decorative gables. The grounds include a formal geometric-style garden. Open daily, April–October. Admission: €

From Portumna, follow the main N52 road south, entering County Tipperary. At the cut-off for local road R489, take a 1.6-km (1-mile) detour to **Lorrha**, a small village that was the site of a monastery founded by St Ruadhan in the sixth century. Even the local lake – Friars' Lough – is a reminder of the early settlement, although no remnants remain.

St Ruadhan's Church of Ireland church, which stands today on the original site, does contain a ruin of a later foundation of the same name built around 1000AD. The town is also home to **Redwood Castle**, a private residence and one of the oldest occupied Norman castles in Ireland (built in 1210). Fully restored in recent years, it is owned by the kinsfolk of the original owners, the MacEgans. It contains 20 rooms spread over five storeys – the top floor is confined to family use. Its features include a thirteenth-century-style banqueting hall, a small oratory, and a unique *sheela-na-gig* (a female figure of uncertain significance but thought to be a pagan fertility symbol) over the main entrance. Open daily, July–August. Admission: €

Returning to the main N52 road, the next stop is **Terryglass**, a hamlet on a stream near the upper reaches of Lough Derg. Its place name – *Tír Dhá Ghlas*, meaning 'land of (the) two streams' – describes it perfectly. Although Terryglass is the site of a monastery founded by St Colman in the sixth century, little remains of its early days except part of the abbey wall. There are, however, two appealing pubs and a picturesque marina.

From Terryglass, follow local road R493 which borders the shoreline of Lough Derg, offering frequent lakeside views and a series of charming small towns and villages, including **Ballin-derry** and **Puckane**, and then the road dips eastward toward **Nenagh**, the chief town of north Tipperary, lying in a fertile valley between the Silvermine and Arra Mountains. Nenagh takes its name from the Irish language, *An tAonach*, meaning 'the assembly place' or 'the fair'. In early Christian times, Nenagh was a major place of gathering; later, the assemblies took the form of horse fairs that are still prevalent today in this horse-happy county.

A signpost northwest of Nenagh town

centre leads to **Ballyartella Woollen Mills** (tel. 067 24278), a family weaving enterprise dating back to 1893, but updated in recent years with modern buildings and equipment. The fabrics produced, made of pure wool and linen, show off the natural colours and hues of the Tipperary countryside, as they are fashioned into coats, scarves, ties, caps and more. A fifteen-minute audiovisual in the shop explains the weaving process, and visitors are also welcome to tour the factory. Open Monday–Saturday. Admission: free

Within the town centre, stop at the **Nenagh Heritage Centre**, off Kickham Street (tel. 067 33850), for an overview display on the whole Lough Derg area. Located in two stone buildings, dating from 1840–42, this site was once a jail, then a convent, and a school. Now, as a museum, it showcases collections of local arts, crafts, photography and memorabilia, as well as genealogical information for people with Tipperary roots. Open Monday– Friday. Admission: €

Depart Nenagh and follow the R495 road to **Dromineer**, a major boating and fishing centre with a wide marina, and then over to the R494 to **Portroe**, a pleasant town on high ground. Follow a short detour off the main road to **Garrykennedy**, to see one of the smallest harbour-front towns on Lough Derg, with a flower-filled marina and two inviting pubs almost side-by-side and known for

their impromptu sessions of Irish traditional music beside the water.

Return to the R495 and follow it south, with wide open vistas of the Lough Derg shoreline on the right. Just under 5 km (3 miles) down, there is a well-placed scenic look-out, with an ample parking area and picnic benches. This place affords some of the best picture-taking angles of the whole 'Lough Derg Drive' circuit.

Continue for less than 8 km (5 miles) to Ballina and then cross over the bridge into Killaloe to complete your tour.

PAT'S PICKS

RESTAURANTS

AN CUPÁN CAIFÉ, Main Street, Mountshannon (tel. 061 927 275). Positioned on the main street of a flower-filled riverside town, this small and art-filled 20-seat bistro features home cooking with a Continental flair, using fresh and organic produce. The menu offers scrumptious puréed vegetable soups, freshly prepared salads, home-baked breads and pastries, and an ever-changing variety of main courses. In summer, there is seating outdoors with a view of Lough Derg and Holy Island. Open for breakfast, lunch and dinner, daily except Wednesday.

BROCKA-ON-THE-WATER, Kilgarvan Quay, Ballinderry (tel. 067 22038). It may not overlook the water, but this small country house merits a devoted clientèle who appreciate fine cuisine in an elegant candlelit setting of crisp linens and heirloom silver. The ever-changing menu features local produce, fresh seafood and farmhouse cheeses, all enhanced by edible flowers and herbs from the garden. Open for dinner only, Monday–Saturday, May–October.

GOOSERS, Main Street, Ballina (tel. 061 376 792). Situated across the road from the riverbank, this thatched-roof restaurant offers seating outside, overlooking the water, or inside in a series of homely rooms, with open fireplaces, and filled with nautical and fishing memorabilia. Bar food is served all day, and full meals at night. Specialities include seafood soups and platters, bacon and cabbage, Irish stew, burgers and steaks. Open for lunch and dinner, daily.

LANTERN HOUSE, Ogonnelloe, near Killaloe (tel. 061 923 034). Panoramic views of Lough Derg and the verdant countryside draw people to this restaurant, set amid palm-tree-lined and flower-filled gardens. The views are exceeded only by the warm hospitality from Liz and Phil Hogan, and their fine Irish cuisine, featuring the best of local ingredients and home-baking. The varied menu ranges from duck à l'orange and pepper steak to fresh wild salmon. Open for dinner, daily, February–October.

GALLOPING HOGAN'S, The Quay, Ballina (tel. 061 376 162). Set in the restored railway station, this bistro-style restaurant offers views of the water and Killaloe from a plant-filled conservatory-style dining room or on an outdoor patio/terrace. The menu offers Irish cuisine with an international slant, with dishes such as Oriental confit of duck, grilled Dover sole, pepper steaks, ham and mushroom vol-au-vents, and pastas. Open for lunch and dinner, daily.

SIMPLY DELICIOUS, Main Street, Ballina (tel. 061 376 883). The name of this shop-front café is an understatement. For a snack, light meal, or picnic ingredients, this is the place to know. Step inside and savour the tempting aromas of freshly baked breads, pastries, scones, fruit tarts and cheese cakes, as well as a wide choice of soups, sandwiches, meat pies, quiches and stuffed baked potatoes. Open for lunch and snacks, Monday–Saturday.

PUBS

CISS RYAN'S PUB AND BEER GARDEN, Main Street, Garrykennedy (tel. 067 23364). Overlooking a picturesque harbour, this stone-faced pub has long had a tradition of evening traditional music sessions and piano sing-alongs. Outdoor seating is available on the front deck, with water views.

DAN LARKIN'S PUB, Main Street, Garrykennedy (tel. 067 23232). With a thatched roof and whitewashed walls outside, this inviting old-world pub has a country-kitchen atmosphere inside, with a traditional half-door, old hutch, open fireplace, vaulted pine ceiling, floors of stone, and wide planks and shelves filled with jugs, crockery and memorabilia. It sits right beside the harbour.

DERG INN, Main Street, Terryglass (tel. 067 22037). Nestled in a lane off the main road, this homely pub is filled with Tipperary memorabilia, from horse pictures and ale posters to vintage bottles, fishing flies and antique baskets. Seating is also offered on a large deck outside.

FRIARS' TAVERN, Main Street, Lorrha (tel. 090 974 7005). Join the locals for a set dance or session of traditional music at this shop-front pub, named after a sixth-century monastery founded by St Ruadhan at nearby Friars' Lough. The owner just happens to be a top-class musician and singer, as are many of the locals who stop by, including Tony Coen, a champion fiddler who leads a weekly Friday-night Céilí & Oldtime Waltz session at the nearby GAA Club (tel. 090 974 7972).

KEANE'S BAR, Main Street, Mountshannon. Situated in the heart of a riverside town, this pub is a community hub. Step inside to see how pubs used to be – it is also the local outlet for vegetables, meat, groceries, newspapers and petrol.

LIAM O'RIAIN, Main Street, Ballina (tel. 061 376 456). For a sampling of 'Old Killaloe' lifestyle, step into this riverside pub–grocery–newsagent. It's the ideal place to meet the locals and join a spontaneous session of traditional music, song or poetry readings.

MOLLY'S, The Quay, Ballina (tel. 061 376 632). Housed in former police station dating back to 1829, this informal plant-decked pub has a country-cottage atmosphere with dozens of pictures and prints of Killaloe in its glory days. It sits at the foot of the bridge on the east bank, offering great views of the river, and picnic tables for outdoor imbibing and snacking as well.

MORAN'S, Main Street, Woodford (tel. 090 974 9063). In the heart of a town known for traditional Irish music, this pub offers music a-plenty and lots of atmosphere, along with an outdoor patio beside the river.

PADDY'S, Main Street, Terryglass (tel. 067 22147). With a lovely cottage décor, this pub is noted for its extensive collection of local antiques, as well as nightly sessions of traditional music. Best of all, it's just a short walk to the marina.

DIGRESSIONS

CRUISING ON THE RIVER – Board a one- or two-deck 50-passenger boat for a floating tour of the River Shannon's largest lake, Lough Derg. Each cruise, averaging 60–90 minutes in duration, includes a commentary about historic sites, plus close-up views of local wildlife, seabirds and plant life. Cruises operate May– September, departing from Killaloe, County Clare, or Dromineer, County Tipperary. Information: The Spirit of Killaloe, Killaloe Marina, Killaloe (tel. 086 814 0559 or www.killaloe.ie/whelans); Derg Princess, Killaloe Heritage Centre, The Canal, Killaloe (tel. 061 376 866); or Ku-ee-tu Waterbus, Dromineer Marina, Shannon Sailing Ltd, Dromineer (tel. 067 24499).

ISLAND HOPPING: In the middle of Lough Derg is Holy Island, known in the Irish language as *Iniscealtra*, meaning 'island of the churches'. Home to no fewer than five ruined churches, this 2-hectare (5-acre) island was the outpost of St Caimin who founded a monastery here in the seventh century. The main building is St Caimin's Church, with a fine Romanesque doorway and chancel that were probably inserted in the twelfth century. West of the church is a roofless round tower believed to have been contemporary with the church, and to the east is a burial ground known as 'the saints' graveyard', which has grave slabs with twelfth-century inscriptions in the Irish language. Although the island is no longer inhabited, it is accessible by a regular ferry service. Information: Holy Island Ferry Service, Mountshannon Marina (tel. 061 921 615 or mobile tel. 086 874 9710 or www.eastclareheritage.com).

22: County Tipperary Touring Trail

Directly east of Limerick and Clare, County Tipperary is one of Ireland's most verdant and undulating areas. Like those two neighbouring counties, Tipperary is also bordered by the River Shannon, along its northwest corner.

As Ireland's largest inland county – and sixth in overall size – Tipperary is rich in pastoral scenery, with green hills and fertile river valleys. Often referred to as 'The Golden Vale', the Tipperary tableau includes the Galtee and Knockmealdown Mountains, and in the middle of the county a broad plain is traversed by the River Suir.

In many ways, Tipperary rivals Kildare as the home of the horse. There are three race courses in the county (Clonmel, Thurles, and Tipperary), and stud farms dot the countryside. There is even a town on the main N8 road, midway between Cashel and Thurles, called Horse and Jockey.

Tipperary's stand-out attractions, however, are historic and man-made – three national monuments that transformed this rural county into one of Ireland's most pivotal gathering areas for well over 1,000 years – the Rock of Cashel, Holycross Abbey and Cahir Castle.

This chapter focuses primarily on central Tipperary, while northern parts of the county, such as Ballina, Nenagh, Terryglass and Roscrea, are included for ease of travel in our chapters on 'The Lough Derg Drive' (Chapter 21) and 'Ely O'Carroll Country' (Chapter 23).

FAST FACTS

Travel Information Offices

CASHEL TOURIST OFFICE, Main Street, Cashel (tel. 062 61333). Open all year.

CAHIR TOURIST OFFICE, Castle Car Park, Cahir (tel. 052 41453). Open May–September.

TRAVEL INFORMATION ONLINE:
www.southeastireland.com and www.tipp.ie

TELEPHONE AREA CODES:
There are at least three different telephone area codes in this region, so the appropriate code will be specified with each number, to avoid confusion.

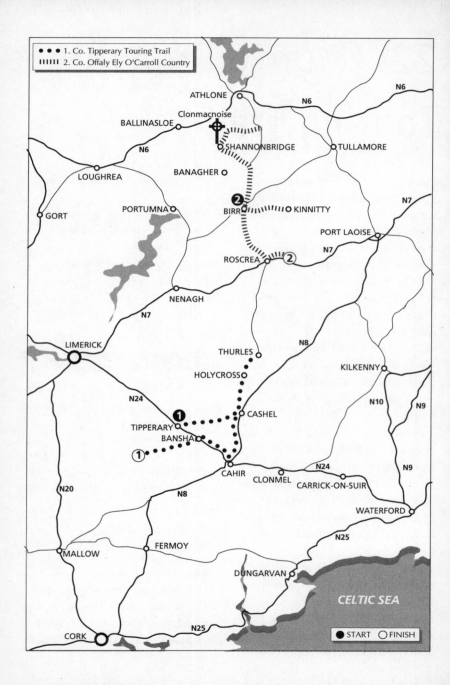

MAJOR EVENTS

CASHEL CULTURAL FESTIVAL – Held each year in the historic heart of Tipperary, this festival offers an array of activities celebrating Cashel's cultural heritage – from free outdoor concerts, art exhibitions and literary events to a family field day and a pub tug-of-war.
Information: Festival Office, City Hall, Cashel, tel. 062 62511. (Mid-July)

GLEN OF AHERLOW WALKING FESTIVAL – Traversing the beautiful Glen of Aherlow, Galtee Mountains and Slievenamuck, this two-day festival caters to walkers of all levels of experience. The programme includes a distance hike, lakeside walk, and also a nature walk for families.
Information: Helen Morrissey, The Glen of Aherlow Fáilte Society Ltd, Coach Road, Aherlow, tel. 062 56331 or www.tipp.ie/aherlow-failte.htm. (First weekend of April)

TIPPERARY TOURING TRAIL DRIVING TOUR

Duration: 3–5 hours plus stops

It's a long way to Tipperary from some places, as the old song goes, but not if you are in the Shannon region. Depart the Limerick or Clare area and follow signs for the main N24 road towards **Tipperary**, the busy marketing town that gives the whole county its name. In the Irish language, Tipperary is known as *Tiobraid Árann*, meaning 'well of (the) river Ara'. Although the River Ara still runs through the town, the original well on Tipperary's main street has long since been covered over.

Dating back to the twelfth century when it was an Anglo-Norman settlement, Tipperary today is primarily known as a dairy-farming centre. Muintir na Tíre, an organised movement to promote all aspects of rural life, was founded here in 1931. It has had a major impact on farming communities throughout Ireland.

From Tipperary, go east onto the N74 main road and travel 19.5 km (12 miles) to the historic hub of the county, **Cashel**, seat of Ireland's kings for over 900 years, and often referred to as 'Cashel of the Kings'. The word 'Cashel', which comes from the Irish language *caiseal*, means 'stone fort'. Because of its great history, Cashel today is one of Ireland's treasured heritage towns.

The focus of the town is a group of medieval ruins known as the **Rock of Cashel** (tel. 062 61437), set on a commanding hill of limestone rising over 60 metres (200 feet) above the surrounding Tipperary countryside. Follow the signs to the 'Rock' and park your car in the ample parking area. Start a tour by climbing the steep hill to the entrance. But before you start your visit to this stunning sight, you might ask yourself: Just what is the Rock?

The Rock of Cashel has been modestly called Ireland's Acropolis. It is the sky-high outpost from whence Ireland's early kings ruled. To enhance it further, Cashel later became intertwined with Ireland's ecclesiastical history.

Cashel's long tale began in the fourth century when local kings chose it to set up a fortress. Even St Patrick came to Cashel. Legend has it that in 448 he baptised King Aengus here. Over the centuries, kings from Cashel conquered much of the surrounding area and were declared rulers of the entire province of Munster. In addition, it is commonly accepted that Brian Ború declared himself the undisputed king of Cashel and was crowned the high king of Ireland here in 977.

Cashel remained a royal capital until the reign of Muirchertach O'Brien who, in 1101, handed over Cashel, in all its glory, to the Church. Within ten years, the archdiocese of Cashel was formally constituted, and a cathedral was built in 1127–34 by Cormac McCarthy, another king, on the site of the former royal palace. By 1169, the cathedral was deemed too small and Dónal Mór O'Brien, king of Thomond, who also built great cathedrals at Limerick and Killaloe, began a new cathedral. This was followed by yet another cathedral in the thirteenth century. But alas, these expansions were stymied in the Middle Ages as English rulers suppressed the power of the Catholic Church in Ireland.

The main buildings were burned in 1495 and yet again in 1647. The structures remained derelict until 1686, when the cathedral was repaired for Anglican use. In 1729, it was re-edified, only to be abandoned again in 1749. In 1874, the ruins were handed over to the Irish government, to be preserved as a national monument. And what a monument it is!

A walk through Cashel is a walk through the centuries. Climb the stone steps and enter the main gateway. A visit starts with a seventeen-minute audiovisual presentation, 'Stronghold of the Faith', presented in the recently restored **Hall of Vicars Choral**, a fifteenth-century building with some seventeenth-century features. To the right of the entrance is **St Patrick's Cross**, reputed to date back to 1150, and which stood for 800 years outside. For safety, it has been brought indoors, and a replica stands outside. It is a rare cross of intricate designs. The carvings include a Crucifixion, and interlacing figures of ribbon-beasts and birds, as well as a Romanesque lion ringed by pellets and concentric circles. Upstairs is a restored dining hall with a minstrel gallery and kitchen, and fifteenth- century furniture.

Nearby is the thirteenth-century **Cathedral**, the largest of the buildings. Standing over the earlier cathedral, built in 1169, this roofless edifice is cruciform in layout, with a long choir and a short nave, two chapels in each transept, and a great tower over the crossing. To the right is a 28-metre (92-foot) **Round Tower** dating back to the tenth century when the Rock was still in the hands of the kings.

The *pièce de resistance* is **Cormac's Chapel**, the twelfth-century cathedral built by King Cormac McCarthy. It is regarded as the finest example of Irish Romanesque architecture, with rich decoration and solid construction. The walls reveal tracings of colourful frescoes, thought to be the only twelfth-century paintings still in Ireland.

Take time outside to explore the many Celtic crosses and burial monuments erected over the centuries, and to enjoy the panoramic views from the Rock, overlooking the surrounding countryside. Guided tours last approximately 45 minutes. Open daily. Admission: €

At the foot of the Rock is **Brú Ború** (tel. 062 61122), a modern glass-enclosed heritage centre dedicated to the preservation of Irish traditional music, dance and song. The displays and exhibits trace the evolution of Irish traditional music, and culminate in a short film showing scenes from Fleadh Cheoil na hÉireann, the annual competition for all-Ireland champion musicians. From mid-June to mid-September, evening shows are staged with performances by top local musicians and dancers. Open Monday–Friday, plus Saturday in summer. Admission: €€

Depart Cashel on the local R660 and drive 16 km (10 miles) north to a national monument with a totally religious focus, **Holycross Abbey** (tel. 0504 43241). Dating back to 1180 and nestling on the banks of the River Suir, this abbey was the fourth to be endowed by Dónal Mór O'Brien, king of Thomond, the same benefactor who erected the cathedral at Cashel and the cathedrals at Limerick and Killaloe. Given to the Cistercian order, the building assumed its name because it housed a relic passed down from the cross of Christ, known as the 'True Cross' or 'Holy Cross'. In the Middle Ages, just as Cashel became a mecca, this abbey also became a hub of religious pilgrimage, drawing the faithful from all over Ireland, who came to pay homage to the relic. It became so popular, in fact, that it was remodelled and enlarged in the fifteenth century to include some new Irish Gothic craftsmanship which remains to this day. Like Cashel and other Catholic foundations, Holycross was suppressed and plundered during the reign of Henry VIII, and its relic was sent to a convent in Cork.

Declared a national monument in 1880, this abbey was restored by the local community in 1971–75 as a parish church, and is still revered as a centre for prayer and reconciliation. A new relic of the 'True Cross', authenticated and sent from St Peter's in Rome in 1977, is now on display in the north transept. The original relic has also been returned and is exhibited in an adjacent reliquary. Other highlights include a medieval sedilia, 5 metres (17 feet) high, with richly carved leaf ornamentation; and a hunting scene mural believed to have originated in the fourteenth century. The grounds include stations of the cross, a glass-enclosed outdoor altar, and gardens dedicated to Padre Pio. Open daily. Admission: free

At this point, you may wish to detour 8 km (5 miles) northeast to **Thurles**, the principal town of east Tipperary, and an agricultural hub. The town's main claim to fame is that in 1884 it was the birthplace of the Gaelic Athletic Association (GAA), the overall sporting body for the games of hurling, Gaelic football, camogie and handball.

To learn more about these native sports, follow signs for **Lár na Páirce**, Slievenamon Road (tel. 0504 23579). When it opened in 1994, it was the first centre of its kind in the country, aiming to tell the story of Gaelic games in an interactive way. Housed in a former bank building, the exhibits include memorabilia from all four Irish provinces, ranging from a large number of hurleys, signed by their owners, to photographs, whistles, jerseys, footballs, newspaper cuttings, trophies, cups and flags, all relating to the history and deeds of great hurlers and footballers. Open Monday–Friday, plus on Saturday during Gaelic games playing season. Admission: €

Retrace your route slightly via Cashel back to the N8 national road, heading south for about 18 km (11 miles) to **Cahir** (pronounced *Kair*), another of Ireland's heritage towns. The Irish for Cahir is *An Chathair*, meaning 'the circular stone fort', which is very similar to the meaning of Cashel. The name originated from the fact that Conor O'Brien, the king of Thomond, built a strong and imposing castle here in the twelfth century. It was around this focal point that the town of Cahir developed.

Some of this original castle has been incorporated in the surviving Anglo-Norman castle, built in the fifteenth–sixteenth century, now known as **Cahir Castle** (tel. 052 41011). Perched on a rocky inlet of the River Suir, this castle is one of Ireland's largest medieval fortresses, with a massive keep, high walls, spacious courtyards and a reat hall.

Unlike its counterparts at Cashel and Holycross, this fortress was a private castle – home of the Butlers – and did not draw hoards of pilgrims for political or religious gatherings. Instead, it attracted a fair share of conquerors, including the earl of Essex who deemed it 'the bulwark of Munster'. The castle was eventually surrendered in 1650 to Cromwell, without a shot being fired. Few conquerors wanted to damage this majestic site.

The size and grandeur of this castle are so impressive that it has often been used as a film location, for productions such as *Barry Lyndon*, *Tristan and Isolde* and *Excalibur*. A visit includes a 45-minute guided tour, a series of exhibits and a seventeen-minute audiovisual presentation on the history of the castle and the area. Open daily, year-round. Admission: €

The nineteenth century saw the growth of a major corn-milling industry, and, in Cahir as elsewhere, this was controlled by the Quaker community. Indeed, Cahir was known as the 'Quaker Town'. The present appearance of the town dates from the 1840s when the earl of Glengall (a member of the Butler family) redesigned the town around **The Square**, often cited as one of Ireland's most successful examples of nineteenth-century town planning. For this project, the earl engaged the famous Regency architect, John Nash, who also designed a fishing lodge known as **Swiss Cottage** (tel. 052 41144), a fanciful thatched-roof *cottage orné* about 1.6 km (1 mile) down the river, east of the castle. Its interior contains a graceful spiral staircase and some elegantly decorated rooms. The wallpaper in the salon, manufactured by the Dufour factory, is one of the first commercially produced Parisian wallpapers. Access is by 40-minute guided tour only, and requires climbing several sets of stone steps. Open daily, May to mid-October; and Tuesday–Sunday, mid-March–April and mid-October–November. Admission: €

From Cahir, it is easy to retrace your route via the N24 road and Tipperary town back to Limerick and the Shannon area. If time allows, follow the signposts through the **Glen of Aherlow**. Fondly called 'Ireland's Greenest Valley', this 26-km (16-mile) route is one of Tipperary's most scenic drives, bounded by the villages of **Bansha** and **Galbally**, and well worth a slight detour. The Glen sits between the **Galtee Mountains** on the south and the **Slievenamuck Ridge** on the north. The Galtees, Ireland's highest inland mountain range, are dominated by a peak named Galteemore, rising to 920 metres (3,018 feet). The name 'Aherlow' is derived from the Irish, *eathralach*, meaning 'between two highlands'.

If you choose not to return to the Shannon area, you can also easily continue eastward via Clonmel and Carrick-on-Suir to Waterford and the Southeast (see Chapters 7–10) or head south to Cork (Chapters 11–14).

PAT'S PICKS

RESTAURANTS

CHEZ HANS, Rockside, Moor Lane, Cashel (tel. 062 61177). For over 35 years, this former Wesleyan chapel in the shadow of the famous Rock has been the culinary domain of Hans-Peter Mattiá. The setting provides a romantic atmosphere, with a cathedral-style ceiling, original stone walls and candlelight, while the menu features Irish ingredients with a French/Irish twist. Specialities include local seafood such as oak-smoked salmon and

Rossmore oysters, as well as free-range chicken with Cashel Blue cheese, and lobster with lemongrass. Open for dinner, Tuesday–Saturday, except first two weeks of January and first week of September.

CLIFFORD'S AT THE BELL, 2 Pearse Street, Cahir (tel. 052 43232). Having operated trend-setting restaurants in Dublin and Cork, Michael and Deirdre Clifford have transferred their culinary expertise and decorative art collection to this small restaurant over 'The Bell' pub. They offer a menu that relies mostly on meats from local butchers, produce from family farms, just-caught fish and local cheeses. Specialities include rack of Tipperary lamb and roast monkfish. Open for dinner, Tuesday–Sunday.

CROCK OF GOLD, 1 Castle Street, Cahir (tel. 052 41951). Across the bridge from Cahir Castle, this multi-level enterprise is a café amid a creatively stocked craft- and book-shop. It offers an all-day menu of fresh salads, soups, sandwiches and home-baked goods. Open for snacks and lunch, daily.

LEGENDS, The Kiln, Cashel (tel. 062 61292). An unbeatable location makes this restaurant a must-do – wide windows look out onto sweeping views of the Rock of Cashel (especially at night when it is floodlit). The location is matched only by the excellent cuisine, offering locally sourced meats, fish and vegetables, prepared in seasonal styles. Open for dinner, Tuesday–Saturday, and for lunch on Sunday, except two weeks in November and two weeks in February.

SPEARMAN'S BAKERY AND TEA ROOM, 97 Main Street, Cashel (tel. 062 61143). With an on-premises bakery producing yummy breads, pastries and cakes throughout the day, this popular café is an ideal stopping place, even if you are only passing through town. Freshly made sandwiches, homemade soups and great just-brewed 'green bean' coffee are specialities. Open for mid-morning and afternoon snacks, and lunch, Monday–Saturday.

PUBS

DWAN'S BREWERY PUB, Slievenamon Road, Thurles (tel. 0504 26007). Occupying a restored nineteenth- century granary, this large four-storey brew pub opened in 1998 and has already gained a far-reaching reputation as one of Ireland's top microbreweries (producing two stouts, an ale and two lagers). It also provides a fun pub atmosphere inside and in its outdoor beer garden.

THE GOLDEN THATCH, Emly (tel. 062 57101). Situated in a small village 16 km (10 miles) west of Tipperary town, this pub has been run by the Mulhall family since 1879. It is a gathering place for fishermen, walkers, golfers and racing enthusiasts.

THE HORSE AND JOCKEY INN, Horse and Jockey (tel. 0504 44303), near Thurles. Dating back over 250 years and originally a horse trainer's home, this pub has long been a landmark on the main Cork–Dublin road. As it sits in the heart of equestrian country, it is frequented by horse trainers and sportsmen who feel right at home amid the décor of horse memorabilia and art.

IRWIN'S YARD, 2 The Square, Cahir (tel. 052 42633). A former grocery store, this vintage pub has a décor of original brickwork, fireplaces and timber beams, with various alcoves, nooks and crannies filled with local memorabilia, including brass pumps, bird cages, spades, pitchforks, brass cash registers and even sack curtains over the windows, all of which give the place a real sense of rustic charm. The outdoor beer garden or 'yard' is an attraction in itself, said to be older than the town's castle walls, and once used for stabling horses for the Bianconi stagecoach services.

KIELY'S BAR, 22 Main Street, Tipperary (tel. 062 51239). Founded in 1912, this pub is one of Tipperary town's oldest licensed premises. It is a favourite with local sporting enthusiasts. Bar food is available during the day and there is music on Thursday and Friday nights.

THE VILLAGE INN, Ballylooby (tel. 052 41705). Situated in a small town just under 5 km (3 miles) southwest of Cahir, this pub is on the tourist trail between the Knockmealdown and Galtee mountains, directly en route to the scenic drive known as 'The Vee'. It has a homely lounge, warmed by a large open fire, and solid country furniture, all on one ground-floor level. There is live music every Saturday.

DIGRESSIONS

EXPLORING BELOW THE SURFACE: If you want to get to the bottom of things, head south of Cahir on the N8 road for 16 km (10 miles) to Mitchelstown Caves, an extensive cave system discovered in 1833 by men quarrying for stone. Although named as the Mitchelstown Caves (since they were found on the then-Mitchelstown Castle Estate), they are actually in south County Tipperary. The caves extend for over a kilometre (half a mile) from the entrance to the innermost cavern. Some rock formations en route are so spectacular that they have names, such as 'The Hanging Gardens of Babylon', 'The Pipe Organ' and 'The Eagle's Wing'. Many fossils are encased in the walls of the passageways inside. Open daily. Information: Mitchelstown Caves, Burncourt, Cahir (tel. 052 67246 or www.mitchelstowncaves.com).

ON A CLEAR DAY, YOU CAN SEE FOREVER: Although often overshadowed by the Ring of Kerry, Antrim Coast and other higher-profile places, one of Ireland's most scenic drives is the Vee Gap, starting out from Clogheen, 8 km (5 miles) southwest of Cahir. It is a drive that should not be missed in fine weather – passing through the Knockmealdown Mountains via the R668, ending at Lismore or neighbouring Cappoquin (via the R669). The broad-brimmed Knockshanahullion (654 metres/2,146 feet) is the highest peak, with the pointed Sugarloaf (653 metres/2,143 feet) to its left. This compact 19.5-km (12-mile) route is covered with rhododendron shrubs in season, and with mountain sheep calmly grazing by the roadside all year round. The road rises to over 609 km (2,000 feet) above sea level and then slowly curves down into County Waterford. There are several lay-by and picnic areas from which to view the surrounding countryside, spread before you in a V-shaped tableau. It is said you can see five counties – Waterford, Tipperary, Limerick, Cork and Kilkenny, and on a clear day, perhaps even more. Information: Cahir Tourist Office, Castle Car Park, Cahir (tel. 052 41453 or www.ballylooby.com/vee.htm).

23: County Offaly – Ely O'Carroll Country

Who or what is Ely O'Carroll?

The name Ely O'Carroll commemorates an ancient Gaelic people, known as the *Éle*, a midlands tribe who settled in parts of Offaly and northeast Tipperary. By the twelfth century, their territory, known as Éile, was divided into two distinct areas – Eliogarty (the land of the Fogartys) and Éile Uí Chearbhaill (the land of the O'Carrolls). The latter district centred around Birr and Roscrea, and hence the area has become accepted as the land of the O'Carroll dynasty or simply, in anglicised form, Ely O'Carroll.

The term gives a special distinction or cachet to County Offaly, an inland county that is not otherwise on the top of tourist 'must-see' lists. When visitors do come to Offaly, however, they realise that it is the home of many significant attractions.

Surrounded by parts of Galway, Roscommon, Westmeath, Meath, Kildare, Laois and Tipperary, County Offaly sits in the middle of Ireland. In fact, Offaly's lovely Georgian town of Birr is often proclaimed as the exact geographic centre of Ireland. It is also the home of the award-winning Birr Castle Gardens and Science Centre, which of themselves are enough to merit a visit to Offaly.

The area's other attractions run the gamut – ranging from one of Ireland's greatest sixth-century monastic settlements at Clonmacnoise, to a vintage car museum and a collage of castles. Bogs are also synonymous with Offaly – as much of the county is devoted to boglands, including the Blackwater Bog, one of the largest sources of fuel for the whole country. A ride on the narrow-gauge Clonmacnoise and West Offaly Railway is an experience not to be missed.

With the River Shannon at its west and the Slieve Bloom Mountains to the east, Offaly has long been an important hub and crossroads of the Irish countryside. This central location makes it a handy base for touring in any direction. *(See map p.214)*

FAST FACTS

Travel Information Offices

ELY O'CARROLL TOURISM LTD, Small Business Centre, Brendan Street, Birr (tel. 0509 20923). Open all year.

TULLAMORE TOURIST OFFICE, Tullamore Dew Heritage Centre, Bury Quay, Tullamore (tel. 0506 52617). Open all year.

BIRR TOURIST INFORMATION OFFICE, Castle Street, Birr (tel. 0509 -20110). Open May–September.

CLONMACNOISE TOURIST OFFICE, Clonmacnoise (tel. 090 967 4134). Open Easter–October.

TRAVEL INFORMATION ONLINE: www.elyocarroll.com, www.offaly.ie and www.ecoast-midlands.travel.ie

TELEPHONE AREA CODES: There are at least three different telephone area codes in this region, so the appropriate code will be specified with each number, to avoid confusion.

MAJOR EVENTS

SLIEVE BLOOM WALKING FESTIVAL – Sponsored by the Slieve Bloom Walking Club, this three-day event welcomes walkers from near and far to traverse 4.8–12.8 km (3–8 miles) on scenic trails along Kinnitty Woodland, Wolftrap Mountain, Clear Lake, the Moonahincha Heritage Walk and other areas. Information: Slieve Bloom Community Centre, Kinnitty, tel. 0509 37299 or www.slievebloom.ie. (First weekend of May)

NATIONAL COUNTRY FAIR – Held at various venues in Birr, this two-day gathering celebrates rural Ireland by combining a traditional country fair with sports events, from fly-casting to ferret racing, and from foxhounds to falconry, as well as sheaf-tossing, tug-of-war, street theatre, face-painting and hunting-horn music. Information: National Country Fair, Birr Castle, tel. 0509 23560 or . www.countryfair.ie(First weekend of June)

BIRR VINTAGE WEEK – Reflecting on an earlier era, this festival draws thousands of people to Birr for a parade of vintage cars, floats and horse-carriages, plus an Olde Time Fair, street-theatre, children's events, sports (including a Georgian cricket match in period costume), live music, pub entertainment and fireworks. Information: Michelle de Forge, Morepark Street, Birr, tel. 0509 20996 or mobile 086 855 1937 or www.birrnet.ie. (Second week of August)

ELY O'CARROLL COUNTRY DRIVING TOUR

Duration: 2–3 hours plus stops

Start a tour in **Birr**, the precise geographic heart of Ireland and the hub of Ely O'Carroll country. Designated as a heritage town, Birr is one of Ireland's finest Georgian towns, picturesquely set beside the River Camcor. It derives its name from the Irish word *biorra*, meaning 'watery place'.

Although dating back to the early Christian period, Birr's main development is attributed to Sir Lawrence Parsons who was assigned the lands during Plantation times in 1620. He named his settlement Parsonstown, and built a large castle on a central site dominating the town. Fourteen generations of this family have lived here, including the present Earl of Rosse.

Although the Parsons' family home, Birr Castle, is not accessible to visitors, the grounds and gardens – known collectively as the **Birr Castle Demesne** (tel. 0509 20336) are open to the public. In particular, the 40 hectares (100 acres) of gardens are a horticultural wonderland, with more than 1,000 species of trees and shrubs, including box hedges featured in the *Guinness Book of Records* as the tallest in the world.

Other facilities open to the public include a giant 1.8-metre (6-foot) reflecting telescope, built in 1845 and the largest in the world for over 70 years, and **Ireland's Historic Science Centre**, located in the nineteenth-century coach house. This unique museum spotlights Ireland's great contributions to science, from astronomy and photography to the invention of the steam turbine engine. Browse through original artefacts, photographs, drawings and letters, and learn from interactive models, audiovisuals and interpretative displays. The galleries here show a much-underrated side of Ireland. It's a fascinating place to visit on a rainy (or a sunny) day. Open daily. Admission: €€

From Birr, it is a 14.5 km (9-mile) detour east via the R440 to **Kinnitty Castle** (tel. 0509 373 180), an authentic castle tracing its roots back to the twelfth century. The original building has been 'reborn' a few times, most notably in 1630 when a 'new' castle was erected, and in 1811 when it was extended by the Pain brothers, who were also architects of Dromoland Castle and Adare Manor. Burned in 1922, it was rebuilt in 1928, into its present Gothic-revival style, with turrets, towers and battlements. Nestled in a sprawling 263-hectare (650-acre) parkland estate at the foothills of the **Slieve Bloom Mountains**, this castle is now a hotel but is open to the public for meals.

For a detour within a detour, travel just over 3 km (2 miles) south of Kinnitty on the Clareen Road (R421) to **Leap Castle** (tel. 0509 31115), an offbeat place whose owner claims it to be 'Ireland's most haunted castle'. Dating back to the fourteenth century when it was a stronghold of the O'Carrolls, this castle is open for tours, but it is wise to phone ahead, especially in the off-season. Open daily. Admission: €

Continuing north from Birr, follow the main N62 road for about 13 km (8 miles) as far as **Cloghan** and then take the R357 northwest for another 13 km (8 miles) to **Shannonbridge**, a small village on the east bank of the Shannon. Take a right turn from the centre of the village, proceeding 6.5 km (4 miles) north to **Clonmacnoise** (tel. 090 967 4195), an impressive sixth-century ruin, standing sombrely on the east bank along a great S-bend of the River Shannon between Lough Derg and Lough Ree. It is the epitome of an early Irish monastery, an everlasting remnant from the days when Ireland was a hub of medieval learning and fondly called the 'Isle of Saints and Scholars'. Even Pope John Paul II made time in his hectic two-day 1979 trip to Ireland to visit Clonmacnoise. 'The very stones speak,' he declared after touring the site.

Founded as a monastery by St Ciarán in 545, this settlement was one of Europe's great centres of learning for nearly 1,000 years, flourishing under the patronage of many kings, including the last high king of Ireland, Rory O'Conor, who is buried here. Great scholars were trained here, and then set forth to bring their knowledge to enlighten the rest of Europe during the Dark Ages. Among the famous alumni of Clonmacnoise was Alcuin, tutor to Charlemagne.

In its heyday, Clonmacnoise was more than a monastery or a university – it was a virtual city, with hundreds of houses and workshops. Because it was superbly situated where the main east–west roadway of early Ireland crossed the prime north–south traffic artery – the River Shannon – Clonmacnoise drew abbots, mentors, and students from all over Ireland. Like other Irish monasteries, it was burned and plundered by many forces, from the Vikings to the English; it was finally reduced to a complete ruin in 1552, and eventually turned over to the Irish government in 1955 to be preserved as a national monument.

Start a visit at the interpretive centre which presents a 23-minute audiovisual on the history and background of the site. Guided tours are then conducted outside. Allow at least an hour to see the remains of the cathedral, eight churches, round towers, high crosses and over 200 other monuments, including the following:

The Cathedral, a blend of tenth- to fifteenth-century architecture. The remains include an early thirteenth-century sacristy; part of a twelfth-century Romanesque doorway that was reconstructed in the fifteenth century; and a fifteenth-century Gothic chancel. Near the high altar are the graves of Turlough Mór O'Conor (who died in 1156), king of Connacht and high king of Ireland, and his son Rory (who died in 1198), the last high king of Ireland.

Temple Ciarán, a small chapel going back to St Ciarán's time, but with many later additions. It is reputed to be the burial place of St Ciarán. In the eleventh century, a collection of early Irish ecclesiastical art treasures was unearthed including the 'Crozier of the Abbots of Clonmacnois', now in the National Museum of Dublin.

Cross of the Scriptures (*Cros na Screaptra*), erected in 914, takes its name from the many biblical scenes that are carved on it, including 'The Crucifixion', 'The Last Judgment', 'Soldiers Casting Lots' and 'Christ Handing the Keys to Peter'.

The South Cross, dating back to the ninth/tenth centuries, is significant because it is covered with panels of interlacing vine-scrolls and other ornaments, as well as a depiction of 'The Crucifixion' on the west face of the shaft.

O'Rourke's Tower, a twelfth-century round tower that rises to almost 19 metres (62 feet). Although impressive, it is imperfect because the top was struck off by lightning in 1135.

Clonmacnoise is open daily. Admission: €€

For a totally different perspective of Irish life, turn left at the exit of Clonmacnoise and follow the signs to the **Clonmacnoise and West Offaly Railway**, Shannonbridge (tel. 090 967 4114), a narrow gauge railway that takes visitors into the boglands, Ireland's unique natural resource formed thousands of years ago. Stretching for miles throughout County Offaly and the neighbouring countryside, the bogs are composed mainly of decayed trees and foliage, which have decomposed over the centuries to form peat or turf, a major source of fuel for the Irish. The one-hour narrated tour follows a 9-km (5.5-mile) circular route around the Blackwater Bog, providing a close-up look at the bog landscape and its flora and fauna, with opportunities to watch turf being cut, stacked, dried and transported. The tours are sponsored by Bord na Móna, the Irish government agency responsible for preserving and mining the bogs. The complex includes a visitor centre that presents displays and a continuous audiovisual about the various facets of the bog as a part of Irish life, including art and sculptures made from bog oak. Trains depart every hour on the hour. It's a great excursion for all ages. Open daily, April–October. Admission: €€

Before departing the Shannonbridge area, you may wish to embark on a short tour 16 km (10 miles) east to **An Dún Transport and Heritage Museum** at Doon, Ballinahown (tel. 090 643 0106), technically just over the county border in County Westmeath, but considered part of 'Ely O'Carroll Country'. It is well worth a visit to see the Hanniffy family's collection of old cars and other forms of transport, including a cable-car display. Vehicles on exhibit include the Bullnose Morris Cowley of the 1920s, a classic Morris Minor, and a rare Shelvoke and Drewry truck of the 1920s, as well as pony sidecars and penny-farthing bicycles. In addition, you can browse through an exhibition of early farm utensils such as early combine harvesters and horse-drawn implements. For train buffs, there is a European model railway. Open daily, May–September. Admission: €

Head back to Birr to begin the southern sector of this tour. Take the N62 south for 19 km (12 miles) to **Roscrea**, another heritage town. It is also one of Ireland's oldest towns, tracing its roots back to the sixth century when St Cronan of Éile founded two monasteries here. The name Roscrea comes from the Irish *Ros Cré*, meaning 'Cré's wood'.

Part of Cronan's second monastery remains to this day, including a round tower and a high cross. The centrepiece of the town, however, is a stone castle, **Roscrea Castle**, Castle Street (tel. 0505 21850), erected in 1280. Visitors can tour the restored gate tower, as well as a polygonal fortification with curtain walls and two D-shaped towers; the courtyard; and a newly laid-out Georgian garden. The complex also includes the eighteenth-century **Damer House**, one of the finest Queen Anne houses in Ireland, with extensive exhibitions about Roscrea heritage. Open daily, April–October. Admission: €

From Roscrea, head east on the main Limerick–Dublin N7 road for about 5 km (just over 3 miles) to **Ballaghmore Castle**, Borris-in-Ossory (tel. 0505 21453). Although technically in County Laois, this castle is considered part of the Ely O'Carroll route, or at least a short detour. Set amid 12 hectares (30 acres) of farmland, it was built in 1480 by the Gaelic Chieftain MacGiollaphádraig (now called Fitzpatrick), meaning son of the servant of Patrick. Among the original stone carvings is an authentic sheela-na-gig on the front facing wall – a pagan fertility symbol to ward off evil. The castle has had a long and turbulent history – partially destroyed by Cromwell's forces in 1647, restored in 1836, and later used as a

granary before falling into disuse until the present owner, Gráinne Ní Cormac, bought it in 1990 and restored it. It is a bit musty and dimly lit but certainly conveys a fifteenth-century atmosphere. Open daily. Admission: €

At this point, along the main N7 road, it is easy to continue east towards Dublin or west to Limerick, or to head south to other parts of Tipperary.

RESTAURANTS

THE MALTINGS, Castle Street, Birr (tel. 0509 21345). Nestled beside Birr Castle grounds along the River Camcor, this building dates back to 1810 when it was used to store malt for Guinness. It was revamped and adapted as a family-run restaurant in 1994. Open for breakfast, lunch, snacks and dinner, daily.

RIVERBANK RESTAURANT, Riverstown (tel. 0509 21528). Views of the Little Brosna river are a focal point at this family-run restaurant, located 1.5 km (1 mile) west of Birr. The décor exudes country-inn charm, with brick walls, fireplace, pink linens and local memorabilia, capped by wide picture windows beside the flower-decked riverbank. The menu offers fresh seafood, free-range meats, and local produce. Lighter items, such as omelettes, soups and salads, are served in the bar all day. Open for lunch, daily; and for dinner, Wednesday–Monday.

SPINNERS BISTRO, Castle Street, Birr (tel. 0509 21673; fax 0509 21672).
Conveniently situated across the street from the Birr Castle estate, this restaurant is housed in a restored nineteenth-century woollen mill, with suitable memorabilia and an adjacent courtyard garden. The menu features Irish cuisine, with specialities such as salmon and potato cakes, and bread and butter pudding. Open for dinner, Tuesday–Sunday, May–September; Wednesday–Sunday, October–April.

THE STABLES, 6 Oxmantown Mall, Birr (tel. 0509 20263). For over 25 years, this restaurant has been a local favourite, set in the converted stables and coach house of a nineteenth-century Georgian house. The décor is rich in old-world ambience, with beamed ceilings, large open fireplace, brick walls, arches and candlelit tables. The menu blends Irish ingredients with French cookery. Open for lunch and dinner, Tuesday–Sunday, June–September; Tuesday–Saturday, October–May; and for lunch on Sunday.

THE THATCH, Crinkill (tel. 0509 20682). Tucked on a country road about 1.6 km (1 mile) south of Birr, this thatched-roof eatery is an unexpected surprise. Having started as a simple pub known as 'Mother Walsh's', it has been in the same family for over 200 years and has gradually expanded into an award- winning restaurant. The menu offers choices such as monkfish piccata, smoked wild boar, fillet of ostrich, veal with smoked chicken, lemon-and-honey roast duck, and rack of lamb. It's very popular with the locals, so reserve in advance. Open for dinner, Tuesday–Sunday, May–September; Wednesday–Saturday, October–April; and for lunch on Sunday.

PUBS

GILTRAP'S BAR, Kinnitty (tel. 0509 37076). Set at the foot of the Slieve Bloom Mountains, this old-style country pub has an inviting atmosphere, with large low windows and beamed ceilings, small stools and wooden tables, and an open brick fireplace. It has been a pub for the past 150 years and has won several awards for current owners, Percy and Phil Clendennen.

HINEY'S, Main Street, Ferbane (tel. 090 645 4344). Located in a small country town southeast of Clonmacnoise, this is a typical old country pub, dating back over 300 years to when it was known as the 'Black Boot Inn'. The current publican, Joe Hiney, is a third-generation proprietor and has left most of the décor intact from earlier days, including its well-worn bar counter. Hearty traditional pub lunches are served during the day.

MICHAEL KILLEEN'S, Shannonbridge (tel. 090 967 4112). Dating back over 400 years, this revered establishment is a pub-cum-grocery store. Step inside and experience yesteryear – from the mellowed bar and open fireplace, to a great collection of vintage prints and photographs along the walls. It is a popular meeting place for local farmers, as well as boatmen from the Shannon. There is traditional music every Thursday.

THE TOWER, Dublin Road, Roscrea (tel. 0505 21774). History surrounds this pub, situated beside a twelfth-century gable and a medieval round tower, the latter of which gives the pub its name. The interior blends a Victorian ambience with walls of brick and dark wood, timber partitions and old coach-house-type seating.

THE VINE HOUSE BAR, West End, Banagher (tel. 0509 51463). Nestled near the edge of the River Shannon, this pub is surrounded by a medieval wall. The interior, a blend of interconnecting brick and wood rooms with low-beamed ceilings, has an eclectic décor of arched windows, pine tables and chairs, flagged floors and stripped walls hung with mirrors. It is a favourite hang-out for boating enthusiasts. From May through September, there is music nightly.

DIGRESSIONS

CRUISING ON THE RIVER: Board the *River Queen*, an enclosed river-bus, for a floating tour of the Ely O'Carroll Country shoreline along the River Shannon. The 90-minute cruise, which includes a commentary, passes under the seven-arched Banagher Stone Bridge and then via Martello towers and fortresses, downstream to Victoria Lock, the largest lock on the entire Shannon system. Cruises operate May–September, departing Banagher Marina, about 13 km (8 miles) northwest of Birr. Information: Silver Line Cruisers Ltd, Banagher (tel. 0509 51112).

TOURING AND TASTING IN TULLAMORE: In the northeast corner of County Offaly is Tullamore, 32 km (20 miles) from Birr and home of Tullamore Dew and Irish Mist. Visit the Tullamore Dew Heritage Centre to learn all about the town and its famous products. It is housed in a four-storey bonded warehouse that was built in the nineteenth century, on the banks of the Grand Canal, to mature the whiskey and load it directly onto canal barges for shipping throughout the world. Visitors can wander through the recreated working stations that were originally at the distillery, such as the malting, bottling and cooperage areas, and the maturating room where oak casks of whiskey were left to mature. A tasting of Tullamore Dew or Irish Mist Liqueur awaits you at the end of the tour. In addition, there is an exhibition on the development of Tullamore from a small village in the 1620s to its present status as a thriving midlands town. Open daily. Information: Tullamore Dew Heritage Centre, Bury Quay, Tullamore (tel. 0506 25015 or www.tullamore-dew.org).

24: Limerick City

Mention *Angela's Ashes* (the prize-winning novel of Limerick-born author Frank McCourt), and images come to mind of a poverty-ridden Limerick of yesteryear. Limerick of today is a totally different story.

Picturesquely situated beside the River Shannon, Limerick is rich in Viking, Norman, medieval and Georgian traditions, making for an interesting and varied landscape. As the fourth largest city in Ireland, it is a busy seaport and manufacturing centre, as well as an important market and communications hub. Limerick is also a key learning centre, home to the University of Limerick and an array of regional, technical, business and language colleges, as well as music academies. In spite of its many facets, however, Limerick is a relatively small and compact city, easy to walk around and to get to know.

Most people associate Limerick with a five-line rhyme known as a 'limerick', although no one knows for sure how or if it originated here. The name Limerick itself is derived from the Irish language *Luimneach*, meaning 'bare area of ground'. Linguists interpret this definition as referring to the land beside the lower reaches of the Shannon, with the 'bare' understood to denote an unprotected and vulnerable location. And indeed Limerick was open to attack – it was plundered by Vikings in the tenth century and by Anglo-Normans in the twelfth century. The Norman conquerors made sure that Limerick would no longer be defenceless by building a mighty castle fortress that survives to this day on the banks of the Shannon.

The castle is only one of Limerick's many buildings and areas to have been recently renewed, restored and enhanced. As the closest city to the international airport at Shannon, Limerick is often the first Irish city that transatlantic visitors encounter. Fortunately, it does make a good first impression and a fitting introduction to Ireland.

FAST FACTS

Travel Information Office

LIMERICK TOURIST OFFICE, Arthur's Quay Park, Limerick (tel. 061 317 522). Open all year.

TRAVEL INFORMATION ONLINE:
www.visitlimerick.com and
www.shannondev.ie/tourism

TELEPHONE AREA CODES:
The area code for all telephone numbers in the Limerick area is 061, unless indicated otherwise.

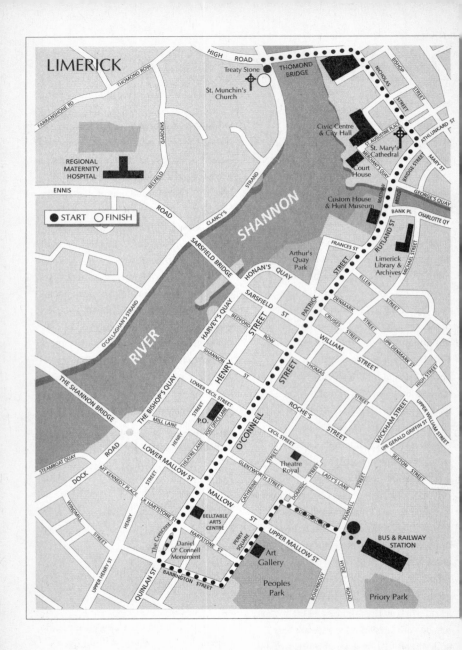

MAJOR EVENTS

FRESH FILM FESTIVAL – Held at Limerick's Belltable Arts Centre, this is a unique event on the Irish cinematic calendar because it caters solely for a youth audience (12–18 age group). The schedule includes showings of classic films featuring children, and also a series of workshops and competitions for kids interested in film-making. Information: Jayne Foley, tel. 319 555 or www.freshfilmfestival.net. (Last week of March)

LIMERICK INTERNATIONAL BAND FESTIVAL – For over 30 years, this gathering has been a highlight of the annual St Patrick's Week festivities. The participants, drawn from Ireland, Europe, the US and other countries, include marching and concert bands, drill and dance teams, and choirs. They perform on the streets of Limerick and at the University of Limerick Concert Hall. Information: Caroline Nolan-Diffley, tel. 410 777 or www.shannon-dev.ie/bandfest. (Mid-March)

LIMERICK CITY WALKING TOUR

Duration: 3–4 hours plus stops

Start a tour at **Colbert Station**, Limerick's bus and rail depot on Parnell Street. By starting here, we are recalling Limerick's history in reverse since this area is the city's newest region, far from the historic original north end of town. If you are a history buff who prefers to retrace a city's progress in chronological order, you might prefer to do this tour in reverse (starting with King's Island).

Continue from the front entrance of the station. Cross over to David Street and walk one block. On the right is the **Tait Clock**, a Gothic octagonal tower with a four-faced clock erected in 1867. Its decorative style sets the tone for the adjacent area.

Turn left at the clock and walk one block to an area known as **Newtown Pery**. Historically, this is Limerick's Georgian quarter and youngest development, compared to the rest of the city centre. Built over a period of 80 years (1760–1840), Newtown Pery was the brainchild of Edward Sexton-Pery, a local gentleman who inherited a large estate and proposed to develop his lands, virtually building a new city, based on a grid of wide streets and squares in the Georgian fashion.

The core of this area, **Pery Square**, contains six houses, numbers 1 through 6. Taken collectively, they are the finest example of Georgian architecture in Limerick, and comprise the only terrace of the city that is symmetrically designed. Notice that the houses at either end have gable entrances.

One of these houses, number 2 Pery Square, has been restored by the Limerick Civic Trust as **The Georgian House** (tel. 314 130). It is a 'show house' open to the public, similar to number 29 Fitzwilliam Street in Dublin. The house, replete with marble walls and ornate plaster work, contains two exhibits – illustrations depicting the history of Georgian Limerick and a display of pictures showing Frank McCourt's Limerick, as well as a life-size reconstruction of the McCourt home. Open Monday– Friday. Admission: €

On the east side of the square is the **Limerick City Gallery of Art** (tel. 310 633), housed in an attractive Romanesque-style building. Enter through a Celtic-patterned door with a stained-glass fanlight incorporating the city arms, a preview of the artistic flair of this establishment. Like many galleries and libraries in the US and Britain, it got off the ground with a little help from Andrew Carnegie who contributed £7,000 towards the construction of the building. The cultural hub of Limerick, this gallery contains a permanent collection of eighteenth-, nineteenth- and twentieth-century Irish art, from acclaimed artists such as Jack B Yeats and Seán Keating. There are also ever-changing exhibitions of paintings, patchwork, architecture and sculpture. Open Monday–Saturday. Admission: free

The gallery is surrounded by the **People's Park**, a tree-shaded square of greenery with a Victorian-style drinking fountain. Walk along the edge of the park or take some time to explore the area. Then continue to Barrington Street

and turn right; walk for two blocks to **O'Connell Street**, a wide thoroughfare that runs through the heart of Limerick. Like its counterparts in Dublin and other towns and cities in Ireland, it is named after Daniel O'Connell, the nineteenth-century Kerry-born lawyer, politician and statesman, who was known as 'The Liberator'. A statue of O'Connell stands in the centre as the street splits in two for one block and forms **The Crescent**. Built in the early 1800s and originally known as Richmond Place, this was designed to be the principal feature of Newtown Pery. The unique design of a double crescent is rare in Ireland. From the Crescent, there is a clear view down O'Connell Street towards the rest of the city.

Walk along O'Connell Street, lined on both sides by Georgian townhouses. To the right on the next block is the **Belltable Arts Centre**, 69 O'Connell Street (tel. 319 866), a hub of Limerick's performing and visual arts. It contains a theatre and two gallery exhibition areas. In addition to evening performances, there are frequent daytime operatic recitals, traditional Irish music sessions, classical concerts, poetry readings and drama workshops. Open Monday–Saturday. Admission charges vary according to event.

If you are walking, follow O'Connell Street for seven blocks in a northerly direction, passing a variety of shops, fast-food eateries, and department stores.

If you are in a car, this is not possible, since traffic flows one-way to the south. You may wish to take a few detours along the route. A left on Mallow Street brings you to the **Shannon Bridge** over the River Shannon, or a left on Sarsfield Street will bring you to the **Sarsfield Bridge**, also providing good views of the river.

A right on Sarsfield Street takes you to **Cruise's Street**, a shopping complex designed in an 'Old Limerick' theme, with 55 shops, restaurants and other enterprises.

As O'Connell Street merges with **Patrick Street**, straight ahead is the **Arthur's Quay Shopping Centre**, an enclosed multi-storey shopping complex with 30 different shops and restaurants.

The adjacent **Arthur's Quay Park**, built on land reclaimed from the river, has a large central paved space for bands and outdoor festivals, and a riverside walk overlooking the Shannon. It is also the setting of the Limerick Tourist Office, well worth a stop for the latest touring information. This section of Limerick south of the turn of the river was the original **Irishtown.**

At this point, you may wish to return to Patrick Street for a detour. Take a right onto Ellen Street, and follow it eastward to **Seán Heuston Place**, passing the old **Milk Market** en route. Dating back to 1830, this outdoor market was once the thriving hub of Limerick's Irishtown. It was begun as a selling area for corn, and later evolved as a market for dairy prod-ucts. Nowadays, on Saturday mornings, it is the site of a country market for mixed vegetables, flowers, cheeses, home-baked goods, jams and preserves.

Retrace your steps to Patrick Street and take a right to see the cultural centrepiece of Limerick – the **Hunt Museum**, Custom House, Rutland Street (tel. 312 833). This world-class collection of historic and archaeological artefacts, fine arts and decorative arts is on display at the former Custom House. The collection contains more than 3,000 art objects, valued at over €50 million. The scope includes statues in stone, bronze and wood; panel paintings; metalwork; jewellery; enamels and ceramics, as well as works by Picasso and Leonardo da Vinci. Irish archaeological material includes Neolithic flints and Bronze Age gold. Rare pieces range from the unique eighth-century Antrim Cross, to penal crucifixes of the eighteenth and nineteenth centuries, and the gold cross worn by Mary, Queen of Scots, on the day of her execution. The Hunt Collection is widely acknowledged as one of the foremost private medieval art collections made in the last century. The Custom House building is worth a visit in its own right. Designed by Italian architect Daviso de Arcort (Davis Ducart), it is a handsome eighteenth-century Palladian-style edifice, standing at the point where the River Shannon meets its tributary, the River Abbey. Open daily. Admission: €€

Cross over the Shannon from Irish-town at **Mathew Bridge**, and enter the area known variously as **King's Island** or **Englishtown**. On **Bridge Street**, walk in a northerly direction. On the left is the heart of Limerick's medieval quarter or 'old city'. On this site, in 922, the Vikings pushed their beaked longships ashore to build their meeting place, *Thingmote*, their most westerly European stronghold.

Two centuries later, Dónal Mór O'Brien, the Irish king of Munster, built a palace on this site. In 1171, he donated it for use as a church. Today this historic ground serves as the setting for the **Cathedral Church of St Mary the Virgin**, Bridge Street (tel. 310 293). Traditionally known as St Mary's Cathedral, this massive Romanesque and Gothic Church of Ireland edifice was completed around 1194, and is Limerick's prime ecclesiastical landmark. It contains many fine antiquities, including a coffin lid reputed to be that of Dónal Mór O'Brien, the king who donated the property to the church and who died in 1194; and an original pre-Reformation stone altar, 4 metres (13 feet) long and weighing 3 tons, reputed the largest in Ireland or Britain. The **Great West Door** is Romanesque in style, and tradition claims that it was King Dónal Mór O'Brien's palace entrance. In addition, there is a reredos erected in 1907, carved by Michael Pearse, the father of 1916 Rising patriot Pádraig Pearse; a wealth of stained-glass windows; a fourteenth-century tower rising to 36.5 metres (120 feet) in height; and a set of 23 medieval carved seats with misericords – the only examples of their kind of furniture preserved in Ireland. The word *misericord* comes from the Latin meaning 'act of mercy'. Carved from oak between 1480 and 1500, the seats were designed to be raised. Each has a lip or ledge that allows the occupant, though standing, to rest during long services. Open Monday–Saturday. Admission: €

Depart the cathedral and turn left onto **Nicholas Street**. Inset into the boundary wall of St Mary's and Nicholas Street is a row of Tuscan columns, the only surviving element of **The Exchange**, a prominent market building built in 1702. To the left also are the Limerick Civic Offices, on the site of the **Old Courthouse** and city jail. Next is **King John's Castle**, Nicholas Street, King's Island (tel. 360 788), the city's signature fortress, erected by the Anglo-Normans in 1210 as a protection beside the River Shannon. Officially known as Limerick Castle, and considered one of the finest examples of fortified Norman architecture in Ireland, this sprawling stone structure was built under orders from King John of England. The castle incorporates some unique features for its time, such as curtain walls; D-shaped towers protecting the castle on the north side; and rounded gate towers. Now the focal point of Limerick's historic quarter, it houses an on-site visitor centre with displays, artefacts and a multi-visual show, 'The Story of Limerick'. The towers and battlements provide spectacular views of the River Shannon, and the undercroft invites visitors to watch the progress of current archaeological digs. Open daily. Admission: €€

Adjacent is **Castle Lane**, an authentic eighteenth- to nineteenth-century street, lined with buildings that represent Limerick's architectural heritage – a granary, two Dutch gable-fronted houses, a labourer's cottage and a tavern. Thousands of bricks from original eighteenth-century Limerick-city buildings were used in the construction of Castle Lane, to ensure an authentic streetscape.

At the forefront of this ancient street is **Limerick Museum** (tel. 417 826), occupying a restored four-storey granary building. This museum presents a collection illustrating the long history of Limerick city and the surrounding areas, from 5000BC to the present. The exhibits range from Stone Age, Bronze Age and medieval times, to examples of Limerick lace, a local enterprise. There is also a trades history display and a currency exhibit, as well as civic artefacts – the city's official sword, maces and charters. Open Tuesday– Saturday. Admission: free

To the left of the castle is **Thomond Bridge**, also built by the Normans. Cross over the bridge. To the left is the symbol of Limerick – the **Treaty Stone**, a rock on a pedestal whereon was signed the 1691 treaty between England and Ireland, a treaty that was breached by England. Afterwards Limerick was referred to as 'the city of the violated treaty'.

Stroll southward along the west banks of the River Shannon via **Clancy's Strand**, for fine views of King John's Castle and the city's other major historic landmarks to the left. Cross over **Sarsfield Bridge** back to the heart of the city to complete your tour.

PAT'S PICKS

RESTAURANTS

AUBARS, 49–50 Thomas Street (tel. 317 799). In a casual yet classy atmosphere, this city-centre bistro offers well- balanced and healthy modern dishes, such as freshly made salads, char-grilled meats, roast fillets of fish, seafood crêpes, and homemade pork and herb sausages. Open for breakfast, lunch, snacks and dinner, daily.

BRULÉES, Henry and Mallow Street (tel. 319 931). Nestled in the heart of the city, this stylish contemporary restaurant specialises in modern Irish cuisine, using locally sourced ingredients and French influences. House favourites include Irish beef fillet on black pudding mash, grilled liver and bacon with champ, and a vegetarian dish of spring rolls on a bed of noodles. Open for lunch, Tuesday– Friday; and dinner, Tuesday–Saturday.

DUCARTES, Old Custom House, Rutland Street (tel. 312 662). Housed in the Hunt Museum, this arty restaurant is a favourite with locals and visitors alike, especially for tables beside the windows or on the outside terrace overlooking the River Shannon marina. The menu offers freshly prepared soups, salads, sandwiches and hot dishes. Open for lunch and snacks, daily.

MANNA, Unit C2, Cornmarket Square, Robert Street (tel. 318 317). Seeking something different? Slightly off the beaten track, this restaurant is situated beside Limerick's traditional Milk Market area. With a décor that is modern – with pale walls, light-wood tables, high-backed chairs and modern art – this restaurant has a menu that is likewise contemporary. Choices include salt-baked sea bass, flambéed king prawns, ostrich, and couscous. Open for dinner, Tuesday– Sunday.

MOLL DARBY'S, 8 George's Quay (tel. 411 511). Wedged beside the River Abbey, a block from St Mary's Cathedral, this restaurant offers an old-world setting of beamed ceilings, brick walls and arches, bent-wood chairs, sconce lighting, and antiques. The menu specialises in seafood and steaks, with added choices of pastas, pizzas and vegetarian dishes. Save room for homemade desserts and ice creams. Open for dinner, daily.

SEAN CARA, 3–4 Dock Road (tel. 314 483). Situated near the Shannon Bridge, this restaurant has a name that means 'old friend'. Living up to its name, this place aims to provide a friendly atmosphere, with brick walls, old photos and other comfortable touches. The menu offers simple traditional fare, such as steaks, traditional Irish stew and boiled Limerick bacon and cabbage, as well as international and vegetarian dishes. Open for lunch and dinner, Tuesday– Sunday.

PUBS

THE LOCKE BAR, 3 George's Quay (tel. 413 733). For a maritime ambience overlooking the riverside quays, step into this vintage pub, dating back to 1724. An old-world décor prevails inside, with many original furnishings and open fireplaces, as well as sporting mementoes (thanks to the current proprietor who played rugby for Ireland). Traditional music is played on Monday, Tuesday and Sunday evenings.

NANCY BLAKE'S, 19 Denmark Street (tel. 416 443). Located between Patrick Street and the Milk Market area, this veteran pub is known for traditional music sessions in the evening, but is an atmospheric place for a drink or snack at any time of day.

PATRICK PUNCH'S, O'Connell Avenue, Punch's Cross (tel. 229 588). It's worth a car or taxi drive to the south edge of town to visit this popular neighbourhood pub. The décor features the best of 'old Limerick' with Tiffany-style lamps, dark woods, open turf fireplaces, and a tin ceiling bedecked with antique model aeroplanes and unicycles. It is also near many of the *Angela's Ashes* street settings.

SCHOONERS, Steamboat Quay, Dock Road (tel. 318 147). Situated overlooking the River Shannon, this bright and modern pub understandably has a nautical décor and ambience, including an outdoor terrace beside the river. It sits in the heart of a developing new Limerick waterside district, between two popular hotels (Jury's Inn and the Clarion). Live music is available almost every night.

TAVERN AT THE CASTLE, Castle Lane, off Nicholas Street (tel. 360 788). Reminiscent of the eighteenth century, this stone-fronted traditional pub sits overlooking the River Shannon, beside King John's Castle. It is an ideal place for a light meal or snack throughout the day, with seating indoors and on picnic tables outside by the river. Traditional music sessions are frequently scheduled.

DIGRESSIONS

CIRCLING THE CITY: Not all tours of Limerick are on foot. Bus Éireann conducts 'The Great Limerick Tour', an open-top bus overview of Limerick city, from medieval and Georgian areas to the rivers, bridges and major landmarks, such as King John's Castle, as well as a look at the *Angela's Ashes* areas of the city. Duration of each tour is 90 minutes, operating daily from mid-June to mid-August. Information: Bus Éireann, Bus Station, Parnell Street (tel. 313 333 or www.buseireann.ie)

HISTORY TRAIL: See the best of 'Old Limerick' on a walking tour with a local guide. Major sites covered include King John's Castle and St Mary's Cathedral, as well as a few off-the-beaten-track places such as the Bishop's Palace, the oldest domestic building in Limerick; Merchant's Quay, once one of the busiest locations in old Limerick; and Sir Harry's Mall, the wall and roadway built by Sir Harry Hartstonge along the River Abbey. Duration of each tour is 90 minutes, with departures Monday– Friday. Information: St Mary's Action Centre, 44 Nicholas Street, King's Island (tel. 318 106 or www.iol.ie/~smidp).

LITERARY LIMERICK: Follow in the footsteps of Limerick-born author Frank McCourt on an *Angela's Ashes* walking tour of Limerick city, with a local guide. The route follows a path through more than 20 settings that were featured in the Pulitzer Prize-winning book, including Roden Lane, Windmill Street, St Joseph's Church, Barrack Hill, Carnegie Library, the Leamy school building, the People's Park, the St Vincent De Paul building, and others. Duration of each tour is 90 minutes, with weekday departures, Monday–Friday. Information: St Mary's Action Centre, 44 Nicholas Street, King's Island (tel. 318 106 or www.iol.ie/~smidp).

25: Adare

Living up to the title 'prettiest village in Ireland' is a tall order, but one that Adare continually meets. Set amid lush countryside beside the River Maigue, Adare is a model estate village lined with ornate thatched cottages, colourful gardens, distinctive Tudor-style stone buildings, and historic abbey ruins. It is cheery and slow-paced, with hardly a trace of the twenty-first century marring the village's old-world image.

No wonder Adare has always been a popular stop for travellers along the busy Limerick and Killarney corridor. It is not surprising that photographers, film-makers, postcard-manufacturers and artists have elevated Adare to the status of a tourism icon.

Not only does Adare look good, but it is a genuine village, not a reconstruction or a prototype. The place name Adare comes from the Irish language, *Áth Dara*, meaning 'ford of (the) oak grove'. It aptly describes the village setting – shaded by great old oak trees beside the river.

The rest of Adare's charm comes from its history, dating back to Norman foundations in the thirteenth century, and enhanced over the years by the building of castles, manors, abbeys and monasteries.

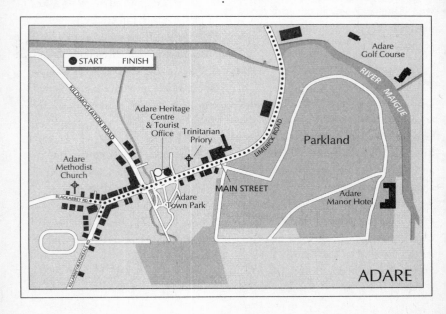

The town owes much to the planning and benevolence of the earls of Dunraven (Quinn family) who have made Adare their home for over 300 years.

So, if you are coming to this part of Ireland, put Adare on your itinerary. Whether you are just passing through or lingering awhile, be sure to walk along the wide flower-rimmed main street – relax, adjust to the local pace, and step back in time. Just being in Adare is a refreshing experience.

FAST FACTS

Travel Information Office

ADARE TOURIST OFFICE, Adare Heritage Centre, Main Street, Adare (tel. 061 396 255). Open all year.

TRAVEL INFORMATION ONLINE:
www.adare-ireland.com

TELEPHONE AREA CODE:
The area code for all telephone numbers in Adare is 061, unless indicated otherwise. Applicable codes for neighbouring areas are specified in each case.

MAJOR EVENTS

LIMERICK SHOW – Looking for a top-notch country fair? Although this event does not actually take place in Adare village, it is only 8 km (5 miles) north at Patrickswell. It is the largest agricultural show in Munster and one of the most important in Ireland, with showings and competitions for pedigree and commercial cattle, horses, sheep and dogs, as well as crafts, horticulture, and entertainment and trade stands. Information: Angela O'Mara, tel. 355298 or www.limerickshow.com. (Last weekend of August)

IRISH COFFEE FESTIVAL – Adare's neighbouring town of Foynes on the Shannon Estuary is the host of this annual salute to one of Ireland's (and the world's) favourite drinks. Irish coffee was invented here more than 50 years ago at the original Shannon Airport, by a barman named Joe Sheridan. The programme includes parades, musical entertainment, street theatre, fireworks, a regatta and the World Irish Coffee Making Championship. Information: Margaret O'Shaughnessy, tel. 069 65416 or www.irishcoffeefestival.com. (Third weekend of July)

ADARE VILLAGE WALKING TOUR

Duration: 1–2 hours plus stops

With plenty of on-site car parking, the most convenient place to start a tour is on **Main Street** at the **Adare Heritage Centre** (tel. 396 666), a relatively new development but built with the goal of blending into the local environment and architecture. Documenting the historical events of Adare from the thirteenth century to the present day, this centre does a good job in setting the tone for a visit to the village. The layout uses a comprehensive exhibition with murals and realistic model enactments, along with a short fourteen-minute audiovisual, to profile the earls of Dunraven and to tell the stories of Adare Castle and Manor and the village's three medieval monasteries – the Trinitarian Monastery, the Augustinian Friary and the Franciscan Friary. Open daily. Admission charge to exhibit: €

Take time to explore the other facilities of the heritage centre, including craft shops, public library and tourist office, or stroll outside amid the well-manicured gardens. Directly across the street is the **Village Park**, with extensive gardens, benches and a thatched gazebo.

Of particular interest is **The Wishing Pool**, a small pool contained in a triangular space, and bounded on two sides by masonry walls, and, on the road side, by a coursed stone parapet wall, with access to **Drehideen Stream** (a small tributary of the River Maigue) on either side. It was used long ago by the women of Adare as a laundry-washing pool, as well as a watering place for horses. Groups of women used to gather regularly at the pool to wash the family clothes and talk about life in the village. Before the days of washing detergents, these women did their washing on 'spittle stones' in the stream bed or by pounding the clothes with wooden beetles. The stream flows under the **Little Bridge** (*An Droichidín*), a small two-arched bridge. The

pool was restored during the European architectural heritage year, in 1975.

From the heritage centre, take a left and enter the grounds of one of the village's trio of church landmarks – **Trinitarian Priory** (tel. 396 177 or 396 172). Officially named Holy Trinity Church, this building incorporates the thirteenth-century nave, chancel, north transept and other parts of the Church of the White Monastery, a house of the Trinitarian Canons of the Order of the Redemption of Captives, the only branch of this order in Ireland. The work of these friars was the ransoming and liberation of Christian captives during the wars of the Crusaders. Why they came to Ireland is uncertain, but they established this monastery in 1230. It is commonly referred to as 'The White Abbey' because of the white habit worn by the monks. Like many similar Catholic establishments, it was suppressed in 1539 during the reign of Henry VIII. It remained in ruins until 1811 when it was restored by the second earl of Dunraven and given to the Catholics of Adare as their parish church. It remains in that usage to this day. In 1852, it was enlarged by the third earl of Dunraven. One of the highlights of the layout is a fine circular dovecote or columbarium behind the church. Open daily. Admission: free

Continue left, walking up Main Street. The next building is the **Parochial House**, a fine stone building dating back to 1852, followed by the **Dunraven Arms Hotel**, a yellow-toned stone inn, set amid palm tree-lined gardens, and dating back to 1792.

After the hotel, continue to the outskirts of town to the **Church of Ireland church** (tel. 396 227), founded in 1316 as an Augustinian Priory, but converted into use as a Church of Ireland place of worship (in 1807) and school (in 1814). Known locally for centuries as **The Black Abbey**, it was suppressed by the forces of Henry VIII in the mid-sixteenth century. The interior contains many interesting features including a fifteenth-century tower and cloister. Open daily. Admission: free

As you move to the left of the church, the River Maigue comes into view. Cross over the bridge, a fine stone work built by the earl of Kildare in the fourteenth and fifteenth centuries, replacing an earlier wooden one.

Across the street is the entrance to the **Adare Golf Club**, part of the Adare Manor estate. Within the golf-club grounds are three significant ruins, not accessible, but visible, from the main street – **Adare Castle**, also known as the Desmond Castle, dating back at least to 1227, built by the Normans and dismantled by Cromwellian forces in 1657; the **Franciscan Friary**, dedicated in 1464 and burned in 1646 by parliamentary forces; and the **Old Parish Church of St Nicholas**, in use from the twelfth century until 1806.

Return to the village, crossing back over the bridge, and to the left is the entrance to **Adare Manor** (tel. 396 566), nestled in a 340-hectare (840-acre) estate beside the River Maigue. The former home of the earls of Dunraven and now a luxury hotel and golf resort, Adare Manor is a nineteenth-century Tudor Gothic mansion. The building of the manor in its present format, which spanned the period 1832 to 1862, under the direction of the second earl of Dunraven, provided work for the villagers during the disastrous potato famine. Walk around outside to see the many unique features: a turreted entrance tower, 52 chimneys to commemorate each week of the year, 75 fireplaces, 365 leaded glass windows, and elaborate decorative stonework – arches, gargoyles, bays and window frames. The interior is equally dazzling, with a 40-metre (132-foot) long minstrel's gallery, inspired by the Hall of Mirrors at Versailles, lined on either side with seventeenth-century Flemish choir stalls. It remained in the hands of the Dunraven family until 1982, and opened as a hotel in 1988.

The grounds are a joy for strolling. The formal gardens, which were laid out in geometric box patterns in the 1850s, comprise an assortment of trees, including a copious 300-year-old Cedar of Lebanon tree on the river bank, 180-year-old beeches, monkey-puzzle trees, cork, and flowering cherries. There is also a display of ogham stones from

County Kerry, dating from the early fifth to the mid- seventh centuries, and an animal cemetery with carved memorials to the Dunraven pets. Open daily. Admission charges sometimes apply for non-guests.

Return to the main road and turn left, strolling along the wide central thoroughfare. To the left are two groupings of thatched cottages, preserved as originally built about 1828. Many of these now serve as restaurants, galleries and shops.

Continue through the village, passing pubs, antique shops, and other local enterprises, until you come to the 'top' or end of the street, as the road branches off in two directions (to Rathkeale or Askeaton). Here, at the apex of the two roads, stands the **Village Hall**, built by the fourth earl of Dunraven in 1911, on the site of the former Fair Green. The earl gave it to the people of Adare as a community centre.

Cross to the other side of the main road and walk back to the Heritage Centre, the starting and finishing point of the tour.

PAT'S PICKS

RESTAURANTS

THE ARCHES, Main Street (tel. 396 246). With an arched doorway and arched windows, this family-run restaurant is a favourite with the locals who come for the home-cooked food, freshly made salads, and community atmosphere. It is located amid the shops in the heart of the village. Open for breakfast, lunch and dinner, Monday–Saturday; and for dinner on Sunday.

DOVECOT RESTAURANT, Adare Heritage Centre, Main Street (tel. 396 449). Named after the dovecote at the adjacent church, this modern sky-lit bistro-style café offers seating both indoors and outside under colourful umbrellas. The menu is international, with a wide array of finger foods, from stuffed potato skins and open sandwiches to Buffalo wings, as well as seafood platters, soups, salads, pizzas, burgers, steaks, and vegetarian dishes such as carrot and almond bake. Open for breakfast, lunch and snacks, daily.

INN BETWEEN, Main Street (tel. 396 633). Wedged amid a row of colourful cottages, this thatched-roof restaurant specialises in innovative Irish cuisine, especially seafood and game dishes. Light items – from burgers to salads and soups – are also offered. There is a choice of seating in cosy rooms inside or on a courtyard outside. Open for lunch and dinner, daily.

THE MUSTARD SEED, Echo Lodge, Ballingarry (tel. 069 68508). Until 1996, this restaurant was the pride of Adare; now it has taken its prize-winning reputation out of town but still within reach (13 km/8 miles southeast of town). Housed in a Victorian country house surrounded by almost 3 hectares (7 acres) of gardens, it offers two dining rooms, each decorated in bold colours, modern art, velvet curtains, tapestries, antiques and flowering plants. The menu, which changes daily, presents an array of creative cuisine, using locally sourced meat and seafood, and vegetables and herbs from the organic kitchen garden. Open for dinner, daily, May–September; Tuesday–Saturday in October–April.

WILD GEESE, Rose Cottage, Main Street (tel. 396 451). Named after the legendary seventeenth-century Irish chieftains and patriots who fled to France and Spain, this Tudor-style cottage sits in the heart of town. Bedecked with rose bushes outside, and with a cheery Victorian décor inside, it offers a diverse menu, with specialties including seasonal salads, roast local Drumcolliher duck, char-grilled meats and seafood, and farmhouse cheeses, as well as a separate vegetarian menu. Open for dinner, Tuesday–Saturday, and for lunch on Sunday, in February–December; and for lunch, Tuesday–Saturday in April–September.

PUBS

BILL CHAWKE'S LOUNGE BAR, Killarney Road (tel. 396 160). This pub is noted for its spontaneous sessions of Irish music, with traditional music every Thursday night and sing-alongs on Friday nights – local and visiting musicians are always welcome. There is also a games room with dart board and pool table, and a beer garden.

CHASER FITZGERALD'S, Pallas Green (tel. 384 203). Located about 24 km (15 miles) east of Adare and convenient for a digression to Lough Gur, this award-winning vintage pub sits on the main Limerick–Waterford road. You can spot it quickly by its eye-catching equestrian-themed murals. Step inside to enjoy a real country-pub atmosphere – with open turf fireplaces, timber- beamed ceilings, flagged flooring, wooden wall panels, stained glass, polished copper, bric-a-brac, antiques, old signs and horsey art. Excellent pub food is available all day.

PAT COLLINS PUB, Main Street (tel. 396 143). Set in the centre of the village, this is a gathering place for locals, golfers and tourists. Friendly and unpretentious, it's a fine country pub for good conversation and local news. Bar food is served throughout the day.

TIMMY MAC'S TRADITIONAL IRISH BAR, Croom Road (tel. 605 100). Although it is part of a hotel (Fitzgerald's Woodland House Hotel), Timmy Mac's has all the trappings and atmosphere of a country kitchen and parlour, with open fireplace, old crockery, vintage photos and lots of local memorabilia. In summer, seating is also available in an outdoor barbecue garden area. From May to October, there are music sessions on many evenings.

DOWN BY THE OLD MILL STREAM: Just 8 km (5 miles) east of Adare is Croom Mills, a beautifully restored nineteenth-century corn-grinding mill, powered by the River Maigue and driven by a 48-metre (16-foot) cast-iron waterwheel. A visit includes a 20-minute film on the history of the mill and the mill workers, plus a walk-through tour of the milling process. Best of all, there is a great restaurant, 'The Mill Race', for home-cooked refreshment at any time of day, from early breakfast onward. Enjoy a snack or a full meal as the mill race flows gently beneath the restaurant. Open daily. Information: Croom Mills (tel. 397 130 or www.croommills.com).

FLYING BOATS: If you have never seen a flying boat, the Foynes Flying Boat Museum is worth a 24-km (15-mile) detour west of Adare. This is actually the 'first' Shannon Airport, the predecessor to the modern airport of today. It commemorates an era begun on 9 July 1939, when Pan Am's luxury flying boat, *Yankee Clipper*, landed at Foynes, marking the first commercial passenger flight on the direct route between the US and Europe. The museum includes the original terminal building, and the radio and weather rooms, with transmitters, receivers and Morse Code equipment. Open daily, April–October. Information: Foynes Flying Boat Museum (tel. 069 65416).

REFRESH THE SPIRIT: East of Adare is one of Ireland's great hubs of learning, art and music – Glenstal Abbey, a nineteenth-century Norman-style castle and home of the Benedictine monks. The abbey sits on a 202-hectare (500-acre) estate and farm, with animals grazing, ancient trees and glorious flowers. The monks, who have recorded several albums of religious music and chant – including the best-selling *Faith of Our Fathers*, with the tenor Frank Patterson (1938–2000) – have also produced two best-selling books in recent years (*The Glenstal Book of Prayer* and *The Glenstal Book of Icons*). The abbey is also a school for boys, and, although the school is not open to the public, visitors are welcome to walk the grounds and attend the music-filled services in the chapel, with over three dozen monks singing. Open daily. Information: Glenstal Abbey, Murroe (tel. 386 103 or www.glenstal.org).

STEPPING BACK IN TIME: Dotted with ancient monuments, Lough Gur is an archaeological gem dating back at least 5,000 years. Excavations have shown that this area, about 16 km (10 miles) southeast of Adare, had continuous occupation from the Neolithic period to late medieval times, and the natural caves nearby have yielded remains of extinct animals such as reindeer, giant Irish deer and bears. The highlights include the foundations of a small farmstead built *c*.900AD; a lake island dwelling built between 500AD and 1000AD; a wedge-

shaped tomb that was a communal grave
*c.*2500BC; and the Grange Stone Circle,
said to be the largest and finest of its kind in
Ireland, built about 2000BC. Open daily,
May–September. Information: Lough Gur
Interpretative Centre, near Grange (tel. 361
511 or www.shannonheritage.com).

SURPRISING CRAFTS: For insight into
southern Limerick's surprising German
connections, head 32 km (20 miles) south
of Adare to the Irish Dresden factory.
This off-the-beaten-track enterprise produces a unique assortment of delicate
figurines made of fine porcelain, sold
throughout Ireland. Founded in the nineteenth century as the Müller-Volkstedt
porcelain company, in Volkstedt, Ger-
many, the business was transferred over
35 years ago to Ireland by the Saar
family. Using 400-year-old German
master-moulds and new patterns inspired
by aspects of rural life in Ireland, Irish
potters, artists and designers work
together as a team to transform a mixture
of clay and lace into intricate works of
art, ranging from collectors' thimbles and
bride/groom pairs, to castles, cottages,
ballerinas, musicians, flowers, animals,
angels and more. Visitors are welcome to
tour the factory, Monday – Friday;
advance reservations are recommended.
Information: Irish Dresden, Main Street,
Drumcolliher (tel. 063 83030).

The West

26: Galway City

As the unofficial capital of the west of Ireland, Galway city has a personality of its own, wholly unlike Ireland's other major cities. There are no Georgian streetscapes like Dublin, no castles like Limerick, no grand parades like Cork, and no Viking towers like Waterford.

Influenced by its remote location amid rocky lands at the head of Galway Bay and the River Corrib, Galway is small and compact, with narrow streets and a style of cut-stone architecture not usually seen in other Irish cities. Galway (pronounced *Gawl-way*) takes its name from the Irish language *Gaillimh*, meaning 'stony', and specifically a 'stony place' or 'stony river'.

Like the rest of Ireland, Galway has been shaped by history, but a history that is unique to its remoteness. The earliest printed references to the area date back to 1124 and describe it as a 'Gaelic hinterland'. Although not conquered by the Vikings like Ireland's other major cities, Galway was invaded by the Anglo-Normans in the thirteenth century. The de Burgos (Burkes) founded a settlement beside a ford on the River Corrib. By 1270, strong stone walls had been added and a great medieval city grew up inside the walls.

Because of its position on the Atlantic, Galway emerged as a thriving seaport for wine, spices and fish, and developed a brisk trade with Spain and other European countries during medieval times. The Galway docks hummed with the arrival of ships from foreign lands. Even Christopher Columbus is said to have landed at the port of Galway, en route to his historic voyage across the Atlantic to 'discover' a New World.

In the fourteenth through mid-seventeenth centuries, Galway was a powerful city state. It became known as the 'City of the Tribes', because of the influence of fourteen wealthy merchant Anglo-Norman families who settled here, ruling the town as an oligarchy for many years. Each of these families (named Athy, Blake, Bodkin, Browne, Darcy, Deane, Font, French, Joyce, Kirwan, Lynch, Martin, Morris and Skerret) had its own street and mansion or castle, with stone-faced designs. Remnants of the buildings and the stonework remain today.

Like the rest of the country, Galway's independence and prosperity was cut short in the late-seventeenth and eighteenth centuries by English rule, with final blows coming during the Great

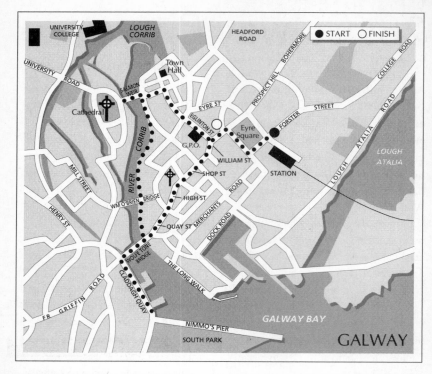

Famine of the 1840s. Two developments helped Galway to rebound – the foundation in 1848 of Queen's College (now officially National University of Ireland – Galway, also known as University College Galway), infusing into Galway all the youthful vibes of a university town; and the establishment of a permanent rail link with Dublin in 1854, reinventing Galway as a true hub of the west.

Growth has been the city's buzzword ever since. Happily, it has been a tempered growth, allowing Galwegians to prosper in the twenty-first century while still preserving their rich heritage. Although the medieval walls have almost disappeared and the city has spread out in all directions, there is still a core of fourteen streets founded by the original tribes. This area, the heart of the city, holds many landmarks that still bear the names of some of these families, such as Lynch's Memorial Window, Blake's Castle, and the Browne Doorway.

Yes, Galway has a unique personality – well aged, yet ever youthful; rich in tradition, yet always embracing innovation. It's a Renaissance city in the truest sense.

FAST FACTS

Travel Information Office

GALWAY TOURIST OFFICE, Forster Street, Galway (tel. 091 537 700). Open all year.

TRAVEL INFORMATION ONLINE:
www.irelandwest.ie

TELEPHONE AREA CODE:
The telephone area code for all numbers in the Galway city area is 091, unless indicated otherwise.

MAJOR EVENTS

GALWAY EARLY MUSIC FESTIVAL – Focusing on medieval, renaissance and baroque music, dance and spectacle, this festival presents concerts, dances, workshops and street performances by internationally acclaimed ensembles. Information: Máiréad Kavanagh, Dún na Mara Drive, Renmore, tel. 086 306 6221 or www.galwayearlymusic.com. (Middle of May)

GALWAY ARTS FESTIVAL – Founded in 1978, this two-week festival is Ireland's largest celebration of the performing and visual arts, bringing a wide variety of international artists to Galway while at the same time showcasing local and national culture. The programme features music, song, drama and dance in the streets, at theatres, in public places and at pubs, plus literary and children's events throughout the city. Information: Elizabeth McDonagh, The Black Box,

Dyke Road, tel. 509700 or www.galwayartsfestival.ie. (Last two weeks of July)

GALWAY INTERNATIONAL OYSTER FESTIVAL – Over 100,000 native oysters are consumed during this three-day event in Galway city. Founded in 1954, it is Ireland's longest-running festival, drawing visitors from all over the world to Galway for the start of the oyster season. The highlight is the Guinness World Oyster Opening Championship and the selection of the 'Oyster Pearl' (a female beauty contest), followed by a programme of parties, a gala ball, concerts, street entertainment and more. Information: Ann Flanagan, tel. 527 282 or www.galwayoysterfest.com. (Last weekend of September)

GALWAY CITY WALKING TOUR

Duration: 2–3 hours plus stops

Walking is the best way to know Galway – streets are narrow, distances are short and much of the core of the city is pedestrianised (but do wear comfortable walking shoes and watch out for uneven pavements, slender footpaths, and some cobbled areas). Start a tour at Galway's rail and bus centre, **Ceannt Station**, Station Road. Turn left and walk half a block to the front entrance of the **Great Southern Hotel**, a lodging landmark dating back to 1845 and well worth a visit or an overnight stay in its own right. The hotel overlooks **Eyre Square**, the city's focal point. Originally a market area known as Fair Green, it was given its current name in 1710 when presented to the city by then-Mayor Edward Eyre who had inherited this grassy patch of land from his father.

Now a pedestrian park, Eyre Square is the city's playground, with pathways and benches, lined by colourful flower-beds and statuary. Take a few moments to reflect at the **Pádraic Ó Conaire Statue**, erected in honour of a Galwegian (1882–1923) recognised as one of Ireland's great short-story writers in the Irish language; or stroll beside **The Browne Doorway**, a fine cut-stone doorway and window, now free-standing and framed in cement, but once the entrance to the mansion belonging to one of Galway's fourteen tribes. There are several carvings on it, including two coats of arms dated 1627, and belonging to the Brownes and the Lynches. Known locally as 'marriage stones', they commemorate the union of two families. Many other city buildings hold similar sets of carved stones with family names.

The adjacent **Quincentennial Fountain**, erected in 1984 to celebrate the 500th anniversary of Galway becoming a city, consists of sheets of iron, mounted to depict the Galway area's distinctive sail boat, the Galway Hooker.

On the west side of Eyre Square is the **Eyre Square Shopping Centre**, one of many such developments in this shop-happy town. This multi-level complex is unique because it includes a section of the city's restored medieval wall. On weekends, markets are held here.

From Eyre Square, head westward to Galway's main thoroughfare, a street that changes its name five times – from **Williamsgate** and **William**, to **Shop**, **High**, and **Quay** streets, before it crosses the River Corrib and changes again. By normal standards for a main city street, it is extremely narrow, with traffic moving at a crawl most of the time. Happily, most of this corridor (from Shop Street through Quay Street) is pedestrianised during prime shopping hours (11am to 7.30pm)

As William Street becomes **Shop Street**, on the right is **Lynch's Castle** (now the Allied Irish Bank), one of the finest surviving town castles in Ireland, dating from the late fifteenth or early sixteenth century, and former home of one of the fourteen original Galway tribe families. On the front is a large framed roundel bearing the arms of the Lynches, plus many decoratively carved windows and projecting gargoyles peering down from the roof.

From Shop Street, turn right onto **Church Lane**, to visit the **Collegiate Church of St Nicholas**, Lombard Street (tel. 564 648) the centrepiece of Galway's medieval heritage. It was founded in 1320, and it is said that Columbus prayed at this church before embarking on his transatlantic voyage. Restored and expanded over the centuries, this church has changed hands from Roman Catholic to Protestant at least four times. Currently under the aegis of the Church of Ireland (Anglican/Episcopal) denomination, it is a showcase of many medieval church furnishings and fixtures, including the **Crusader's Tomb**, a twelfth- or thirteenth-century burial vault with a rare Norman-French inscription; a beautifully carved baptismal font, dating back to the sixteenth or early seventeenth century, with different designs on each side; a lectern with 'barley sugar' twist columns of fifteenth- or sixteenth-century vintage; and a free-standing *bénitier* or holy-water stoup, uncommon in Ireland and one of the most unusual features of the church, made in the late fifteenth or early sixteenth century. Open daily, April–September. Admission: free

Return to Shop Street and make a right onto **High Street**. Notice the occasional decorative or arched-stone doorways and family crests of the fourteen original Galway names, now adapted and incorporated into the shop-front façades of Galway's commercial enterprises. On the left is **O'Maille's**, 16 High Street (tel. 562 696), a family-run tweed shop established in 1938. It became world-famous by producing the clothing for the classic film, *The Quiet Man*, and has done a brisk trade ever since. Next on the left is the Malt Arcade, a cobbled laneway from bygone days, and several doors along on the left is **Kenny's Book Shop**, 20 High Street (tel. 562 739), a family-operated bookshop and art gallery. A Galway fixture for over 50 years, this shop is a treasure-trove of old and new books, maps, prints, engravings and volumes about Galway history.

Next is **Quay Street**, the heart of Galway's colourful 'Left Bank', lined with interesting curio shops and cafés reflecting the latest hip trends.

On the right is **Kirwan's Lane**, one of the city's surviving medieval laneways. Just beyond is Jury's Inn, a 1990s addition to the Galway scene. It sits beside the remnants of seventeenth-century **Blake's Castle**, a fortified residence tower house that once belonged to one of Galway's fourteen tribes. Over the years, it has had many uses, ranging from a jail to a distillery and a fertiliser factory. The bar of the hotel preserves two stone carvings from the building – the coats of arms of the Lynch and Browne families, dated 1645 and displayed over a door and a fireplace.

Directly opposite Jury's is the **Fishmarket**, an outdoor area beside the River Corrib (sometimes referred to by the locals as the Galway river) which used to attract local fishmongers to sell their wares. This is the heart of the city's medieval quarter. Behind the market area is the **Spanish Arch**, built in 1594, and one of Galway's most-photographed landmarks. It was the focal point of the landing dock area where Spanish ships unloaded their cargoes of wine and brandy from their galleons in the heyday of trading between Galway and Spain.

Beside the arch, off Flood Street, is the **Galway City Museum** (tel. 567 641), displaying a collection of local memorabilia, photographs and documents. Open daily, May–September; and more limited schedule in off-season – phone in advance. Admission: €

On the opposite side of the River Corrib is **The Claddagh**, a residential area now, but once a small fishing village of uncertain origin and possibly older than Galway itself. It gets its name from the Irish language *An Cladach*, meaning 'the sea-shore'. The original settlers were native Irish who spoke the Gaelic tongue, as distinct from the Anglo-Norman families within the walled city. The Claddagh residents, who made their living by fishing, sold their wares at the Fishmarket beside the Spanish Arch. They lived in small thatched cottages of mud walls, haphazardly arranged amid cobbled streets. Although they lived in poverty, they had one treasure. Legend has it that they originated the Claddagh ring, a wedding ring cast in the form of two hands clasping a heart with a crown at the top. Over the years, the ring has become a popular piece of jewellery for Galwegians and visitors alike. Although the world of the Claddagh fishing community came to an end in 1934 with the construction of a modern housing development, the tradition of the Claddagh ring lives on and thrives.

Cross back over the **Wolfe Tone Bridge**. From the front of Jury's, take a right and walk along the side of the hotel. This is the beginning of **Riverside Walk**, a path that borders the east side of Lough Corrib. Walk north as far as the **Salmon Weir Bridge**, a popular landmark that allows people to stop and watch the salmon leaping upstream. Cross over the bridge to see one of the city's newest buildings, the **Catholic Cathedral of Our Lady Assumed into Heaven and St Nicholas**, University and Gaol Roads (tel. 563 577), completed in 1965. Dominating the Galway skyline with its huge dome, it is a modern Renaissance-style edifice that is made of limestone and marble from local quarries and enhanced by the work of contemporary Irish artisans who designed the statues, stained-glass windows and mosaics. It sits on the site of the former city jail. Open daily. Admission: free

Cross back over the bridge and take a right to St Vincent's Avenue. On the left is another of Galway's newest additions, **Town Hall Theatre**, Courthouse Square (tel. 569 777), Galway's major performing arts venue, formerly the town hall.

Cross over **St Vincent's Avenue** to **St Francis Street**. Halfway up the block on the right is the **Franciscan Abbey**. The current building sits on part of a site that was occupied by an earlier friary founded in 1296. Continuing on, the street name changes to

Eglington Street, a busy commercial thoroughfare, and the **General Post Office** is on the right. Straight ahead is **Williamsgate Street** and a left turn will bring you back to Eyre Square, completing the tour.

In addition, one of Galway's top attractions is located outside town, beyond a walking tour route. If you do not have access to a car, it is less than a five-minute taxi or local bus journey away from Eyre Square.

Either way, head to the **Galway Crystal Heritage Centre**, Merlin Park, Dublin Road (tel. 757 311), aptly called a 'museum of Irish crystal'. Step inside and be dazzled by the huge Georgian-style **Great Hall**, the reception area, decorated with intricate glasswork, crystal chandeliers, and a ceremonial staircase. Tours start with an audiovisual on the craft, followed by a tour of workshops, to see craftspeople design, etch and inscribe the delicate patterns and tracings. In addition, there are four other exhibits: **The Celtic Room**, housing scroll work of early artists; the **Hall of Tribes**, outlining the history of the great Galway families; **Boatbuilders' Workshop**, focusing on the traditional boats of the west, including the Galway Hooker; the **Claddagh Village**, a prototype of the city's famous old quarter, and birthplace of the Claddagh ring. To all of this, add a terrace balcony with sweeping views of Galway Bay. Open daily. Admission: €

THE COBBLESTONE, Kirwan's Lane (tel. 567 227). Tucked into one of Galway's oldest lanes, this indoor/outdoor café is one of the city's brightest stars on the cuisine scene, with emphasis on vegetarian soups, quiches and salads, as well as 'beany shepherd pie' or vegetable and walnut bake. Seafood and meats are also available, as is a wide array of baked-on-premises croissants, breads, muffins, cakes and cookies. On many evenings, proprietor Kate Wright hosts cooking classes after closing hours. Open for snacks and lunch, daily.

CONLON'S, 3 Eglinton Street (tel. 562 268), just off William Street. For fresh local seafood, head to this long-established restaurant (opposite the General Post Office), specialising in traditional fish-and-chips or wild Corrib smoked salmon, as well as oysters, scallops, mussels, crab and lobster. Take-out is also available if you feel like a picnic. Open for lunch and dinner, daily.

GBC – THE GALWAY BAKING COMPANY, 7 Williamsgate Street (tel. 563 087). It's hard to match the value of this landmark shop-front restaurant for a snack or a full meal from morning till night. Freshly baked breads and pastries are featured here, as are Irish traditional dishes such as Irish stew and steaks, as well as quiches, crêpes, omelettes, salads and real 'tea-leaf' tea. Downstairs is a coffee-shop, and upstairs is a full-service restaurant. Open daily.

KC BLAKE'S BRASSERIE, 10 Quay Street (tel. 561 826). Opposite the Spanish Arch and next to Jury's Inn, this stylish restaurant is nestled in a fifteenth-century medieval tower house. The menu offers Irish dishes such as beef and Guinness stew and black-pudding croquettes, as well as international fare such as *sole meunière*, siki shark, and chicken fajitas. Open for dinner, daily.

MALT HOUSE, High Street (tel. 567 866). An 'old Galway' atmosphere prevails at this cosy whitewashed restaurant, positioned on a cobblestone alley off the main street. The menu features modern Irish cuisine, with emphasis on fresh seafood, including monkfish, lobster, prawns, scallops, mussels and Galway Bay oysters. Open for lunch and dinner, Monday–Saturday.

MCDONAGH'S SEAFOOD HOUSE, 22 Quay Street (565 001). Established in 1912, this seafood market-cum-restaurant is synonymous with fresh seafood. With a choice of settings – an informal fish-and-chips bar or a full-service restaurant, it offers the best of the local catch. Shellfish platters are a house speciality, as is barbecued or grilled salmon. Arrive early, though – this place is very popular and no reservations are accepted. Open for lunch and dinner, daily.

MOCHA BEANS, 2 Cross Street (tel. 565 919). Tucked beside Quay Street, this coffee house has an international ambience, and serves a choice of coffees and teas from all around the world. The menu also offers freshly squeezed juices, open sandwiches, salads, soups, bagels and more. Open for breakfast, lunch and snacks, daily.

SCOTTY'S, 1 Middle Street (tel. 566 400). Popular with university students, this casual café brings the flavours of the USA to Galway. The menu offers fresh salads, deli-style sandwiches, burgers and subs, with accompaniments of your choice – mayo, lettuce, tomatoes, pickles, olives, peppers, onions and more. Ice-cream sundaes are a speciality. Open for lunch and snacks, daily.

PUBS

AN PÚCÁN, 11 Forster Street (tel. 561 528). Located one block east of Eyre Square, and named after a type of fishing boat, this old fashioned nautically themed pub has been a mecca for Irish traditional music in Galway for over 50 years. The nightly sessions usually start at 9.30 or 10pm. A talented mix of local musicians plays here and travelling musicians are always welcome.

BUSKER BROWNE'S, Cross Street (tel. 569 402), at Kirwan's Lane. Housed in two of Galway's oldest buildings – a slate house dating back to 1615, and a former convent – this multi-room pub offers lots of

Right: Street signs in the village of Ballyvaughan, pointing the way to many different destinations in the Burren area of County Clare.

Below: Western County Clare is known for its Irish traditional music, including regular sessions at the Hyland's Burren Hotel in Ballyvaughan.

Above: A cow grazes along the western shores of Lough Derg, the largest lake of the Shannon River, near Tuamgraney, County Clare
.Below: The picturesque County Clare town of Killaloe is an historic place on the River Shannon that claims to have been the Irish capital during 1002–14, when Brian Ború reigned as High King of Ireland. St. Flannan's Cathedral, dating back to the twelfth century, is on the left.

Above: Set on a hill rising 200 feet above the surrounding countryside, the Rock of Cashel dates back to the fourth century. Over the years, it has been both a seat of Irish kings and a stronghold of Christianity.

Below: Unimpressed by the ancient stone ramparts at the Rock of Cashel, County Tipperary, two local dogs pose for a photo.

Above: Set beside the River Shannon in Limerick city, King John's Castle dates back to 1210 and is considered one of the finest examples of fortified Norman architecture in Ireland.

Left: Glenstal Abbey at Murroe, County Limerick, is a nineteenth-century Norman-style castle, now the home of Benedictine monks who run a school for boys. It is one of Ireland's great hubs for learning, art and music. The monks, who have recorded several albums of sacred music, have also produced bestselling books.

Above: A leisurely mode of transport on Inis Móŕ, the biggest of the Aran Islands, thirty miles out to sea at the mouth of Galway Bay.

Below: Built in 1864 as a private home and now a school for girls, Kylemore Abbey is a popular oasis in the middle of Connemara, County Galway. Visitors can tour the ground floor rooms, stroll in the newly restored Victorian walled gardens, spend time in the Gothic chapel or meander around the lakeside pathways.

Left: Buskers play traditional music to attract the attention (and perhaps a few euro) of shoppers passing by on High Street, Galway City.

Below: One of County Donegal's most pristine stretches of shorelines is at Malin Bay, just west of Glencolumbkille in the southwestern part of the county.

Above: Reflecting life in northwestern Ireland over the past 300 years, the cottages at Fr. McDyer's Folk Village Museum at Glencolumbkille, County Donegal, are open for guided tours.

Right: Set beside the beach and mountains, the Folk Village at Glencolumbkille is named for Fr. James McDyer, a local priest who inspired the local people to build this museum and furnish it with implements and memorabilia from their own homes.

Above: Dating back to 1870, Glenveagh Castle is the centrepiece of Glenveagh National Park, near Letterkenny in County Donegal. The surrounding gardens are famed for a rich variety of exotic and rare plants from as far away as Tasmania, Madeira and Chile.

old-world atmosphere in a choice of seating areas, snugs and alcoves. Traditional Irish music is the norm, but Dixieland jazz is also played as background to Sunday brunch.

THE CRANE, Sea Road (tel. 587 419). Although this landmark Victorian-style pub is not in the middle of town, it always draws a steady flow of serious practitioners and followers of traditional music from near and far. Sessions are held on both the ground level and first floor every night. In addition, there is both step and set dancing three nights a week, and a singers' club every third Saturday of the month. The décor lends itself to a festive atmosphere – brightly coloured walls, sturdy country furniture, and posters and photographs of Galway musicians and festivals.

MCSWIGGAN'S PUB, 3 Eyre Street (tel. 568 917). Located one block from Eyre Square, this pub oozes an authentic old-world atmosphere, thanks to a décor of brick, stone and wood-panelled walls, beamed ceilings, snugs, nooks and crannies, and timeworn ale posters. A unique focal point is an actual 10.5-metre (35-foot) tree, branching up to the first floor. Music is on tap on many nights.

THE QUAYS, 11 Quay Street (tel. 568 347). Dating back almost 400 years, this popular pub offers two bars, each with its own character – the Old Bar, with antiques, old clocks, polished timber and check-tiled floor; and The Claddagh, a spacious split-level bar with authentic timber, brickwork and church artefacts, including a stained-glass window, pulpit and a series of arches. Traditional music sessions are held on Friday and Saturday nights year-round; and there is Irish dancing on Monday and Tuesday (June–September).

TIGH NEACHTAIN, 17 Cross Street (tel. 568 820). This old-world pub is housed in a seventeenth-century building that was once the townhouse of Richard Martin, the founder of the Royal Society for the Prevention of Cruelty to Animals. The décor reflects an earlier era – low-beamed ceilings, tiny snugs, alcoves, flagstone floors, open fireplaces, and walls lined with a complete collection of Galway Arts Festival posters. Traditional Irish music is played on Friday and Saturday, and folk/jazz on Sunday, and impromptu sessions can happen on any night.

SNUG-GARAVAN'S, William Street (tel. 562 831). Housed in the former home of a Spanish merchant, this place is two pubs in one. The entrance leads to the snug, distinguished by its huge medieval fireplace (3.7 metres by 6.7 metres /12 feet by 22 feet), granite walls, dark-wood beams, and cave-like atmosphere. Continue through a corridor to Garavan's which has the feel of a spiffy saloon with contemporary luxury. Galwegians alternate between the two settings, depending on their mood.

CRUISING ON THE RIVER: See Galway from a different perspective by cruising on the River Corrib on board the double-deck ship, the *Corrib Princess*. These narrated cruises last 90 minutes, taking in a variety of riverside sights, from historic ruins and castles to wildlife. Departures are from Wood Quay, daily, April–October. Information: Corrib Tours, Furbo Hill, Furbo, Co. Galway, (tel. 592 447 or www.corribprincess.ie).

ISLAND-HOPPING: It seems that almost everyone yearns to visit the Aran Islands, three islands sitting 48 km (30 miles) out at sea where Galway Bay meets the Atlantic Ocean: Inishmore (*Inis Mór* – Great Island); Inishmaan *(Inis Meáin* – Middle Island); and Inishere (*Inis Oirr* – Eastern Island). Although the islands have been modernised in recent years, they are still far-flung outposts of Gaelic culture, language and lifestyle, with a resident population of just over 1,500 people. A regularly scheduled ferry boat operates services from Rossaveal (the shortest crossing – 40 minutes) or Galway City Dock (90 minutes); schedules vary according to season, weather and sea conditions. Tickets can be purchased at the Galway Tourist Office. Information: Island Ferries (tel. 568 903 or www.aranislandferries.com); Inis Mór Ferries (tel. 566 535 or www.queenofaran2.com); and O'Brien Shipping (tel. 567 283 or www.doolinferries.com). Air taxi service to the islands is also available (flight time is less than ten minutes), depending on the weather, from Inverin, 26 km (16 miles) west of Galway city. Information: Aer Arann (tel. 593 034 or www.aerarann.ie).

TOURS GALORE: Tired of walking? Galway offers a wide array of all-day hop-on/ hop-off tours and one-hour narrated sightseeing tours. See more than a dozen highlights of Galway city (Eyre Square, Salmon Weir Bridge, Galway Cathedral, Galway Bay, the Claddagh and more). Most tours operate daily, departing from the Galway Tourist Office on Forster Street or from Eyre Square. Reservations are not needed; pay on the bus or at the tourist office. Information: Healy Tours (tel.770 066 or www.healybus.com); Lally Tours (tel. 562 905 or www.lallytours.com); or O'Neachtain Tours (tel. 553 188 or www.oneachtaintours.com). In addition, these three firms operate sightseeing tours of Connemara and the Burren, as does Bus Éireann (tel. 562 000 or www.buseireann.ie), from mid-May to the end of September.

27: Galway Bay and Connemara

Galway Bay needs no introduction. Celebrated in story and song, it automatically draws visitors to see its splendid sunsets and azure waters. While you can enjoy glimpses of the bay from the city centre, it is the coastline west of Galway that presents the most panoramic views of this famous bay. Once you have travelled a short distance west to see Galway Bay, a bonus awaits – Connemara.

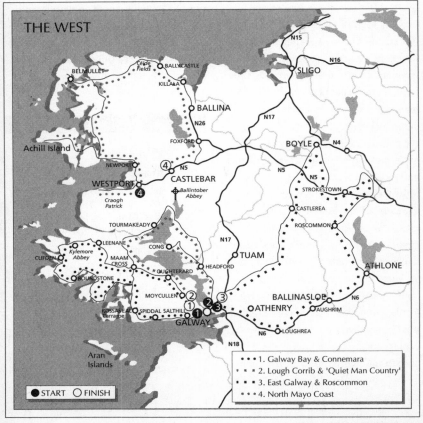

THE WEST

1. Galway Bay & Connemara
2. Lough Corrib & 'Quiet Man Country'
3. East Galway & Roscommon
4. North Mayo Coast

● START   ○ FINISH

Connemara – The very name sounds alluring. The place name is derived from the Irish-language *Cuain na Mara*, meaning 'harbours of the sea'. And indeed there are many harbours along Connemara's richly curved coast. A large part of Connemara is also designated as a Gaeltacht, an Irish-speaking district. Signs and road markers are printed primarily in Irish – this can be viewed as charming or confusing by visitors who do not know Irish.

Connemara is neither a city nor a town. It is a region, the section of County Galway that sits west of Galway city. After the Ring of Kerry, it is one of the most popular 'must see' drives in Ireland. Connemara does not have any outstanding museums, landmarks, great houses or national monuments, but it is synonymous with stunning scenery – wide and open, rugged and natural. This is the picture-postcard image of Ireland that most visitors think of. The coast is indented with little bays, inlets and beaches. At almost every turn, there are lakes, waterfalls, rivers and streams, while a dozen glorious mountains, known as the Twelve Bens, rise at the centre to overshadow a rocky landscape dominated by bog. Gorse, heather, rhododendron, fuchsia and wildflowers enliven acres of dreary useless rock.

As in the rest of Ireland, the people of this remote region have progressed and prospered in recent years. Traditional whitewashed cottages are topped by TV antennae, slate roofs have replaced much of the original thatching, and a car is in almost every driveway. Still, there are vestiges of days gone by – stone fences, piles of newly cut turf, and an occasional donkey-cart on a back road. Sheep graze on the hillsides, and Connemara ponies frolic in the meadows. The sweet aroma of turf fires permeates the countryside.

Shops are filled with the sounds of lively conversations in the Irish language, and pubs ring with native music, song and dance. Cottage industries carry on ageless crafts. Old ways are treasured. People have time to stop and chat. Tradition is indeed alive and well in Connemara.

FAST FACTS

Travel Information Offices

GALWAY TOURIST OFFICE, Forster Street, Galway (tel. 091 567 700). Open all year.

CLIFDEN TOURIST OFFICE, Galway Road, Clifden (tel. 095 21163). Open March–October.

SALTHILL TOURIST OFFICE, Promenade, Salthill (tel. 091 520 500). Open April–October.

TRAVEL INFORMATION ONLINE:
www.irelandwest.ie,
www.connemara.net or
www.connemara-tourism.org

TELEPHONE AREA CODES:

There are two area codes for telephone numbers in the Galway and Connemara areas, 091 and 095. To avoid confusion, an area code will be specified with each number.

MAJOR EVENTS

CONNEMARA INTERNATIONAL MARATHON – Join hundreds of runners on a full 42-km (26.2-mile) marathon or a 21-km (13.1-mile) half-marathon. The route wends its way from Lough Inagh to Killary Harbour and Leenane, and ends in the Maam Valley. It's a great way to see Connemara! Information: Ray O'Connor, tel. 091 565 154 or www.connemarathon.com. (Last Sunday of March)

ROUNDSTONE OPEN ARTS WEEK – Held at the picturesque village of Roundstone on the Galway Bay coast, this ten-day festival presents a continuous programme of music, with concerts and *céilí* bands, as well as a parade, country market, tug-o-war, mini-marathon and fun run, treasure hunt, dance workshops, herbal walks, and readings by Connemara authors. Information: Richard Marquis de Stacpoole, tel. 095 35834 or www.roundstone-connemara.com. (Last week of June to first week of July)

CONNEMARA PONY SHOW – Drawing owners and spectators from all over Ireland and the world, this annual event is the world's largest showing of Connemara ponies. The day also features a crafts fair, a dog show and Irish dancing competitions. Information: Michael Ward, Showgrounds, Clifden, tel. 095 21863. (End of August)

GALWAY BAY AND CONNEMARA DRIVING TOUR

Duration: 5–6 hours plus stops

Depart Galway city from the west side of town, beside the famous Spanish Arch and the River Corrib. Cross over the **Wolfe Tone Bridge** and follow the signs for **Salthill**, a popular beach resort with a 4 km (2.5 mile) long promenade and easily walkable stretch of beach overlooking Galway Bay. Salthill's seafront is home to two family-oriented attractions, in case you have the kids travelling with you. **Galway Atlantaquaria – National Aquarium of Ireland** (tel. 091 585 100) is an aquarium focusing on native Irish aquatic life, in both saltwater and fresh-water categories. The 170 species on display range from the familiar (crabs, sea bass, plaice, turbot, flounder and sole) to the exotic (conger eels, ray, bullhuss and more). Special exhibits include the life of an Irish salmon and an 18-metre (60-foot) skeleton of a fin whale, one of the largest inhabitants of the ocean. Open daily, April–September; Wednesday–Sunday, October–March. Admission: €€

  Leisureland (tel. 091 521 455) is an indoor swimming centre, with pools of various sizes and depths, water slides, pirate ships, water cannons and a bubble pool, as well as outdoor amusements and rides in the summer months, including roller-coasters, miniature train rides and more. Open daily. Admission: €€

Continue from the hustle and bustle of Salthill westwards to **Barna**, spelled *Bearna* in the Irish language, a word that means 'gap'. This begins a rugged Irish-speaking area known as **Cois Fharraige** (beside the sea). From here on, for about 24 km (15 miles), there are splendid open views of Galway Bay to the left. On a clear day, you can easily see the coast of County Clare and the Aran Islands.

Many homes, in which the women knit the traditional Aran *báinín* sweaters, display signs outside saying, 'Handknits for sale', and most shops in the area offer locally made knitwear. In this area, road signs are more likely to appear only in the Irish language. To make identifying places easier, we'll include both spellings, when appropriate, with the English first.

Spiddal, or **An Spidéal**, is in the heart of the Irish-speaking area. The Irish place name refers to a hospital that once stood here. Today the town is known for its views of Galway Bay and two very fine craft centres. On the left side of the road is **Standún's** (tel. 091 553 108), the granddaddy of the sweater stockists. Having operated for over 50 years on this site, this craft centre is a hub and clearing house for hand-knit Aran fishermen's sweaters, made by local residents in their cottages. Besides knits, there is a good selection of tweeds, pottery, glassware, books and other souvenirs. The views of the bay from the rear of the store make shopping a scenic treat. Open Monday–Saturday, and sometimes on Sunday in busy summer months.

Continue on the road for a few hundred metres, and to the right is **Spiddal Craft Centre – Ceardlann An Spidéil** (tel. 091 553 376), a cluster of cottage shops where craftspeople ply their trades each day. The selection includes wood-turning, stone sculpture, screen printing, pottery, weaving, floral art and Celtic-design jewellery. See your souvenir being made before you buy. Open daily, March–October. Admission: free

Return to the R336, with dramatic views of Galway Bay to the left. Dry stone walls, called *claíocha*, are the most striking aspect of the landscape. These walls, which enclose individual plots of land, are a relic of a time when small farmers laboured doggedly to clear their tiny fields for tillage. In the waters around Galway Bay and Connemara, you will see various conventional boats, as well as two types of local craft – the *currach*, a long canoe-like vessel, originally used for fishing, and the *huicéir*, or 'hooker', which is a heavy timber-hulled sailboat, mainly used for carrying turf, and easily recognisable by its large colourful sails.

The next town is **Inverin** or **Indreabhán**, derived from the Irish word for 'estuary'. It is the home of Connemara Regional Airport, which is the gateway for flights to the Aran Islands via Aer Arann (see Chapter 26, 'Galway City – Digressions'). Here the road swings in a northerly direction, passing **Rossaveal** or **Ros an Míl**. This place name means 'peninsula of the whale or sea-monster'. Although there may not be any monsters lurking at Rossaveal today, it is the chief fishing harbour of Connemara, with a series of new quays used by the many modern fishing trawlers that dock here. High-speed ferries, bound for the Aran Islands, also depart daily from this busy port.

At the end of the bay lies the crossroads at **Costelloe** or **Casla**, which means 'small harbour'. The Udarás na Gaeltachta (Gaeltacht Authority) has established an industrial estate here beside the headquarters of Raidió na Gaeltachta and Telefís na Gaeilge, the Irish-language radio and television broadcasting services. A 5-km (3-mile) detour southeast on the R343 leads to **Carraroe** or **An Ceathrú Rua**, the 'red-coloured quarter', a popular hub for Irish-language summer schools and for the promotion of Irish culture. It also enjoyed a measure of American literary fame as the hometown of the character 'Nuala Anne McGrail' in many of Fr Andrew Greeley's recent mass-market novels.

Continue north on the R336 to **Screeb** (or *Scríb*, which means 'track' or 'furrow').

Turn left onto the R340 and follow this scenic road along the **Iorras Ainteach** peninsula to **Gortmore** (*Gort Mór*, meaning 'great field') and **Kilkieran** (*Cill Ciarán*, meaning 'St Ciarán's church'), a small village named after St Ciarán of Clonmacnoise (See Chapter 23, 'County Offaly'). It is said that he passed through this area after visiting the Aran Islands. Seaweed processing, salmon farming and sea fishing are the main activities of the area today. It is now a short journey of less than 8 km (5 miles) to **Carna**, a place name that is the same in English and Irish, the main centre of the peninsula. A prime lobster fishing centre and home of the University College Galway's marine biology station, Carna is surrounded by rocky hills, lakes, sandy beaches and a cluster of offshore islands, including **St MacDara's Island**, revered locally and known for its seventh-century early Christian oratory.

Continue northwards on the R340 via **Glinsk** (*Glinsce*) and **Gowla** (*Gabhla*), turning left onto the R341 to **Cashel Bay**, a lush oasis in the midst of Connemara's barren landscape – and a return to place names that are used commonly in English only. This is the setting for several hotels, including Cashel House, a luxurious country inn known for its exotic gardens and woodlands. It has attracted many famous media stars and politicians who seek an out-of-the-way retreat, including President Charles de Gaulle of France in 1969.

Follow the R341 when it wends to the left at **Toombeola**, whose Irish name means 'tomb of the giant Beola', to **Roundstone**, whose Irish name translates as 'rock of the seals'. Considered by the locals to be the most picturesque of Connemara's many sea villages, Roundstone was founded and designed in the early nineteenth century by a Scottish engineer, Alexander Nimmo, who constructed the pier and the delightful streetscape. If the town tableau looks familiar, that's because it was used as a setting for the 1997 Hollywood film *The Matchmaker*.

The focal point is a local craft village that houses local artisans plying traditional crafts, including **Roundstone Musical Instruments** (tel. 095 35875). Step into this small shop, housed in the former Franciscan monastery, and watch as master craftsman Malachy Kearns hand-fashions bodhráns (traditional one-sided drums) from goatskins that have been treated with an age-old formula. Each drum is then hand-decorated with Celtic designs, initials, family crests or names. Tin whistles, flutes, harps and other musical instruments are also for sale. Open daily, April–October; Monday–Saturday, November–March.

The road continues for 14.5 km (9 miles) west to **Ballyconneely**, a small hamlet on an isthmus between Ballyconneely Bay and Mannin Bay where there is a beautiful coral beach. A kilometre and a half (1 mile) north on the left is a stone monument commemorating the landing in 1919 of John Alcock and Arthur Whitten Brown who crash-landed here after the first-ever west-to-east transatlantic flight.

Eight kilometres (5 miles) to the north is **Clifden**, derived from the Irish word *An Clochán*, meaning 'stepping stone'. A busy marketing hub founded in the nineteenth century, Clifden is the largest town in Connemara and is considered the region's unofficial 'capital'. To enjoy panoramic views of the Clifden skyline with the mountains in the background, take a short detour on the **Sky Road**, a well-signposted 11-km (7-mile) circuit leading west of town to the Atlantic, with both a high road and a low road that meet in the middle. Clifden is a good shopping town, with an array of fine restaurants as well.

For insight into what it has been like to live in Connemara over the centuries, take a 6.5-km (4-mile) detour east of town to the **Connemara Heritage & History Centre**, Lettershea (tel. 095 21246). Surrounded by the Roundstone bog and views of the **Twelve Bens** mountains, this 3.2-hectare (8-acre) site blends ancient history with pre-famine days. It contains a reconstructed Bronze Age crannóg (fortified lake dwelling), an authentic megalithic tomb, and a dolmen, all dating back to prehistoric times. The focal point is a pre-famine farm, worked in the 1840s by Dan O'Hara, who was eventually forced to emigrate to the US because he couldn't pay the high rents of the local landlord, a case repeated over and over among the poor tenant farmers of Connemara.

The present-day farmer, Martin Walsh, takes visitors on a tractor-pulled trolley ride up the side of a mountain for panoramic views and a walk-around tour of the original farm buildings, including demonstrations of traditional methods of cutting turf, tilling the land, or digging the potatoes. The visitor centre, which presents a short audiovisual on the area, is entered by crossing a bridge that is also of historic interest. Moved here from Clifden, it is known as **O'Connell's Bridge**, because the great Irish Liberator, Daniel O'Connell entered Clifden over this bridge in 1843. Open daily, April–October. Admission: €€

Retrace your route back to Clifden and follow the main N59 road north almost 16 km (10 miles) for one of the area's prime natural wonders, the **Connemara National Park**, Letterfrack (tel. 095 41054), a 1,620-hectare (4,000-acre) kaleidoscope of wondrous scenery. With very little man-made development, it is a blend of mountains, bogs, heaths, grasslands, rivers, waterfalls and nature trails. Connemara ponies run wild, and assorted wildlife, including a herd of red deer, roam the gentle landscape. Some of the park's mountains, such as **Benbaun**, **Bencullagh**, **Benbrack** and **Muckanaght**, are part of the famous **Twelve Bens** mountain range. **Glan-more**, which means large glen, forms the centre of the park, as the River Pollladirk flows through. A visitor centre offers an exhibition on the Connemara landscape and an audiovisual show, 'Man and the Landscape', on the park. The visitor centre is open daily, April–mid-October. Admission: €

Return to the main N59 road and continue 8 km (5 miles) to Connemara's finest building, **Kylemore Abbey** (tel. 095 41146). Overlooking Kylemore Lake, this splendid castellated mansion was originally built in 1864 as a private residence for Mitchell Henry, a wealthy merchant from Manchester, who presented it as gift to his wife who died shortly afterwards. The entire estate was given in 1922 to the Benedictine nuns who operate it as a girls' school and as a visitor attraction. Although the abbey itself is not open to the public, visitors are encouraged to take pictures, picnic, or tour the grounds, including a recently restored Gothic chapel, considered a mini-cathedral, which was erected in Mrs Henry's memory between 1877 and 1881. Admission includes an audiovisual on the history of the abbey. Try to be on the grounds at noon or 6pm, when bells ring out calling the nuns to prayer, adding an enchanting *Sound of Music* aura to the entire estate. Open daily. Admission: €€

Visitors can also tour the 2.5-hectare (6-acre) walled **Kylemore Victorian Garden**, 1.5 km (1 mile) west of the abbey entrance. Singled out as a winner of a *Europa Nosta* award in 2002, this serene lakeside sanctuary was originally laid out in 1867, and took three years to complete, transforming a wilderness of rock and bog into a feast of flowers and plants set in geometrically designed borders and beds, along with hundreds of thousands of trees. Unfortunately, the garden fell into disuse for over a century, until its recent restoration commissioned by the nuns. The garden is divided into two sections – a formal flower garden for leisurely strolls and the kitchen garden, containing fruit, vegetables and herbs for use in cooking. Reduced-price joint admission tickets are available for a combined visit to the abbey and garden. Open Easter–October. Admission: €€

From Kylemore, follow the main N59 road east for 13 km (8 miles) to **Leenane**, a small village aptly described by its Irish place name, *An Líonán*, meaning 'the shallow sea-bed'. It sits in the shadow of the Maamturk Mountains, between Killary Harbour, Ireland's only natural fjord, and the Inagh Valley. This scenic area was used as the setting for the 1991 film *The Field*, starring Richard Harris.

At the north edge of town, overlooking the harbour, is the **Leenane Cultural Centre**, Main Street (tel. 095 42323), a museum that focuses on the 20 different kinds of sheep that are indigenous to the Galway and Mayo area.

Through a series of exhibits and hands-on presentations, it tells the story of the local wool industry, including carding, spinning, weaving and using natural dyes. Daily demonstrations of sheep-shearing are given outdoors in the summer months. There is also a thirteen-minute audiovisual, shown continuously, on local history and places of interest. Open daily, March–October. Admission: €

If you take a short detour north of the town, as the road gradually wends its way along the shores of Killary Harbour into the Delphi Valley, you will see the picturesque **Aasleagh Falls**, on the River Erriff.

There are two routes back to Galway city. The most scenic choice starts just beyond Kylemore, on the R344, heading south. This route leads through the **Inagh Valley**, a sheltered area where the Maamturk mountains rise up on the left, with Derryclare Lough and Lough Inagh on the right beside the Beanna Beola mountains. This road ends at **Recess**, signposted locally by its Irish name of **Sraith Salach**, which means 'fenland of the willows', a very fitting description of the area. From Recess, it's just over 56 km (35 miles) back to Galway city, via Maam Cross, Oughterard and Moycullen.

An alternative route, the R336 straight from Leenane, heads south to Maam and Maam Cross. Then turn left and join the main N59 road for the final 40 km (25 miles) back to Galway city. (For information on Maam, Maam Cross, Oughterard and Moycullen along these routes, see Chapter 28, 'Lough Corrib and *Quiet Man* Country'.)

PAT'S PICKS

RESTAURANTS

BLACKBERRY CAFÉ, Main Street, Leenane (tel. 095 42240). Overlooking Killary Harbour, this café exudes a welcoming country-kitchen atmosphere and is a reliable stop for quality food on the Connemara circuit. The menu, which changes daily, features oysters and mussels farmed in adjacent waters, with excellent seafood chowders, quiches and salads. Other specialities include fishcakes and Irish stew, all accompanied by home-baked breads. Open for lunch, dinner and snacks, daily, June–August; Wednesday–Monday, April–May and September.

BOLUISCE, Main Street, Spiddal (tel. 091 553 286). With a name that means 'patch of grazing by the water', this restaurant is a mainstay along the Galway Bay route. There are no water views, but the atmosphere is homely, with brick walls, fireplace and local art. Specialities include mussels and lobsters, as well as steaks, duckling and vegetarian dishes. The house seafood chowder alone is worth a visit. Open for lunch, snacks and dinner, daily.

FOGERTY'S, Market Street, Clifden (tel. 095 21427). Sporting an authentic thatched-roof and stone façade, this little restaurant stands out on the Clifden streetscape. Step inside and enjoy a meal in a homely setting in a choice of rooms spread over two floors. The menu offers traditional favourites – chowders, steaks, Irish lamb stew and local seafood. Open for dinner, daily, February–December.

HIGH MOORS, Ballyconneely Road, Dooneen, Clifden (tel. 095 21342). Dine in a private home at this restaurant run by John and Eileen Griffin, just 1.5 km (1 mile) from town, sitting atop a hill with panoramic views of the countryside. Specialities include Connemara lamb, Carna Bay scallops, and vegetables and herbs from the family garden. Open for dinner, Wednesday–Sunday, June–September.

KYLEMORE ABBEY RESTAURANT, Kylemore (tel. 095 41146). With seating indoors and outside, this flower-bedecked self-service restaurant is no ordinary café. The food, all prepared fresh daily, is set out like a banquet – salads, soups, casseroles, quiches, sandwiches, home-baked breads, cakes, pies and more. Much of the produce comes from the abbey's own gardens. Open for lunch and snacks, daily.

MITCHELL'S, Market Street, Clifden (tel. 095 21867). A reliable fixture in the centre of town since 1991, this shop-front restaurant has a turn-of-the-century ambience, with a cosy décor of brick and stone walls, open fireplace and local memorabilia. House specialities range from Irish stew and fishcakes to mussels, oysters, salmon and creative combination dishes such as smoked salmon quiche and seafood pastas. Open for snacks, lunch and dinner, daily, March–October.

O'GRADY'S, Lower Market Street, Clifden (tel. 095 21450). For over 40 years, this bistro-style restaurant has been a stand-out on the Connemara circuit. The updated décor is bright and contemporary, featuring oil paintings, prints and sculptures by local artists. The menu offers whatever is fresh from the sea, prepared in creative ways, such as tempura of plaice, cod with black olive tapenade, scallops over sweet chilli linguine, or salmon, shrimp and mussel paella, as well as beef, lamb and poultry choices. Open for dinner, Monday–Saturday, April–October.

O'GRADY'S ON THE PIER, Sea Point, Barna (tel. 091 592 223). Owned by a member of the same family as the restaurant (above) in Clifden, this little gem sits right on the harbour, with views of Galway Bay and distant mountains. Seafood is the star on the menu, with innovative choices, such as cod with lemon grass, baked sea bass, grilled black sole or baby shark, as well as token meat entrées. Open for dinner, daily; and for lunch on Sunday.

O'DOWD'S SEAFOOD BAR AND RESTAURANT, Main Street, Roundstone (tel. 095 5809). Overlooking the harbour, this family-run place has been a local fixture since 1840 when it was Kelly's hotel, pub and grocery shop. It became 'O'Dowd's' in 1906 and has been in the same family ever since. If the traditional wood-panelled interior of the pub looks familiar, that's because it was featured in the 1997 film *The Matchmaker*. The menu offers a selection of international meat and vegetarian dishes but specialises in locally caught seafood – hot-buttered Connemara lobster, ocean rolls (fillets of plaice stuffed with seafood), Killary Bay prawns, Connemara oak-smoked salmon, and Roundstone crab. Open for lunch and dinner, daily.

PUBS

EJ KING'S BAR, The Square, Clifden (tel. 095 21330). Established in 1832, this place began as a general merchant's store and bar, originally owned by EJ King, a well-known local figure. The interior décor reflects the pub's long history – stone walls, timber ceiling, subdued lighting and solid country furnishing, with captains' chairs and dark-wood tables. It is a gathering spot for writers, artists, film-makers, and naturalists. Traditional music is played on most nights, all year round.

GRIFFIN'S BAR, Main Street, Clifden (tel. 095 21190). In contrast to the many traditional music pubs of the region, this place is known for its sporting atmosphere. It is home to the 'Connemara Blacks', a local rugby team. To round off the 'sports bar' attributes, there is a pool table, as well as a darts board, and a big-screen TV for viewing live matches and games.

MANNION'S BAR, Market Street, Clifden (tel. 095 21780). Nestled in the middle of town, this vintage pub is synonymous with traditional music – played nightly from April to October (with two sessions on Sunday); and at weekends from November to March.

THE TWELVE PINS BAR, Barna (tel. 091 592 368). Known to the locals as 'The Pins', this landmark hotel pub offers a rural country atmosphere. It has a large and rambling bar with an open log fireplace, and there is seating outside in the summer. Traditional hot bar food is served throughout the day.

DIGRESSIONS

FLOATING ON A FJORD: View Connemara from a different perspective on the waters of Killary Harbour, Ireland's only natural fjord, a 14.5-km (9-mile) stretch of sheltered water in northwest Connemara between Galway and Mayo. Cruises are conducted on board the *Connemara Lady*, a luxury 132-passenger two-deck catamaran. In addition to affording the opportunity to view the scenery, the 90-minute tour follows a route that passes wildlife habitats of seals, otters, dolphins and seabirds. Operates April–October from the dock 1.5 km (1 mile) south of Leenane on the N59. Information at the Leenane dock or Killary Cruises, 56c Bowling Green, Galway (tel. 091 566 736 or www.sea-cruiseconnemara.com).

ISLAND HOPPING: In addition to the Aran Islands (see Digressions in Chapter 26 – Galway City), the west coast of Connemara is also flanked by many smaller islands, such as Inishbofin, a 5-km (3-mile) long island known for archaeological remains, rare flora and fauna, and impressive cliff scenery. Nestled in the Atlantic 11 km (7 miles) northwest of Clifden, Inishbofin was chosen by St Colman in the seventh century as the site for a monastery, and was also a favoured haunt of the celebrated sixteenth-century pirate queen, Grace O'Malley. Today, about 200 inhabitants remain. Passenger ferries operate from Cleggan, April–October. Trips average 30 minutes. Information: King Ferries, Cleggan (tel. 095 44642 or www.inishbofinkingferries.com).

WALKING OFF-THE-BEATEN-PATH: 'Let's walk.' That's the simple but inviting motto of archaeologist and folklorist Gerry MacCloskey who leads visitors on walks into the remote terrain that he knows like the back of his hand – to meet the locals, explore ancient ruins, and see wild dolphins, grey seals, gannets, basking sharks and more. The walks, which include boat excursions to offshore islands, are conducted

from April to September on five- or
seven-day treks, and include accommodation, meals, picnics, musical entertainment and guided sightseeing.
Information: Gerry MacCloskey, Connemara Safari Walking Holidays, c/o
Abbeyglen Hotel, Clifden (tel. 095
21071 or www.walkingconnemara.com).

28: Lough Corrib – *Quiet Man* Country

Tourists may flock to sing the praises of Galway Bay, but this famous bay is only the beginning of Galway's liquid assets. Lesser known but equally beguiling is Lough Corrib, the Republic of Ireland's largest lake at 17,000 hectares (42,000 acres) in size. Stretching from the River Corrib in Galway city, up along the eastern half of the county, this lovely lake is picturesque, unspoiled, and fish-filled, providing some of Europe's best fishing waters for salmon and brown trout. If you like to cast a rod, it's hard to find better waters.

Great fishing is only half of the story here. Straddling Counties Galway and Mayo, Lough Corrib is home to Ashford Castle, one of Ireland's great resorts, and is the gateway to some of the west's most splendid scenery – the Maam Valley, Partry Mountains, and the legendary Joyce Country, a wild territory ruled from the thirteenth to nineteenth centuries by the Joyce clan, one of Galway's fourteen original tribes. It is said that exactly 365 islands, one for every day of the year, float in Lough Corrib, including Inchagoill Island, site of an early Christian monastic settlement dating back to the fifth century.

Importantly also, Lough Corrib is celebrated as the home of Cong, the small village that served as the setting for the legendary 1952 film *The Quiet Man*. *(See map p.259)*

FAST FACTS

Travel Information Offices

GALWAY TOURIST OFFICE, Forster Street, Galway (tel. 091 537 700). Open all year.

CONG TOURIST OFFICE, Old Courthouse, Cong, Co. Mayo (tel. 094 954 6542). Open June–September.

OUGHTERARD TOURIST OFFICE, Town Centre, Oughterard (tel. 091 552 808). Open May–September.

TRAVEL INFORMATION ONLINE:
www.irelandwest.ie, www.lakedistrict.ie, www.oughterardtourism.com, www.cong-ireland.com and www.quietman-cong.com

TELEPHONE AREA CODES:
There are two area codes for telephone numbers in this region, 091 and 094. To avoid confusion, the area code will be specified with each number.

QUIET MAN COUNTRY CELEBRATIONS –
First convened for the fiftieth anniversary of the release of *The Quiet Man*, this weekend gathering has become an annual meeting for fans of the film. The activities consist of appearances by John Wayne and Maureen O'Hara lookalikes, discussions, celebrity speakers, walking tours and visits to the settings of the film. Information: Paddy Rock, West Clonbur, Co. Galway, tel. 094 954 6155 or www.quietmancelebrations.com. (Last weekend of September)

DRIVING TOUR OF LOUGH CORRIB – QUIET MAN COUNTRY

Duration: 3–5 hours plus stops

Depart Galway city or another nearby origination point in the west. Follow the signs to national road N84, and follow this road on the eastern shore of Lough Corrib, towards **Headford**, a small market village 27 km (17 miles) to the north.

From Headford, bear left onto local road R334 and travel northwest 19 km (12 miles) into County Mayo and **Cong**, a picturesque village nestled on the northeast corner of Lough Corrib. The place name, which comes from the Irish language *Conga*, meaning 'isthmus', describes Cong's position on a large 6.5-km (4-mile) isthmus of land that separates Lough Corrib and Lough Mask.

For such a small and out-of-the-way town, Cong has many claims to fame, not the least of which is the fact that it was the setting for the classic 1952 movie *The Quiet Man*, starring John Wayne, Maureen O'Hara and Barry Fitzgerald. Naturally, the town has not forgotten its moment of glory. Follow the main street to the river and turn right to see **The Quiet Man Heritage Cottage**, Circular Road (tel. 094 954 6089). This authentic whitewashed cottage, complete with an emerald-green half-door and thatched roof, is a museum built to perpetuate the memory of the film. The ground floor has been designed as a replica of the original cottage set, where the interior scenes were filmed. All of the costumes, implements and furnishings – from the four-poster bed to the tables and chairs, are authentic reproductions of those used in the film. Scenes and life-size figures add to the nostalgia. The upstairs rooms serve as an exhibition hall for local archaeological and historical displays. Open daily, March–October. Admission: €

Long before *The Quiet Man*, Cong was making history as the site of **Cong Abbey**, a monastery founded by St Féichín in the sixth century, and rebuilt as an abbey of the Augustinians by King Turloch Mór O'Conor in the twelfth century. Turloch's son, Rory, the last high king of Ireland, retired to the abbey in 1183, and died there in 1198; he is buried at Clonmacnoise (See Chapter 23, 'County Offaly').

From this abbey came the **Cross of Cong**, created in the 1120s. A masterpiece of twelfth-century religious art, the cross was hidden for many years after the suppression of the monasteries in the fifteenth and sixteenth centuries, and then discovered in the early nineteenth century in a chest in the village. Made of oak, plated with copper and decorated with gold filigree in a Celtic pattern, it is considered as one of the great processional crosses of Ireland, now on display at the National Museum in Dublin.

Of the abbey church, only the chancel survives, entered from the car park through a north doorway built of stones reassembled there in the 1860s. In contrast, the doorways along the eastern side of the cloister are genuine examples of twelfth-century masonry work, with delicate Romanesque-early Gothic carvings. The details of these doorways are classified among the finest products of Irish medieval stone carving. The ruins of the abbey are in the centre of town opposite the tourist office.

On the edge of town are the entrance gates to **Ashford Castle** (tel. 094 954 6003), dating back to the thirteenth century and today serving as one of Ireland's major five-star hotel resorts. Drive along the long entrance pathway, park your car, and then cross over the drawbridge on foot to enter the fairytale world of Ashford, a broad vista of turrets and towers, arches and battlements. Over the years it has served as a residence to the De Burgos (Burkes), one of the original fourteen tribes of Galway, who conquered the surrounding land. In the eighteenth century, owned by the Oranmore and Browne families (the latter also of the original Galway tribes), it was enlarged to include a château-style section. Much of the current façade was added in the late nineteenth century by the Guinness family, of brewing fame, who lived here until 1939 when it was transformed into a hotel. The name derives from the Irish language, *Áth na Fuinseoige*, meaning 'ford of the ash' – a fitting name, as this great fortress/residence, which sits on the northern edge of Lough Corrib, is surrounded not only by ash, but also by dozens of other ancient trees, shrubs and flowers of all kinds. The grounds and gardens are open to the public, for a fee, and boat trips on Lough Corrib are also available from the pier next to the hotel (see Digressions below). Open daily, year round. Admission: €€

From Cong, take a slight detour northward around the eastern shore of Lough Mask, via **Ballinrobe**, a small market town that is a hub of outdoor sports activity. Home to the only racetrack in County Mayo, it also hosts the World Wet Fly Angling Championships each year.

From here, follow the main N84 road for 11 km (7 miles) to **Ballintubber Abbey** (tel. 094 30934), known as 'the abbey that refused to die'. This story of determination began in 1216 when

Cathal O'Conor, king of Connacht, built the abbey on the site of an earlier church attributed to St Patrick in 441. The word Ballintubber comes from the Irish language, *Baile Tobair Phádraig*, meaning 'the townland of St Patrick's well'. Like other abbeys in Ireland, Ballintubber was suppressed by Henry VIII. After destruction by Cromwell in 1653, the abbey was roofless, but not deserted. For 250 years, the people attended services in the wind, rain and other elements, making Ballintubber one of the few Irish churches in continuous use for nearly 800 years. The first attempts at restoration came in 1846, but work was abandoned because of the Famine. Eventually, the abbey was completely restored in 1966. Proud of their heritage, volunteers offer a 20-minute audiovisual on the history of the abbey, and guided tours of the building and garden-filled grounds. Open daily. Admission: free

If you are a capable long-distance walker, from the grounds of Ballintubber you can also follow **Tóchar Phádraig**, an old pilgrim road leading to Croagh Patrick, 35.5 km (22 miles) west. Although named after Ireland's patron, St Patrick, the road actually predates Christianity and was probably built around 350AD, as a route for the kings of Connacht to reach Cruachán Aigle (the pagan name for the mountain now known as Croagh Patrick).

From Ballintubber, retrace your route southwards as far as **Partree** and then turn right onto a local road along the western shore of **Lough Mask**, with the **Partry Mountains** on your right, entering into a Gaeltacht or Irish-speaking district. Follow this scenic drive via **Tourmakeady**, passing from County Mayo back into County Galway. This is the heart of **Joyce Country**, the far-flung lands inhabited in medieval times by the Joyces, one of Galway's fourteen original tribes. It is said that the Joyces were of princely Welsh stock, very tall in stature. Tom Joyce, the patriarch of the Irish sept, who came from Wales to Ireland and settled in Connemara during the reign of Edward I, is reputed to have been over 2 metres (7 foot) tall, a gigantic height for the times. But don't look for any giants along the route now. The clan eventually dispersed and resettled all over Ireland, including Dublin from whence came the great twentieth-century scribe, James Joyce. His wife, Nora Barnacle, was from Galway city, but he claimed no Galway connections other than his surname.

The road leads to **Maam**, also known as Maam Bridge, in the heart of the Maam Valley, an isolated spot, flanked by the craggy **Maamturk Mountains** on the right and upper reaches of Lough Corrib on the left. The curious place name derives from the Irish *An Mám*, meaning 'the mountain pass'. There is a small bridge here over a body of water known appropriately as the **Joyces' River**. Follow the R336 south for 8 km

(5 miles) to **Maam Cross**, a crossroads at the intersection of the main N59 road.

Turn left onto the main road and head east, driving though desolate and bare rock-strewn lands, with a lake-studded valley flecked with purple heather to the right, and distant views of Lough Corrib on the left. After 16 km (10 miles), straight ahead is **Oughterard**, a fishing town nestled between the Owenriff river and one of Lough Corrib's most pictur-esque points. The place name comes from the Irish language, *Uachtar Árd*, meaning 'upper height'. Surrounded by trees, Oughterard is a mix of substantial Geor-gian houses and small fishing cottages.

From Oughterard, you can take a boat trip (see Digressions below) to see **Incha-goill Island**, the most famous of Lough Corrib's 365 islands, located in the centre of the lake, halfway between Oughterard and Cong. Uninhabited since the 1940s, Inchagoill Island contains the remains of **Teampall Phádraig** (St Patrick's church), believed to have been built of wood or wattle and daub by St Patrick. The present stone church was erected in the fifth century by his nephew, Lugnaed, who is buried on the island. A unique 'ru-dder stone', so-called because of its shape, marks Lugnaed's grave, reputed to be the oldest inscribed Christian stone in Europe outside the Catacombs of Rome.

Before leaving Oughterard, consider one of the favourite local drives – north-west of town to see the **Hill of Doon**.

Follow the signposts from town for the **Glann Road**. The road winds along the Corrib's shores and moves inland before returning to the shore and a picnic spot. After this, it narrows and climbs for another 3 km (2 miles), before reaching a car park overlooking Lough Corrib, and giving panoramic views of the Lough and the Hill of Doon. The drive totals about 14.5 km (9 miles) more, each way.

From Oughterard, travel about 3 km (2 miles) south of town and make a left at the signpost for **Aughnanure Castle** (tel. 091 552 214), a six-storey tower house dating back to *c*.1500. Standing on a rocky island along the shores of Lough Corrib, this well-preserved stone fortress was the home of the O'Flahertys, a ferocious Irish clan who were the masters of West Connacht – the area between Lough Corrib and the sea. The site also con-tains the remains of a banqueting hall, a watch tower, two bawns and a dry harbour. Open daily, June–September; Saturday–Sunday, May and October. Admission: €

Return to the main road and con-tinue for 16 km (10 miles) east to the village of **Moycullen**, a picturesque spot with an equally evocative place name. In the Irish language, *Máigh Cuilinn* means 'plain of holly'. From here, it is just 13 km (8 miles) back to Galway city.

RESTAURANTS

ECHOES, Main Street, Cong, Co. Mayo (tel. 094 954 6059). Housed in a shop-front location in the centre of town, this long-established restaurant is known for its superb cut-to-order beef fillets and rack-of-lamb entrées (the family butcher's shop is next door) and seafood dishes such as sole on the bone, and scallops and bacon. Open for dinner, daily, May–October; Thursday–Sunday, November–April.

MOYCULLEN HOUSE, Mountain Road, Moycullen, Co. Galway (tel. 091 555 566). Surrounded by 12 hectares (30 acres) of woodland, rhododendrons and azaleas, this place sits on one of the highest points in the area, overlooking Lough Corrib about 2.5 km (1.5 miles) from the village. It was built as a home in the 'arts and crafts' style over a cen-tury ago, and adapted for use as a restau-rant in 1998. The menu runs the gamut of classic Irish favourites – from steaks, roast lamb and pork fillets to supreme of chicken, fillet of salmon and roast duck, with vegetarian tartlets as well. Open for dinner, Thursday–Tuesday; and for lunch on Sunday.

QUIET MAN COFFEE SHOP, Main Street, Cong, Co. Mayo (tel. 094 954 6034). Established in 1951 when *The Quiet Man* was being filmed, this small and homely restaurant is as popular with the locals as it is with visitors. Sit in the front room with a view of the town, or in the back room overlooking flower-filled gar-dens and the river. Paintings of Mayo and photos of *The Quiet Man* scenes decorate the walls. The menu features homemade soups, freshly made sandwiches and salads and an ever-changing selection of hot dishes. Open for lunch and snacks, Thursday–Tuesday.

RIVERSIDE CAFÉ, Bridge Street, Oughter-ard, Co. Galway (tel. 091 552 404). Over-looking the river, this contemporary café specialises in freshly baked pastries, cakes and breads, as well as deli-style meats, salads and snacks. Open for lunch and snacks, daily; and for dinner, Friday–Saturday.

WHITE GABLES, Clifden Road (N59), Moycullen, Co. Galway (tel. 091 555 744). Nestled in the centre of the village, this restaurant is housed in a beautifully restored cottage, and decorated through-out with antiques and original artwork. The menu features fresh seafood – lobster from a seawater tank, crab, oysters, scal-lops, monkfish, turbot and John Dory sole, as well as steaks and poultry. Open for dinner, Tuesday–Sunday; and for lunch on Sunday.

PUBS

JOSEPH KEANE, Maam Bridge, Co. Galway (tel. 091 571 110.). In the middle of nowhere, this pub is a welcome source of refreshment for visitors coming from many directions. Hearty hot soups and baskets of sandwiches are served in a homely fireside atmosphere. In typical country fashion, the proprietor also operates a newsagent, general store and petrol station, and a wool dealership.

KELEHAN'S PUB, Bushypark, Co. Galway (tel. 091 522 134). Situated on the N59, overlooking Lough Corrib, this pub sits on the main road between Oughterard and Galway. It is one of the oldest family-run pubs in the area, and the décor reflects its long history – nooks, crannies and archways, dark woods, stone walls, and lantern lighting. It's a favourite with fishermen and horse riders, as well as passing motorists.

KEOGH'S BAR, Main Street, Oughterard, Co. Galway (tel. 091 552 222). With a licence dating back to 1915, this pub has long been a fixture in the middle of town. Step inside to enjoy a cosy and well-settled atmosphere, with subdued lighting, a long and narrow bar, alcove seating, and lots of old photographs on the walls. Proprietor Mick Keogh also operates a bureau de change, supermarket and delicatessen on the premises.

PEACOCKE'S, Maam Cross, Co. Galway (tel. 091 552 306). Sometimes called the Piccadilly or Celtic Bazaar of Connemara, this place sits at a busy crossroads. The diverse facilities include a bog-themed bar with open turf fireplace, a 20-metre (66-foot) tower that provides panoramic views of the four quarters of Connemara, and a replica of *The Quiet Man* cottage, plus an on-site supermarket and petrol station. There are plenty of reasons to start a friendly conversation here.

TÍ BHURCA – BURKE'S BAR, Clonbur, Co. Galway (tel. 094 954 6175). Immersed in the heart of Joyce Country between Lough Corrib and Lough Mask, this pub is 8 km (5 miles) west of Cong. Originally known as Mount Gable House, it is run by the fourth generation of the Burke family. Bar food is available all day, and traditional music is on tap most nights.

DIGRESSIONS

CRUISING ON THE CORRIB: No visit to this area is complete without a boat cruise on Lough Corrib, famed for its scenic shorelands, 365 islands, and mountain vistas. From Oughterard or Cong, you can embark on two-hour guided sightseeing cruises. The trips, operated on double-deck boats with sun decks, bars and narrated commentary, include a visit to Inchagoill Island, the most famous of the lake's 365 islands, located in the centre of the lake. Cruises operate daily, May–October, from Oughterard; and all year from Cong. Information: Corrib Ferries, Oughterard Pier (tel. 091 552 808) or Cong Pier (tel. 094 954 6029 or www.corribcruises.com).

GETTING BELOW THE SURFACE: Travel 3 km (2 miles) west of Oughterard to visit Glengowla Mines, a silver and lead mine dating back to the nineteenth century. Reputed to be one of the richest and most productive mines of its time, Glengowla has been restored to a level of 20 metres (65 feet) underground. Guided tours take visitors down, via steps with handrails and lighting, into the marble chambers and caverns, to see silver, lead, calcite, quartz and many other mineral formations in the walls of the mine. Facilities include a visitor centre with mineral samples from the mine, demonstrations of gold panning, and a rock and gem shop. Open daily, March–November. Information: Glengowla Mines, Oughterard, Co. Galway (tel. 091 552 360).

29: East Galway and County Roscommon

As many cross-country visitors to Ireland's west coast drive across the N6 to Galway city and Connemara, or the N5 to County Mayo, they pass by the unpretentious area of East Galway and part of County Westmeath. Inland and unsung, this part of Ireland is not high on tourists' lists of 'must sees'. Few travel guides do justice to the heritage attractions of this uncommercialised area.

Likewise, directly east of Galway, in the heart of the Irish midlands, lies the equally overlooked County Roscommon. Set beside the western shores of Lough Ree and Lough Allen, the River Shannon's second- and third-largest lakes, Roscommon offers wooded and lakeland scenery, refreshing but not spectacular. The place name Roscommon comes from the Irish language, *Ros Comáin*, meaning 'St Comán's woods'. The eighth-century saint is said to have found the area so pleasant that he built a monastery among the trees.

Unlike the rocky coastal lands of western Galway and Mayo, Roscommon is adorned with relatively fertile and pastoral lands. During the seventeenth to nineteenth centuries, it proved attractive to the British aristocracy and their agents who became unpopular landlords while the Irish tenant farmers worked the land.

As a result, the Roscommon countryside is flecked with great houses and country manors – a rich legacy of Gothic, Georgian, Victorian and Italianate architecture, once owned by the landed gentry, the earls and lords of long ago. Many of the houses have been sold into private hands, and a few have passed to the Irish government or local organisations to maintain as museums and testimonies of the past.

Indeed, you will quickly discover that the lesser-travelled roads of East Galway and County Roscommon are roads well worth taking.

(See map p.259)

FAST FACTS

Travel Information Offices

ATHLONE TOURIST OFFICE, Athlone Castle, Co. Westmeath (tel. 090 649 4630). Open April–October.

AUGHRIM TOURIST OFFICE, Aughrim, Co. Galway (tel. 090 967 3939). Open April–October.

ROSCOMMON TOURIST OFFICE, Main Street, Roscommon (tel. 090 662 6342). Open May–September.

BOYLE TOURIST OFFICE, Main Street, Boyle, Co. Roscommon (tel. 071 966 2145). Open May–October.

TRAVEL INFORMATION ONLINE:
www.irelandwest.ie,
www.ecoast-midlands.travel.ie,
www.visitroscommon.ie and
www.galwayeast.com

TELEPHONE AREA CODES:
There are at least three area codes for telephone numbers on this route. To avoid confusion, the area code will be specified with each telephone number.

MAJOR EVENTS

STROKESTOWN INTERNATIONAL POETRY FESTIVAL – Political satire in verse, Irish-language poems, and other poetic works are the feature of this event, drawing competitors from Ireland, Britain and the US. Pub poetry and traditional music also add to the festivities. Information: Merrily Harpur, Festival Office, Bawn Street, Strokestown, Co. Roscommon, tel. 071 963 3690 or www.strokestownpoetryprize.com. (First weekend of May)

BOYLE ARTS FESTIVAL – With workshops and activities for adults and children, this annual event is a feast of visual arts, drama, comedy, literature and music of many genres (traditional, classical and jazz). Information: Festival Office, Boyle, Co. Roscommon, tel. 071 966 3085 or www.boylearts.com. (Last week of July)

BALLINASLOE INTERNATIONAL OCTOBER FAIR AND FESTIVAL – One of Europe's oldest horse fairs, this eight-day event includes horse and pony events, showjumping, agricultural show, street entertainment, fireworks, tug-of-war and vintage parade. Information: Mary Phelan, Festival Office, 4 Duggan Avenue, Ballinasloe, Co. Galway, tel. 090 964 4793 or www.ballinasloe.com. (Late September–early October)

EAST GALWAY AND COUNTY ROSCOMMON DRIVING TOUR

Duration: 4–6 hours plus stops

From Galway city, drive along the main N6 road for 35.5 km (22 miles) to **Loughrea**, a picturesque market town on a lake. The town, in fact, is named after its lake. The Irish-language words, *Baile Locha Riach*, mean 'the town of the grey lake'. In the Middle Ages, Loughrea was the principal seat of the MacWilliam Uachtair Burkes, leading chieftains of the west. To see the lake and the highlights of the town, turn right at **West Bridge** as you enter from the main road.

Go one block south to **Barrack Street**, which runs along the lake. Here, on the left side, is the thirteenth-century **Town Moat**, the only functioning water-filled medieval moat in Ireland. Turn left and continue, with the lake on your right, to see **St Brendan's Cathedral**, Barrack Street (tel. 091 841 212), built during the period 1897–1903. A treasure house of Celtic Renaissance art, it contains an unrivalled collection of stained-glass windows by leading Irish artists including Evie Hone, Sarah Purser and Michael Healy; 30 embroidered banners made to the designs of noted Irish artist Jack B Yeats; and benches with individual carvings at the ends of each seat; as well as noteworthy metalwork in the lamps. Open daily. Admission: free

Return to the main N6 road going east. After 8 km (5 miles), a sign on the left side of the road points to **Dartfield – Ireland's Horse Museum and Park**, Kilreekill (tel. 091 843 968). For anyone interested in horses, this place is made-to-order. Developed and owned by renowned Galway horseman Willie Leahy, Dartfield is a tribute to horses and their role in Irish life. It is housed on a nineteenth-century estate consisting of 142 hectares (350 acres) of parklands and a quadrangle of buildings. The museum contains a walk-around exhibit with a 20-minute audiovisual, art gallery, hall of fame, library, café and equestrian-themed gift shop. In the outdoor stable area, horses can be seen at work and at rest. In addition, there is a forge and tack room, and carriage and pony rides are available, as are horse-riding lessons. Guided tours are available on request. It is located about 8 km (5 miles) east of Loughrea, off the N6. Open daily. Admission: €€

Continuing on from Kilreekill via the N6 for 9.5 km (6 miles), the next town is **Aughrim**, a small village with a very interesting history. It was the scene of the bloodiest battle of Irish history – the Battle of Aughrim on 12 July 1691. Sometimes referred to by US visitors as the 'Gettysburg of Ireland', the Battle of Aughrim involved a confrontation between 45,000 soldiers from eight European countries, and cost 9,000 lives. The **Battle of Aughrim Interpretative Centre** (tel. 090 967 3939) enables visitors to relive the battle via a high-tech three-dimensional audiovisual presentation and 'hands-on' multi-sensory displays. Afterwards, go outside and walk the adjacent battlefield area which is signposted for visitors. Open Tuesday–Sunday, June–September. Admission: €

After Aughrim, it is just 6.5 km (4 miles) to **Ballinasloe**, the main commercial and industrial centre for East Galway, and an important crossroads town from ancient times. The town's October Horse Fair, dating back to 1722, was once the largest fair of its kind in Europe, and today it is still the largest livestock fair in Ireland (see Major Events).

It is just 24 km (15 miles) east to **Athlone** in County Westmeath, a thriving commercial hub and the largest town on the River Shannon. Athlone is perhaps best known, however, as the birthplace of the great Irish tenor, Count John McCormack (1884–1945).

The Athlone streetscape is dominated by the high profile of **Athlone Castle** (tel. 090 649 2912), a sprawling stone fortress with turrets, towers and cannons, sitting on the edge of the river. It is well signposted from the main road. Built in 1210 for King John of England, this huge castle played an important part in Athlone's history, first as the seat of the presidents of Connacht and later as the headquarters of the governor of Athlone during both the first Siege of Athlone in 1690 and the second in 1691. Declared a national monument in 1970, the castle is noted for its original medieval walls and authentic cannons and mortars. The interior now houses a museum and visitor centre with exhibits including an audiovisual presentation on the Siege of Athlone, displays on the castle itself, the town of Athlone, the flora and fauna of the River Shannon region, and a review of the life of John McCormack. Open daily, April–October. Admission: €

For a change of pace and a scenic drive along the western shores of Lough Ree, follow the N61 north for 32 km (20 miles) to **Roscommon**, the chief town of County Roscommon and a busy market centre. Follow the N61 through the town, going eastward towards Ballyclare, and then take a left turn onto the R368 to **Strokestown**, an eighteenth- and early nineteenth-century village, laid out for Maurice Mahon (1738–1819), also known as the Baron Hartland. The Mahon family had been granted these lands in the 1650s in return for their support of the English colonial campaign.

To learn more about how the family lived, visit **Strokestown Park House** (tel. 071 963 3013). A prime example of a gentleman farmer's country house, this huge 45-room Palladian mansion was built in the 1730s for Thomas Mahon, and incorporates many parts of an earlier tower house. It is the focal point of an estate that was the seat of the Pakenham-Mahon families for over 300 years until 1979 – reflecting how the landed gentry pampered themselves at the expense of the native population. The centre block of the house, fully furnished as it was in earlier days, contains the private residential rooms. It is surrounded by two wings that contain the service areas, including Ireland's last galleried kitchen in the north wing, and an elaborate vaulted stable, described as an 'equine cathedral', in the south wing. The galleried kitchen, now a tea room, illustrates how each day's menu was dropped to the cook from the gallery, so the lady of the house did not have to encounter the commotion of the kitchen staff. Open daily, Easter–October. Admission: €

Outside, the stable yards have been converted into the **Irish Famine Museum** (tel. 071 963 3013). In contrast to the grandeur of the main house, this museum spotlights one of the most far-reaching events of Irish history – the Great Famine of the 1840s. The exhibits illustrate how and why the famine started and was allowed to spread, reducing the Irish population of 8.1 million people by almost a third, through death and mass emigration. The exhibits range from photographs, letters, documents, and satirical cartoons of the times to farm implements and a huge cauldron that was used for soup to feed the starving people in a famine-relief programme. Open daily, Easter–October. Admission: €

Leaving Strokestown, follow the main N5 road west for 8 km (5 miles) via **Tulsk**, and then turn right onto the N61 for 24 km (15 miles) to **Boyle**, a busy market town beside the Boyle river. As you approach the town, on the right is the entrance to **Lough Key Forest Park** (tel. 071 966 2363). Spanning 340 hectares (840 acres) along the shores of the Shannon's third largest lake, this was originally part of an estate that belonged to the King-Stafford-Harman family, influential local landowners. In 1788, they built here a magnificent lakeside country house, known as 'Rockingham', which burned down in 1957. Shortly afterwards, the grounds were turned over to the Irish government's Forest and Wildlife Service, for public use. It has since become one of Ireland's foremost lakeside parks, containing mixed woodlands, with cypress groves and diverse foliage, and bog gardens with peat-loving plants. The grounds include a lake with more than a dozen islands, extensive nature walks, tree-identity trails, ancient monuments, ring forts, a central viewing tower, picnic grounds and more. Open daily during daylight hours. Admission: €

The town of Boyle is also the setting of **King House**, Main Street (tel. 071 966 3242). Built for Sir Henry King in 1730, this Palladian-style residence was considered as one of the finest town houses in rural Ireland. It is thought to have been the work of Sir Edward Lovett Pearce who also designed the Irish Parliament House on College Green, Dublin, now the Bank of Ireland. Highlights include a long entrance gallery with tripartite windows and an original fireplace, plus extensive vaulted ceilings on all floors. In 1788, the family built a new and grander house, 'Rockingham' (see above), and moved outside town beside Lough Key; this building then became the headquarters of the Roscommon Militia. It was occupied by the Connaught Rangers and used as a barracks until 1930. In 1989, the Roscommon County Council began restoration work, and the house was opened to the public in 1994. Displays in the various rooms reflect the house's varied history, including its military usage and recent restoration. A room has been left partially restored so that visitors can see the fabric of the house. In addition, there are exhibits on the King family and families of local kings. An audiovisual, 'Kings of Connaught', uses special effects and life-sized models to tell the stories. Open daily, April–October. Admission: €

Boyle is also the home of **Boyle Abbey** (tel. 071 966 2604), one of Ireland's best-preserved ecclesiastical ruins. Founded in 1161 by Cistercian monks from Mellifont Abbey in County Louth, the abbey was a transitional creation, bridging the Romanesque and Gothic periods. This is graphically illustrated by the juxtaposition of a row of rounded arches on one side of the nave and a row of pointed arches on the other side. Although suppressed and mutilated in the seventeenth and eighteenth centuries, the Abbey still retains a remarkable framework, including a church, cloisters, kitchens, sacristy, cellars, and a gatehouse which houses an interpretative centre. Open daily, April–October. Admission: €

From Boyle, depart on local road R361 and travel southwest for 24 km (15 miles) to **Castlerea**, a busy market town famous for its connections to the last high king of Ireland. Drive through the town and follow the signposts west on the main N60 road for 4 km (2.5 miles) to visit **Clonalis House** (tel. 094 962 0014). One of Ireland's great stately houses, this is the ancestral home of the O'Conors, kings of Connacht, and home of the O'Conor Don, the direct descendant of the last high king of Ireland. Standing on land that has belonged to the O'Conors for more than 1,500 years, this house was built in 1880, a combination of Victorian, Italianate and Queen Anne architecture, with mostly Louis XV-style furnishings. The dis-

plays include ancient portraits and documents, a rare harp said to have belonged to the legendary poet and bard, Turlough O'Carolan, antique lace, horse-drawn farm machinery, and other memorabilia. The grounds, with terraced and woodland gardens, also hold the O'Conor inauguration stone, the Irish version of the Stone of Scone – the revered Scottish royal stone dating back to the ninth century. Open Tuesday–Sunday, June–mid-September. Admission: €

Return to Galway via the N83 and N17, or continue on to other parts of Ireland.

PAT'S PICKS

RESTAURANTS

THE ABBEY, Abbey Hotel, Galway Road, Roscommon (tel. 090 662 6240). The atmosphere of an eighteenth-century manor prevails at this restaurant on the edge of town amid private gardens. The bar menu offers soups, sandwiches and salads, while the main dining-room serves full-service meals in the Irish tradition. Open for lunch and dinner, daily.

CRUACHÁN AÍ CAFÉ, Tulsk, Co. Roscommon (tel. 071 963 9268). Nestled at the crossroads of the N5 and N61 roads, this café is part of a local heritage centre whose Irish name translates into 'a place of mystery and legend'. The café, which overlooks the River Ogulla, serves gourmet coffees, teas, cakes, sandwiches, soups and more. Open for snacks and lunch, daily.

GLEESON'S CAFÉ, Market Square, Roscommon (tel. 090 662 6954). Conveniently located next to the tourist office overlooking the town square, this café is set in a nineteenth-century townhouse with large archway, turf-fire stove and local limestone masonry. The menu features freshly made soups, salads, sandwiches, casseroles and baked goods – homemade cakes, brown bread and scones are a speciality. Open for breakfast, lunch and snacks, daily.

RESTAURANT LE CHÂTEAU, St Peter's Port, The Docks, Athlone, Co. Westmeath (tel. 090 649 4517). Housed in a former Presbyterian church near Athlone Castle on the banks of the River Shannon, this restaurant has a décor reflecting an ecclesiastical theme (stained-glass windows, candlelit tables) with nautical overtones (lighthouse pillars and galleon-style upper floor). The menu, which blends Irish and French cuisine, offers specialities such as Angus beef, rack of lamb and local seafood. Open for lunch and dinner, daily.

WINEPORT, Glasson, Co. Westmeath (tel. 090 648 5466). Overlooking the shoreline of Lough Ree almost 5 km (3 miles) north of Athlone, this nautically-themed restaurant has grown in recent years to include a covered boardwalk. The menu blends international recipes with locally sourced ingredients such as freshwater fish from the River Shannon, especially eel and pike, as well as certified Angus beef, free-range poultry, garden-grown herbs, organic vegetables and farmhouse cheeses. Open for lunch, Monday–Friday; and dinner, daily.

PUBS

BIRCH GROVE, Athlone Road, Ballinasloe, Co. Galway (tel. 090 964 4014). For a rest or snack in transit, this pub is a good stopping place on the main N6 road. The interior is unusually spacious, open-plan and comfortably plush with plenty of windows, a wooden beamed ceiling, and a series of built-in snugs, ideal for a quiet chat. Bar food is available all day, and traditional music is played on Thursday–Sunday nights.

KEENAN'S PUB, Tarmonberry, Co. Roscommon (tel. 043 26098). Situated just west of the Shannon, east of Strokestown, this pub dates back to 1840 and has been run by the Keenan family for five generations. Step inside and sample the past – take a seat at the large L-shaped timber bar, or browse amid the old-style grocery shelves and glass cases containing various bric-a-brac and old prints. There is music every Monday evening.

RAFTERY'S – THE BLAZERS' BAR, Craughwell, Co. Galway (tel. 091 846 708). Nestled on the busy N6 road, this pub has been owned for over a century by the Raftery family, and has connections to Hollywood and to the sports world. Over the years, it has welcomed its share of actors and writers as it is the closest pub to St Cleran's, one-time home of Hollywood film director John Huston. Many local horse-owners, jockeys and trainers also gather here. The décor is suitably plush, with dark mahogany and royal blue seating, and pictures and bric-a-brac related to horses and hounds. It is also the meeting place for the Blazers Golf Society.

SEÁN'S BAR, 13 Main Street, Athlone, Co. Westmeath (tel. 090 649 2358). Standing in the shadow of Athlone Castle's walls, this pub claims to be the oldest pub in continuous use in Ireland, with a documented history going back to 1600. Much of the history is reflected in the décor – open fireplace, mirrored shelving, time-worn mahogany bar, church-pew seating, and walls covered with memorabilia. Music is played, Sunday–Thursday nights, year-round.

DIGRESSIONS

CRUISE ALONG THE SHANNON: With both Lough Ree and Lough Key along this route, there are several opportunities for a narrated boat trip on the Shannon. Most cruises last 60 to 90 minutes and operate June–September. Information: MV *Ross*, Jolly Mariner Marina, Coosan, Athlone (tel. 090 647 2892 or www.acl.ie) and Lough Key Boat Tours, The Harbour, Lough Key Forest Park, Boyle, Co. Roscommon (tel. 071 966 7037).

DISTILLERY TOUR: For a bit of history and liquid refreshment, head 32 km (20 miles) east of Athlone on the N6 road to visit Locke's Distillery at Kilbeggan. Established in 1757, the original distillery on this site operated for almost 200 years, producing triple-distilled malt whiskey, until it closed in 1953. It has since reopened as a museum of whiskey-making. A 25-minute tour reveals the step-by-step process – from the grinding of the grain to the casking of the final product. All tours end in the 'tasting room' for a sample. Open daily. Information: Locke's Distillery Museum, Main Street, Kilbeggan, Co. Westmeath (tel. 0506 32134 or www.lockesdistillerymuseum.com).

IN THE FOOTSTEPS OF ST BRENDAN: A detour south of Loughrea or Ballinasloe leads to the isolated monastery foundation and burial ground of St Brendan the Navigator (*c*.558), the same intrepid saint who is revered in County Kerry as the first 'discoverer' of America. Other than early grave slabs, little remains of the original foundation. The site does have a small stone church (*c*.1200), known as St Brendan's Cathedral (Church of Ireland), noted for its Gothic chancel and Gothic windows. The west doorway, considered one of the finest specimens of Hiberno-Romanesque art in existence, is replete with columns and arches, and surmounted by pilasters and a throng of carved human heads. Open daily. Information: Galway East Tourism, Old Church Street, Athenry, Co. Galway (tel. 091 850 687 or www.galwayeast.com).

30: North Mayo Coast

Looking for something different? Off the beaten path? Go west, as the old adage recommends. And to go really west, head beyond the popular paths of County Galway into the upper reaches of County Mayo – along the coast from Clew Bay to Killala Bay.

The North Mayo Coast presents an ever-changing route of beaches and bays, lakes and rivers, hillsides and mountains. Clew Bay, in particular, is a stand-out for great scenic beauty. Spanning a distance of over 24 km (15 miles) long and 11 km (7 miles) wide, Clew Bay is dotted with hundreds of small islands that form a fascinating archipelago. The focal point is Achill Island, Ireland's largest offshore island, and a favourite resort.

Historically, this area has been drawing people for many centuries. Céide Fields, said to be the most extensive Stone Age monument in the world, is on this route. St Patrick trudged his way here in the fifth century and climbed the nearest mountain overlooking Clew Bay, setting a spiritual precedent that is still followed today at Croagh Patrick. In the sixteenth century, the pirate queen Grace O'Malley used Clew Bay as her base. The English also found their way here in the seventeenth and eighteenth centuries, building two picturesque Georgian towns – Westport and Newport.

In addition, this area came close to changing Irish history in August 1798 when France's General Humbert landed at Killala with 1,000 men, in an unsuccessful attempt to lead the United Irishmen in a full-scale rebellion against the English. In recent years, the late American writer Thomas Flanagan used the incident as the focal point for his successful book and film set in this corner of Ireland, *The Year of the French*.

The North Mayo coast is also home to the remote region known as Bangor Erris, a Gaeltacht or Irish-speaking area. You'll know you are in the Gaeltacht when the usual 'B & B' (bed and breakfast) signs are noticeably outnumbered by '*B agus B*' signs.

(See map p.259)

FAST FACTS

Travel Information Offices

ACHILL ISLAND TOURIST OFFICE, Keel, Achill Island (tel. 098 45384). Open June–early September.

BALLINA TOURIST OFFICE, Cathedral Road, Ballina (tel. 096 70848). Open April–early October.

BELMULLET TOURIST OFFICE, Belmullet (tel. 097 81500). Open June–September.

CASTLEBAR TOURIST OFFICE, Linenhall Street, Castlebar (tel. 094 902 1207). Open June–August.

WESTPORT TOURIST OFFICE, James Street, Westport (tel. 098 25711). Open all year.

TRAVEL INFORMATION ONLINE:
www.irelandwest.ie,
www.visitmayo.com, or
www.mayo-ireland.ie

TELEPHONE AREA CODES:
At least three area codes are used for telephone numbers in this area. To avoid confusion, the area code will be listed with each number.

MAJOR EVENTS

CASTLEBAR INTERNATIONAL FOUR DAYS' WALKS – Walkers from all over the world gather in Castlebar for these annual walks into the surrounding countryside. Each participant carries a flag or wears a T-shirt from his or her country to promote having fun and forging global friendships. Information: Elaine Devereux, Festival Office, New Antrim Street, Castlebar, tel. 094 902 4102 or www.castlebar4dayswalks.com. (First weekend of July)

BALLINA STREET FESTIVAL AND ARTS WEEK – A family-oriented festival, this annual gathering draws over 50,000 people to Ballina for a continuous programme of music, song, sport, a Mardi Gras, street spectacle and fireworks, as well as children's events including a teddy bears' picnic. Information: Mark Winters, Parochial Hall, Kevin Barry Street, Ballina, tel. 096 79814 or www.ballinastreetfestival.com. (Second week of July)

FÉILE IORRAS – INTERNATIONAL FOLK ARTS FESTIVAL – The Barony of Erris on the northwest coast of Mayo plays host to this annual gathering, combining the best international folk art groups with local and Irish artists. Events include workshops, concerts, carnival night, busking, literary readings and more. Information: Festival Office, Belmullet, tel. 097 20977 or www.feileiorras.org. (Late July–early August)

CROAGH PATRICK PILGRIMAGE (REEK SUNDAY) – Each year, thousands of pilgrims, visitors and curiosity-seekers climb Croagh Patrick in the tradition of Ireland's patron saint, on the final Sunday of July. The two-hour climb can be done any other day as well. 'Everyone has to do it at least once,' they say. Information: Croagh Patrick Centre, Murrisk (tel. 098 64114 or www.croagh-patrick.com. (Last Sunday in July)

NORTH MAYO COAST DRIVING TOUR

Duration: 5–6 hours plus stops

Start this tour from **Castlebar**, a busy industrial town and the administrative capital of Mayo. Take the N5 west for almost 18 km (11 miles) to **Westport**, one of the west of Ireland's few purpose-planned towns. Designed by the English architect James Wyatt *c*.1780, it has a long boulevard, known as **The Mall**, with a colonnade of trees on both sides of the River Carrowbeg. The streets, lined with handsome Georgian buildings, converge around a central octagon-shaped monument. It is well worth taking the time to walk around Westport. If you happen to be in town on a Thursday, don't miss the weekly country market at the **Town Hall** on **The Octagon** from 9.30am to 1pm. Admission: free

At the western edge of the town is **Westport House**, off Quay Road (tel. 098 25430), an eighteenth-century Georgian country mansion that is the home of Lord Altamont, a descendant of Grace O'Malley, the famous sixteenth-century pirate queen of the Irish seas. Conceived by German architect Richard Castle, the house was completed in 1778 by James Wyatt. Interior highlights include an ornate staircase of white Sicilian marble, a wide selection of family portraits and other paintings, early nineteenth-century Waterford Glass chandeliers, eighteenth-century hand-painted Chinese wallpaper, and Irish silver. In an effort to appeal to a wide range of visitors, the grounds include an antique shop, children's zoo, miniature train, camping park, and pitch-and-putt and tennis facilities. Open daily, June–September; Sunday, April and May. Admission: €€

The front gate of Westport House faces the harbour. It is worth a stroll along the quay to see the variety of pubs, restaurants and other local enterprises. This is also the embarkation point for cruises to Clare Island (see Digressions below).

For a short but essential detour, depart Westport and travel via the local R335 road, with panoramic views of Clew Bay to the right. After 8 km (5 miles), the glorious profile of **Croagh Patrick** rises on the left to a height of 765 metres (2,510 feet). Known locally as 'the Reek', it is an isolated quartzite cone-shaped peak, considered one of the most striking features of the west-of-Ireland landscape. The name of the mountain, which literally means 'St Patrick's Hill', has its origins in legend – St Patrick is said to have spent 40 days and nights on the summit, fasting and praying for the people of Ireland during the mid-fifth century. To commemorate the event, each year Christian pilgrims gather here on the last Sunday in July, to climb the mountain, many in bare feet, in the footsteps of Patrick. On the summit of Croagh Patrick is a church, built in 1905 on the site of a small oratory that dated back to 842. The present edifice was built over a period of a year at the cost of £1,000. Materials for construction were prepared at the foot of the mountain and transported to the top by donkey.

At the foot of the mountain is **Croagh Patrick Centre/Teach na Miasa**, Murrisk (tel. 098 64114). In addition to providing guidance and facilities for those who venture out to climb the 765-metre (2,510-foot) mountain, this purpose-built centre also serves as an information source for non-climbing visitors, giving details about the mountain and its traditions. The exhibits include a photo gallery and displays on the archaeological, social and religious history of the mountain. Guided tours of the mountain are also available from the centre. Open daily, March–October. Admission: €

Return to Westport and drive via the N59 to **Newport**, a distance of 13 km (just over 8 miles). Hugging the northeast corner of Clew Bay, Newport is a prime fishing centre for salmon on the Newport river and other nearby waters. A focal point of the town is the unique seven-arch viaduct over the river, a blend of red sandstone and limestone. Newport's main claim to fame is that it is the ancestral home of Princess Grace of Monaco, the former Hollywood actress Grace Kelly, whose grandfather was a Newport native before he emigrated to the US. Princess Grace and Prince Rainier often visited Newport, although nothing remains of the original homestead today. During her visits, the Princess usually stayed at **Newport House**, a lovely eighteenth-century Georgian-style country inn beside the river.

From Newport, it's just over 27 km (17 miles) to Achill Island via the N59. Before you reach the island, you will pass through **Mulrany**, a delightful seaside village located on an isthmus between **Clew Bay** and **Blacksod Bay**. Bordered by colourful giant fuchsias, rhododendrons and exotic palms, Mulrany has an almost Mediterranean atmosphere. Its place name, which comes from the Irish *An Mhala Raithní*, means 'the hilltop of (the) ferns'.

Achill Island is Ireland's largest offshore island, 22.5 km (14 miles) long and 19.5 km (12 miles) wide. Joined to the mainland by a bridge at **Achill Sound**, Achill is not as isolated as the Aran Islands or other offshore outposts around the Irish coast. Yet it is relatively undeveloped and unspoiled except for holiday homes dotting the hillsides. Home to about 3,000 people, this island is blessed with an amazingly diverse assortment of scenery, from sandy Blue Flag beaches and steep seaside cliffs, to bog lands and farmlands, as well as mountains, lakes, valleys and moors, all adorned with heather and fuchsia hedges. Part of the area is a Gaeltacht, where the local people speak Irish as their everyday language.

Follow the main R319 road westward for about 16 km (10 miles) to **Keel**, a popular beach village. Beyond Keel is **Trawmore**, a fine 3.5 km (2-mile) long beach, and the **Cliffs of Menawn** which rise to a height of 244 metres (800 feet), taller than the highly touted Cliffs of

Moher of County Clare. At the western tip of the island is **Croaghaun**, a peak rising to 668 metres (2,192 feet) in height.

On the return drive, you may wish to detour northward towards **Slievemore** (672 metres/2,204 feet), a cone-topped mountain of quartz and mica. In the waters behind **Slievemore Mountain**, seals bask on hot summer days in caves and on little islands that have been carved out by the erosion of the waves. At the foot of the mountain is **Dugort**, another popular resort village.

Return to the mainland and retrace your route to Newport, and then via the main N59 road northward, with Clew Bay on your left, towards Bangor. This remote region, collectively called **Bangor-Erris** or the Barony of Erris, is one of Europe's least inhabited areas. Steeped in tradition and culture, this region is a Gaeltacht or Irish-speaking area, and road signs give place names primarily in Irish. Four different colleges in the region offer courses in the Irish language in the summer months.

Drive first to Bangor, a picturesque village on the Owenmore river, and then take the R313 out to **Belmullet**, one of the most westerly points in Ireland. Its place name, derived from the Irish *Béal an Mhuirthead*, literally means 'entrance of the Mullet Peninsula'. Founded in 1825, Belmullet is a pleasant town situated on the narrow neck of land between Broad Haven and Blacksod Bays. The surrounding peninsula is an area of wild

seacoast with a variety of sea birds. Fishing is popular here, with over 39 varieties of fish known to inhabit the waters off the coast.

Moving back to the mainland, follow the R314 along the northern coast. At various points, you will pass evocative free-standing sculptures along the roadside – created to reflect the landscape, earth, rock and growing things in this part of Mayo. These are part of the **North Mayo Sculpture Trail**, created by Irish and international artists to illustrate their impressions of the local landscape and folklore. The fifteen-sculpture trail extends from Belmullet to Ballina.

Between Belderrig and Ballycastle is **Céide Fields**, Ballycastle (tel. 096 43325), one of Ireland's oldest developments, rated as the most extensive Stone Age site in the world. Preserved in a blanket of bog, this 5,000-year-old farm is believed to pre-date the pyramids of Egypt and Stonehenge of Britain. It consists of a 1,012-hectare (2,500-acre) parcel of land that was a thriving village in the Stone Age (3500–3000BC). It has been unearthed from the bog, to show stone walls, rectangular fields, tombs, houses, hearths, pottery and tools. Start a tour in the visitor centre, an attraction it itself in this remote area. It is a pyramid-shaped building, made partly of limestone and partly of peat, with a glazed lantern apex. Step inside and watch a 20-minute audiovisual, 'Written in Stone', which presents valuable archaeological background in layman's terms. Exhibits also provide helpful insight into the geology, botany and wildlife of the region, as well as shedding light on the level and nature of the social organisation of this ancient civilisation. Guided walking tours are conducted around the actual site outside. (Note: Céide is pronounced *Kayd-ja*). Open daily, mid-March–November. Admission: €

On departing the visitor centre, take note that the R314 road runs close to the edge of **Céide Cliffs**, offering spectacular coastal views, comparable to the Cliffs of Moher and often deemed more stunning and expansive.

Continue for 8 km east on the R314 to **Ballycastle**, a small resort village that takes its name from the Irish *Baile an Chaisil*, meaning 'homestead of the stone fort'. This name is appropriate because the town is surrounded by stone forts and court-tombs dating from the Neolithic period.

A scenic 3.5-km (2-mile) detour signposted from Ballycastle goes to **Downpatrick Head**, a cliff rising to 38 metres (125 feet) above **Killala Bay**, providing panoramic views in all directions. The ruins of a church and holy well attributed to St Patrick are here, giving the area its name. Straight ahead is *Dún Briste*, a fragment of a cliff broken off during some natural cataclysm and now isolated at sea.

The next significant town, 9.5 km (6 miles) to the southeast, is **Killala** on the west shore of Killala Bay. The place name, taken from the Irish language, *Cill Ala*, meaning 'church of St Ala', refers to a foundation dating back to the fifth century and the time of St Patrick. It was at this tiny port in August of 1798 that General Humbert of France landed with 1,000 men to help the United Irishmen, under patriot Theobold Wolfe Tone, in their quest for freedom from English rule. Although Humbert took Killala and Ballina, his efforts eventually met defeat as the forces marched further south. Killala's moment of glory is chronicled in the late Thomas Flanagan's *Year of the French*, a bestselling book and film.

Continue 10.5 km (6.5 miles) south to **Ballina**, the largest town in County Mayo, sitting beside the River Moy, and synonymous with salmon and trout fishing. The place name is derived from the Irish *Béal an Átha*, meaning '(place at the) mouth of the ford'.

End your day's touring here, in the heart of the North County Mayo, or continue south via the N26 towards Castlebar, stopping after 16 km (10 miles) at Foxford to see one of Ireland's oldest craft centres – **Foxford Woollen Mills**, St Joseph's Place (tel. 094 925 6756). Founded in 1892 by a local nun, Mother Agnes Morrogh-Bernard, to provide work for a community ravaged by the effects of the Irish Famine, these mills have brought prosperity to the area. The

Foxford label – on colourful blankets, rugs and tweed clothing – has become a benchmark of fine woollen fabrics throughout the world. A visit starts with a walk-through audiovisual with life-like figures recounting the history of the town and the nun's trail-blazing efforts. Afterwards, visitors can take a tour of the mills and watch the weaving process. Open daily. Admission: €

End the tour at your starting point of Castlebar or continue on to other destinations.

PAT'S PICKS

RESTAURANTS

THE BEEHIVE, Keel, Achill Island (tel. 098 43134). This informal café-craft shop is a beehive of activity, serving snacks and light meals in a setting filled with locally made pottery, knitwear, jewellery and art. There are four rooms to choose from inside, and picnic tables outside. The self-service menu features seafood salads, soups, sandwiches and casseroles. Open for lunch and snacks, daily, Easter–November.

CALVEY'S, Keel, Achill Island (tel. 098 43158). A favourite with the locals, this casual restaurant is known for its extensive seafood menu – featuring 20 varieties of Achill fish and shellfish, from crab and oysters to turbot and wild salmon. Organic certified Achill Island lamb, raised on the Calvey family farm, is also featured. Open for lunch and dinner, daily.

ENNISCOE HOUSE, Castlehill, Crossmolina (tel. 096 31112). Overlooking Lough Conn, this Georgian-style country inn offers an elegant yet relaxed setting, with antiques, family heirlooms and open fireplaces. The menu changes daily, but usually features fresh local salmon and other fish caught from the adjacent waters of the Cloonamoyne Fishery. Organically grown vegetables and herbs come from the garden outside. Open for dinner only, March–mid-October.

GRACELAND, Keel, Achill Island (tel. 098 43510). No, there is no Elvis connection here – a relative of the owner is named Grace. This is a simple coffee shop, although it does have stunning views of the sea and an elegant décor, with a Georgian-style interior, including chandeliers, fireplace and mantel, Wedgwood trim, and paintings and photos from a local gallery. The menu offers fresh scones, muffins and international breads, soups, sandwiches and salads. Open for lunch and snacks, daily, April–November.

KELLY'S KITCHEN, Main Street, Newport (tel. 098 41647). Set in the heart of town next to the Kelly family butcher's shop, this busy café is a delight, with simple country charm, and pictures of Newport on the walls. The menu features fresh salads, soups (including a signature Clew Bay chowder) and sandwiches, as well as hot dishes such as Irish stew, using prime meats from the butcher's shop. Open for lunch, snacks and dinner, daily, May–September; and for lunch and snacks, Tuesday–Saturday, October–April.

THE LEMON PEEL, The Octagon, Westport (tel. 098 26929). With a décor of deep primary colours, this modern shop-front bistro offers a creative international menu with tasty choices such as Cajun-crusted salmon, Barbury duck with chilli and orange sauce, stir-fried vegetables with shrimp, homemade seafood ravioli, and chicken *au poivre*. Open for dinner, Tuesday–Sunday, March–January.

QUAY COTTAGE, The Harbour, Westport Quay (tel. 098 26412). Set on the quay beside Clew Bay, this award-winning restaurant presents top-quality cuisine in a comfortable cottage-style setting, with four different rooms furnished in nautical style. The menu offers fresh Clew Bay seafood, local free-range beef, lamb and poultry, and creative vegetarian delights, attractively presented with edible flowers, and accompanied by home-baked breads. Open for dinner, daily, May–September; Wednesday–Sunday, October–April.

PUBS

THE ASGARD TAVERN, The Harbour, Westport Quay (tel. 098 25319). Standing on the quayside overlooking Clew Bay, this vintage pub offers a real nautical atmosphere amid a display of sea-faring memorabilia in a series of small cosy rooms. Bar food is available throughout the day.

GAUGHAN'S, O'Rahilly Street, Ballina (tel. 096 21151). Located in the heart of town just over a block from the River Moy, this cosy enclave has all the trappings of a traditional pub and has been in the Gaughan family since 1936. It's a popular spot for bar-food lunches.

LAVELLE'S ERRIS BAR, Main Street, Belmullet (tel. 097 82222). Deep in the heart of the Mullet Peninsula, this remote pub is a welcome oasis for travellers in northwest Mayo. In addition to a traditional atmosphere, it offers the modern diversion of a big-screen TV for watching sporting matches. Bar food specialises in fresh local seafood such as crab claws, mussels and chowders.

MATT MOLLOY'S, Bridge Street, Westport (tel. 098 26655). Dating back to 1896, this pub is a mecca for traditional music, with music memorabilia on the walls, and the sounds of flutes, fiddles, concertinas, tin whistles, spoons, bodhráns and uilleann pipes wafting in the air. The prime reason for this pub's reputation for good music is its owner – Matt Molloy of The Chieftains, who leads the sessions whenever he is home from his worldwide performing travels.

THE TOWERS, The Harbour, Westport Quay (tel. 098 26534). Situated at the edge of the Clew Bay waters, this pub is housed in an old castle-like tower with a beer garden on the outside. It dishes up not only a relaxing nautical atmosphere, but great pub food as well. Traditional music is played nightly during the summer months.

DIGRESSIONS

AWARD-WINNING MUSEUM: The first branch of Ireland's National Museum located outside Dublin is at Turlough Park, on a hillside 6.5km (4 miles) east of Castlebar. Housed in a €12 million custom-designed building, the National Museum of Country Life depicts the traditions of rural life throughout Ireland during the years 1850–1950, with more than 50,000 items, divided into categories of domestic furniture, agricultural implements, religious items, dress and footwear and educational gear, plus archival film footage. Open Tuesday–Sunday. Information: National Museum of Country Life, Turlough Park, Castlebar (tel. 094 903 1589 or www.museum.ie).

ISLAND-HOPPING: With a current population of 150 people, Clare Island has had a long and colourful history for over 5,000 years, but its main claim to fame is that it was the sixteenth-century base of operations for Grace O'Malley, or Granuaile, Ireland's legendary pirate queen. According to local lore, Grace is buried in the grounds of a twelfth-century abbey on the island. Ferries operate May–September from Westport Quay and year-round from Roonagh Pier. Information: Clare Island Ferries Ltd, Westport Harbour, Westport (tel. 098 28288); and O'Malley Ferries, Roonagh Pier, Roonagh Quay, near Louisburgh (tel. 098 25045).

PLACE OF PILGRIMAGE: Rarely does a tour bus or car arrive in County Mayo without making a detour to Knock, 19 km (12 miles) southeast of Castlebar. A hub of religious pilgrimage, this small one-street town was thrust into the spotlight on 21 August 1879 when local residents reported seeing a vision of the Blessed Mother. Ever since, Knock has become an internationally recognised shrine, ranked with Lourdes or Fatima as a major place of Catholic pilgrimage. Not surprisingly, Knock has grown from one humble site to a major enterprise, complete with a huge basilica, folk museum, hotels, international airport and dozens of shops. Open daily. Information: Knock Shrine Information Centre, Knock (tel. 094 938 8100 or www.knock-shrine.ie).

TRACKING A PIRATE QUEEN: From Westport, head 16 km (10 miles) west to Louisburgh, an eighteenth-century town on Clew Bay. The focal point is the Granuaile (Grace O'Malley) Centre, a museum dedicated to the memory of Grace O'Malley (1530–1600), Ireland's legendary pirate queen. Housed in the former St

Catherine's Church of Ireland building, it includes exhibits, paintings and an audiovisual on Grace's daring exploits, seafaring travels, and achievements in the male-dominated society of the six-teenth century. Open Monday–Saturday, June–September. Information: Granuaile (Grace O'Malley) Centre, off Main Street, Louisburgh (tel. 098 66341).

The Northwest

31: Sligo Town and Yeats Country

A large and lively market town, Sligo (pronounced *Sly-go*) is the gateway to Ireland's remote northwest. Ideally situated, Sligo sits in a valley between the two mountains of Ben Bulben and Knockarea, at the mouth of the River Garavogue, with Sligo Bay and the Atlantic on its western shores and Lough Gill to the east. The place name for Sligo is indeed fitting – from the Irish Sligeach, meaning 'shelly place'.

Dating back to the early Christian period, Sligo was probably founded *c*.450 by Bishop Bronus, a disciple of St Patrick. Although Sligo, like the rest of Ireland, has had its ups and downs historically, it is literature and art that have given a distinctive character to this town and county.

For many years, the town and its environs were the source of inspiration for Ireland's Nobel Prize-winning poet William Butler Yeats and his painter brother Jack. Hence Sligo's main fame has been as the hub of Yeats Country. Visitors come from all over the world to see this little corner of Ireland that Yeats described as 'the land of heart's desire'.

Six-and-a-half kilometres (4 miles) south of Sligo town is Strandhill, a beach resort sitting at the foot of Knockarea Mountain (330 metres/1,083 feet). If you are fit for mountain climbing, you can start a signposted walk here. The route leads to a gigantic cairn or gravesite, known as *Miscaun Meadhbh* (Maeve's Mound), 61 metres (200 feet) in diameter and 10.5 metres (34 feet) high. It is traditionally considered as the resting place of an Irish queen who reigned in the first century BC. From the summit, there are panoramic views of Sligo and Sligo Bay. Nearby is Carrowmore, the largest cemetery of Megalithic remains in Ireland.

FAST FACTS

Travel Information Offices

SLIGO TOURIST OFFICE, Temple Street, Sligo (tel. 071 916 1201). Open all year.

TRAVEL INFORMATION ONLINE: www.irelandnorthwest.ie and www.sligotourism.ie

TELEPHONE AREA CODES: The area code for telephone numbers in the Sligo area is 071.

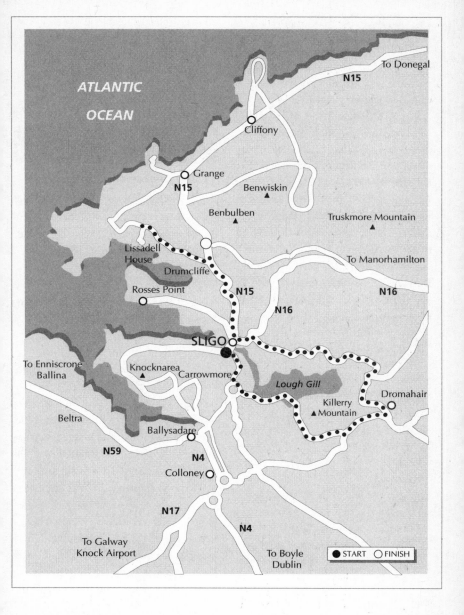

MAJOR EVENTS

YEATS INTERNATIONAL SUMMER SCHOOL –
For almost half a century, this has been
one of Ireland's leading summer
schools, focusing on the poet William
Butler Yeats who said that Sligo was
'the place that has influenced my life
most'. It is a two-week gathering of students, teachers, scholars, musicians,
dancers and interested visitors from
around the world, for lectures, seminars,
tours, poetry readings and workshops. A
shorter winter school also takes place on
the first weekend of February. Information: Maura McTighe, Yeats Memorial
Building, tel. 914 2693 or www.yeats-
sligo.com. (Last week of July and first
week of August)

**QUEEN MAEVE SUMMER SCHOOL OF TRADI-
TIONAL MUSIC, SONG AND DANCE** – Named
in honour of a powerful local queen who
ruled the area in the first century BC, this
event offers classes and workshops to
beginners and experienced musicians in
tin whistle, flute, fiddle, button accor-
dion, banjo, traditional singing (in English and Irish) and set dancing.
Festivities include recitals, sessions,
céilithe, and concerts. Information:
Carmel Gunning, Sligo Institute of
Technology, Ballinode, tel. 916 2008 or
www.cisl.ie/tradmusic. (First week of
August)

SLIGO BAROQUE FESTIVAL – This weekend festival draws to Sligo practitioners
and followers of Baroque music from
all over Ireland and abroad, for concerts,
workshops and other events. Information: Ms Joe Conway, Model and Niland
Gallery, The Mall, tel. 914 1405 or
www.modelart.ie. (Last weekend of
October)

WALKING/DRIVING TOUR OF SLIGO AND YEATS COUNTRY

Duration: 4–6 hours plus stops

A tour of Sligo and Yeats Country comes
in two parts – a walk in the town and a
drive around the surrounding countryside.

Begin with a walk around Sligo town.
Park your car in one of the designated
areas, including two car parks within one
block of the bus and rail station on **Lord
Edward Street**. From the station, turn
left and cross over to **Adelaide Street**.
Walk one block and take a left to see
Sligo's two cathedrals, both side-by-side
on **John Street**. On the corner is the
**Cathedral of the Immaculate Concep-
tion** (tel. 916 2670), a Romanesque-style
edifice dating back to 1874 and noteworthy for an interior of 69 stained-glass
windows. Adjacent is the **Cathedral of
St John the Baptist** (tel. 916 7260), a
Gothic building designed in 1730 by the
German architect Richard Castle. The
north transept contains a brass tablet in
memory of Susan Mary Yeats, mother of
William Butler Yeats and Jack Butler
Yeats. She married John Butler Yeats in
this church in 1863. Open daily. Admission: free

Return to **Temple Street** and walk one block south to the Sligo Tourist Office, a large complex that also includes the **Hawk's Well Theatre** (tel. 916 1526), a hub of theatrical activity year-round. The theatre, which derives its name from one of Yeats's one-act plays, carries on the legacy of Sligo's great literary traditions.

Turn left at the corner and walk half a block to make a right onto **Church Street**. Across the street is the **Sligo Presbyterian Church** (tel. 916 2337), built in 1828, and straight ahead is **Harmony Hill**, high ground that offers fine views of the rest of the town. Continue for half a block to **High Street**, one of Sligo's oldest streets, which dates from medieval times or earlier, although no traces of its ancient buildings remain.

Turn right here to see the **Dominican Church** (tel. 914 2700), commonly known as 'the friary'. It is one of Sligo's most modern structures, opened in 1973. It sits on the grounds of an early Renaissance Gothic edifice of 1845, and incorporates the apse of the older church in the rear section. Open daily. Admission: free

Walk half a block and turn left onto **Old Market Street**, although nothing really remains from Sligo's old market days except the place name. Turn left onto **Teeling Street**, passing the courthouse and post office on the left, and then make a right turn onto **Abbey Street**. The focal point of this street is **Sligo Abbey** (tel. 914 6406), Sligo's only surviving medieval building. Built for the Dominicans in 1252, the abbey was the burial place of the kings and princes of Sligo. It is now in ruins, but the nave, choir, arched tower, and three-sided cloister survive. The fifteenth-century altar is one of the few medieval altars still intact in Ireland. Access to the site is via a stone stairway. Open daily, April–October. Admission: €

Turn left after the Abbey and straight ahead is the River Garavogue, which runs through the heart of the town. Turn left onto **Kennedy Parade**, named after the former US president John F Kennedy, who visited Ireland, though not Sligo, in 1963. Cross the river at **Bridge Street** and walk one block straight ahead.

Then take a left to visit the **Sligo County Museum and Art Gallery**, Stephen Street (tel. 914 2212), which displays the first editions of William Butler Yeats's complete works and his Nobel Prize for Literature (1923), as well as a collection of oils, watercolours and drawings by Jack B Yeats. Open Monday– Friday. Admission: free

Follow **Stephen Street** westward, passing a statue of William Butler Yeats on the right, and then cross over the **Douglas Hyde Bridge**, named after Ireland's first president, a major figure in the Irish cultural revival at the turn of the century. Straight ahead on the left is the **Yeats Memorial Building**, Hyde Bridge at O'Connell Street (tel. 914 5847), containing an extensive collection of Yeats memorabilia. Open Monday– Friday. Admission: free

For a detour from the bridge, walk two blocks east via Stephen Street to the **Model Arts and Niland Gallery**, The Mall (tel. 914 1405), a former school and now Sligo's main centre for twentieth-century art. The collection comprises over 250 works, including paintings by Jack B. Yeats, Paul Henry, Mainie Jellett, Louis Le Brocquy, Maurice McGonigle, Mary Swanzy and AE (George Russell), as well as international works. Open Tuesday–Saturday. Admission: free

Returning to Hyde Bridge, walk one block along **Wine Street**, named after the wine vaults that once stood here, and turn right on **Quay Street** to see the façade of **Town Hall**, dating from 1865 and a fine example of Italian Renaissance style. On this site in 1245, a castle was built by the Anglo-Norman leader, Maurice Fitzgerald, signalling the official birth of Sligo as a town. In 1995, the 750th anniversary of Sligo Castle was celebrated, although no trace of the building remains.

Retrace your steps to Wine Street, and on the left is **Wesley Chapel** (tel. 914 2346), dating back to 1832. It replaced an earlier site begun by the Methodists in Sligo in 1775. It is said that the founder of Methodism found fertile ground in Sligo and visited fourteen times between 1758 and 1789. Opening times are posted outside. Admission: free

Straight ahead is Lord Edward Street and the completion of the walking phase of the tour. The rest of the route requires a car. From the bus and train station, drive south on Adelaide and Temple Streets to the main road, also known as **Pearse Road**. Proceed approximately 1.5 km (1 mile) south and make a left at the sign for the **Lough Gill Drive**, a 42-km (26-mile) route east of town, which encircles **Lough Gill**, the beautiful lake that figured prominently in Yeats's writings. Like Sligo town itself, Lough Gill is also well named. The place name comes from the Irish language, *Loch Gile*, meaning 'lake of brightness'. It is a constant and unspoiled panorama of silvery blue waters, encircled by wooded hills and lush foliage.

Drive the 42-km (26-mile) route in a counter-clockwise direction, with the lake always at your left. Signposted highlights include **Dooney Rock**, with its own nature trail and lakeside walk (inspiration for the Yeats poem 'Fiddler of Dooney'); and the **Lake Isle of Innisfree**, one of the lake's 22 islands. The poem of the same name is one of Yeats's most famous works, almost an anthem for Sligo.

As the road swings to the east and north sides of the lake, you are temporarily in County Leitrim. Stop at **Parke's Castle**, Fivemile Bourne (tel. 916 4149), a fine example of a seventeenth-century fortified manor house. Named after the English family who gained possession of the land during the 1620 plantation of Leitrim, the castle was recently restored with an Irish oak interior, showing great craftsmanship. Distinctive features include a diamond-shaped chimney, mullioned windows, parapets and a courtyard that pre-dates the castle. The visitor centre presents an audiovisual on the history and restoration of the building, 'Stone by Stone', plus a series of colourful exhibits. Open daily, mid-March–October. Admission: €

The next point of interest is **Hazelwood Forest**, signposted to the left off the road. The grounds include the **Hazelwood Sculpture Trail**, a forest walk along the lake, with thirteen sculptures carved out of local wood by Irish and international artists. Created in 1985–87, it was the first permanent sculpture trail in Ireland.

The road now wends its way back into Sligo. Turn right and go north along the main N15 for 6.5 km (4 miles). Soon the unmistakable loaf-like profile of **Ben Bulben** (527 metres/1,730 feet) comes into view on the right. One of Ireland's most famous mountains, Ben Bulben is featured prominently in Yeats's writings. As he requested, the poet is buried at the foot of the mountain in **Drumcliffe Churchyard**. A simple stone marks the grave of William Butler Yeats (1865–1939), who wrote his own bleak, if poetic, epitaph: 'Cast a cold eye on life, on death; horseman, pass by.' He is buried with his wife, George. Open during daylight hours. Admission: free

The church on the grounds, a former Church of Ireland edifice, has been turned into the **Drumcliffe Visitors Centre** (tel. 914 4956), with a permanent exhibition that outlines the history of the church and the surrounding area before if became synonymous with Yeats. The interactive displays go back to 574 when St Columbcille founded a monastery here. An audiovisual traces the history of a battle that took place in the middle of the sixth century on the banks of the Drumcliffe river, between the high king of Ireland and leaders of the O'Neill clan. Open daily. Admission: €

Continue on the main road for four more miles to **Lissadell House**, Drumcliffe (tel. 63150), a fine example of a large nineteenth-century home in the Grecian Revival style. The focal point of the house is a two-storey hallway lined with Doric columns leading to a double staircase of Kilkenny marble. A favorite country retreat for Yeats, the house was owned by his friends, the Gore-Booth family, who beguiled Yeats with their diverse interests. Eva was a distinguished poet and book collector, Sir Josslyn was a keen horticulturist who planted the grounds, and Constance was a political activist who took part in Ireland's 1916 Easter Rising and married Count Markievicz, a Polish nobleman. She was the first woman ever elected a member of the British Parliament, but took a seat instead in the newly formed

Irish Parliament and was the Minister for Labour in the first Irish government. The house and its contents were on view to the public until 2003 when the remaining members of the Gore-Booth family sold it. The new owners plan to make the house accessible to the public, but details are not available at time of going to print. Phone in advance of your visit for opening times and admission fees.

From Lissadell, retrace your route to the main N15 road and turn right to return to Sligo or turn left to continue on towards Donegal or other northern parts of Ireland.

PAT'S PICKS

RESTAURANTS

AUSTIES, Rosses Point (tel. 917 7111). Overlooking Sligo Bay 6.5 km (4 miles) north of Sligo town, this restaurant is housed in a 200-year-old building with a seafaring décor. The walls are covered in maps, ships' wheels, ropes, telegraph signals, miniature ships and nautical bric-a-brac. As might be expected, the menu features seafood – mussels, prawns, crab, sole, trout, mackerel and salmon, all presented as entrées or in chowders, salads or sandwiches. Steaks, burgers and poultry dishes are also available. Open for bar food and dinner, daily, April–August; Wednesday–Sunday, September–March.

CAFÉ BAR DELI, Rear of 15–16 Stephen's Street, Sligo (tel. 914 0100). Set beside the Garavogue river, this modern two-storey bistro is spacious and airy, with large windows and lots of lush hanging plants. The menu combines Irish ingredients with Mediterranean influences, offering soups, salads, pastas, pizzas, club sandwiches, chicken wings, steaks and nachos. Open for snacks and lunch, daily; and for dinner, Wednesday–Sunday.

COACH LANE RESTAURANT, 1–2 Lord Edward Street, Sligo (tel. 916 2417). With stone walls, hardwood floors, open fireplace and candlelight, this cosy restaurant is located in an old laneway over a pub. Specialities include chargrilled steaks, local lobster and salmon, as well as international choices such as spicy Cajun chicken. Seating is also available on an outdoor terrace in good weather. Open for dinner, daily; and for lunch on Sunday.

THE COTTAGE, 4 Castle Street, Sligo (tel. 914 5319.). Situated in the heart of town, one block from Sligo Abbey, this homely restaurant offers creative and healthy meals and snacks. House specials include hot open sandwiches, quiches, chillis, pizzas and baked potatoes with various fillings. Vegetarian and wholefood dishes are also featured. Open for lunch and snacks, daily; and for dinner, Friday–Sunday.

MARKREE CASTLE, Collooney (tel. 916 7800). Dating back to 1640, Sligo's only castle hotel-restaurant is nestled in a fairytale setting 11 km (7 miles) south of Sligo, amid meadows, woods and gardens reaching to the River Unsin. The formal dining room, enhanced by splendid gold-filigree plasterwork and chandeliers, offers French cuisine with fresh Irish ingredients and creative sauces. Open for dinner, daily; and for lunch on Sunday.

PUBS

HARGADON'S, 4 O'Connell Street, Sligo (tel. 917 0933). Dating back over 130 years, this centrally located pub is a Sligo tradition, with well-preserved snugs, wooden benches, stone floors, coloured glass, old barrels and bottles, and a pot-belly stove. Bar food is served all day.

THE HARP TAVERN, Quay Street, Sligo (tel. 914 2473). Overlooking the River Garavogue, just 46 metres (50 yards) from the Town Hall, this popular pub retains many vestiges of yesteryear – stone and pine floors, wood-beam ceilings, a stone fireplace and many nooks and crannies. As it is named after Ireland's national musical instrument, it is not surprising that locals gather for traditional music on Monday nights year-round, plus Wednesday and Sunday nights in summer.

YEATS TAVERN, Drumcliffe Bridge, Drumcliffe (tel. 916 3117). Named after the Nobel Prize-winning poet and located across the road from his grave, this pub is a popular stop on the local circuit. The décor features Yeats memorabilia and vintage furnishings. It is on the main N15 road, 6.5 km (4 miles) north of Sligo.

THE THATCH, Dublin Road, Ballysadare (tel. 916 7288). As its name proclaims, this pub is a traditional thatched cottage, dating back to 1638 and originally a coaching inn. Sit by the fireside and enjoy a drink or snack at any time of day, or stop by in the evening and hear some traditional music (Thursday–Sunday in summer months). It is situated 8 km (5 miles) south of Sligo on the Dublin Road, in a small village at the mouth of the Owenmore river.

DIGRESSIONS

CRUISING LOUGH GILL: For close-up views of many scenic landmarks immortalised in poetry by William Butler Yeats, including the Lake Isle of Innisfree, the *Wild Rose* Waterbus operates 60-minute cruises on the waters of Lough Gill on the edge of Sligo town. The cruise commentary includes recitations of Yeats's poetry by ship's captain George McGoldrick. Departures are from Doorly Park and Parke's Castle. Operates March–October. Information: Wild Rose Waterbus (tel. 071 916 4266 or mobile 087 259 8869).

GUIDED TOURS: If you'd like to leave the driving to someone else, a company called 'Discover Sligo' provides full-day and half-day minibus tours, concentrating on three different themes – Cottages and Castles (Monday, Wednesday and Friday), Landscapes and Legends (Tuesday, Thursday and Saturday), and Majestic Views (Sunday). Tours depart from various hotels in the area, and from the Sligo Tourist Office. Advance reservations are required. Information: Discover Sligo Tours, Calry, Sligo (tel. 914 7488 or www.discoversligo.com).

PREHISTORIC TRAIL: About 8 km (5 miles) south of town is one of Sligo's oldest treasures – Carrowmore, a Megalithic burial ground considered the largest cemetery of its kind in Ireland, and one of the largest in Europe, containing over 60 tombs, dolmens, small passage graves and stone circles. Archaeologists claim that some of the graves are at least 700 years older than those at Newgrange. For background information, a restored cottage at the site houses a small exhibition and slide show. Open daily, Easter–October. Information: Carrowmore Megalithic Cemetery, Carrowmore, Sligo (tel. 916 1534 or www.heritageireland.ie).

32: Donegal Town

Tweed is the lifeblood of Donegal town. No one knows exactly when the industry originated, but one thing is certain – the making of beautiful hand-woven tweed has put Donegal town on the map. Although beautiful tweeds are produced all over the county, the most famous name in tweed production is Magee, located in the heart of Donegal town since 1866. Indeed, once people come here for the tweed, they find many other reasons to be glad that they have made the long journey.

And it is a long journey. Sitting on a sheltered curve of land where Donegal Bay meets the River Eske, Donegal town is the most remote of Ireland's major towns – almost 226 km (140 miles) out of Dublin and nearly 290 km (180 miles) from Shannon. Remote, yes, but not isolated or deserted. Donegal has always drawn people up to Ireland's northwest coast, no matter how long or difficult the journey.

Even the Vikings found their way to Donegal, establishing a fort there in the ninth century. The area was then known as *Tír Conaill*, meaning 'the land of Conall' – Conall being an ancestor of the O'Donnells, powerful Gaelic chieftains. In time, the native Irish described the Viking fort as *Dún na nGall*, meaning 'fort of the foreigners'. And hence the place name of Donegal evolved.

In the fifteenth century, the O'Donnells, led by Red Hugh O'Donnell, built a Norman-style castle on the site of the original Viking fort. With his wife, Nuala, Red Hugh is also credited with having erected a monastery in 1474 on the banks of the river, for use by the Franciscan friars. Known as Donegal Abbey, the monastery prospered as a scholarly hub for over 150 years. One of Ireland's most important records of history, the Annals of the Four Masters, was written here.

Like other parts of Ireland, Donegal also felt the domination of the English. After the Battle of Kinsale in 1607, when the O'Donnells and other Irish chieftains were forced to leave Ireland during the 'Flight of the Earls', the O'Donnell territory of Donegal was granted to Sir Basil Brooke. He laid out the town as it exists today, with a central square or 'Diamond', and expanded the castle by adding a Jacobean-style wing.

During the subsequent Famine years and other times of economic hardship, Donegal has survived, thanks to the tweed industry. Whether produced in homes or in factories, the tweeds of Donegal are part of a great tradition. It's a tradition that melds old ways into everyday life. So, come to Donegal for the tweed – and while you are here, enjoy a rich heritage of other crafts, plus music and song as well.

FAST FACTS

Travel Information Offices

DONEGAL TOURIST OFFICE, The Quay, Donegal (tel. 074 972 1148). Open all year.

TRAVEL INFORMATION ONLINE:
www.irelandnorthwest.ie,
www.donegaltown.ie and
www.donegaldirect.ie

TELEPHONE AREA CODE:
The area code for telephone numbers in Donegal is 074.

MAJOR EVENT

DONEGAL INTERNATIONAL WALKING FESTIVAL – Walkers from near and far and of all levels of experience join in this three-day programme of walks from Donegal town,

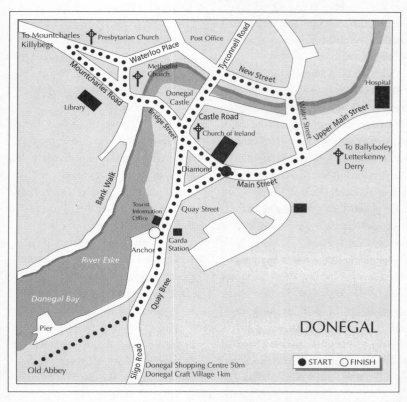

To Mountcharles Killybegs
Presbytarian Church
Post Office
Waterloo Place
Tyrconnell Road
New Street
Mountcharles Road
Methodist Church
Hospital
Donegal Castle
Library
Castle Road
Church of Ireland
Water Street
Upper Main Street
To Ballybofey Letterkenny Derry
Bridge Street
Bank Walk
Diamond
Main Street
Tourist Information Office
Quay Street
Anchor
Garda Station
River Eske
Quay Brae
Donegal Bay
Pier
Sligo Road
Old Abbey
Donegal Shopping Centre 50m
Donegal Craft Village 1km

DONEGAL

● START ○ FINISH

through the Bluestack Mountains and Barnesmore Gap and beside Lough Belshade and Mountcharles Shore, as well as a night walk along Murvagh Beach. Information: John McGrory, Northwest Walking Guides, Clunarra, Letterbarrow, Co. Donegal, tel. 973 5967 or www.northwestwalkingguides.com. (Third weekend of October)

DONEGAL TOWN WALKING TOUR

Duration: 1–2 hours plus stops

The best place to start a tour is at the Donegal Tourist Office on **The Quay**, beside the **River Eske**. From here, take a right turn and walk along the Quay. On the right is **The Anchor**, a 4.5-metre (15-foot), one-ton Napoleonic anchor manufactured in France. Local lore says that it belonged to the French frigate, the *Romaine*, which was part of a squadron that had come in 1798 to join the Irish in battling the English. When the French and Irish forces met with defeat, the *Romaine* left behind its anchor in the waters of Donegal Bay and hastened back to France. The anchor was brought to Donegal town in 1951 and put on display in its present position.

Less than half a kilometre (a quarter of a mile) downriver are the remains of **Donegal Abbey**, otherwise known as the Friary of Donegal. It was founded in 1474 by one of the great Gaelic chieftains of the area, Red Hugh O'Donnell, and his wife, Nuala, who invited the Franciscans to take up residence. In time, great gatherings of clergy and lay leaders assembled at this peaceful spot beside the river. It was from this friary that four scholars – Michael and Peregrine O'Clery, Peregrine Duignan and Fearfeasa O'Mulconry – undertook to salvage old Gaelic manuscripts and compile the Annals of the Four Masters, now recognised as the most comprehensive early history of Ireland. It took them four years to write the book (1632–36), a year-by-year narrative that goes back to the time of Noah's grandmother, and chronicles the events until 1616. Judged of utmost importance in documenting Ireland's Celtic heritage, the Annals are housed today in the National Library in Dublin. Unfortunately, little remains of the abbey's great stone structure, except part of a church and a cloister arcade. Open daily. Admission: free

From the Abbey, turn left and retrace your steps along the Quay, past the tourist office, for half a block to **The Diamond**, the diamond-shaped centrepiece of Donegal town. Part of the town plan laid out by Sir Basil Brooke in the early seventeenth century, the Diamond was originally designed as a market square for livestock and produce. No trace of the market house or market yard remain. It was redeveloped in the spring of 1993 as a pedestrian area. Around the Diamond today are three- and four-storey shops, hotels and private houses, built of local sandstone.

The most significant monument on the Diamond is the **Four Masters Memorial Obelisk,** a 7.5-metre (25-foot) high red granite structure in the Irish Romanesque style. It was erected in 1937 to honour the men from Donegal Abbey who wrote the Annals of the Four Masters. Their names are inscribed on the obelisk in the Irish language.

On the opposite side is **Magee of Donegal** (tel. 972 2660). Established in 1866, the Magee name is synonymous with Donegal tweed. In the time-honoured tradition, most of the tweeds are woven by hand in the homes of the weavers, and are assembled at a factory two blocks away (not open to the public), but a weaver gives demonstrations of the craft in this large shop (June–September). Browse amid the racks of colourful tweeds and get a feel for the diversity of colour, texture and style of Donegal tweeds. Here's a little local trivia: the famous novelist James Joyce, while still a struggling writer living in Italy, acted as a sales agent for Magee. Open Monday–Saturday. Admission: free

Take a left to **Bridge Street** and straight ahead is the town's major focal point – **Donegal Castle,** Castle Street (tel. 972 2405). Once the stronghold of Irish chieftains, later the seat of an English overlord, and now a national monument, this castle is Donegal's centrepiece, recently restored and opened to the public in 1996 after a century of neglect and eight years of restoration. It was built *c*.1470 in the format of a tower house, by Red Hugh O'Donnell, head of a powerful Donegal clan. In the early seventeenth century, during the Plantation era, it came into the possession of Sir Basil Brooke, who added an extension of ten gables and mullioned windows in the Jacobean style. Most of the restoration work focused on the painstaking repair of the original stonework and windows. The castle is furnished inside with authentic period pieces – from Persian rugs and French tapestries to boars' heads and stuffed pheasants, as well as informative display panels that chronicle the history of the structure. Open daily, mid-June to mid-September. Admission: €

From the castle's front gates, take a right turn onto **Bridge Street**. Follow the street across the river to see two of Donegal's old churches. On the right is the **Methodist church,** Waterloo Place (tel. 972 1825), more than a century old; and also on the right a block further west is the **Presbyterian church,** Meetinghouse Street (tel. 972 1113), founded in 1824. Opening hours are posted on the notice boards in front of each church. Admission: free

While on the west bank of the river, you may wish to take a slight detour. Follow the sign on **Mountcharles Road** for **Bank Walk,** a pleasant 2.5-km

(1.5-mile) walk along the River Eske as it empties into Donegal Bay. From this side of the river, you can enjoy sweeping views of the town, Donegal Abbey and Donegal Bay.

Return to Mountcharles Road, cross back over the bridge onto Bridge Street, passing the castle and continuing in a northward direction. On the right-hand side, opposite the castle entrance, is the **Church of Ireland church**, Castle Street (tel. 972 1075), notable for its tall spire and façade of hand-cut stone. It was built in 1828 and completed in its present form in 1890 when the chancel and vestry were added. Opening hours are posted on a notice board outside. Admission: free

Continue as Castle Street becomes **Tirconnail Street** (sometimes spelled *Tyrconnell*). Straight ahead on the left is the **Donegal Railway Heritage Centre** (tel. 972 2655). Housed in the town's **Old Station House**, this museum focuses on local railroad history, going back to the days when narrow gauge railways connected Donegal town to many other parts of the county, for transporting animals, produce and people. Although the system closed in 1959, members of the South Donegal Railway Restoration Society are currently restoring old carriages and a steam locomotive in the hope of providing a segment of narrow-gauge service as a tourist attraction. The displays include a continuous video showing, photo archive, facsimile posters, artefacts, old tickets and more. Open daily, June–September; Monday–Friday, October–May. Admission: €

From Tirconnail Street, turn right onto **New Row**, following the river, and then right again on **Water Street**. Water Street leads to Donegal's prime thoroughfare, **Main Street**. To the left, on a hillside, is **St Patrick's Church of the Four Masters**, Upper Main Street (tel. 972 1026). Designed to commemorate the four scholars who wrote the Annals of the Four Masters at Donegal Abbey, this church was built in 1935, in an ornate Irish Romanesque style, with a distinctive façade of local Barnesmore red granite. Open daily. Admission: free

From the front entrance of the church, turn left, and walk the length of Main Street, a continuous row of colourful shop fronts, restaurants and pubs, many of which offer traditional music at night. Main Street brings you back to the Diamond and the Quay, to complete the walking tour.

PAT'S PICKS

RESTAURANTS

THE BLUEBERRY TEA ROOM, Castle Street (tel. 972 2933). Overlooking the Diamond, this cosy upstairs restaurant is the perfect spot for a proper afternoon tea (or cappuccino or espresso) or a light meal. It is also an internet café. Open for snacks, lunch or early dinner, Monday–Saturday.

THE GRANARY, The Mullins, Killybegs Road (tel. 972 880). With open fireplace, vintage clocks, bric-a-brac, rafters and old photos of early Donegal, this popular restaurant has an old-world atmosphere, yet it is housed in one of the town's newest hotels, The Mill Park. The menu offers local seafood and traditional hearty fare, such as steaks and roast lamb, as well as soups, salads and burgers. Open for lunch and dinner, daily.

THE HARBOUR, Quay Street (tel. 972 1702). Located across from the tourist office, this popular restaurant offers views overlooking the water, and a seafood menu, as well as steaks and pizzas. House speciality is baked potatoes with a choice of fillings. Open for lunch and dinner, daily.

JUST WILLIAM'S, The Diamond (tel. 972 1027). Fast service, combined with a cornucopia of freshly prepared foods is the secret of success for this brasserie-style restaurant at the Central Hotel. The menu offers soups, salads, sandwiches, meats carved-to-order, and all sorts of pastries, pies and sweet treats. Open for lunch and dinner, daily.

THE OVEN DOOR, The Diamond (tel. 972 1511). Freshly baked breads, cakes, pastries, pies and other treats are the mainstay of this popular café. The menu also offers a variety of homemade, soups,

salads, sandwiches and hot meat or seafood dishes. Open for lunch and snacks, Monday–Saturday.

PUBS

DON BRESLIN'S PUBLIC BAR, Quay Street (tel. 972 2719). One of the newest establishments in town, this large multi-level 'super-pub' is housed in a quayside complex known as Pier 1. Breslin's offers six different nautically themed bar settings, many with views of Donegal Bay. Live music is on tap every night during the summer months. Bar food is available all day.

O'DONNELL'S BAR, The Diamond (tel. 972 2519). In the hub of town, this old stone-faced pub is a favourite gathering spot for sports fans after local games or for watching national matches on the big-screen TV. Music sessions, sing-songs and pub quizzes are almost always on the schedule.

THE OLDE CASTLE, Castle Street (tel. 972 1062). Situated across from Donegal Castle, this rustic pub is a popular place for traditional atmosphere. The interior has several intriguing old-style snugs, and the décor features timber beams, lantern-style lighting, a stripped-brick circular bar with cosy cushioned stools, and lots of nooks and crannies.

SCHOONER INN, Upper Main Street (tel. 972 1671). True to its name, this pub is designed in the interior style of a galleon, with nautical fixtures and furnishings, model ships and seafaring memorabilia. Besides the nautical theme, it is also a gathering spot for local musicians, and there are traditional sessions nightly from June to September. Just for diversion, there is also reputed to be a ghost in the building.

DIGRESSIONS

CRUISING AROUND DONEGAL – Savour the sights of Donegal aboard the *Donegal Bay* Waterbus, a 62-seat glass-enclosed vessel. It offers 70-minute sightseeing cruises with commentary – along the shoreline, to see abbeys, estates, the old coast-guard station, castles, and even a wind farm and oyster/mussel farm, as well as islands and a seal colony. Operates May–September. Information: Donegal Bay Waterbus, Harbour Office, The Quay (tel. 972 3666).

HISTORIC WALKS: Explore the historic sites of Donegal town in depth on a guided walking tour with a local historian. Tours operate June–August, departing from the tourist office on the Quay. Information: John McGrory, Northwest Walking Guides, Clunarra, Letterbarrow (tel. 973 5967 or www.northwestwalkingguides.com).

SOURCING DONEGAL CRAFTS: See the wide range of crafts for which Donegal is famous. Drive 1.5 km (1 mile) south of town to the Donegal Craft Village. Housed in a small cluster of cottage-style buildings surrounding a central courtyard, this craft-producing complex reconstitutes the true atmosphere and creative environment of Donegal's cot-

tage industries. Walk from cottage to cottage, and watch as young artisans practise traditional and modern crafts – ranging from porcelain and ceramics to hand-weaving, batik, crystal, jewellery, metalwork and visual art. Open daily, April–October. Information: Donegal Craft Village, Ballyshannon Road (tel. 972 2225).

33: Along Donegal Bay

Donegal Bay is the surfing capital of Ireland.

Did we say surfing? Yes! Surprising as it may seem, this beautiful bay is synonymous with surf, thanks to its wide sandy beaches and formidable waves roaring in off the Atlantic. Even the World Surfing Championships have been held here.

Galway Bay may have its sunsets, Bantry Bay its palm trees, Clew Bay its islands, but Donegal Bay has its churning foam-edged waters. Each year, thousands of visitors come and suit up, to ride the waves into Rossnowlagh, Bundoran and other Donegal Bay beaches. These waters are also among the clearest and most unpolluted in Ireland, winning European Blue Flag status.

The best part about Donegal Bay is that it has a lot to offer over and above the surf. Bordered by cliffs and mountains, the bay is home to a diverse collection of resorts and fishing ports, old abbeys and pilgrim sites, craft centres and folk museum cottages. Remote and rural, Donegal Bay presents some of Ireland's most photographic coastal views – whether the surf's up or not!

DONEGAL TOURIST OFFICE, The Quay, Donegal (tel. 074 972 1148). Open all year.

BUNDORAN TOURIST OFFICE, The Bridge, Bundoran (tel. 071 984 1350). Open all year.

TRAVEL INFORMATION ONLINE:
www.irelandnorthwest.ie and www.donegaldirect.ie

TELEPHONE AREA CODES:
There are at least two area codes for telephone numbers in the Donegal Bay region. To avoid confusion, the appropriate area code will be given for each number.

MAJOR EVENTS

CUP OF TAE FESTIVAL – Classes and workshops in learning to play the fiddle and flute are the focal point of this annual gathering where the folklore of each tune is passed on, as well as the music. It is named in honour of a local musician, John 'The Tae' Gallagher, whose family

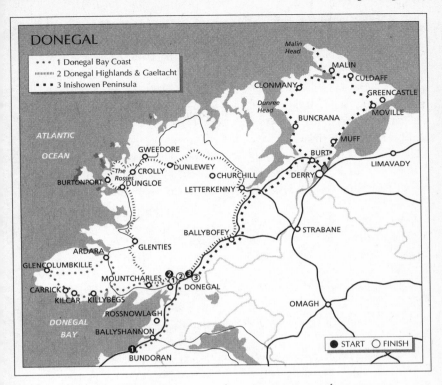

was well known for generations for making tea on fair days and at other local gatherings. Information: Stephen McCahill, Ardara, tel. mobile 087 242 4590. (First weekend of May)

OIDEAS GAEL – IRISH LANGUAGE AND CULTURE COURSES – Held in the heart of the Donegal Gaeltacht at Glencolumbkille, this summer school extends over many months and offers one-week classes in the Irish language (for beginners and advanced) as well as dancing, hill walking, tapestry making, Celtic pottery, marine painting, archaeology, and playing of the bodhrán, flute, and tin whistle.

Information: Liam Ó Cuinneagáin, Oideas Gael, Glencolumbkille, tel. 074 973 0248 or www.Oideas-Gael.com. (April–October)

BALLYSHANNON FOLK AND TRADITIONAL MUSIC FESTIVAL – Ever since 1977, this festival has drawn the top Irish and international performers in folk and traditional music. In addition to concerts, there is also a non-stop programme of street and pub entertainment. Information: Ray Gaughan, Festival Office, Ballyshannon, tel. 071 985 1088 or www.ballyshannonfolkfestival.com. (First weekend of August)

Duration: 4–6 hours plus stops

Start this tour in Bundoran, equidistant from Sligo town and Donegal town, about 32 km (20 miles) in either direction, on the main N15 road. This tour can also be followed when en route from Sligo to Donegal.

Bundoran is one of Ireland's main seaside resorts, thanks to its lovely location on a crest of Donegal Bay, and its wide sandy Blue Flag-winning beach, known as **Tullan**, which is among the cleanest in Europe. At the south end of the beach are unique rock formations, carved by the erosive motions of the sea, with descriptive names such as **Puffing Hole**, the **Wishing Chair** and the **Fairy Bridge**.

Six-and-a-half kilometres (4 miles) north on the main N15 road is **Bally-shannon**, a busy seaport and market town, sitting on a steep bank overlooking the river Erne. It has a fitting place name, derived from the Irish language, *Béal Átha Seanaidhm* meaning 'ford--mouth of the hillside'. Founded in the seventeenth century, the town is full of character, with well-kept Georgian-style houses, narrow and hilly streets, and a backdrop of mountains, waterfalls and river views.

Two local enterprises are worth a visit. On the main road, to the right, is **Donegal Parian China** (tel. 071 985 1826), producing delicate wafer-like parian china, handcrafted from the mould to decorating stages, in patterns of Irish flowers and Celtic designs. The complex includes an exhibition room, showing off the best of Donegal Parian's own wares, as well as samples from its parent company, Belleek China, and sister company, Galway Crystal. In addition, there is a continuous audiovisual presentation, art gallery, and guided tours of the workshops. Open daily, May–September; Monday–Friday, October–April. Admission: free

Follow the signposts to the right off the main road to **Celtic Weave**, Cloghore (tel. 071 985 1844). This company, run by the Daly family for four generations, specialises in handcrafted and hand-painted china baskets in patterns of Irish roses. Open Monday–Saturday. Admission: free

Continuing north of the N15, follow the local road R231 for approximately 6.5 km (4 miles) to **Rossnowlagh**, as the vistas to the left reveal a 3-km (two-mile) long crescent of dune-edged beach.

Before descending to the beach, on the left is the **Franciscan Friary** (tel. 071 985 1342), home of the **Donegal History Society Museum**. This museum contains a variety of displays on the area, including two volumes of the 1848 English translation of the Annals of the Four Masters, as well as historical artefacts, photographs and memorabilia. In addition, the Friary, founded in 1946, is an attraction in itself, with various outdoor shrines and gardens, including a

Christmas garden. The grounds – perched on a cliff overlooking the sea, offer sign-posted walking trails, prayer paths, and a viewing point that overlooks the broad expanse of Rossnowlagh beach. Open daily. Admission: free

From the Friary grounds, turn left and follow signposts to **Rossnowlagh** beach. Derived from the Irish language, *Ros Neamhlach*, this place name is interpreted variously to mean 'wood of the apple trees' or 'the heavenly cove'. Either way, it is a picturesque place, ideal for surfing, windsurfing, board-sailing and other watersports. If time allows, walk or drive along the beach – yes, cars are encouraged to drive along the hard and wide expanse of sand. Riding horses along the beach is also a favourite pastime with the locals.

Continue north, as the road parallels the coast for a while. Turn right at the sign for Ballintra, leading back to the main N15 road. Make a left onto the N15 main road and go north. This road will lead you around Donegal town and to the N56 road for the rest of the tour.

After passing around Donegal town, continue west on the N56. Views of Donegal Bay appear on the left as you approach the fishing village of **Mountcharles**. A small lake, **St Peter's Lough**, can be seen on the right, as you proceed toward **Iver**, the next village. Continue on to **Dunkineely**, where the bay opens up on the left. Enjoy lovely coastal views of Donegal Bay on the left for the next 8 km (5 miles).

Take note that the roads on this part of the tour are narrow and hilly, often curving around scenic mountain passes, deep valleys and coastal cliffs. Expect to average no more than 48 km (30 miles) per hour, and sometimes less.

Next is **Killybegs**, one of Ireland's busiest fishing ports and an important herring-fishing station. Strong salty fish aromas fill the air as you pass through the town.

As you depart Killybegs, the main N56 road swings north, but instead follow local road R263. This road goes west and there is a viewing point that offers panoramic views at Fintragh Bay, with Donegal Bay in the distance. Continuing west, enjoy wonderful seascapes to the left, and the great profiles of Crownarad and Mulnanaff mountains looming ahead.

As you approach **Kilcar**, you enter a Gaeltacht or Irish-speaking area. This means that road signs will appear in both the Irish and English languages, with a preference for the former. Signs for **Kilcar** will also say **Cill Charthaigh**. The place name, which means 'St Carthach's church', commemorates a church built here in the sixth century by a bishop named Carthach.

Continue to follow the coast road to **Carrick** – *An Charraig*, which means 'the rock', appropriately given the rocky land which surrounds the town, including the stony peaks of **Slieve League** to the left, towering over Donegal Bay.

These are said to be the highest marine cliffs in Europe (230.5 metres/756 feet). You can gain access via signposted roads from the villages of Carrick or Teelin. The cliff face, extending for about 3 km (2 miles) has been carved by the Atlantic to give a variety of shapes and colours. **Bunglas** is a spectacular place to view the sea cliffs, and you can easily spend a day walking from Bunglas, through the somewhat spine-chilling **One Man's Path**, to **Malinbeg** near Glencolumbkille. This is for experienced climbers and walkers only.

Travel 11 km (7 miles) west, and next is **Glencolumbkille** or **Gleann Cholm Cille**, meaning 'St Columba's valley' or 'the glen of St Columba's church', a reference to the fact that St Columba established a monastery here in the sixth century. It is a very remote and peaceful valley, where sheep far outnumber the people. Up until the early 1960s, local industry was almost non-existent, and young people were emigrating at a rapid rate. To stem the tide of emigration and create employment in the area, a man with great foresight and business acumen came on the scene. Fr James McDyer, although born in the region, had been away for many years doing priestly work in England. When he returned to Glencolumbkille, he was saddened at the lack of opportunity amid such scenic beauty. He set about converting the area's natural attributes into local enterprises, and organised the people into self-reliant co-operatives for knitting, farming, fishing, fish-processing, and other small industries. He saw great potential for tourism, but realised that no one would make the journey out to this far-flung corner of Donegal for scenery alone, so he conceived the idea of a 'living history' museum.

In 40 years, it has grown to be the area's major attraction (and is now named after the industrious priest) – **Fr McDyer's Folk Village Museum** (tel. 074 973 0017). Designed, assembled, and maintained by the people of Glencolumbkille, this outdoor village seeks to recreate life in the town over the past 300 years. The complex includes a cluster of cottages or *clachan*, built and thatched in the traditional rounded Donegal style – tied down to withstand the prevailing winds off the Atlantic. Each cottage represents a different era and way of life – eighteenth, nineteenth and twentieth centuries – and is furnished with the tools, implements and utensils appropriate to that period. Other buildings include a nineteenth-century school, a craft shop, a tea house and a bakery. A walk-through tour aims to acquaint visitors with local customs and traditions, while maintaining the community's rich culture. The grounds, set into a hillside overlooking the sea below, feature a herb garden and a nature walk incorporating replicas of local history, including standing stones, a limekiln, mass rock, hedge school, sweat house and round tower. The shops in the complex offer the craft work of the local community. Open daily, Easter–October. Admission: €

Take the road signposted to Ardara, a distance of 26 km (16 miles). It will bring you through a scenic drive known as **The Glengesh Pass**, a high gorge between the steep-sided Glengesh and Mulmosog mountains overlooking **Loughros Beg Bay**.

Ardara (*Árd an Ratha*, meaning 'height of the ringfort') appears to be named after a nearby fort on top of a cliff, although Ardara itself is in a deep valley. Today Ardara is noted as a major centre for the manufacture of hand-woven tweeds and hand-knit garments. The main street is lined with shops selling woollen goods.

The **Ardara Heritage Centre**, Main Street (tel. 074 954 1704), a small museum, tells the story of tweed from the sheep to the wool and eventually into woven cloth. It consists of a series of walk-around exhibits, old photographs, displays and models of equipment used in the process. In addition, a weaver is frequently on duty to answer questions and demonstrate how to work a loom. Open daily, Easter–September. Admission: €

From Ardara, return via the N56 south. The road presents good views of Donegal Bay as it descends toward Killybegs. Retrace your route from Killybegs back to Donegal town, a distance of 27 km (17 miles), for the completion of the tour, or to travel onward.

THE FORGE, Rossnowlagh Road, Ballyshannon (tel. 071 982 2070). Country-inn charm prevails in this restaurant, with a décor of brick walls, old pine furnishings, carriage wheels, saddles, harnesses, open fireplaces and a distinctive mural depicting an old-time forge. The menu offers modern Irish cuisine, with emphasis on steaks, free-range chicken and duck, and local seafood, such as grilled salmon, baked cod, king prawns, and scallops in their shells. It is conveniently located less than 5 km (3 miles) north of Ballyshannon. Open for lunch and dinner, daily.

THE GATE HOUSE, Glencolumbkille Road, Carrick (tel. 074 973 9366). Feel like a good cup of tea? Head to this old house, facing Slieve League and overlooking Teelin Bay, 1.5 km (1 mile) west of town. Built in 1865, it was crafted from hand-cut stone, and still retains many of its early furnishings, from a cast-iron fireplace to an old-world kitchen with flagstone floor. It's an ideal place to stop for tea and scones, homemade bread and jam. Open for tea and snacks, daily, May–September.

KITTY KELLY'S, Largy, Killybegs (tel. 074 973 2386). Sitting on the coast road about 5 km (3 miles) west of Killybegs, this homely restaurant was originally a farmhouse, and it dates back over 200 years. It has kept many of its authentic trappings, from an old cutlery dresser and wood stairs to cosseting rooms for storage. The menu features local seafood as a speciality, but also offers traditional Irish fare and a sprinkling of other dishes such as pastas. Open for dinner, daily, May–December; Sunday–Thursday, January – April.

THE SANDHOUSE, Coast Road, Rossnowlagh (tel. 071 984 1204.). Set on a crescent of beach overlooking Donegal Bay, this local landmark has long been a focal point of the area, first as a fishing lodge in 1886, later a thatched pub from 1906, and then expanded into a stellar hotel since 1949. Enjoy a snack or light meal in the nautically-themed Surfers' Bar or the antique-filled lounge, by a turf fireplace. The main dining room specialises in local seafood harvested in Donegal Bay, such as lobster, oysters, scallops and mussels. Open for dinner, daily, February–November.

SMUGGLERS' CREEK INN, Coast Road, Rossnowlagh (tel. 071 985 2366). For a nautical décor, panoramic views of Donegal Bay, and great seafood, this is the place. The bar menu offers oysters and mussels harvested from local beds, as well as soups, salads and sandwiches. House dinner specials include Smugglers' Sea Casserole (scallops, salmon and prawns), deep-fried squid, and tiger prawns. Open for lunch and dinner, daily, Easter–October; Wednesday–Sunday, November–April.

THE TEA HOUSE, The Folk Village, Glencolumbkille (tel. 074 973 0017). Come through the half-door and step back in time at this thatched-roof cottage, furnished with tables and chairs handcrafted by the local people. Operated as a charitable trust, this homely self-service restaurant offers the best of local produce and freshly baked goodies, produced by members of the community. The menu emphasises traditional Irish recipes for Guinness cake, scones, brown bread and apple tart, as well as homemade soups and salads. Open for lunch and snacks, daily, April–October.

PUBS

COPE HOUSE 'SHIPS INN', Main Street, Killybegs (tel. 074 973 1836). Decorated with a nautically themed copper façade, this vintage pub fits right into the seafaring atmosphere of this busy fishing port. The interior sports an equally maritime décor – ship wheels and murals, propellers, bells and a collection of model ships and seafaring memorabilia. It's an ideal spot to linger over a quiet drink while looking out at the ships pulling in to the harbour.

DICEY REILLY'S PUB, Market Street, Ballyshannon (tel. 071 985 1371). Dating back to 1856, this is the oldest pub in town. Originally known as the 'Anchor Bar', it has changed names many times since, taking its present name in 1996. In the passing of the years, it has accumulated many tales to tell – for example, Guinness used to be bottled on the premises, and whiskey was delivered in barrels before being bottled. It has long been a popular watering hole, especially for fishermen in this port town.

JOHN JOE'S, Main Street, Kilcar (tel. 074 973 8015). Located in the middle of the village, this homely pub is now in its third century of trading as a public house. It is a gathering place for local sports fans and for spontaneous sessions of traditional music.

NANCY'S BAR, Front Street, Ardara (tel. 074 954 1187). Tradition is the keynote of this cottage-style inn, which has been in the same family for seven generations and is named after the great-grandmother of the current owner. The décor is replete with open fireplaces, antiques, bric-a-brac and memorabilia. Bar food is available all day, and chowder is a speciality.

THE PIPER'S REST, Kilcar (tel. 074 973 8205). Set amid the rugged mountainous countryside and the panoramic seascapes, this 200-year-old pub is the epitome of an earlier era – thatched roof, half-doors, flagged floors, stone walls and an open turf fireplace. Bar food includes hearty seafood chowders, and traditional music is played on most nights.

THE SLIEVE LEAGUE BAR, Main Street, Carrick (tel. 074 973 9333). Originally a shebeen dating back to 1779, this pub takes its name from the nearby cliffs. Although recently renovated, it still retains many original features, including a wood and brick interior, walled seating, flagged-and-timber floor and sturdy country furniture. Locals gather here to use the pool table or for the nightly sessions of traditional music.

DIGRESSIONS

DONEGAL BAY CRUISING: The fishing boats *Nuala Star* and *Assaroe Star* offer one-hour sightseeing cruises in Donegal Bay beside the Slieve League Coast and the Cliffs of Bunglas. These boat trips also provide opportunities for watching dolphins, whales and bluefin tuna in nearby waters, and seals sunning themselves on the rocks. Boats depart from Teelin Pier, May–September. Information: Paddy Byrne, Teelin (tel. 074 973 9365 or www.nwcsa.com/nualastar).

PILGRIM TRAIL: North of Rossnowlagh, take a detour at Laghy on local road R232, to visit one of Ireland's main sites of Christian pilgrimage, Lough Derg or Station Island. For some background, first proceed to the village of Pettigo to visit the Lough Derg Journey, a heritage centre that profiles the famous pilgrimage – so visitors can experience the sights, sounds, and feelings, without having to go through all the rigours. The story of Lough Derg goes back to St Patrick's time, in the mid-fifth century, when Ireland's patron saint is said to have come here to do penance on an island in the middle of the lake. Christian pilgrims have followed in his footsteps ever since, coming to the same island, now known as 'St Patrick's Purgatory', for a day or more of prayer and fasting each spring and summer. To see the actual pilgrimage site, head 6.5 km (4 miles) north to the pier for Station Island. The centrepiece of the island is an octagonal church built in 1921. One-day retreats are held in May and September, and traditional three-day pilgrimages from June through mid-August. It is customary to fast and walk around in bare feet. Boats take visitors to the island regularly, daily in May–September; at weekends in March–April. Information: The Prior, St Patrick's Purgatory, Lough Derg, Pettigo (tel. 071 986 1518 or www.loughderg.org) or Lough Derg Journey, Main Street, Pettigo (tel. 071 986 1565).

34: Donegal Highlands and Gaeltacht

The ruggedly rural highlands of Donegal hold many surprises. You wouldn't expect to find an art gallery housing works by Picasso here, but you will, just as you'll encounter a national park with exotic edible plants and a castle with links to Tabasco sauce.

Most of all, this remote territory, extending beyond Donegal town out into the hinterlands along the Atlantic, holds incredibly beautiful scenery – endless lakes and bays, peninsulas and headlands, islands and inlets, bog lands and valleys, all dominated by the Blue Stack and Derryveagh Mountains.

More than half of this area is part of a Gaeltacht or Irish-speaking district. This not only enhances the rural character of these far-flung communities, but, more importantly, it preserves the native culture and crafts. It also adds music to the air. Some of Ireland's finest contemporary singers and musicians were nurtured here, from Daniel O'Donnell to Enya and the folk groups, Altan and Clannad.

Because of the vast scope of this territory, it would take weeks or even months to follow every road, drive every peninsula, or explore every byway. This chapter presents a sample of the most interesting towns and experiences. It is a road less travelled, but indeed full of surprises.

(See map p.315)

FAST FACTS

Travel Information Offices

DONEGAL TOURIST OFFICE, The Quay, Donegal (tel. 074 972 1148). Open all year.

DUNGLOE TOURIST OFFICE, Main Street, Dungloe (tel. 074 952 1297). Open June–September.

LETTERKENNY TOURIST OFFICE, Neil T. Blaney Road, Letterkenny (tel. 074 912 1160). Open all year.

TRAVEL INFORMATION ONLINE:
 www.irelandnorthwest.ie and
www.donegaldirect.ie

TELEPHONE AREA CODES:

The area code for all numbers in this part of Donegal is 074, unless noted otherwise.

MARY FROM DUNGLOE INTERNATIONAL FESTIVAL – Commemorating a local woman of great beauty, this arts and music festival includes a pageant to select a 'Mary from Dungloe' to reign over the ten-day event. Activities range from readings by Donegal authors and art exhibitions to street music, parades, vintage car and bike displays, concerts, a carnival and fireworks. Information: Judy Lee, Festival Office, Dungloe, tel. 952 1254 or www.maryfromdungloe.info. (End July–early-August)

FÉILE AN EARAGAIL – More than 100 cultural events are staged in 20 northwest Donegal towns and villages at this annual festival. Presenting a mix of international and local talent, the programme includes touring theatre, concerts, visual arts, comedy shows, literary readings and children's events. Information: Festival Office, Central Library, Oliver Plunkett Road, Letterkenny, tel. 912 9186 or www.donegalculture.com. (Mid-July)

HARVEST FAIR – For a real autumn country-fair atmosphere, head to this five-day gathering at Glenties. It attracts people from all over County Donegal to its 'Fair Day' events of animal shows, music, crafts and celebrations. Information: Kevin O'Donnell, Glenties, tel. 955 1158. (Mid-September)

DONEGAL HIGHLANDS AND GAELTACHT DRIVING TOUR

Duration: 6–8 hours plus stops

Before setting out on this drive, be aware that much of the Atlantic Highlands area (like part of the Donegal Bay region) belongs to a Gaeltacht (Irish-speaking district), so the road signs are printed in the Irish language first, followed by the English words. In some of the more remote sections, signs are in Irish only. Often the Irish word for a place bears no resemblance to the English equivalent – for example, *An Clochán Liath* in Irish is Dungloe in English. This can be daunting, but our itinerary gives the place names in both languages. Remember that the Irish language is also used for pub and shop signs.

Overall, the driving is slow and tedious in many places because of poor roads and the variety of bogland, mountain and seacoast terrain. Mileage will average 48 km (30 miles) per hour, although in some places it will be more.

If starting out from Donegal town, take the main N56 road west as far as **Mountcharles**, and then make a right onto the R262, a scenic road with the **Blue Stack Mountains** rising on the right. In just over 16 km (10 miles) you will reach **Glenties** or **Na Gleannta**, nestled in the hills where two glens and two rivers meet. Not surprisingly, the Irish place name for this delightful village means 'the glens'. The attractive layout of the village, which has four times been a national award winner in Ireland's annual 'Tidy Towns' competition, includes an early nineteenth-century courthouse and a market house. Glenties is considered as the official gateway to the Donegal highlands and to the Donegal Gaeltacht. This area is home to the largest native Irish-speaking population in Ireland. From now on, the route passes shops and pubs with signs in the Irish language.

From here, rejoin the main N56 road as it wends northwards. After about 13 km (8 miles), the road crosses the **Gweebara Bridge** or **Droichead Gaoth Barra**, over the Gweebara river. Another 13 km (8 miles) takes you to **Dungloe** or **An Clochán Liath**, meaning 'the grey stepping stone'. This name is appropriate, as the rocks around this small fishing port have a distinctive grey hue.

Dungloe is celebrated as the 'capital' of **The Rosses**, an area of countless promontories, islands and headlands of rock-strewn land tucked amid bays and inlets. The bleakness of the large and lonely stretches of uninhabited land draws many visitors who seek solitude. A detour of 8 km (5 miles) to the left will bring you to one of Donegal's major fishing ports, **Burtonport**, otherwise known as **Ailt an Chorráin**, which means 'ravine of the curve'. It is said that more salmon and lobster are landed at this port than anywhere else in Ireland.

The next town, 11 km (7 miles) to the north, is **Crolly** or **Croithlí**, the place name meaning 'quagmire', because of the marshy boglands nearby.

Since 1939, Crolly has been the home of the **Crolly Doll Factory** (tel. 954 8466), a local enterprise producing distinctive porcelain collector dolls, dressed in outfits incorporating County Donegal's hand-knitted woollens, hand-woven tweeds and linens. Open Monday–Friday. Admission: free

This area marks the end of the Rosses and the beginning of a new Gaeltacht district or parish known as **Gweedore** or **Gaoth Dobhair**, meaning 'water inlet'. Outside the towns and villages, the houses and cottages are very scarce in this territory.

Three kilometres (2 miles) north is the hamlet of Gweedore, gateway to a promontory known as **Bloody Foreland**. The term has nothing to do with ancient battles or massacres, but is used to describe the reddish hue given to the rocks by the evening sun. Take a detour on the R257 to do the complete Bloody Foreland circuit (about 19 km/12 miles), for broad views of the Atlantic and the massive Horn Head cliffs rising to the east, as well as a picturesque collection of offshore islands including Inishbofin, Inishdooey, Inishbeg and Tory.

Although more peninsulas, such as Rosguill, Ards and Fanad lie ahead, they must await another day. This tour now turns inland, following the R251 road to

Dunlewy or **Dún Lúiche**, simply meaning 'Lughaidh's fort'. **Mount Errigal**, Donegal's highest peak (751.6 metres/2,466 feet), rising on the left, presents a scenic backdrop to this tiny village, set in a shallow peat valley and bordered by two lovely lakes.

Take time to visit a local community development that has given new life and the hum of activity to this area – **The Lakeside Centre – Ionad Cois Locha** (tel. 953 1699). Once the small homestead of a local weaver named Manus Ferry, this place has evolved into 'an oasis in the Gaeltacht' for visitors in search of a lovely setting to enjoy a bit of history, some fresh air on a boat ride, or a cup of tea by a fireside. The old farmhouse has been converted into a visitor centre with exhibits and demonstrations on weaving, from carding and dyeing to spinning. It is furnished just as it would have been in Manus Ferry's day, complete with a time-worn loom, and a kitchen with cupboard bed and a hob for grilling over the fire. After a tour of the house, step out into the farmyard to see the animals or the herb and vegetable gardens, watch sheep being sheared, or take a boat ride on the lake. Old-fashioned Irish storytelling is part of the guided tour, as is traditional music and dance of the most authentic kind. There is a relaxed aura about the place, a welcome change after a long drive. Listen as the locals speak in the Irish language. You'll be encouraged to try a few Gaelic words, too. Open daily, mid-March–November. Admission: €

Return to the R251 and travel east along this scenic valley for almost 13 km (8 miles) to reach the area's prime natural attraction, **Glenveagh National Park** at Churchill (tel. 913 7090). It is hard to imagine that one of Ireland's finest national parks is secluded out in these Donegal hinterlands, but here it is – 9,712 hectares (24,000 acres) of gardens, moor lands, lakes, woods and mountains, including the two highest mountains in Donegal – **Errigal** and **Slieve Snacht**. This vast natural expanse was not always a happy place. In 1857, the estate was created by Englishman John George Adair, who added a Gothic-style granite castle in 1870. He drove over 200 families from their homes on the land so that he could live by himself. Although he died in 1885, his wife remained here until 1921. In the 1930s, it was purchased by Henry McIlhenny, of the Tabasco sauce family, who was also a distinguished art historian and chairman of the board of the Philadelphia Museum of Art. The grandson of a Donegal emigrant, McIlhenny restored the castle and made many artistic improvements in the buildings and gardens, spending several months a year here until 1983 when he presented the castle and gardens as a gift to the Irish nation.

A tour starts at the visitor centre with a 25-minute audiovisual which presents background on the castle and estate. Mini-buses then take visitors on a short ride to the castle and gardens. If you prefer to walk, it takes about 45 minutes between the two sites. Guided tours of the castle are conducted every 20 minutes and last about half-an-hour. Save time to explore the gardens to savour the rich variety of exotic and rare plants from as far away as Madeira, Tasmania and Chile. In addition, there are themed sections such as the Belgian Walk, Swiss Walk, Italian Garden, Rose Garden, View Garden, and Vegetable Garden with edible and ornamental vegetables. The grounds provide a variety of nature trails and a lush habitat for wildlife, including the largest red deer herd in Ireland. Open daily, mid-March–early November. Admission: €

Return to the R251 and turn right. Three more surprises await 6.5 km (4 miles) away on the shores of Lough Gartan. A right turn will bring you to the **Glebe House and Gallery** (tel. 913 7071). This is the art hub of Donegal, donated to the people of Ireland by English artist Derek Hill (1916–2000), who lived and painted in this area. Glebe House, a fine Regency-style building that was formerly Hill's home, is a museum of masterpiece art, including more than 300 works by leading twentieth-century artists such as Picasso, Bonnard, Kokoschka and Jack B. Yeats, plus Donegal folk art, Japanese and Islamic art, and papers and textiles by William Morris. Outside, the former stables have been converted into a gallery showing selec-

tions of Derek Hill's paintings, as well as a changing programme of visiting exhibits. Open daily, mid-March–October. Admission: €

Turn right and follow signs for **Colmcille Heritage Centre** (tel. 913 7306). Situated beside **Lough Gartan**, this heritage centre tells the story of the life and times of Donegal's patron saint, Colmcille (521–597). Born in Gartan, he first spent time spreading Christianity in the area around Glencolumbkille and then set up at least three religious foundations in Ireland – Derry, Durrow and Moone – before he went on to bring Christianity to Scotland, becoming known there as St Columba of Iona. The story is told via several media including artistically designed banners, stained glass, illustrated panels, artefacts, and wax models in authentic clothing. There is also a step-by-step explanation of how ancient manuscripts were produced by the monks. Open daily, May–September. Admission: €

This point also marks the end of the Gaeltacht area. Turn right and the local road links up with the N56 for the next 11 km (7 miles) to **Letterkenny**, a large and busy town with a 1.5-km (1-mile) long main street at the head of **Lough Swilly**. The place name is taken from the Irish *Leitir Ceannan*, which means 'white-faced hillside'.

It is the home of the **Donegal County Museum**, High Road (tel. 912 4613), a treasure-trove of exhibits about all facets of life in the county, from folk life to history, geology, archaeology and local railways. Open Monday–Saturday. Admission: free

Continue through Letterkenny, turning south onto the N56 for the 48-km (30-mile) trip back to Donegal town. En route, the road will merge to become the N15 as you pass through the 'twin towns' of **Stranorlar** and **Ballybofey**, separated by the River Finn. The road is particularly scenic south of Ballybofey as you drive through **Barnesmore Gap**, with the Blue Stack Mountains and Lough Eske on the right. If you are not heading back to Donegal, Letterkenny is also an easy gateway to the Inishowen Peninsula or to Derry and Northern Ireland.

PAT'S PICKS

RESTAURANTS

DANNY MINNIE'S, Teach Killindarragh, Annagry (tel. 954 8201). Deep in the heart of the Gaeltacht area 8 km (5 miles) west of Crolly, this restaurant has a country-inn atmosphere, with antiques and candlelit tables. The menu, offered in Irish and English, presents local seafood as the speciality, including lobster and other shellfish, as well as Donegal lamb and beef, and vegetarian dishes. Open for dinner, daily, June–September; Tuesday–Saturday, October–May.

GALFEES, 63 Upper Main Street, Letterkenny (tel. 912 8535). For a quick snack, a picnic or a relaxing meal, this bistro is a local gem in the centre of town. It is a food emporium, offering baked goods, preserves and other goodies for sale, as well as being a gourmet take-away and restaurant. The menu, which has options for weight-watchers, presents freshly made salads, soups, pastas, vegetarian dishes, meats and seafood, as well as sweets of all kinds. Open for lunch and snacks, daily; and for dinner, Monday–Saturday.

LOBSTER POT, Burtonport (tel. 954 2012). In a fishing port known for its big catches, this restaurant wisely specialises in lobster, Atlantic wild salmon, and other local seafood platters, as well as hearty soups and chowders. The atmosphere is cosy, with dark woods, open fireplaces, brass poles, old copper lamps, and lots of memorabilia. It is situated near the harbour 8 km (5 miles) west of Dungloe. Open for lunch and dinner, daily.

MILL RESTAURANT, Dunfanaghy (tel. 913 6985). Built as a flax mill between 1880–1900 by the Stewards of Ards, who were the landlords at that time, and later converted into a home by a well-known watercolour artist, this restaurant is in a picturesque setting on the shore of New Lake. The location and décor provide a welcoming setting – lakeside views, fresh flowers, soft lighting, antiques and original paintings. The menu, which changes every six weeks, offers a cuisine based on fresh local produce in season, with emphasis on fish and shellfish such as Sheephaven Bay salmon and Doe Castle mussels. Open for dinner, Tuesday–Sunday, mid-March–December.

QUIET MOMENTS TEA ROOM, Upper Main Street, Letterkenny (tel. 912 8382). For a cup of tea in a serene setting, head to this shop-front café in the centre of town. It also offers pastries, breads, soups, salads and sandwiches made to order. A second location stands at the other end of the town at Lower Main Street (tel. 912 7401). Open for lunch, snacks and tea/coffee, daily.

SILVER TASSIE RESTAURANT, Ramelton Road, Letterkenny (tel. 912 5619). Located almost 6.5 km (4 miles) north of the town, this restaurant is popular with the locals, especially for its carvery-style lunch. The menu features traditional favourites such as roast chicken, seafood, lamb and steaks. Open for lunch and dinner, daily.

PUBS

BIDDY O'BARNES, Barnesmore Gap (tel. 972 1402). In the wilderness along the main N15 road between Ballybofey and Donegal town, this is a good pub to know, with the scenic backdrop of the Blue Stack Mountains to the west. The country cottage décor includes blazing turf fires, wooden beams, stone floor and local memorabilia, plus a picture of the original 'Biddy' (a legendary landlady) over the mantelpiece. Snacks, soups and sandwiches are served.

LEO'S TAVERN, Meenaleck, Crolly (tel. 954 8143). Locals and visitors alike flock to this pub for the music and the Gaelic hinterland atmosphere. The owner, an accomplished musician, is the father of the well-known Irish songstress Enya and her siblings of the traditional music group Clannad. The walls of the tavern display the gold, silver and platinum discs of this talented family. Stop in for some music, a drink, a snack or just for a good conversation.

MCGILLOWAY'S, Main Street, Dunfanaghy (tel. 913 6438). Music, played here most nights, is the main attraction here – the walls are lined with photographs of famous musicians and dozens of brass horns. The décor also features well-placed accordions, fiddles, guitars and a piano.

MOLLY'S, Main Street, Dunfanaghy (tel. 913 6127). Having been trading for over 200 years, this rustic pub harks back to an earlier era – one small room with original brass stair rods, a tiny snug, antique whiskey mirrors; and the other room with a mixture of vintage furniture, a Victorian fireplace and hand-painted wall murals of classic Guinness ads. Music is played all year –Thursday and Saturday, June–September; and every second Saturday, October–May.

SKIPPER'S TAVERN, Burtonport (tel. 914 2234). Situated in a fishing port, this pub has a nautical atmosphere, with low-beamed timber ceilings, wooden floors, lots of nooks and crannies, and a bar-food menu featuring fish dishes. Most of all, this landmark pub is known for its afternoon music sessions, from 4pm onwards, on Wednesday, Saturday and Sunday.

DIGRESSIONS

GUIDED TOURS: If you'd prefer to leave the driving to someone else, Bus Éireann conducts narrated sightseeing tours of the north Donegal area. The tour is through the Barnesmore Gap, and includes a visit to Glenveagh National Park before returning via Dunlewey, Gweedore and Glenties. Tours operate Monday–Saturday in July and August, departing from Donegal town. Information: Bus Éireann (tel. 912 1309 or www.buseireann.ie).

ISLAND-HOPPING: The waters off the Donegal coast are flecked by islands of all sizes. Two of the most popular are Tory and Aranmore, both havens of Gaelic culture and language. Tory, 11 km (7 miles) west of the mainland, is accessible by boat from Bunbeg, Magheraroarty or Portnablagh. Aranmore, about 3 km (2 miles) from the mainland, is reached from Burtonport. Ferry services to Aranmore operate daily; and to Tory operate daily in April–October, and five days a week in November–March. Information: Donegal Coastal Cruises Turasmara, Bunbeg Pier Office, Bunbeg (tel. 953 991); or Aranmore Ferry, Leabgarrow, Arranmore (tel. 952 0532).

35: Inishowen Peninsula

The largest of County Donegal's many peninsulas, Inishowen sits at the top of the county, the most northerly point of the entire island of Ireland.

Very few visitors ever get this far, but those who do make the journey are well rewarded. Bounded on three sides by water, Inishowen is almost triangular in shape, between Lough Swilly and Lough Foyle, and facing the Atlantic. It is a collage of dramatic seacoasts, dune-filled beaches, challenging mountain drives, deep green valleys, and cliff-etched headlands. With such rich scenery plus a fine collection of ancient forts and monuments, traditional craft centres, and a dozen friendly towns, many people consider Inishowen to be a miniature Donegal or even a miniature Ireland.

The area takes its name from the Irish language, *Inis Eoghain*, meaning 'Owen's island'. Owen was an early member the Uí Néill or O'Neill clan. In medieval times, Inishowen was part of the great northern kingdom of the O'Neills, ruled from the royal palace at Grianán Aileach.

In spite of its remote location, the Inishowen Peninsula is compact and easy to tour, making it a very good choice for a quick sampling of Irish landscape. The entire peninsula is bordered by a well-signposted 161-km or 100-mile drive, aptly named the 'Inishowen 100'.

(See map p.315)

FAST FACTS

Travel Information Offices

BUNCRANA TOURIST OFFICE, Railway Road, Buncrana (tel. 074 936 2600). Open June–September.

INISHOWEN TOURISM SOCIETY LTD, Chapel Street, Carndonagh (tel. 074 937 4933). Open all year.

TRAVEL INFORMATION ONLINE:
www.irelandnorthwest.ie,
www.donegaldirect.ie and
www.visitinishowen.com

TELEPHONE AREA CODES:
The area code for telephone numbers on the Inishowen Peninsula is 074, unless stated otherwise.

MOVILLE VINTAGE CAR RALLY – For over 30 years, this rally has drawn car enthusiasts to Moville's town square – an average of 80 to 100 vehicles take part. The day also includes music by various folk groups, and a parade of marching bands. Information: Seán Rawdon, Malin Road, Moville, tel. 938 2225. (First Sunday of July)

BUNCRANA MUSIC FESTIVAL – Featuring a variety of musical artists performing in open-air concerts on the streets of Buncrana, this week-long gathering also includes a fireworks display on the banks of Lough Swilly, a scavenger hunt, a sand-castle-building competition, a treasure hunt and children's activities, such as a teddy bears' picnic and indoor ice-skating. Information: Catherine McDaid, Festival Office, Buncrana, tel. 936 1397 or www.buncranafestival.com. (Last week of July)

CLONMANY FAMILY FESTIVAL – Since 1967, this annual festival has been a highlight of the Inishowen calendar. The one-week programme features more than a dozen open-air concerts by Ireland's top bands, as well as an arts and crafts exhibition, vintage car and machinery rally, sheepdog and agricultural show, hill walks, and song-writing and pub talent competitions. Information: Hugo Boyce, Festival Office, Clonmany, tel. 937 6477 or www.clonmany.com. (First week of August)

INISHOWEN PENINSULA DRIVING TOUR

Duration: 4–6 hours plus stops

The Inishowen Peninsula drive is one of the best signposted routes in Ireland, with signs and directions clearly printed in English as well as Irish, and all distances shown in miles and kilometres. However, the roads can be steep, narrow and hilly, and the driving is tedious and slow in many spots. Expect to average no more than 48 km (30 miles) an hour.

Start out early from Donegal town, driving approximately 64.5 km (40 miles) via the N15, N56 and N13, to the small village of **Burt**, the gateway to the Inishowen Peninsula. *Note:* if travelling in Northern Ireland, it is a lot easier to start this tour from Derry, just over the border and less than 8 km (5 miles) from Burt via the main N13 road.

However, assuming that you have made your way to this area, your first stop is **Grianán Aileach**, Burt (tel. 936 8000). One of Ireland's greatest ringforts, this mighty stone structure sits 228.5 metres (750 feet) above sea level atop the Donegal countryside, at the southern tip of the Inishowen Peninsula. The place name, derived from the Irish *Grianán Ailigh*, is usually interpreted to mean 'the stone fort of the sun'. Archaeologists maintain that the fort itself dates from 500BC or earlier, but the circular ramparts may go back as much as 5,000 years. Considering its commanding position, it is thought to have originally been a pagan temple. From the fifth century to the twelfth century, it was the royal residence of the Ulster chieftains, the O'Neills. Although greatly ravaged in medieval times, it was partly restored in the 1870s. It is still one of the most impressive circular ringforts in Ireland, with a diameter of 23.5 metres (77 feet) and walls that are 5 metres (17 feet) high and almost 4 metres (13 feet) thick. The fort itself is a great vantage point for taking panoramic pictures – it is said you can see five counties and two rivers from it.

A visit starts at the heritage centre, built in a circular stone layout much like the fort itself. It contains an exhibit depicting the story of Grianán Aileach, using models, photos, artefacts and storyboards. While it is not as inspiring as seeing the actual fort, the exhibit is ideal for anyone not able to climb a hilly and steep landscape. For those who are fit, a ticket for a shuttle-bus ride to the fort is provided as part of the admission to the visitor centre. Open daily. Admission: €€

From the fort, return to the main road and continue to **Burnfoot**, a small village overlooking Lough Swilly. The rather unusual place name is derived from the Irish language *Bun na hAbhann*, meaning 'mouth of the river', an apparent reference to its position by the water. This village marks the start of the circular drive around the peninsula known as 'Inishowen 100' or 'Inis Eoghain 100'.

In just over 4.5 km (3 miles), the road leads into the picturesque marina village of **Fahan** overlooking Lough Swilly. The name comes from the Irish language *Fathain*, which means 'grave'. It is probably so named because the local cemetery may hold the remains of St Mura, the first recorded abbot here in the early seventh century. A 2-metre (7-foot) high stone cross is known locally as St Mura's cross, and dates from about the seventh century. It contains a rare Greek inscription, said to be the only one of its kind known to date from early Christian Ireland. St Mura's crosier, which was found here, is on display in the National Museum in Dublin.

Continue north for 8 km (5 miles), heading towards **Buncrana**, whose name derives from the Irish language, *Bun Cranncha*, which simply means 'mouth of the River Cranna'. In addition to its proximity to the river, the town also overlooks Lough Swilly and has a 4.5-km (3-mile) long sandy beach, making it a focal point for visitors. As the largest town on the peninsula, Buncrana has always been a centre of industry, particularly for textiles, tweeds and knits.

Buncrana's prowess in the textile industry is profiled at **Tullyarvan Mill** (tel. 936 1613), signposted as you cross over the River Cranna a little over half-a-mile north of town. Housed in a nineteenth-century converted corn mill, this centre illustrates the town's 250-year-old involvement in the textile industry. It includes a complete textile museum, with displays of knitwear, wools and other cloths, as well as the tools and implements used to make them. Open daily, Easter–September. Admission: €

Depart Buncrana and follow the 'Inishowen 100' signs on local road R238. As the road swings right, you may wish to take a slight detour to the left to **Dunree Head**. This will bring you to **Fort Dunree Military Museum**, Dunree (tel. 936 1817), Ireland's first public military museum. It is located on the site of First World War defences on the north Irish coast. Even if you have no interest in military history, this is a worthwhile diversion because of its location. Perched high on a cliff overlooking Lough Swilly, this old fort has one of the best vantage points in Donegal, an ideal spot to take pictures or just to enjoy sweeping sea views on a clear day. The museum incorporates a Napoleonic Martello tower that houses a wide range of exhibits, an audiovisual centre and a restored forge. Open daily, May–September. Admission: €

Retrace your path back to the R238 road and continue going north. The road swings left for the **Gap of Mamore**, a scenic roadway that passes between two almost equal hills – **Mamore Hill** (421 metres/1,381 feet), and **Croaghcarragh** (420 metres/1,379

feet), part of the Urris Hills. The road rises to a height of almost 244 metres (800 feet) above sea level before following a spiralling corkscrew descent. In the process, it offers panoramic views of the entire northern coastline.

At the bottom, the road comes to a fork. Keep right to stay on the 'Inishowen 100' drive, and pass through **Clonmany** and **Ballyliffin**, two small villages less than 3.5 km (2 miles) apart, both with fine beaches overlooking **Pollan Bay**.

Follow the road east for just over 8 km (5 miles) for **Carndonagh**, a busy market village. It takes its name from the Irish words, *Carn Domhnach*, meaning 'cairn of the church'. The church in question is a Church of Ireland edifice about half-a-kilometre (a third of a mile) west of town. It is the site of some interesting ancient monuments, grouped together on a roadside platform on the church grounds. The focal point is **St Patrick's Cross**, a primitive ringless cross decorated on one side with interlaced ornamentation, and on the other with an interlaced cross and a simple crucifixion scene. The cross has frequently been estimated to date back to the seventh century, making it among the oldest High Crosses in Ireland, although it may be two or three centuries younger. The cross is flanked on either side by small pillars. The first has two carved figures – the harpist David and the warrior Goliath – while the second pillar is not as readily identifiable, showing a figure with unusual ears.

The 'Inishowen 100' now takes a northerly direction, following the R238 and R242 for almost 5 km (3 miles) to **Malin**, a lovely village with a ten-arched bridge on **Trawbreaga Bay**. Malin takes its name from the Irish word *Malainn*, meaning 'brow', because it sits at the brow or forehead of the peninsula.

Planned and laid out in the seventeenth century, Malin is built around a triangular village green, lined with lime, sycamore and cherry trees. The local beach on Trawbreaga Bay is known as Five Fingers Strand because it is marked by five standing rocks, jutting out into the bay. The sand dunes along the bay are reputedly the highest in Europe, formed by the sea and wind over a period of 5,000 years.

Follow the R242 for 13.5 km (8.5 miles) to **Malin Head**, Ireland's most northerly point. As the road rises, a stunning panorama appears, with views of Trawbreaga Bay to the south, **Dunaff Head**, **Fanad Head** and **Horn Head** to the west, and wild sea-ravaged seascapes to the north. On a clear day, the hills of Scotland are visible to the east.

As might be expected, the Irish Meteorological Service has a weather station here. There is little else, except for a nineteenth-century signal tower, several shops, holiday homes, a 200-year-old thatched cottage with tea rooms and a small interpretative centre.

Return to the 'Inishowen 100' drive, going southeasterly via the R242 and R243 towards **Culdaff**, a resort village with a descriptive place name in the Irish language – *Cúill Dabhcha*, meaning 'secluded place of the sand hills'.

Follow the 'Inishowen 100' as it switches back to the R238 in descent to the shores of **Lough Foyle**. Turn left for **Greencastle**, a thriving commercial fishing port, perched at the point where the Foyle narrows and Northern Ireland is only a mile away across the water. A ferry service connects Greencastle with Macgilligan in County Derry (see Digressions below). The place name is derived from the Irish *An Caisleán Nua*, meaning 'the new castle', referring to a castle built in 1305 by Norman earl, Richard de Burgo. No longer new, it lies in ruins north of the town.

The centrepiece of the town is the **Inishowen Maritime Museum and Planetarium** (tel. 938 1363), located in a former coastguard station overlooking the harbour. Recipient of several 'museum of the year' awards, it contains a variety of seafaring exhibits, paintings, documents, photographs and maritime memorabilia, including boats ranging in size from 1.8 metres (6 feet) to 15.2 metres (50 feet). It also has a state-of-the-art planetarium for exploring the stars, which indeed seem very close in this northerly part of the world. Open daily, May–September. Admission: €

Continue south on the R241 for 3 km (2 miles) to **Moville**, an attractive eighteenth-century town and resort overlooking **Lough Foyle**. Prior to the Second World War, it was a popular port of call for transatlantic liners. The place name is derived from the Irish language, *Maigh Bhile*, meaning 'the plain of the ancient tree'.

The 'Inishowen 100' now follows the R238 for 16 km (10 miles), southward to **Redcastle**, a resort area popular with families because of its children's amusement and play centre and challenging golf course. Continue driving south for about 13 km (8 miles) to **Muff**, an unusual name derived from the Irish *Magh*, meaning 'a plain'. From the shoreline, you can see Derry city in the distance. In the early part of this century, a US Naval air service station was located here.

From Muff, follow the R239 back to Burnfoot, to complete the 'Inishowen 100' circuit. From here, head back to Donegal town, Letterkenny or Derry, or to other parts of Ireland.

PAT'S PICKS

RESTAURANTS

THE CORNCRAKE, Millbrae, Carndonagh (tel. 937 4534). Situated at the edge of town, this well-established restaurant is run by a pair of accomplished chefs, Bríd McCartney and Noreen Lynch, who also operate a cookery school on the premises. The menu presents the freshest of local ingredients, with tradiional recipes such as nettle and fresh herb soup, mature cheddar and chive soufflé, fresh crab bake, roast rack of Donegal lamb, and wild salmon with foaming hollandaise. Open for dinner, Wednesday–Sunday, July–September; Saturday–Sunday, October–June (except closed from Christmas to St Patrick's Day).

KEALY'S SEAFOOD BAR, Greencastle (tel. 938 1010). Perched on the harbour front beside the Foyle Fishermen's Co-op, this informal restaurant is known for fresh local seafood, particularly seafood chowder, oysters, lobsters and Atlantic salmon, as well as organic vegetables and farmhouse cheeses. And yes, even fish and chips. Open for lunch and dinner, Tuesday–Sunday, June–September; Thursday–Sunday, October and December–May.

MCGRORY'S OF CULDAFF, Culdaff (tel. 937 9104). Established in 1924, this inn restaurant was recently enlarged and updated, resulting in a modern art nouveau and art deco style, combined with original natural stone work and rich cherry and oak timber furnishings. The menu reflects locally sourced produce, with an emphasis on seafood, steaks and lamb with vegetarian options. Open year-round for dinner, Tuesday–Saturday; and for lunch 'all day' on Sunday.

RESTAURANT ST JOHN'S, Fahan (tel. 936 0289). Overlooking Lough Swilly, this Georgian-house restaurant offers an elegant ambience beside a cosy fireplace, and seating in the conservatory extension also offers water views. The menu concentrates on fresh vegetables and local produce. Specialities include Swilly salmon, baked turbot, stuffed mussels, Donegal lamb and crispy roast duckling. Open for dinner, Tuesday–Sunday; and for lunch on Sunday.

PUBS

THE FRONT BAR, Culdaff (tel. 937 9104). As a part of McCrory's inn (see Restaurants above), this pub offers an old-world ambience, with an open fireplace in the corner, natural stone walls, rugged pine beams and locally sourced flagstones. Opened in 1924, it was originally a pub with general merchant store, drawing customers from near and far to buy everything from a bicycle to a clay pipe. Since the 1960s, it has developed as a venue for traditional music, with sessions held throughout the year every Tuesday and Friday night, and also on Thursday in the summer. Many sessions have been featured on television and radio broadcasts.

HARRY'S BAR, Bridgend (tel. 936 8544). At the start or finish of an Inishowen tour, this roadside pub on the Letterkenny–Derry road awaits, with a relaxing country-cottage décor – bright wood, stained-glass partitions, polished brass and an open fireplace. Bar food is popular at lunchtime.

THE QUIET LADY, Malin Street, Carndonagh (tel. 937 4777). For a relaxing drink, snack or even breakfast, stop into this cosy pub with a homely atmosphere enhanced by an open turf fireplace, soft lighting and comfortable banquette-style seating. On Wednesday to Sunday evenings, it is a good choice for traditional music.

RAWDON'S BAR, Malin Road, Moville (tel. 938 2225). Licensed since 1887, this vintage pub has been in the Rawdon family for four generations, and the décor shows it. The walls are lined with old photographs, maps, ships' posters, and antique mirrors. Traditional music is played on Friday.

SEAVIEW TAVERN, Ballygorman, Malin Head (tel. 937 0117). Claiming to be Ireland's most northerly tavern, this place overlooks the harbour at the top of the peninsula, with views of Inistrahull Island and the hills of Scotland on a clear day. Bar food includes plates heaped with local oysters and mussels.

DIGRESSIONS

CRUISE ACROSS LOUGH FOYLE: Save time and mileage (approximately 80 km/50 miles) when travelling between the Inishowen Peninsula and Northern Ireland. A car-ferry service provides a direct link between Greencastle on the Inishowen peninsula and Magilligan, north of Derry city. The ferries run throughout the day, from approximately 7.20am on weekdays and 9am at weekends until 7.50pm or later, depending on the time of year. It's a continuous shuttle drive-on/drive-off service; no reservations are needed; crossing time is about fifteen minutes. Information: Lough Foyle Ferry Co. Ltd, The Pier, Greencastle (tel. 938 1901 or www.loughfoyleferry.com).

FAMINE VILLAGE: Between Ballyliffin and Carndonagh, follow a signposted local road to Doagh Island. The island is actually a peninsula, so no crossing of water is involved to reach it. The island is home to a reconstructed famine village, with over 20 thatched cottages, farm buildings and other sites (caves, mass rocks, hedge schools, sod houses and turf hovels, to name a few). You can walk around on your own or take a guided tour to learn what Ireland was like in the eighteenth, nineteenth and early twentieth centuries, especially during the time of famine and emigration. See samples of local foods, plants and herbs used for cures. During the summer, local people play traditional music and recreate special events such as matchmaking, evictions and 'wakes', all designed to bring history to life. Open daily, Easter–October. Information: Doagh Visitor Centre, Doagh Island, Inishowen (tel. 937 8078 or www.clonmany.com/doaghcentre).

The North

36: Belfast City

In the last three decades of the last century, newspaper headlines and TV reports kept Belfast in the news, but not for happy reasons. As the 'capital' of Northern Ireland, Belfast was synonymous with guns and tanks, armed patrols and civil strife. Media summaries were quick to point out the worst, but each time the city has bounced back brilliantly to be better than ever. Spunky and spirited, Belfast has always been a survivor.

And why not? Bordered by mountains and hills and nestled beside the River Lagan and Belfast Lough, Belfast is an appealing city, in spite of its war-torn image. As more and more visitors who come here learn, 'the Troubles' are confined to certain off-centre areas, usually far out of reach to the average traveller.

To a large degree, Belfast has kept humming because of its role as the industrial and business hub of Northern Ireland. Unlike Dublin, which thrives on tourism, Belfast can exist without it. Purpose-built 'tourist attractions' are few and far between in Belfast.

Although only 161 km (100 miles) north of Dublin, Belfast is a world apart, even in history and appearance. While Dublin basks in its strong Viking, Norman, and Georgian façades and traditions, Belfast is a much younger city, with distinctive Victorian and Edwardian flavours.

As late as the seventeenth century, in fact, Belfast was still a village. In the 1800s, however, it came into its own as a driving force in the industrial revolution in Ulster. With the development of industries like linen, rope-making, engineering and ship-building (ships built here include the *Titanic*), Belfast doubled in population every ten years. By 1888, as the census topped 300,000 people, Belfast was finally given the status of a city.

Today, Belfast has a population of over 500,000 people, one third of the citizens of Northern Ireland. It is a big and busy city, home of the world's largest dry dock and countless industries. Above all, it is an optimistic place. In early 1997, a superb new convention and performing arts centre, Waterfront Hall, opened as the keystone of a massive urban-development project along the river, and the city has continued to thrive and grow ever since.

FAST FACTS

Travel Information Offices

BELFAST VISITOR AND CONVENTION BUREAU, 47 Donegall Place, Belfast (tel. 028 9023 9026). Open all year.

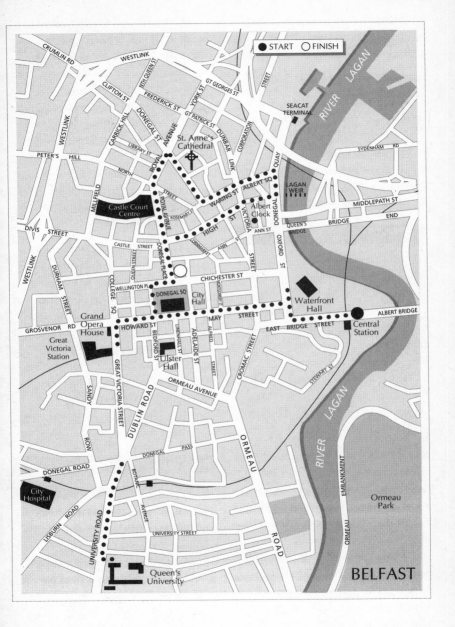

START ● FINISH ○

BELFAST

NORTHERN IRELAND TOURIST BOARD, 59 North Street, Belfast (tel. 028 9023 1221). Open all year.

TRAVEL INFORMATION ONLINE:
www.discovernorthernireland.com, www.gotobelfast.com and www.tourism.belfastcity.gov.uk

TELEPHONE AREA CODE:
The telephone area code for all of Northern Ireland is 028, or 048 from the Republic. All local numbers have eight digits.

MAJOR EVENTS

BELFAST FILM FESTIVAL – The programme is packed with exciting Irish premières, new European and international films, classics, panel discussions and workshops. Film types include documentaries, avant-garde video, local archives, short films, and music. Information: AnneMarie, Belfast Film Festival Office, Unit 18, North Street Arcade, tel. 9032 5913 or www.belfastfilmfestival.org. (Last week of March)

BELFAST MARATHON – More than 10,000 runners step off from City Hall and follow a trail around Donegall Square, Royal Avenue and the rest of the city at this annual event. Associated activities include a wheelchair marathon, team relay, marathon walking, fun run, and pasta party. Information: Marathon Office, Belfast City Council, tel. 9027 0345 or www.belfastcity.gov.uk/marathon. (First Monday of May)

CATHEDRAL QUARTER ARTS FESTIVAL – Based in Belfast's historic north city centre, this festival features fringe-type contemporary events appealing to younger, less mainstream arts audiences. The mix includes music, comedy, literature, film, circus, visual and performance arts, and street theatre, plus themed bus tours, boat cruises and sculpture tours. Information: Seán Kelly, Festival Office, 20 North Street, tel. 9023 2403 or www.cqaf.com. (First ten days of May)

BELFAST FESTIVAL AT QUEEN'S – As the largest arts festival on the island of Ireland, this annual gathering presents over 300 events, with participation by stars of classical music, opera, jazz, folk, rock, traditional music, theatre, dance, comedy and the visual arts, from all over the world. Information: Margaret McKee, Festival Office, Queen's University, University Road, tel. 9066 5577 or www.belfastfestival.com. (End of October and first two weeks of November)

BELFAST CITY WALKING TOUR

Duration: 3–4 hours plus stops

Start a tour at the Central Rail Station, **East Bridge Street**. As you depart the front (north) door of the station, straight ahead is the new Laganbank development, a burst of urban renewal along the River Lagan.

In an effort to refocus the city around the beauty of its river, Belfast created the

Lagan Weir in 1993. It has helped to keep the river's water level up, to beautify the waterfront, and to encourage wildlife to return. It has also spurred investment and building on a large scale. The centrepiece along the riverfront is now the striking round-domed façade of **Waterfront Hall**, Oxford Street (tel. 9033 4400), a state-of-the-art concert hall and conference centre with a 2,235-seat main auditorium and many smaller rooms. It is the first purpose-built meeting and performing arts centre of its kind ever built in Northern Ireland, and already it has acted as a magnet for additional waterfront attractions including Lagan Weir and **The Odyssey Centre**.

From **Oxford Street**, take a left turn onto **May Street**. On the left is **St George's Market** (tel. 9032 0202) – this is Belfast's original 'Variety Market', dating back to the nineteenth century. Completely restored in 1999, it is a genuine covered market for fresh fruit, home-baked goods and pastries, preserves, spices, flowers, fish, vegetables, bargain clothing, crafts, CDs and more. Even if you are not buying, it is fun to savour the aromas, listen to the local accents, and see the colourful commodities. Stroll from stall to stall to take it all in, and perhaps snap a few pictures. Open Friday. Admission: free

Continue to head west on May Street. After two blocks, take a left to visit **St Malachy's Church**, 24 Alfred Street (tel. 9032 1713), the most central of Belfast's Catholic churches. Opened in 1842, this is one of the most original Tudor Revival churches in Ireland, with a unique façade of red brick, stone-dressed castellation, and octagonal corner turrets. The interior is even more interesting, designed on a lateral plan with the carved white marble altar on one of the longer walls. The lace-like fan-vaulted ceiling was inspired by Henry VII's chapel at Westminster Abbey. Open daily. Admission: free

Return to May Street and walk half a block east to **Donegall Square**, the focal point of the city-centre area and the setting for **City Hall** (tel. 9027 0456). With its great green 52.7 metre (173-foot) high dome visible for miles, this huge edifice is a vast Renaissance-style structure of Portland stone, modelled after St Paul's Cathedral of London. It opened in 1906, almost 20 years after Queen Victoria had granted Belfast the status of a city. Her statue stands at the front entrance of the palace-like building which was erected as a symbol of the city's wealth and self-confidence. It is also impressive inside, with a décor of Edwardian-style stained glass and marble, ornate plasterwork, and a mural by Belfast artist John Luke, depicting the industries such as ship-building and linen-making that have made the city prosperous. Tours, which last about 45 minutes, require advance reservations. Open Monday–Saturday. Admission: free

From Donegall Square South, take a short detour west along **Howard Street** for two blocks to **Great Victoria Street** and turn left. On the right is the **Grand Opera House** (tel. 9024 1919), an ornate Victorian gem of a building dating back to 1894. The exterior is rich in fanciful turrets and curlicues, while the interior is a panorama of brass rails, gilded balconies and exotic motifs. It is the home of Opera Northern Ireland and has an ever-changing programme of ballet and concerts. Open to the public for performances only, Monday–Saturday.

Still more Victoriana awaits directly across the street at the **Crown Liquor Saloon**, 44 Great Victoria Street (tel. 9027 9901), the veritable benchmark of Belfast pubs. It is such a classic that it is maintained by the National Trust and revered with a museum-like awe by its regular patrons and visitors from near and far (*see* Pubs below).

Retrace your steps back to Donegall Square to visit the **Linen Hall Library**, 17 Donegall Square North (tel. 9032 1707), Belfast's oldest library, founded in 1788 as an independent charitable institution. Now housed in an old linen warehouse, the library was originally across the street at the old White Linen Hall, which was demolished a century ago to make way for the coming of City Hall. This building was designed in a distinctly Edwardian style by Charles Lanyon, a Belfast architect who is cred-

ited with many of the city's finest buildings. The shelves are lined with old and rare books, as well as current volumes. Items of particular note include a Robert Burns collection, an Irish collection of over 20,000 volumes, and a political collection of over 80,000 documents on every aspect of political life in Northern Ireland since 1968. Open Monday–Saturday. Admission: free

Turn left at the Library and left again onto **Donegall Place**. On the left is the Belfast Visitor and Convention Bureau (*see* Travel Information Offices above), which marks the beginning of a pedestrian area, delightful for strolling. It is lined with interesting stores featuring local crafts, including linen shops. After two blocks, Donegall Place becomes **Royal Avenue**, the prime shopping street of Belfast. Take some time to browse. On the left is the **Castlecourt Centre** (tel. 9023 4591), the main city-centre multi-storey enclosed shopping mall.

Take a right onto the **North Street Arcade** and follow it to **North Street**. On the left is the Northern Ireland Tourist Board, another good source of information about Belfast and beyond. Continue for half a block to **Donegall Street**, and turn left. Walk half a block, and straight ahead on the right is **St Anne's Cathedral** (tel. 9032 8332), Belfast's principal Anglican cathedral. It took 86 years to build it completely – from 1899 to 1985 – so it combines several architectural styles, but Irish Romanesque predominates. The interior is dominated by a long and lofty nave, and the baptistry ceiling features a striking mosaic commemorating the landing of St Patrick at Gaul in 432. Open daily. Admission: free

Take a left and walk one block south to **Waring Street**, then turn left. This street displays some of Belfast's distinctive architecture. Take note of the **Ulster Bank** (1860), which looks like a Venetian palace, with sculptured rooftop figures of *Britannia*, flanked by *Justice* and *Commerce*, and a dozen smaller classical figures.

From Waring Street, cross over to **Albert Square**. On the right is the **Albert Memorial Clock Tower**, Belfast's Big Ben, a Gothic Revival landmark erected in 1867–69. Continue east on Albert Square. To the right is the E-shaped **Custom House**, a large mellow yellow edifice, built in 1857 to a design by Charles Lanyon. The front of the building, which faces the River Lagan, features a sculptured pediment with *Britannia*, *Neptune* and *Mercury* gazing out to sea. To the right, stretching over the river, is the Lagan Weir, erected in 1993 to improve the waterfront.

Make your way across the busy thoroughfare of **Donegall Quay** to visit the **Lagan Lookout** (tel. 9031 5444), a visitor centre focusing on the River Lagan and its weir. Using a series of high-tech and hands-on videos, computers, exhibits and illustrations, visitors can explore the industrial, engineering and folk history of the harbour. Huge wrap-around windows look out onto the river and all of its activities. Open daily. Admission: £

Retrace your steps back to the Clock Tower and then take a left onto **High Street**, one of the city's oldest streets. High Street becomes **Castle Place**, as it melds into a pedestrian area. Make a left onto Donegall Place, and straight ahead is Donegall Square. Walk to the east side of the square and board bus number 69, 70 or 71 (or take a taxi) to complete the rest of this tour.

A bus (or taxi) will take you to **Queen's University**, University Road (tel. 9033 5252), Belfast's hub of learning. Established in 1845, the same year as the universities in Cork and Galway, as part of the national system, this college became independent in 1909. Charles Lanyon, who designed so many of Belfast's buildings, was the architect of this red-brick Tudor complex. It is said that the central college building was modelled after Magdalen College in Oxford. The main features here are a Tudor cloister and mullioned windows. Each November, the university hosts a leading musical and arts event open to the public, 'The Belfast Festival at Queen's'. Although most buildings are not open to the public, the visitor centre features various exhibits of interest about the university. Open Monday–Saturday, May–September; and Monday–Friday, October–April. Admission: free

Directly south of the campus is Belfast's star attraction, the **Ulster Museum**, Stranmillis Road (tel. 9038 3000). As the national museum for Northern Ireland, this graceful classical-style four-storey building is a treasure-trove of history, geography, science and culture, reflecting 9,000 years of information and discoveries. Highlights include a section on Ulster with samples of original spinning wheels used in linen-making, currency dating back to the thirteenth century, and watercolours and oil paintings of Belfast's early days. In the antiquities section, you'll find everything from Neolithic tools and gold pieces dating from Ireland's Bronze Age, to an authentic Egyptian mummy named Takabuti. The Botany and Zoology sections display not only specimens of Irish flora and fauna, but exotic rare butterflies and a giant bird-eating spider as well.

Other collections range from contemporary international art (including the Saatchi collection of works by young contemporary artists), to Irish furniture, glass, silver, ceramics and costume. Of special interest is a gold and silver jewellery collection recovered by divers in 1968 from the Armada treasure ship *Girona*, wrecked off the Giant's Causeway in 1588. Allow two to three hours at a minimum to take it all in. A free 'route map' is yours for the asking. Open daily. Admission: free

Directly behind the museum is Belfast's chief horticultural attraction – the **Botanic Gardens**, University Road and Stranmillis Road (tel. 9032 4902). Located between the grounds of the university and the River Lagan, this 11.5-hectare (28-acre) verdant setting was established in 1829 by the Belfast Botanic and Horticultural Society as a place of natural beauty for the local people to enjoy. It has grown ever more beautiful over the years, particularly the rose garden and herbaceous borders sections. The grounds include two buildings that shelter exotic and tender plants. **The Palm House**, designed in 1839 by the ubiquitous Charles Lanyon, is the earliest surviving example of a curvilinear cast-iron glasshouse. Lanyon created the building with the Dublin iron founder Richard Turner, who went on to build the palm houses at Kew Gardens in London and the Botanic Gardens at Glasnevein in Dublin. Restored in 1983, it is well stocked with exotic palms and other delicate plants from around the world. **The Tropical Ravine**, or Fernery, added in 1889, is designed in grand Victorian style, with a sunken glen overlooked by a balcony, to provide a steamy atmosphere for exotic warm-weather ferns and jungle plants such as sugar cane, coffee, cinnamon, banana, aloe, ivory nut, rubber, bamboo and guava. Open daily. Admission: free

Return to Donegall Square in the city centre via bus, taxi, or by strolling the 1.5 km (1 mile) north via University Road to **Shaftsbury Square**, and then via Great Victoria Street, or via Dublin Road and Bedford Street, to complete the tour.

RESTAURANTS

CAYENNE, Ascot House, Shaftsbury Square (tel. 9033 1532). As its name implies this award-winning restaurant has a spicy ambience – with dramatic lighting, hip background music and moving artwork. The menu has a global appeal, using fresh Irish ingredients with Oriental and Mediterranean influences, producing creative and tasty dishes such as seafood risotto, chargrilled squid, salmon with lemongrass, and eel teriyaki. Open for lunch, Monday–Friday; and for dinner, Monday–Saturday.

CAFÉ EQUINOX, 32 Howard Street (tel. 9023 0089). Nestled at the back of a household gift shop, this small eatery is a favourite with shoppers. The menu offers creative sandwiches, pastas and salads, as well as pastries, milkshakes, fresh-baked scones and six different kinds of farmhouse apple juice from local sources. Open for lunch and snacks, Monday–Saturday.

CAFÉ PAUL RANKIN, 27–29 Fountain Street (tel. 9031 5090). Sitting in the heart of the prime shopping area, this continental-style café (a sister operation to the highly-acclaimed Cayenne) offers first-rate soups, pastas, croissants, pastries and other speciality baked goods. A second location is at 12–14 Arthur Street, near Donegall Square North (tel. 0931 0108). Open for breakfast, lunch and snacks, Monday–Saturday; and for dinner, Thursday (late shopping night).

DEANE'S BRASSERIE, 38 Howard Street (tel. 9056 0000). Located behind City Hall, this ground-floor eatery is named after its chef, Michael Deane, a Michelin-star award winner. The décor is ornate and Baroque in style, and the food is simply delicious – a fusion of Irish and international cooking, with dishes such as Thai spiced salmon, ravioli of lobster, roast cod with ratatouille, and a chic fish and chips, as well as a vegetarian menu. Upstairs is a clubby 40-seat dining room known simply as **Restaurant Michael Deane** (tel. 9033 1134), offering gourmet eight-course dining at higher prices. Open for lunch and dinner, Monday–Saturday; upstairs restaurant is open for lunch on Friday, and dinner, Wednesday–Saturday.

FEASTS, 39 Dublin Road (tel. 9033 2887). In a shop-front location south of City Hall, this little gem is aptly named. It is a gourmet deli café, offering the usual sandwiches, soups and salads, as well as speciality dishes using freshly made pasta and farmhouse cheeses. Open for lunch and snacks, Monday–Saturday.

HARD ROCK CAFÉ, The Odyssey Pavilion, 2 Queen's Quay (tel. 9076 6990). For those who are devotees of this brand, this is the first-ever 'Hard Rock' on the island of Ireland. As might be expected, it offers classic American-style burgers, steaks and salads, in an atmosphere of high-energy music, late into the night. For collectors of Hard Rock memorabilia, there is an adjoining retail shop. Open for lunch, snacks and dinner, daily.

NICK'S WAREHOUSE, 35 Hill Street (tel. 9043 9690). Situated near St Anne's Cathedral, this wine bar-cum-restaurant offers trendy cuisine, such as haddie leekie soup, open prawn hoagie, grilled loin of rare-breed pork, spiced squid, and mixed-nut bake, as well as local standards such as steaks, and sausages and mash. Owner Nick Price has transformed an old whiskey warehouse into a relaxing setting, with brick walls, open kitchen, and wrought-iron culinary sculptures. Open for lunch, Monday–Friday; and dinner, Tuesday–Saturday.

PUBS

THE BEATEN DOCKET, 48–52 Great Victoria Street (tel. 9024 2986). Opened in 1985, this is one of Belfast's newest pubs. With a bright brick exterior and glass dome, it presents a modern contrast to its classic Victorian neighbour next door, the Crown Liquor Saloon (*see* below). Step inside and see its attractive mahogany bar with solid brass rail and elephant heads, not to mention bevelled mirrors, stained-glass panels, and a traditional snug. 'Real ale' is a speciality here.

CROWN LIQUOR SALOON, 44 Great Victoria Street (tel. 9027 9901). Maintained by the National Trust, this classic pub is a feast of Victorian décor. Step inside and sit in one of the ten authentic carved-oak snugs on the right, each with its own bell and doors topped by lions or griffons; or take a place along the long bar with inlaid coloured glass and marble trim. Savour your favourite beverage and enjoy the décor of richly coloured tiles, stained and smoked glass, gas lights, bevelled mirrors, wooden arches and red-and-yellow tin ceiling. It's a true taste of 'old Belfast'.

KELLY'S CELLARS, 30 Bank Street (tel. 9032 4835). Dating back to 1720, this pub is one of Belfast's oldest taverns in continuous use, located just half a block from Royal Avenue. It is a classic and unpretentious specimen of the way pubs used to be – with vaulted ceilings, paned windows, arches and alcoves, and walls covered with memorabilia.

MCHUGH'S BAR, 29–31 Queen's Square (tel. 9024 7830), near Albert Clock. By a few years, this place claims to be Belfast's oldest pub, dating back to 1711, as well as the city's oldest building. It was recently refurbished and reopened in 1998, with lots of memorabilia and mementos of the past. Enjoy traditional music entertainment on most evenings.

WHITE'S TAVERN, 2–4 Wine Cellar Entry (tel. 9024 3080), with access off Lombard Street, High Street and Rosemary Street. Located on a cobbled lane, this tavern was established in 1630 as a wine and spirit merchant's shop, and was rebuilt in 1790. Step in, order your favourite beverage, and enjoy the old Belfast ambience amid the brick arches, ornate snugs, old barrels, and framed newspaper clippings dating back at least 200 years.

DIGRESSIONS

CIRCLING THE CITY: See the best of Belfast on board an open-topped or glass-topped double-decker bus. Two companies operate guided sightseeing tours with narrated commentaries covering historic and cultural sights, political murals, gardens and more. Tours depart from Castle Place, corner of Castle Street, daily, May–September. Information: Citybus Tours, (tel. 9045 8484 or www.translink.co.uk); and Belfast City Sightseeing (tel. 9062 6888 or www.city-sightseeing.com).

GUIDED WALKS: Tour the streets of Belfast, led by knowledgeable local guides. Five different themes are explored: '*Titanic* Trail', exploring landmarks from the shipbuilding era; 'The Old Town', tracing the original ramparts of the city and tracking the origins of Belfast with emphasis on the period 1660–85; 'City Centre Walk', strolling through Victorian Belfast; 'Blackstaff Way', meandering in the heart of the city; and 'Bailey's Historical Pub Tour', visiting six of Belfast's historic pubs. Tours operate May/June–September, but dates and times vary. Information: Belfast Welcome Centre (tel. 9268 3665).

RIVER LAGAN CRUISES: See the skyline and main sites of Belfast from the waters of the River Lagan on board the *Joyce*, a 40-seat passenger boat. The route starts at the Lagan Weir and travels along the waterfront to Stranmillis and back. An alternative cruise is also available along the harbour to sites associated with the building of the *Titanic*, including the historic shipyards. Boats depart from piers at the Lagan Lookout, the Royal Mail Building or the Odyssey Centre. Departures run in March–December. Information: Lagan Boat Company, 1 Donegall Quay (tel. 9033 0844 or www.laganboatcompany.com).

SCIENTIFIC ADVENTURES: Looking for a rainy-day detour? Head across the river to the W5 ('Who-what-where-when-why') Museum, with over 100 scientific exhibits. The name says much about its mission – it focuses on the 'who, what, where, when and why' of science, exploring many facets and discoveries, appealing to the curious of all ages. Step inside and encounter different types of experience – from a simulated tornado and a kinetics display of flying tennis balls, to a lie-detector test. Or you can play music on a laser harp, make an animated cartoon, build a racing car, or see yourself in the past with a video delay. W5 is at the Odyssey Centre, a sprawling glass-and-metal complex along the docklands, which also houses shops, bars, restaurants, an ice hockey arena and an IMAX cinema. Open daily. Information: W5 Museum, 2 Queen's Quay (tel. 9046 7700 or www.w5online.co.uk).

TAXI TOURS: Sit comfortably in a London-style black taxi and tour familiar areas of Belfast, as well as parts of the city not seen on conventional tours. One of the most popular routes is the Falls and Shankill Roads sections to see the Peace Wall and the colourful political wall murals that decorate the sides of shops and housing estates. Tours operate daily. Information: Black Taxi Tours (tel. 9064 2264 or www.belfasttours.com).

37: Glens of Antrim Coast

As the home of the Giant's Causeway and Old Bushmills Distillery, the coast of County Antrim probably does not need anything else to draw visitors. But those two popular attractions are only the beginning. On the same route, you can take in all the beauties of the nine Glens of Antrim, plus endless coastal vistas, and an enchanting assortment of colourful harbour towns and seaside villages, not to mention two of Ireland's most impressive castles at Carrickfergus and Dunluce.

How to do it all in one day? Start early.

FAST FACTS

Travel Information Offices

CARRICKFERGUS TOURIST OFFICE, Heritage Plaza, Antrim Street, Carrickfergus (tel. 028 9336 6455). Open all year.

CAUSEWAY COAST AND GLENS TOURIST OFFICE, 11 Lodge Road, Coleraine (tel. 028 7032 7720). Open all year.

BALLYCASTLE TOURIST OFFICE, 7 Mary Street, Ballycastle (tel. 028 2076 2024). Open all year.

GIANT'S CAUSEWAY TOURIST OFFICE, Giant's Causeway, Bushmills (tel. 028 2073 1855). Open all year.

LARNE TOURIST OFFICE, Narrow Gauge Road, Larne (tel. 028 2826 0088). Open all year.

PORTRUSH TOURIST OFFICE, Dunluce Centre, 10 Sandhill Drive, Portrush (tel. 028 7082 3333). Open all year.

TRAVEL INFORMATION ONLINE:
www.discovernorthernireland.com,
www.antrim.net and
www.causewaycoastandglens.com

TELEPHONE AREA CODE
The telephone area code for all of Northern Ireland is 028, or 048 from the Republic. All local numbers have eight digits.

MAJOR EVENTS

WALK THE GLENS – This is a walking festival focusing on the scenic paths of the Antrim and Cushendall glens. Walks range from 3 to 24 km (2 to 15 miles), for experienced and beginner walkers. Information: Maria Lavery, Old School House, 25 Mill Street, Cushendall, tel.

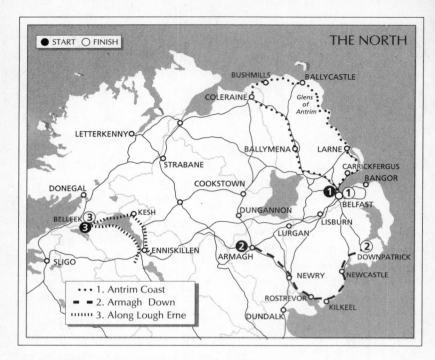

The North map legend:

● START ○ FINISH

THE NORTH

··· 1. Antrim Coast
- - 2. Armagh Down
····· 3. Along Lough Erne

2177 1378 or www.nacn.org/cushendall. (Second weekend of June)

HEART OF THE GLENS FESTIVAL – Held annually in the peak of summer, this community festival features open-air concerts, cultural, social and environ-mental events. Information: Maria Lavery, Old School House, 25 Mill Street, Cushendall, tel. 2177 1378 or www.nacn.org/cushendall. (Second week of August)

OUL' LAMMAS FAIR – Ever since 1606, Ballycastle has been the focal point for this event – acknowledged as Ireland's oldest traditional market fair, with horse-trading, market stalls and street

entertainment. More information: Festival Office, Ballycastle, tel. 2076 2024. (Last week of August)

ANTRIM COAST DRIVING TOUR

Duration: 4–6 hours plus stops

Depart Belfast in a northerly direction on the main M1 road, accessible from most parts of the city, including Donegall Square via Howard Street. Continue north through pleasant residential sections, bearing right to join the A2, with Belfast Lough visible on the right.

Follow the A2 to **Carrickfergus**, almost 19.5 km (12 miles) up the coast. One of the oldest towns in Northern Ireland, it is named after a sixth-century Gaelic king called Fergus. It is said proudly by the locals that Carrickfergus was a thriving town when Belfast was a sandbank. Be that as it may, it was indeed the north's main port until Belfast began to expand in the seventeenth century.

The principal structure of the town is built on an outcrop of basalt rock standing watch over the harbour – **Carrickfergus Castle**, Antrim Street (tel. 9335 1273). Acknowledged as Northern Ireland's largest and best-preserved Norman castle, this massive stone fortress was started in 1180 by John de Courcy, the first Norman lord of Ulster. It has had a long and glorious history and was garrisoned until 1928. The focal point is a much-photographed square keep, 27.5 metres (90-feet) high (five storeys) with 2.5-metre (8-foot) thick walls. Enter through a gate flanked by two round towers. Inside, well-versed guides explain the castle's history, and show off various highlights such as an old castle well and a dungeon. Take time to explore the interior, refurbished and containing many exhibits and a ten-minute audiovisual. In addition, there are opportunities to try your hand at medieval writing, dressing up in armour or taking part in medieval games. In the summer months, the grounds hold medieval fairs, crafts markets and pageants, as well as ever-changing exhibitions and events including archery and military tattoos. Open daily. Admission: £

Continue on the A2 for 13.5 km (8.5 miles), skirting around **Larne**, a busy manufacturing town and seaport, second only to Belfast as a port. It is the closest point to Britain – just about 19.5 km (12 miles) west of Scotland – so there are many super-speed car ferries, huge freight ships and pleasure craft coming and going in the harbour.

Proceed north along the A2. This stretch of road, the 40 km (25 miles) from Larne to Cushendall, was widely recognised as a great engineering feat when it was constructed in the 1830s. The magnificent coast curves around the base of steep headlands, with the Irish Sea on the right and the Glens of Antrim rising on the left. It is one of Ireland's most spectacular drives.

As you travel north of Larne, to the left, in the distance, is **Slemish Mountain** (438 metres/1,437 feet), where St Patrick, captured as a boy and brought to Ireland, is said to have been a shepherd. Next on the left, after 6.5 km (4 miles), is **Ballygalley Head**, rising to 300 feet and offering panoramic coastal views of Ballygalley Harbour.

Within 8 km (5 miles), on the left, the road begins to reveal the verdant panoramas of the **Glens of Antrim**, nine lovely valleys, formed 20,000 years ago by retreating glaciers. Each glen has an individual name, based on the original Gaelic language or on local legends and lore. Although not all of the meanings are absolutely known for certain, the popular translations are as follows:

Glenarm, from the Irish *Gleann Arma*, meaning 'glen of the army'. It is thought to refer to some battle or military gathering that might have taken place here, which is highly likely since the glen was the home of the Irish MacDonnell clan for many centuries. This glen is deemed to have been the first and oldest of the glens.

Glencloy, from the Irish *Gleann Claidhe*, meaning the 'glen of the fences', thought to imply a stone fence, or possible 'glen of the hedges'. This glen is dotted with a lattice of stone barriers, interspersed with streams and waterfalls.

Glenariff, from the Irish *Gleann Aireamh*, meaning 'glen of the arable land' or 'ploughman's glen'. It is a lovely blend of farms and waterfalls, once described by William Makepeace Thackeray as 'Switzerland in miniature'. At the foot of Glenariff is **Red Bay**, which takes its name from its sloping red sandstone cliffs.

Glenballyeamon, from the Irish *Gleann Bhaile Éamainn*, meaning 'glen of Éamainn's homestead' or, to be more Anglicised, 'glen of Edward's homestead'. This glen is said to be the barest of all, with traces of ancient forts throughout the countryside.

Glenaan, from the Irish *An Gleann*, meaning 'the valley' or 'glen of the rush lights'. This glen is famed as the location of the grave of the legendary Oisín, a poet warrior of the third century, who was said to have been the son of the mythological Irish hero, Fionn Mac Cumhail.

Glencorp, thought to mean 'glen of the slaughter', but probably based on legend more than language. It is known today for its lovely hill farms and white-clad slopes.

Glendun from the Irish *Gleann Duinne*, meaning 'valley of the river Dunn' or, traditionally, 'the brown glen'. The most characteristic feature today is its wealth of bridges and fords over the river.

Glenshesk, from the Irish *Glean Seisc*, meaning 'glen of the sedges'. This glen is deemed the wildest and most unspoiled of all.

Glentaisie, traditionally taken to mean 'Taisie's glen'. The overall characteristic of this glen is that it is neat and tidy.

Many of the people who live here are descended from the ancient Irish and their Hebridean cousins, the Scots, and this area is one of the last places in Northern Ireland where Gaelic is still a spoken language.

As you drive from one glen to another, you'll see that the geological variety of the glens provides an ever-changing pattern of scenery, so that each glen has its own particular profile and personality, while the whole area has a unity seldom found in nature.

Better than any guide, the glens speak for themselves in a language of lush natural beauty and wide open vistas. There are also several towns to look out for and to explore. Between Glencloy and Glenariff is **Carnlough**, an old limestone quarry town with a sandy bay and picturesque harbour with an enticing ivy-clad old-world inn dating back to 1848. Known as **The Londonderry Arms**, it was once owned by Winston Churchill (*see* Restaurants below).

Near the foot of Glenballyeamon is **Cushendall**, a quiet resort village whose streets are lined with stately Georgian and Regency houses. It takes its name from the River Dall which runs through it. In the village centre is a curious structure called **Curfew Tower**, built as a jail in 1809.

Just under 5 km (3 miles) to the north is **Cushendun**, sitting on the shore where Glendun and Glencorp sweep together towards the sea. It is one of the most picturesque villages in all of Ireland, and certainly one of the smallest, with a population of only 50. Almost everyone stops to take a picture of its lovely Cornish-style whitewashed cottages. The entire village is now maintained by the National Trust.

From Cushendun, you have a choice of taking the coast road via **Torr Head** and **Fair Head**, both looking out toward the Scottish Isle of Mull, or following the main A2 road, to Ballycastle. Either way, it is just over 19 km (12 miles), but your choice should be dictated by timing, weather visibility and interests, as the coastal route will take longer.

Ballycastle, a popular beach resort village, stands at the junction of Glenshesk and Glentaisie, north of Knocklayd Hill (517 metres/1,696 feet). The town is built around **The Diamond**, a central area that was the original setting of the Scottish MacDonnell family castle. Today, the Diamond is surrounded by shops, pubs and other enterprises. Each August it is also the setting for the 'Oul' Lammas Fair', one of the oldest traditional festivals in all of Ireland (*see* Major Events).

Take the coastal road from Ballycastle, B15, heading west for about 19 km (12 miles). After passing **White Park Bay** on the right, all signs lead to the **Giant's Causeway**, Causeway Head (tel. 2073 2143). Extending for almost 5 km (3 miles) along the coast, this unique natural rock formation is undoubtedly Northern Ireland's most photographed attraction. Often called the eighth wonder of the world and listed on the UNESCO World Heritage List of sites, it consists of more than 37,000 tightly packed basalt columns, almost like stone steps. The tops of the stones begin at the foot of the coastal cliffs and reach into the sea, disappearing under the water. Most of the stones are six-sided in shape and vary in size, with some as tall as 12 metres (40 feet). They were formed by quick cooling and shrinking lava that burst to the earth's surface about 70 million years ago, according to geologists, but local lore has a different view. It is believed that Fionn Mac Cumhail, a legendary Irish giant, put the stones in place as a causeway or highway across the sea to Scotland – hence the name, 'Giant's Causeway'. No matter what explanation you accept, it is a one-of-a-kind site, not duplicated anywhere else in Ireland.

Start a tour by looking at the various exhibits and displays in the visitor centre, maintained by the National Trust. The 25-minute audiovisual provides a thorough overview on the history and geology of the area. Then step outside and explore the rocks for yourself. You can walk down a graded pathway, which takes about half an hour, but the walk back up the hill can be strenuous and take even longer. The best plan is to buy a round-trip fare on the minibus which departs every fifteen minutes from the back door of the centre. This ride down takes less than five minutes, and once you are at the site, you can stay as long as you wish, taking the minibus of your choice back up the hill, on a first-come basis. It is breezy and open at the site, so dress warmly, and bring rain gear in case of a sudden shower. If you want to do some climbing on the rocks, wear appropriate footwear. Once you are down at the rock site, there is no place to take shelter until you return to the visitor centre. In spite of these minor cautions,

it is well worth making the trek down to the actual coastline site – a definite 'must see' on a tour of Northern Ireland. Allow about two hours between the visitor centre and the actual site itself. Open daily. Admission: free. Minibus, audio-visual and parking: £

From the causeway, rejoin the A2 road, heading just over 3 km (2 miles) south-west to **Bushmills**, a small town on the River Bush, made famous around the world through its whiskey. Take time to visit the **Old Bushmills Distillery**, Main Street (tel. 2073 1521). Officially licensed in 1608, this landmark distillery is the oldest of its kind in the world. Visitors are welcome to take a walk-through tour of the plant to view the whole process, essentially unchanged over the centuries. Escorted by well-versed guides with informative and amusing commentaries, the tours begin with the barley. You'll see ripe golden Irish barley as it is examined, graded and cleaned. The chosen barley is then poured into tanks of water supplied by the River Bush which runs alongside the distillery. Next the barley is spread out to sprout and become malt. After the malt is dried in a kiln that is kept separate from any smoke or heat, it is stored in great bins to mellow for several weeks. The tour then moves on to the fermenting process, followed by triple distillation, as the whiskey-to-be flows through three consecutive copper-pot stills. The resulting spirits are then placed in oak casks to mature. The final step is the assembly line for bottling, labelling and boxing. The tours, which last about one hour, culminate in the **Potstill Bar**, a pub-style 'tasting room' where guests are invited to sample the results. Open daily, April–October; Monday–Friday, November–March. Admission: £

Return to the A2 road, and about 3 km (2 miles) west is **Dunluce Castle**, Portrush (tel. 2073 1938), another of Northern Ireland's well-photographed castles. Built c.1300, by Richard de Burgh, earl of Ulster, it is a splendid structure sitting on basalt rock jutting out over the sea, reached by a wooden walkway. Like most castles, it has an interesting history. It was captured by the Irish MacDonnells, chiefs of Antrim, in 1584 and remained their base of power for many years. In 1639, the kitchen fell off into the sea, along with several domestic staff. That unfortunate incident signalled the demise of the castle, and it declined into ruin shortly afterwards. A curtain wall and two towers are still in remarkable shape, as is a gatehouse. Open daily, April–September; Tuesday–Sunday, October and March; Tuesday–Saturday, November–February. Admission: £

It is just under 5 km (3 miles) west to **Portrush**, a popular seaside resort and home of the world-class Royal Portrush Golf Club. If time allows, take a stroll on the beach or visit **Dunluce Centre**, 10 Sandhill Drive (tel. 7082 4444), a visitor centre that is geared toward families, with multimedia shows and thrill rides. For adults, it is a good comfort stop, with a Victorian-style arcade of shops and restaurants. It also has a viewing tower, offering panoramic views of the whole northern coast. Open daily, June–August; Saturday–Sunday, April, May and September. Admission to the centre is free but there are fees for rides and activities.

At this point, the day must draw to a close. Follow signs south towards Coleraine and take the ring-road leading to the A26 towards Ballymena, and then link up with the M2 main road into Belfast, or continue on to Derry or another destination.

PAT'S PICKS

RESTAURANTS

BUSHMILLS INN, 9 Dunluce Road, Bushmills (tel. 2073 2339). Dating back to the seventeenth century, this inn is a popular spot for a snack or full meal, within walking distance of the famous distillery. Relax amid an old-world décor of open fireplaces, gas lamps, antiques and a circular library. The bar food ranges from creative salads to hearty soups and sandwiches, while the main dining room offers specialities such as peppered beef fillet flamed in Bushmills whiskey and cream, or local River Bush salmon. Open for lunch (in bar) and dinner (in restaurant), daily.

HARBOUR LIGHTS, 11 Harbour Road, Carnlough (tel. 2888 5950). For lunch or just a cup of coffee or tea and a freshly baked scone, this is a good stop along the scenic Glens of Antrim drive. Situated on the second floor of a harbour-front building overlooking both the town and the sea, this charming café offers views to match the excellent home-baked food. Open daily, July and August; Friday–Sunday, September–March; Wednesday–Sunday, April–June.

LONDONDERRY ARMS, 20 Harbour Road, Carnlough (tel. 2888 5255). Dating back to 1848 and once in the hands of Winston Churchill who inherited it, this historic ivy-clad inn is hard to pass by. It overlooks the harbour, at the foot of Glencloy. Bar food ranges from soups and sandwiches to a ploughman's platter of local cheeses, while full meals focus on traditional dishes such as roast chicken and bacon, or rib of beef with horseradish sauce, or salmon from nearby waters. Open for snacks and dinner, daily; and lunch on Sunday.

RAMORE, Ramore Street, Portrush (tel. 7082 4313). Overlooking the harbour of a popular seaside resort, this modern bistro offers international fast-food cuisine prepared in an open kitchen, with gourmet flair. House specialities range from jumbo prawn salad to chilli steak, tortilla chips and dips, or pastas and vegetarian dishes. Open for lunch and dinner, daily.

THE VICTORIANA, Dunluce Centre, 10 Sandhill Drive, Portrush (tel. 7082 4444.). Located in a busy and conveniently located visitor centre near the beach, this self-service restaurant on two levels offers light meals all day in a Victorian setting. Specialities include North of Ireland favourites such as Ulster fry, steak and onion pie, and sausage rolls, as well as beef or chicken burgers, baked potatoes with a choice of fillings, and home-baked pastries, croissants, biscuits and scones. Open for lunch and snacks, daily, May–September.

WYSNERS, 16–18 Ann Street, Ballycastle (tel. 2076 2372). This small family-run restaurant is known for dishes featuring fresh local ingredients such as North Atlantic salmon caught in the waters off Carrick-a-Rede, or Bushmills malt cheesecake. Lunch and snacks are served in a downstairs café, and full dinners in an upstairs dining room. Open Monday–Saturday.

PUBS

THE HOUSE OF MCDONNELL, 71 Castle Street, Ballycastle (tel. 2076 2975). In this land of the McDonnell clan, it is not surprising to find this aptly named local landmark. Opened in 1766 as a grocery shop with bar, this classic pub has been in the same family since its first day. Step inside and enjoy the vintage décor – mahogany bar, tiled floor and photographs of yesteryear. Traditional music is on tap every Friday evening.

SWEENEY'S PUBLIC HOUSE, 6B Seapoint Avenue, Portballintrae, Bushmills (tel. 2073 2405). For a drink with a view, head to this old stone building, converted from a seventeenth-century stable. It offers sweeping panoramas of the sea from its wide conservatory windows. Bar-food snacks (with emphasis on local seafood) are available all day and evening. On Friday and Saturday nights, there is live folk or country music.

MCCOLLAM'S PUBLIC HOUSE (JOHNNY JOE'S), 23 Mill Street, Cushendall (tel. 2177 1992). Originally a coaching inn, this vintage pub has been in the same family for the past four generations. The layout is reminiscent of a typical house that evolved into a pub – with a big old range in the kitchen and an open fire in the parlour. It has long been a favourite for local farmers attending the sheep sales, and many a good deal has been struck under this roof.

DIGRESSIONS

CIRCLING THE COAST: For those who prefer to let someone else do the driving, Ulsterbus operates narrated sightseeing tours of the Antrim Coast and Giant's Causeway from Belfast, late June–September. Or you can opt for a 'Bushmills Open Topper' public bus from Coleraine, stopping along the coast at Portstewart, Portrush, Portballintrae, Bushmills and the Giant's Causeway, July–August. Information: Ulsterbus (tel. 7032 5400 or www.translink.co.uk).

CROSSING THE OLD (ROPE) BRIDGE: Feel like a bit of exercise in the great outdoors? Take the coastal road, B15, between Ballycastle and the Giant's Causeway, and follow signs for the Carrick-a-Rede Rope Bridge, a swaying 19-metre (63-foot) wooden-plank bridge with a wire handrail, positioned over 24 metres (80 feet) above the sea, spanning an open chasm between the mainland and Carrick-a-Rede Island. Each spring fishermen put up the bridge to give them access to a salmon fishery on the island, but the general public is welcome to use the bridge, just for the thrill of it. Access is from Larrybane car park, where there is a visitor centre operated by the National Trust. After parking your car, you'll have to walk 1.5 km (1 mile) (about 15–20 minutes) along a cliff path to get to the bridge. Bridge open, early spring–mid-September in daylight; visitor centre open daily, June–August; Saturday–Sunday, May. Information: National Trust (tel. 2073 1159 or www.nationaltrust.org.uk).

ISLAND HOPPING: Less than 10 km (6 miles) off the Antrim coast sits Rathlin Island (population: 100), almost 13 km (8 miles) long and less than 1.5 km (1 mile) wide, and just under 26 km (16 miles) from the Mull of Kintyre in Scotland. Said to have been the first place in Ireland attacked by Vikings (in 795AD), the island is shaped like a boot and surrounded by limestone and basalt sea cliffs reaching 143 metres (470 feet) in places. It is also a haven for sea birds. Ferries depart Ballycastle daily for the island, with more frequent sailings in June–September. Travel time is approximately 45 minutes. Information: Caledonian MacBrayne Ferries, 14 Bayview Road, Ballycastle (tel. 2076 9299 or www.calmac.co.uk).

VINTAGE RAIL TRIPS: For a nostalgic train trip, climb aboard the recently restored Giant's Causeway and Bushmills Railway. This narrow-gauge train follows part of the original rail route travelled in 1883–1949 by the 'Causeway Tram', the world's first hydroelectric railway. The equipment includes two steam locomotives – *Shane* (1949) and *Tyrone* (1904) – plus a diesel engine (*Rory*). The route passes beside a scenic valley, seashore, coastline, woodlands and the River Bush. Trains operate daily, April–October; and some weekends, November–March. Information: Giant's Causeway and Bushmills Railway, Giant's Causeway Station, Runkerry Road, Bushmills (tel. 2073 2844 or www.giantscausewayrailway.org).

38: Armagh and Down – St Patrick's Country

Who has not heard of St Patrick? Each year, on 17 March, people all over the western world mark St Patrick's Day in some way, whether it be by marching in parades, wearing little green shamrocks, singing Irish songs or drinking green beer. No other European saint, except perhaps St Nicholas, has such wide recognition.

Although no one knows exactly where or when Patrick was born, most people agree that he was one of Ireland's most frequent travellers between 432 and 461, the years when he went about spreading Christianity to every city and town, mountain and hillside, nook and cranny of the country.

It is certainly impossible to come to Ireland without hearing of Patrick. Although churches, shrines, monasteries and holy wells of various sizes and types are attributed to Patrick all over the Emerald Isle, nowhere are there more Patrick connections than in Armagh, the main city of County Armagh, about 64 km (40 miles) southwest of Belfast.

Of all the high and mighty spots of Ireland, Patrick chose Armagh as his base from which to spread the new religion of Christianity, probably c.445. He began his mission by asking the local chieftain, Daire, for permission to build a church. At first, Daire gave him a site near the base of the hill, but later when the chieftain saw how well the evangelist was doing, he gave Patrick a hilltop, and Patrick built a great church, later to become known as St Patrick's Cathedral. It was henceforth considered as his principal church and bishopric.

As history shows, Patrick's foundation was only the beginning. Many other churches, schools and colleges grew up around the original site as the settlement developed into one of the greatest-known centres of religion and learning during the Dark Ages. By the eighth century, Armagh was generally accepted as the ecclesiastical capital of Ireland, surpassing Cashel, Clonmacnoise and all others. In c.807, the great Book of

Armagh was written by Ferdomnach, a scribe at the School of Armagh. That treasured manuscript, like the Book of Kells, is now on display in Dublin's Trinity College.

Unfortunately, in the middle of the ninth century, this 'city of saints and scholars' experienced unwelcome raids and plundering by the Vikings. With its reputation of learning and wealth, Armagh proved an irresistible target, with at least ten attacks recorded between 831 and 1013. The power of the Vikings was finally broken at Clontarf in 1014 by the Irish high king, Brian Ború, who perished in that battle. Brian's dying wish was to be buried in Armagh at St Patrick's original church site, and the burial of the high king at Armagh magnified the importance of the city even more. In 1152, the Synod of Kells bestowed on the archbishop of Armagh the title of Primate of All Ireland, an epithet that is still used today.

Like the rest of Ireland, Armagh endured raids and conquests by the Normans and English forces from medieval times onwards. It did not begin to recover until the eighteenth century when it was rebuilt in a largely Georgian style, thanks to a resident primate, Archbishop Robinson. He employed Thomas Cooley and Francis Johnston, two architects responsible for some of Ireland's finest Georgian buildings including those in Dublin, both of whom created a legacy of beautiful streetscapes and terraces in Armagh.

Even with Georgian enhancements, the focal point of Armagh today remains the site of the fifth-century church. A house of God has stood on the hill since Patrick's time, over fifteen centuries, and Armagh is still the ecclesiastical capital of Ireland. Today, however, there are two St Patrick's cathedrals – the original site which now belongs to the Church of Ireland (Anglican) and a Catholic edifice, less than half-a-mile away.

The city of Armagh offers a number of attractions that help to illuminate the story of Patrick. But the story does not end here. From Armagh, it is an easy drive eastward to County Down and a region known as St Patrick's Vale – a beautiful area of countryside that also embraced the saint. This area is the place where he completed his ministry. St Patrick was laid to rest in the cemetery of Downpatrick Cathedral in the shadow of the Mourne Mountains.

(See map p.352)

FAST FACTS

Travel Information Offices

ARMAGH TOURIST INFORMATION CENTRE, 40 English Street, Armagh, Co. Armagh (tel. 028 3752 1800). Open all year.

DOWNPATRICK TOURIST INFORMATION CENTRE, St Patrick Centre, 53a Market Street, Downpatrick, Co. Down (tel. 028 4461 2233). Open all year.

NEWCASTLE TOURIST INFORMATION CENTRE, 10–14 Central Promenade, Newcastle, Co. Down (tel. 028 4372 2222). Open all year.

TRAVEL INFORMATION ONLINE:
www.discovernorthernireland.com, www.armagh.gov.uk/tourism and www.kingdomsofdown.com

TELEPHONE AREA CODE:
The telephone area code for all of Northern Ireland is 028, or 048 from the Republic. All local numbers have eight digits.

MAJOR EVENTS

APPLE BLOSSOM FESTIVAL – With events in Armagh city and other towns, this is a county-wide celebration of the local orchards in full bloom, with music, exhibits, and apple craft workshops. Information: Armagh Tourist Information Centre, 40 English Street, Armagh, tel. 3652 1800. (May)

ULSTER DERBY – Run at Down Royal Racecourse for more than 40 years, this is Northern Ireland's richest flat race, comparable to the Irish Derby at the Curragh of Kildare. This course also hosts the Northern Ireland Festival of Racing on the first weekend of November. Information: Down Royal Racecourse, Maze, Lisburn, Co. Down, tel. 9262 1258 or www.downroyal.com. (Third weekend of June)

ALL-IRELAND BUSKING COMPETITION – A small village 5 km (3 miles) north of Newcastle is the setting for this annual two-day competition, drawing street entertainers from all over Ireland – singers, musicians, clowns, fire eaters, bed-of-nails artists, portrait artists and pavement artists. Information: Patrick Burns, Festival Office, 89 Decourcey Way, Dundrum, Co. Down, tel. 4375 1412 or www.dundrumfestival.com. (Middle weekend of August)

ARMAGH AND DOWN – ST PATRICK'S COUNTRY WALKING AND DRIVING TOUR

Duration: 3–5 hours plus stops

The best way to do this tour is in two parts. Drive to Armagh, and then spend the morning touring the sights of the city, primarily on foot. Park your car at the parking area next to the tourist office and walk around the town. In the afternoon, return to your car to drive the scenic route through St Patrick's Vale in County Down.

As you arrive in Armagh, follow the signs for the Tourist Information Office at 40 English Street, and park your car in the adjacent car park. From here, make a sharp right turn to start a tour where St Patrick started, the focal point of Armagh – **St Patrick's Church of Ireland Cathedral**, Cathedral Close, off Abbey Street (tel. 3752 3142). Set on high ground, this is the site on which Patrick built his principal church and headquarters c.445. Although little is left of the original structure, there has been a house of worship in Patrick's name here for over 1,500 years. Today, rebuilt at least seventeen times, it melds a mixture of architecture, with a rich variety of carved heads forming a frieze around the exterior. The predominant structure is from an 1834 restoration of a thirteenth-century church. Highlights include an old medieval stairway in the south transept; sections of an eleventh-century Celtic Cross; an ancient granite figure known as the **Tandragee Idol**, an Irish warrior believed to date back to Celtic times; and a baptismal font that is a copy of a curiously carved octagonal stone font found in 1805, 2 metres (7 feet) underground near the west door of the cathedral. Most visitors head straight to the north transept where a tablet on the west wall marks the **Grave of BrianBorú**, Ireland's great high king of the tenth and eleventh centuries. Open daily. Admission: free

To get an overview of the city of Armagh and its other connections with St Patrick, return to the tourist office and walk through for access into **St Patrick's Trian**, 40 English Street (tel. 3752 1801).

Who was St Patrick? Where did he come from? What did he do? How and why did he make Armagh his headquarters? These and many other questions about the 'Apostle of the Irish' are answered in this impressive three-part heritage centre. Start with a walk-through tour of **The Armagh Story**, an interpretative area that relates the history of the city even before St Patrick, in prehistoric and Celtic times. The focus then shifts to Patrick and his life and times in Armagh, followed by the Viking and Georgian eras. From here, enter an audio-visual theatre to see the 20-minute film, *Belief*, which profiles the many types of beliefs held by humanity. The final segment, a particular favourite with children, is **The Land of Lilliput**, a hands-on exploration of Jonathan Swift's world as outlined in his book, *Gulliver's Travels*, which was partly written in Armagh. The centre also includes art galleries, craft shops and a permanent display on the Book of Armagh, a biblical manuscript written in 807 by the Irish scribe Ferdomnach. Open daily. Admission: £

From here, take a left onto **English Street** and then a right on **College Street**. This will bring you to **The Mall**, Armagh's tree-lined Georgian centrepiece. This area, originally a race course, was also used for bull-baiting, cockfighting and other sports, as well as a common grazing land. In 1773, these pursuits ceased, and this grassy area evolved into its present state. The star feature of the Mall is the Georgian architecture of the buildings that line either side. The townhouses and terraces are ranked as the finest Georgian work in Northern Ireland. Here you can also visit the **Armagh County Museum**, The Mall East, Armagh (tel. 3752 3070), for an in-depth look at the natural and social history of Armagh. Originally built, in 1833, as a national school, this museum also has an art gallery and extensive map collection. Open Monday–Saturday. Admission: free

Return to English Street, and walk one block north to **Cathedral Road**. To the left is **The Shambles Market** (tel. 3752 8192), a local market area topped by an elegant cupola clock tower. Built in 1827, the Shambles still hosts a market with an average of 35 traders dealing in clothing, fruit, vegetables, flowers, household fabrics, music, tools and more. Open Tuesday and Friday, with car-boot sales on Saturday. Admission: free

Straight ahead is a steep climb up another hill to the **Roman Catholic Cathedral of St Patrick**, Cathedral Road (tel. 3752 2802), the 'other' and much younger Patrician namesake which was built a little over a century ago (1840–73). Perched high above the rest of the city, this Byzantine-style building, with two loft spires and a carillon of 39 bells, is in complete architectural contrast to the 'original' cathedral. The interior is rich in lavish colouring, mosaics, and carvings. The pale blue ceiling and walls are painted and etched with the image of every Irish saint and a multitude of angels. Panoramic city views from the top of the cathedral's front steps are alone worth the trip to this site. Open daily. Admission: free

If you have not already retrieved your car for the trip up Cathedral Road, do so

now, and depart the city-centre area, heading to the south end of the city to visit the **Palace Stables**, Friary Road (tel. 3752 9629). Although this site has little to do with St Patrick, it does offer some enjoyable 'hands-on' insight into Armagh as an ecclesiastical capital. This living-history museum – a former stable on the grounds of a bishop's residential palace – surrounds a cobbled courtyard, recreating an eighteenth-century ambience. Built by Archbishop Robinson when he came to Armagh in 1765, the palace itself today comprises the offices of the Armagh District Council. The interior of the stables hosts a walk-through tour of life in Armagh in 1776, using a 'day in the life' format, with life-like figures in period dress, an audio commentary and colourful murals. The tour also takes you into the **Primate's Chapel**, completed in 1786, one of the finest examples of Georgian neo-classicism in Ireland; as well as the coachman's house, tack room, servants' tunnel and ice house. Open daily. Admission: £

From this point, travel southeast via the A28 to County Down. It's just 19 km (18 miles) to **Newry**, a busy manufacturing and mercantile town with a lovely setting in the centre of a mountainous region divided in two parts by **Carlingford Lough**, a long arm of the Irish Sea. Mountains are visible from both sides of the town. On the west is **Slieve Gullion** (579 metres/1,900 feet), and on the east are the legendary **Mountains of Mourne**, immortalised in the Percy French song of the same name.

From Newry, follow the A2 road for the scenic drive beside the Mourne Mountains, a 40-km (25-mile) sweep along the coast of Carlingford Lough. To the left, fifteen summits rise to over 609 metres (2,000 feet), providing an ever-changing panorama in every mile. This is the start of the area known as **St Patrick's Vale**.

This splendid drive along the A2 passes through a series of delightful seaport and fishing towns, including **Rostrevor**, the most sheltered place in Northern Ireland, known for the Mediterranean plants that grow by the seashore; **Warrenpoint**, with a lively waterfront and yacht marina; and **Kilkeel**, a fishing port specialising in prawns and herrings.

The drive culminates at **Newcastle**, a nineteenth-century Victorian seaside resort, with the Mourne Mountains on one side and the Irish Sea on the other. It is here that **Slieve Donard** (852 metres/2,796 feet), the highest mountain in the Mourne range and the highest peak in Northern Ireland, 'sweeps down to the sea'. Nearby is the **Royal County Down Golf Course**, one of the top-rated golf courses in the world.

The temptation is to linger, but the final chapter on St Patrick still awaits. Take the A24 road 16 km (10 miles) north to **Downpatrick**. The place name is derived from the Irish *Dún Pádraig*, meaning 'St Patrick's fort'. The focal point of the town is **Downpatrick Cathedral** on the **Hill of Down**, off the Mall, a place of Christian prayer and worship since the time of St Patrick. Successive churches have been built, replaced and restored on this site, culminating in the present building. In the twelfth century, relics of St Patrick were discovered here, giving rise to the belief that the intrepid saint must have spent a lot of time here, after Armagh. As evidence for the theory, a slab of rock engraved simply with one word, *Pádraig*, sits in the cathedral graveyard.

The adjacent modern building puts a modern focus on the life of Ireland's favourite saint. The **Saint Patrick Centre**, Market Street (tel. 4461 9000) invites visitors to cross over a 'time bridge' to the fifth century to follow the story of Patrick in his own words, with a little help from state-of-the-art sound and visual-art technology – including word walls, sculptures, recorded readings from Patrick's own writings, and interactive computer exhibits. The tour ends with an enlightening multimedia presentation on a 180-degree-shaped screen, with voices from past and present analysing the many aspects of Patrick. Open daily. Admission: £

From Downpatrick, it is just over 32 km (20 miles) back to Belfast via the A7 road. Alternatively, you can continue on to other destinations in County Down or beyond.

RESTAURANTS

In the heart of apple-orchard country, Armagh is noted for dishes such as potato apple bread and apple pudding. County Down, on the edge of the sea, is a seafood haven, with local specialities such as Strangford oysters, and Kilkeel herring and prawns.

CHARLEMONT ARMS, 63–65 Lower English Street, Armagh (tel. 3752 2028). An eighteenth-century atmosphere prevails at this long-established inn. Bar snacks, available all day, feature local favourites such as minced-steak pie, steak and kidney pie, stuffed bacon rolls and chips, and Irish stew, as well as burgers and sandwiches. More formal dining is available at night. Open for lunch and dinner, daily.

HESTER'S PLACE, 12 English Street, Armagh (tel. 3752 2374). Situated in the heart of town, this daytime café is near the tourist office. Specialities range from home-baked scones to Irish stew, bacon and cabbage, and (a local favourite) Armagh apple tart and cream. Open for breakfast, lunch and snacks, Monday–Saturday.

PILGRIM'S TABLE CONSERVATORY RESTAURANT, 40 English Street, Armagh (tel. 3752 1814). Housed within the St Patrick's Trian complex, this restaurant offers indoor and outdoor seating overlooking the city and its cathedrals. The self-service menu offers an ever-changing array of fresh salads, soups, casseroles, sandwiches and tempting pastries. Open for lunch and snacks, Monday–Saturday, and on Sunday afternoon.

SEA SALT BISTRO, 51 Central Promenade, Newcastle, Co. Down (tel. 4372 5027). As its name suggests, this resort restaurant sits facing the water on a sea-front terrace. The eclectic menu ranges from gourmet sandwiches and chowders to local seafood, such as Ardglass crab and Dundrum Bay mussels, as well as steaks and vegetarian dishes. Open for lunch, daily, and dinner, Wednesday–Sunday in June–September; and for lunch, Tuesday–Sunday, and dinner, Wednesday–Sunday in October–May.

PUBS

THE OLD COMMERCIAL, 2 Kildare Street, Ardglass, Co. Down (tel. 3968 41236). Located in a village known for its herring fishing, this pub dates back to the 1800s. Consequently, it has a comfortable nautical ambience with a low-beamed ceiling, granite fireplace, vintage whiskey barrels and, in the middle of the floor, an old well with a glass cover. Thanks to the present owner who was a master mariner in the merchant navy, it also has antiques from around the world.

DUFFERIN ARMS COACHING INN, 35 High Street, Killyleagh, Co. Down (tel. 4482 8229). Dating back over 200 years, this old inn offers a choice of different rooms and alcoves, including an old traditional public bar and a cellar bar which has a 15-metre (50-foot) stable bar, stone-flagged floors, and pitch-pine ceiling. Music is played most weekends, ranging from jazz, Cajun, Irish traditional and blues, to Russian gypsy, and there are occasional impromptu traditional sessions midweek. It sits about 8 km (5 miles) north of Downpatrick on Strangford Lough.

PERCY FRENCH, Downs Road, Newcastle, Co. Down (tel. 4372 4830). An old-world atmosphere prevails at this seaside pub, named after the famous songwriter who composed the signature tune in praise of the Mountains of Mourne, which 'sweep down to the sea' outside. It is a favourite gathering spot for golfers after eighteen holes at the adjacent Royal County Down Golf Links.

DIGRESSIONS

LEARN ABOUT LINEN: The linen industry, long synonymous with Northern Ireland, is the focus at the Irish Linen Centre, a museum occupying a restored seventeenth-century market building in Lisburn, a prosperous town about 32 km (20 miles) northwest of Downpatrick or 40 km (25 miles) northeast of Armagh.

Take a tour and trace the production of linen from the earliest days of the seventeenth century to the high-tech industry of today. There are opportunities to see linen in all its stages of production, from spinning to weaving with hand-looms, and an audiovisual presentation, 'Flax to Fabric'. Open Monday–Saturday, year-round. Information: Irish Linen Centre, Market Square, Lisburn (tel. 9266 3377).

SCENIC PENINSULA: For a scenic lakeside drive, head east of Downpatrick to the Ards Peninsula. This finger of land curls around the eastern shore of Strangford Lough, a 29-km (18-mile) long lake. A place of great natural beauty, the lough is home to more than 100 different species of marine life and fish, as well as being a bird sanctuary and wildlife reserve. Two roads border the peninsula – the A20 (the lough road) and the A2 (the coast road). At the southern tip of the peninsula is Portaferry, a delightful harbour town with an aquarium and seal sanctuary. To reach Portaferry, there is a continuous car-ferry service from Strangford, about 16 km (10 miles) east of Downpatrick. Information: Strangford Ferry (tel. 4488 1637).

STROLL INTO THE PAST: For an educational excursion that works for all ages, detour 40 km (25 miles) north of Downpatrick to the Ulster Folk and Transport Museum. Bringing together many aspects of Ulster's past into a unique outdoor setting, it contains a series of nineteenth-century buildings, all saved from ruin and moved intact from their original sites in various parts of Northern Ireland. Walk among nineteenth-century farmhouses, mills, churches, rural schools, a forge, a bank, a paint shop and more. There are demonstrations of cooking over an open hearth, ploughing the fields, thatching roofs and practising traditional Ulster crafts such as textile-making, quilting, lace-making, printing, spade-making and shoe-making. In addition, there are exhibits on Irish railways and on the *Titanic*, built just 12.5 km (8 miles) away in Belfast Harbour. Open daily. Information: Ulster Folk and Transport Museum, Cultra, Co. Down (tel. 9042 8428 or www.nidex.com/uftm).

TASTY TOUR: Are you hooked on potato crisps (known as chips in the US) as a favourite snack? If so, you'll enjoy a detour about 16 km (10 miles) east of Armagh to the Tayto factory. Step inside the factory, which occupies a 300-year-old castle, and take a tour to see the transformation of potatoes into crispy snacks. Tours, available Monday–Friday, last around 90 minutes and must be prebooked. Information: Tayto (NI) Ltd, Tandragee Castle, Main Street, Tandragee, Co. Armagh (tel. 3884-0249 or www.tayto.com).

39: Derry City

Perched on a hillside overlooking the Foyle Estuary, Derry is one of Ireland's oldest and most beautiful locations, and unequivocally the finest example of a walled city. Yet life has not always been easy here.

Derry, the second largest city of Northern Ireland (population: 90,000) and the unofficial 'capital' of the north-west, has had many faces, both happy and sad. For almost 400 years, it has also had two names. Its original place name, from the Irish *Doire*, meaning 'oak grove', was given by its founder, St Columbcille (also known as Columba), in the sixth century, while the name Londonderry was conferred in 1613 by a group of wealthy English companies collectively known as the Honourable Irish Society.

Not only did the Society rename the city, but its members also built a strong 1.5-km (1-mile) long wall around it and populated it with settlers from Britain. In the turbulent sixteenth and seventeenth centuries, the walled city of Londonderry resisted siege after siege, but never surrendered to a would-be conqueror, earning it the title of 'Maiden City'.

During the eighteenth and nineteenth centuries, Londonderry became the principal point of embarkation for emigrants leaving Ulster for the New World, giving it many lasting links with America. It also grew as a great port, shipbuilding hub, and shirt-manufacturing centre. During the Second World War, the city was one of the major naval bases used by the Allied forces.

In the latter part of the twentieth century, Derry was deeply embroiled in 'the Troubles', almost torn apart as a geographic and political buffer between Northern Ireland and the Republic. The famous walls were closed off and sealed with barbed wire. It became a city divided, as the Unionists (mostly Protestants) gravitated to the east side of the Foyle, to an area known as the Waterside, while the Nationalists (largely Catholics) remained on the west side of the water in an area known as the Bogside.

In spite of age-old animosities, things have brightened in recent years. Mutual agreements have done much to restore harmony and hope to the people. Buildings have been repaired, new attractions and shopping centres have been added to the cityscape, the celebrated walls have opened once again for unlimited pedestrian access, and new hotels have enhanced the city skyline. Tourism attractions in the city have won major awards. The Derry City Council has voted to drop

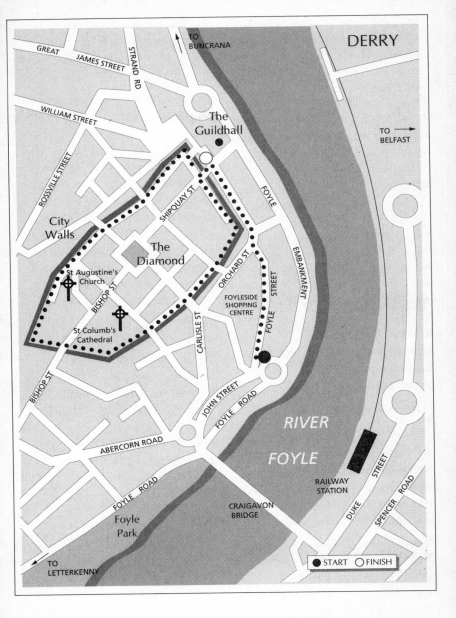

TO BUNCRANA

DERRY

GREAT JAMES STREET

STRAND RD

WILLIAM STREET

The Guildhall

TO BELFAST

ROSSVILLE STREET

City Walls

SHIPQUAY ST

FOYLE

The Diamond

St Augustine's Church

ORCHARD ST

EMBANKMENT

BISHOP ST

St Columb's Cathedral

CARLISLE ST

FOYLESIDE SHOPPING CENTRE

FOYLE STREET

BISHOP ST

JOHN STREET

FOYLE ROAD

RIVER

ABERCORN ROAD

FOYLE

FOYLE ROAD

RAILWAY STATION

DUKE STREET

SPENCER ROAD

Foyle Park

CRAIGAVON BRIDGE

TO LETTERKENNY

● START ○ FINISH

the 'London' from its name. Optimism and enthusiasm have filled the air. And, on the world stage, Derry people have earned much-deserved plaudits, with Nobel Prizes going to poet Seamus Heaney and statesman John Hume.

Derry-born songwriter and musician Phil Coulter has won wide recognition for his song about Derry – 'The Town I Loved So Well'. In many ways, his words have become a new anthem for Derry: '... deep inside (is) a burning pride ... they carry on ... their spirit's been bruised, but never broken ... They will not forget, but their hearts are all set on tomorrow, and peace once again ...'

FAST FACTS

Travel Information Office

DERRY VISITOR AND CONVENTION BUREAU, 44 Foyle Street, Derry (tel. 028 7126 7284). Open all year.

TRAVEL INFORMATION ONLINE:
www.discovernorthernireland.com and www.derryvisitor.com

TELEPHONE AREA CODES:
The telephone area code for all of Northern Ireland is 028, or 048 from the Republic. All local numbers have eight digits.

MAJOR EVENTS

CITY OF DERRY JAZZ FESTIVAL – One of Ireland's top jazz festivals, this four-day programme draws top solo artists, quartets and bands in jazz and blues from Ireland, Europe, the US and beyond. Information: Festival Office, tel. 7137 6545 or www.cityofderryjazzfestival.com. (First weekend of May)

BANKS OF THE FOYLE HALLOWEEN CARNIVAL – Established in 1986, this one-day festival is reputed to be the oldest outdoor Halloween party in Ireland. The focal point is a free street party, drawing at least 30,000 costumed participants from near and far, masquerading (and competing for cash prizes) as ghosts, witches and warlocks. Face-painting, balloon-modelling and music are part of the fun, too. Information: Halloween Carnival Office, tel. 7126 7284 or www.derrycity.gov.uk/halloween. (31 October)

FOYLE FILM FESTIVAL – Since 1987, this cinema event has drawn entries from around the world, converging on Derry for a week of screenings, awards and celebrations. Categories are for best film, best Irish short, best international short, best animated short and best documentary. Information: Festival Office, Nerve Centre, 7–8 Magazine Street, tel. 7126 7432 or www.foylefilmfestival.com. (November)

DERRY CITY WALKING TOUR

Duration: 1–2 hours plus stops

Small and compact, the walled city of Derry, also referred to as the 'Inner City', is ideal for walking, although it is built on a hill and the streets within the walls are steep. Walking 'on the walls' requires climbing steps in the ascent and descent.

Parking within the walled city is difficult and spaces are scarce. The best plan is to park your car at one of the city's many enclosed parking areas, such as the Foyleside Shopping Complex, Foyle Street and Orchard Street, or the Quayside Centre, Strand Road. Both are within easy walking distance of an entrance to the walled city. Once your car is securely parked, set out on foot for touring.

Start a tour on **Foyle Street**, named after the river beside it, the setting for the Derry Visitor and Convention Bureau (*see* above). Directly east, along the water, is **Foyle Quay**, originally known as Derry Quay, from whence the many emigrant ships docked and departed in the nineteenth century.

From Foyle Street, walk one block north to **Shipquay Place**, gateway to the walled city. Before entering through the gate, take a right to visit **The Guildhall**, Guildhall Square (tel. 7137 7335). One of Derry's most significant buildings outside the walls, this richly decorated Tudor-Gothic sandstone structure stands out with mullioned windows and is topped by a four-faced chiming spire clock, one of the largest in Ireland or Britain. The original Guildhall, built in 1890 but badly damaged by fire in 1908, was rebuilt in 1912, only to be bombed in 1972. It was reconstructed in recent years, and now is a civic and cultural centre for Derry. The interior offers a feast of stained-glass windows, each depicting a different segment in the long history of the city. Open Monday–Friday. Admission: free

After visiting the Guildhall, walk straight ahead, between **Shipquay Gate** and **Magazine Gate**, to the **Tower Museum**, Union Hall Place (tel. 7137 2411. This award-winning heritage centre depicts 'The Story of Derry', through a series of exhibits, life-sized figures, holograms, tableaux, audiovisual displays, historical artefacts and re-enactments. Enter through a stone and brick tunnel, one of the original passageways of the city, a legacy of the seventeenth century. The displays bring to life the city's eras of monasticism, Irish chieftains, English Plantation, wall-building, sieges, emigration, ship-building and industry, as well as current social history. The museum takes its name from the adjacent **O'Doherty Tower**, site of a castle built by the O'Doherty family of Ulster in the sixteenth century. The tour ends with the screening of *In Our Lifetime*, a well-documented film chronicling 'the Troubles' of the last 30 years of the twentieth century. Open daily, July–August; Tuesday, September–June. Admission: £

The Tower Museum also provides access to the adjacent complex known as **The Craft Village**, Shipquay Street (tel. 7126 0329), a shopping and entertainment complex that combines retail, workshop and residential units. It is laid out in a format that portrays life in Derry from the sixteenth to the nineteenth centuries, including an authentic thatched cottage that provides informal *Teach Ceoil* (Music House) sessions of music, song and dance regularly throughout the summer. One of the most distinctive features of the village is the individual style of the windows – each window represents a particular period of Irish history and illustrates the various changes that have taken place in design and appearance. Open Monday–Saturday. Admission: free

Delay no further. It's time to 'walk the walls'. From Shipquay Gate, you can climb the steps up to enter **The Walls of Derry**, the city's pride and joy. These 5.5-metre (18-foot) thick walls enclose the entire inner city with a 1.5-km (1-mile) long raised terrace walk, lined with seven arch gates, six bastions and many cannons. The walls provide a great platform for a panoramic view of the entire city – both inside and outside the walls. Built between 1614 and 1619, the walls were made by London stonemasons using earth, lime and local stone, some of which came from ruined medieval monastery buildings, all skilfully constructed as thick defensive ramparts with angular artillery bastions. Despite sieges in 1641, 1649 and 1689, Derry's walls were never breached. Today, Derry is widely recognised not only as Ireland's finest intact walled city, but also as one of the best in Europe.

Originally there were just four entrances (or gates) into the walled city – Bishop's Gate, Shipquay Gate, Ferryquay Gate and Butcher's Gate – arranged in a cross pattern, with the Diamond as its centre. Drawbridges were used to protect some of the gates when under attack. Later additions were New Gate (1789), Castle Gate (1803) and Magazine Gate (1865). Walk the entire circuit on your own or with a guided tour (*see* Digressions below). Open daily. Admission: free

After completing your walk on the walls, take time to explore some of the sights that you have seen from the heights. Return to Shipquay Gate and enter the inner city, heading up **Shipquay Street**, passing the streetside entrance to the Craft Village on the right. On the left is the **Richmond Centre**, a complex of 30 shops, and the largest merchant trading centre of its kind within the inner city. It's a steep walk up a big hill for two blocks, and then you arrive at **The Diamond**, the inner city's hub. Currently occupied by a war memorial statue erected in 1927, this area was the site of Derry's first town hall. The winged centrepiece figure represents *Victory*. Notice that many of the buildings that surround the Diamond are of relatively recent vintage, with eighteenth-century Georgian origins and some nineteenth-century Victorian façades, including **Austin's**, Derry's landmark department store, on the left.

Walk around the Diamond to **Bishop Street**, and then take a left onto **London Street**, and follow the path to **St Columb's Cathedral** (tel. 7126 7313), Derry's ecclesiastical focal point. Built on the highest ground within the walled city, this church is named after Derry's founder, St Columb, also known as Columbcille and Columba (521–597), who built a monastery here in 546. Although he went on to found other monasteries in Ireland and Scotland, this place is synonymous with him. The present Anglican cathedral was the first in Britain or Ireland to have been built after the Reformation, and is a fine example of planters' Gothic. Built by the Irish Society between 1628 and 1633, this edifice houses many interesting relics of Derry's early days, including the locks and keys of the four original city gates, and the bishop's consecration chair of 1633. Open Monday–Saturday. Admission: £

In architectural contrast, just beyond the cathedral is the **Derry Court House**, one of Ireland's best examples of Greek Revival (1813) building.

Retrace your steps to complete the tour. On the return trip, take time to visit each of the city's gates and examine the various styles, arches and stonework.

PAT'S PICKS

RESTAURANTS

BEAN-THERE.COM CAFÉ, 20 The Diamond (tel. 7128 1303). Situated in the centre of the city, this internet café is a haven for gourmet coffees (espresso, cappuccino, café latte) along with fresh-baked pastries, muffins, cakes, pies, scones, bagels and breads. Speciality and 'make-your--own' sandwiches range from prawn cocktail and chicken Caesar salad to vegetarian delight and BLT. Check your e-mail while eating well. Open for lunch and snacks, daily.

BOSTON TEA PARTY, Shipquay Street (tel. 7126 4568). Ensconced in the heart of the Derry Craft Village, this delightful café offers a lot more than tea – soups, salads, sandwiches, sausage rolls, fish and chips, stews and more. Open for lunch and snacks, Monday–Saturday.

LASOSTA RISTORANTE, 45a Carlisle Road (tel. 7137 4817). Since 1995, this Italian restaurant has been a dependable local favourite, located just outside the walls beside Ferryquay Gate. The décor is reminiscent of a homely villa, with open fireplace, tile floors, dark woods and framed posters of Italy. The menu offers a selection of authentic antipasto and pastas, as well as main courses of duck, seafood, beef, chicken and lamb, prepared with traditional sauces and herbs. Open for dinner, Tuesday–Sunday.

THOMPSON'S ON THE RIVER, Queen's Quay (tel. 7136 5800). For a romantic setting with panoramic views of the walled city and the River Foyle, treat yourself to a meal at this wide-windowed restaurant in the new Great

Southern City Hotel. The décor, conveying a nautical ambience, is enhanced by unique art pieces and contemporary furnishings. Menu choices vary with the season, but always include fresh seafood, free-range meats and locally sourced produce. Open for lunch and dinner, daily.

PUBS

ANCHOR BAR, 38 Ferryquay Street (tel. 7136 8601). One of Derry's oldest bars, this themed pub is located inside the city walls beside the Ferryquay Gate. As its name suggests, it has a nautical ambience, with ships' wheels, lanterns, fishing nets, tankards and seafaring murals on the walls. Pub grub is available on weekdays, and traditional music and other entertainment are featured on many nights.

BECKETT'S BAR, 44 Foyle Street (tel. 7136 0066). Nightly entertainment is the major draw to this pub situated close to the Foyleside Shopping Centre. The repertoire ranges from jam sessions and salsa, to Frank Sinatra nights and music of the 1960s, 1970s and 1980s, with a DJ.

THE LINENHALL BAR, 3–5 Market Street (tel. 7137 1665). Situated inside the Derry walls next to Ferryquay Gate, this pub has lots of atmosphere and is a favoured gathering spot for the locals. Sporting events are shown on a big-screen TV, and pub grub is served at lunchtime.

RIVER INN BAR AND CELLARS, 36–38 Shipquay Street (tel. 7137 1965). Dating back to 1684 and claiming to be the oldest pub in Derry city, this place was originally operated as an inn, and the bar was named 'Gluepot' in honour of a London pub. The walls are lined with a collection of wine bottles and local Derry memorabilia, including a map showing the streets of Derry in 1690. Pub grub includes daily lunches and evening meals (Wednesday–Sunday).

DIGRESSIONS

CRUISING ON THE RIVER: See the Derry city skyline from the waters of the River Foyle on a 75-minute boat cruise on board the *Toucan One*. Departures are available from the Cruise Berth on Queen's Quay, daily, May–September; and other times subject to weather and demand. Information: Foyle Cruise Line Ltd, Harbour Museum, Harbour Square (tel. 7136 2857).

POETIC PATH: Follow the footsteps of Nobel Prize-winning poet Seamus Heaney by visiting Bellaghy Bawn, 56 km (35 miles) east of Derry. This literary museum focuses on the works of Heaney, who grew up in Bellaghy and wrote his earliest poetry about the surrounding countryside. A visit starts with the fifteen-minute audiovisual, 'Where Are You Now?', written and narrated by Heaney, with some of his poetry reflecting on his memories of the area. Then wander upstairs through the Heaney Archives and see mounted copies of his works, rare publications, and original manuscripts. Open daily, April–September; Tuesday–Saturday, October–March. Information: Bellaghy Bawn, Castle Street, Bellaghy, Magherafelt (tel. 7968 6812).

STEPPING BACK IN TIME: For insight into the story of emigration from this part of rural Ireland to America in the eighteenth and nineteenth centuries, take an excursion to Omagh, about 48 km (30 miles) south of Derry, to visit the Ulster American Folk Park. This museum comprises authentic reconstructions of the thatched cottages that emigrants left behind, and prototypes of the log cabins that became their new homes in the frontiers of America. Walk-through exhibits include a forge, weaver's cottage, smokehouse, schoolhouse, post office, and typical Ulster and American streets of the time. Open daily. Information: Ulster American Folk Park, 2 Mellon Road, Omagh, Co. Tyrone (tel. 8224 3293 or www.folkpark.com).

WALKING THE WALLS WITH A GUIDE: Learn the history of Derry as you walk around the walls with a local guide. Highlights on the 90-minute route include the original gates of the city, the Guildhall, Tower Museum and St Columb's Cathedral. Tours operate Monday–Friday, departing from the visitor bureau. Information: Derry Visitor and Convention Bureau, 44 Foyle Street, Derry (tel. 7126 7284 or www.derryvisitor.com).

40: Along Lough Erne

Dominating County Fermanagh deep in the southwest corner of Northern Ireland, Lough Erne is a lakeland paradise, stretching for 80.5 km (50 miles), with over 154 islands and countless alcoves and inlets. Silvery-blue waters, lush leafy greenery and unspoiled wooded shorelines are the trademarks of Lough Erne, offering an ever-changing array of scenic views, and easily earning its reputation as 'the Killarney of the North'. Not surprisingly, it is a favourite resort destination for boating fans and fishing enthusiasts.

Although a little off the beaten track for some tourists, Lough Erne is a link between the north and the south. Many tour buses heading from Dublin travel via Lough Erne to reach Donegal.

Unlike some resort areas, the Lough Erne district is a lot more than water and fish. It is the setting for some of Northern Ireland's finest stately homes and castles, as well as one of the best cave networks in Europe. Most of all, this is the home of Belleek, the benchmark of Irish pottery, and a name that ranks with Waterford at the top of its craft.

(See map p.352)

FASTS FACTS

Travel Information Office

FERMANAGH TOURIST INFORMATION Centre, Wellington Road, Enniskillen (tel. 028 6632 3110). Open all year.

TRAVEL INFORMATION ONLINE: www.fermanaghlakelands.com and www.fermanagh-online.com

TELEPHONE AREA CODE: The telephone area code for all of Northern Ireland is 028, or 048 from the Republic. All local numbers have eight digits.

MAJOR EVENTS

JAZZ AND BLUES FESTIVAL – Top jazz bands and groups from Ireland, Europe and the US converge on Enniskillen to play for three evenings at this annual event. Information: Festival Office, Ardhowen Theatre, Dublin Road, Enniskillen, tel. 6632 5440 or www.ardhowentheatre.com. (Early June)

COOLE FEST – This annual music festival presents an array of concerts, all with the scenic backdrop of Castle Coole House and estate. Music includes big bands, tenor solo artists and jazz groups. Information: Festival Office, Castle Coole, Dublin Road, Enniskillen, tel. 6632 2690 or www.nationaltrust.org.uk. (Late June)

LOUGH ERNE DRIVING TOUR

Duration: 2–3 hours plus stops

Geographically, Lough Erne is divided into two parts – Upper and Lower Lough Erne. The 'upper' part is actually the bottom or southern portion of the water, while the 'lower' section is on the northern end. The bottom or 'upper' part of the lough is replete with tiny islands and coves – a haven for watersports. Lower Lough Erne, in contrast, has a more scenic unbroken shoreline, with a couple of easily accessible islands. Lower Lough Erne, 29 km (18 miles) long, is also bordered by a variety of attractions that are open to the public. In the interest of time and reasonable mileage, our daytrip concentrates on Lower Lough Erne.

The ideal place to start this tour is at **Belleek**, a small village on the River Erne whose name in the Irish language is *Béal Leice*, meaning 'ford-mouth of the flagstone'. This curious name originated from the fact that a flat rock in the river bed appeared as a smooth level floor when the water became shallow in summer.

The prime industry of the town is also the region's chief tourist attraction – **Belleek Pottery**, Main Street (tel. 6865 8501). Established in 1857, Belleek is one of the names identified throughout the world as a symbol of ultimate Irish craftsmanship.

Tours are conducted every half-hour, to show visitors how the delicate 'basket weave' creamy-white porcelain china is manufactured, starting with the raw materials – china clay, feldspar, ground flint glass, water and a few other ingredients. These are ground and mixed into a thick substance called 'slip'. After the slip is put through giant sieves, it is poured into moulds that absorb water and shape the pieces into vases, ornaments, tableware and statues. When dry, the shaped pieces are decorated with Irish motifs. The production line also demonstrates how the intricate strands of basketware are woven together, and how tiny petals, stems and twigs are created by hand. Firing is next, followed by rigorous inspection. In addition to the behind-the-scenes tour, there is an audiovisual presentation and a museum that illustrates the history of Belleek, and displays some of the oldest and rarest pieces, including an earthenware collection that dates back to the pottery's earliest days almost 150 years ago. Open daily, April–October; Monday–Friday, November–March. Tours available, Monday–Saturday, June–August; Monday–Friday, September–May. Admission: £

Adjacent to the pottery factory is the **ExplorErne Exhibition**, Erne Gateway Centre (tel. 6865 8866), a heritage centre that tells the story of Lough Erne, from its formation to the present day. Open daily, April–September; Monday–Friday, October–March. Admission: £

From Belleek, commence a drive around Lower Lough Erne. Take the A47 heading east on the northern side of Lower Lough Erne. The road follows a route across a bridge onto **Boa Island**, an 8-km (5-mile) long landmass that has been incorporated into part of the roadway. To the right is a sign for **Caldragh Cemetery**. If time allows, follow the signposts over some uneven grounds to see one of Ireland's oldest stone figures – **Janus**, a human figure with a face on each side. It is thought to date back to pagan times, perhaps the first century.

Continue in an easterly direction for 16 km (10 miles) to **Kesh**, a small town whose name is derived from the Irish *An Cheis*, meaning 'wattle causeway'. It is thought to be a reference to an early bridge crossing over the town stream. From Kesh, make a right and travel for just under 5 km (3 miles) to the Lough Erne shoreline to **Castle Archdale Country Park**, Kesh (tel. 6862 1588), for some close-up views of the lough.

Drive another 8 km (5 miles) along the shore to **Trory Point**, for views of **Devenish Island**, a 28-hectare (70-acre) island that was chosen in the sixth century by St Molaise as the site for a monastery that remained functional until the sixteenth century. The remains are considered today to be the most extensive early and medieval Christian settlement in Northern Ireland. The layout includes a well- preserved 24.5-metre (81-foot) twelfth-century round tower with four

carved heads, a fifteenth-century high cross, an oratory with Romanesque angle pilaster bases, and various other buildings. Ferries to the island operate April–September. For details, contact the Environment and Heritage Service (tel. 9023 5000).

Continue eastward via the B82, with Lough Erne on the left, for almost 5 km (3 miles) to **Enniskillen**, a large lakeside town that is actually an island, separating Lower Lough Erne from Upper Lough Erne. The place name in the Irish language, *Inis Ceithleann*, means 'Cethlenn's island'. According to legend, Cethlenn was a local pirate's wife who owned the island.

Because of its strategic location, Enniskillen was always a place of military importance. It was the stronghold of the Irish Maguire clan in the Middle Ages, and in the seventeenth century it was given to Sir William Cole of England, who built the town as it is today. The British army regiment known as the Iniskilling Fusiliers took its name from Enniskillen where it was raised in 1689 (the regiment is now part of the Irish Rangers).

The centrepiece of the town is **Enniskillen Castle** (tel. 6632 5000), a mighty stone fortress with a long and colourful history, overlooking Lough Erne on the western edge of town. Originally built in the fifteenth century by the Maguire chieftains, it remained their stronghold until passing into English hands in 1594 after an eight-day siege. In 1612, Sir William Cole, who was appointed constable, founded the town and rebuilt the castle. He added the distinctive 'watergate' feature to the outer walls; it is not, in fact, a gate, but a twin turreted tower that is a favourite with photographers today. In the eighteenth century, the castle became an artillery barracks. The interior exhibitions reflect all facets of the castle's history, from the Maguires to its military importance as the one-time home of the Royal Iniskilling Fusiliers and the Fifth Dragoon Guards. Open daily, July–August; Monday–Saturday, May, June and September; Monday–Friday, October–April. Admission: £

Take time to walk the town or take a short 1.5-km (1-mile) detour south of Enniskillen via the A4 road to **Castle Coole** (tel. 6632 2690), a building that has been rated by some experts as the finest classical mansion in Ireland. Erected in 1789–98 for the first earl of Belmore, this stately mansion was designed by James Wyatt in a tranquil setting, overlooking the east bank of Lough Erne. White Portland stone transported from England was used on the exterior, including the magnificent Palladian front. Now in the care of the National Trust, the home is marked by elaborate plasterwork, stucco and carvings. A tour takes in the ground-floor reception and dining rooms, furnished with many original Regency pieces, plus an ornate silk-panelled state bedroom,

servants' tunnel, five of the original stables in the grand yard, and an elaborate private coach in the original coach house. The grounds, which encompass mature oak woodlands, provide a habitat for a rare flock of grey geese, introduced c.1700. Open daily, July–August; Monday and Wednesday–Sunday, June; and Saturday–Sunday, March–May and September. Admission: £

Return to Enniskillen and begin the second lap of the scenic route around Lower Lough Erne via the A46. Before starting out, depending on time, you may wish to make another detour just under 13 km (8 miles) southwest via the A4 and A32 to visit another great house in the care of the National Trust, **Florence Court** (tel. 6634 8249). Built by the earls of Enniskillen in the eighteenth century, this Georgian building is noted for its fine rococo plasterwork and walled garden. The adjacent park features Irish yew and oak trees planted about 200 years ago. Open daily, June–August; Saturday–Sunday, March–May and September. Admission: £

Six and a half kilometres (4 miles) further west via the A32 are **Marble Arch Caves**, Marlbank (tel. 6634 8855), an extensive cave system, recognised as one of the best in Europe. Access is via underground boat tours that allow visitors to explore a natural underworld of stalactites, stalagmites, rivers, waterfalls, winding passages and lofty chambers.

Tours last 75 minutes and also include geology exhibitions and an audiovisual. Open daily, late March–September (weather permitting). Admission: £

If you have taken both options, it will require a 19-km (12-mile) drive via the A32 and A4 to bring you back to the Lough Erne shoreline. At Enniskillen, join the A46 road heading west for the 38.5-km (24-mile) drive back to Belleek. This route is the most scenic stretch of Lower Lough Erne, with a constant panorama of lakeside views on the right. There are very few man-made attractions on this road, so sit back and relax as some of Northern Ireland's most memorable scenery unfolds before you.

From Belleek, it's easy to continue on to Sligo or Donegal, or return to Derry or Belfast, or other parts of Ireland.

PAT'S PICKS

01~87U9LD7

RESTAURANTS

BELLEEK CAFÉ, Belleek Pottery, Main Street, Belleek (tel. 6865 8501). Although housed in the landmark china-producing factory, this Georgian-style self-service restaurant deserves special mention in its own right. Soups, fresh salads, sandwiches, pastries and other treats are served, naturally, on delicate Belleek china. In this part of Ireland, everything tastes better when it's served on Belleek! Open for snacks and lunch, daily, April–October; Monday–Friday, November–March.

LE BISTRO, Erneside Shopping Centre, Enniskillen (tel. 6632 6954). Located at the Erneside Shopping Centre, this dependable self-service café overlooks Lough Erne. The menu includes soups, salads and sandwiches of all kinds. Open for breakfast, lunch and snacks, daily.

FRANCO'S, Queen Elizabeth Road, Enniskillen (tel. 6632 4424)). Ensconced in a series of restored buildings along the riverfront, this lively restaurant is decorated with colourful wall murals, hand-painted by a local artist. The menu features a blend of Italian dishes, such as pizza and pasta, plus steaks and local seafood – salmon, crab, oysters and mussels. Open for lunch and dinner, daily.

KILLYHEVLIN REGATTA, Dublin Road, Enniskillen (tel. 6632 3481). Set on its own garden-filled grounds 1.5 km (1 mile) south of town, this restaurant at the Killyhevlin Hotel is the best bet for wide-windowed views of Lough Erne. The menu offers steaks, rack of lamb, duckling and fresh local seafood. There is a bountiful buffet during the day and full-service dining in the evening. Open for lunch and dinner, daily.

SADDLERS, 66 Belmore Street, Enniskillen (tel. 6632 6223). Located at the south end of town near the Fairgreen, this restaurant is upstairs above the Horseshoe pub. Not surprisingly, the interior has an equestrian theme and décor. The menu offers hearty choices, such as steaks, surf-and-turf, barbecued ribs, burgers and mixed grills, as well as local seafood. Open for lunch and dinner, daily.

THE THATCH, 20 Main Street, Belleek (tel. 6865 8181). As its name indicates, this small café is set in an authentic thatched cottage, claiming to be the only original thatched building in any town or-village in County Fermanagh, and providing a distinctive old-world atmosphere. The menu offers home-baked scones and cakes, and freshly made soups and sandwiches with various fillings, including wild smoked salmon. Open for snacks and lunch, Monday–Saturday.

PUBS

BLACK CAT COVE, Main Street, Belleek (tel. 6865 8942). Looking for a good traditional pub? Step inside this colourful shop-front pub, and savour the ambience of yesteryear – open-hearth fire, antiques and lots of local memorabilia. Music is scheduled every night in spring and summer, and at weekends during the rest of the year.

BLAKE'S OF THE HOLLOW, 6 Church Street, Enniskillen (tel. 6632 2143). A landmark in the centre of town, two blocks from the castle, this pub dates back to the 1880s. It has an authentic Victorian décor, with a long marble-topped bar, pinewood snugs, and lots of local memorabilia.

CROW'S NEST, 12 High Street, Enniskillen (tel. 6632 5252). Nestled in the heart of the main shopping area, this pub claims to be the oldest licensed inn in the area. The décor includes local artefacts and a collection of antique books. Traditional music is played on weekend afternoons.

DIGRESSIONS

CRUISING ON LOUGH ERNE: Cruise along the shores of Enniskillen and see the highlights of Lower Lough Erne from on board the MV *Kestrel*, a glass-enclosed waterbus. The narrated trip lasts for almost two hours and includes a 30-minute stop at Devenish Island. Cruises depart from Round O Jetty, Enniskillen, daily, July–August; at weekends, May–June and September; or according to demand. Information: Erne Tours, Brooke Park, Enniskillen (tel. 6632 2882).

FOLLOWING VIKING TRADITIONS: Explore the waters of Upper Lough Erne on board the *Viking Voyager*, a powered longship. The 90-minute route includes Crom Castle, Gad Island and Innis Rath. Boats depart at weekends, April–September, from Share Centre, Lisnaskea. Reservations required. Information: Share Centre, Lisnaskea (tel. 6772 2122) (B127 road).

LEARNING ABOUT LACE: For insight into Ireland's great lace-making traditions, drive 6.5 km (4 miles) south of Enniskillen via the A509 to the Sheelin Antique Irish Lace Museum. Tracing the history of lace-making in Ireland, this museum conveys the importance of the industry to the country as a whole, and to Irish women in particular. It houses approximately 400 antique lace items dating from 1850 to 1900, including wedding dresses and veils, shawls, parasols, collars, baby bonnets, christening gowns, flounces and jackets. Samples of lace from Ireland's great lace-making centres (such as Limerick, Youghal, and Carrickmacross) are also on display. Open Monday–Saturday. Information: Sheelin Antique Irish Lace Museum, Bellanaleck, Enniskillen (tel. 6634 8052 or www.irishlacemuseum.com).